TRAVELER'S FLORIDA COMPANION

The 2000–2001 Traveler's Companions

ARGENTINA • AUSTRALIA • BALI • CALIFORNIA • CANADA • CHILI • CHINA • COSTA RICA • CUBA • EASTERN CANADA • ECUADOR • FLORIDA • HAWAII • HONG KONG • INDIA • INDONESIA • JAPAN • KENYA • MALAYSIA & SINGAPORE • MEDITERRANEAN FRANCE • MEXICO • NEPAL • NEW ENGLAND • NEW ZEALAND • PERU • PHILIPPINES • PORTUGAL • RUSSIA • SOUTHERN ENGLAND • SOUTH AFRICA • SPAIN • THAILAND • TURKEY • VENEZUELA • VIETNAM, LAOS AND CAMBODIA • WESTERN CANADA

Traveler's FLORIDA Companion
First Published 1997
2nd Edition 2000
Published in the United Kingdom by Kümmerly+Frey AG,
Alpenstrasse 58, CH 3052 Zollikofen, Switzerland
in association with
World Leisure Marketing Ltd
Unit 11, Newmarket Court, Newmarket Drive,
Derby, DE24 8NW, England
Web Site: http://www.map-world.co.uk

ISBN: 1-8400-6089-1

Created, edited and produced by
Allan Amsel Publishing, 53, rue Beaudouin, 27700 Les Andelys, France.
E-mail: Allan.Amsel@wanadoo.fr
Editor in Chief: Allan Amsel
Editor: Samantha Wauchoupe
Original design concept: Hon Bing-wah
Picture editor and designer: Roberto Rossi

Printed by Samhwa Printing Co. Ltd., Seoul, South Korea

TRAVELER'S FLORIDA COMPANION

By Donald Carroll and Julia Clerk
Photographs by Nik Wheeler

Kümmerly+Frey

Contents

MAPS

BEACON

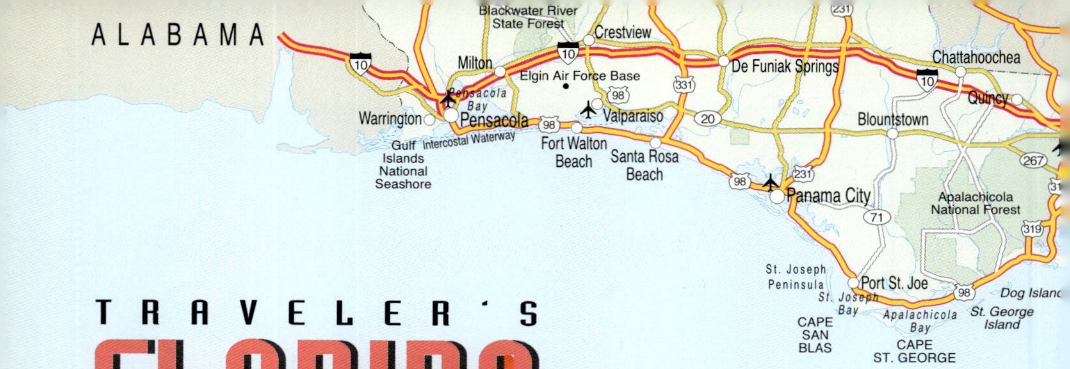

TRAVELER'S FLORIDA COMPANION

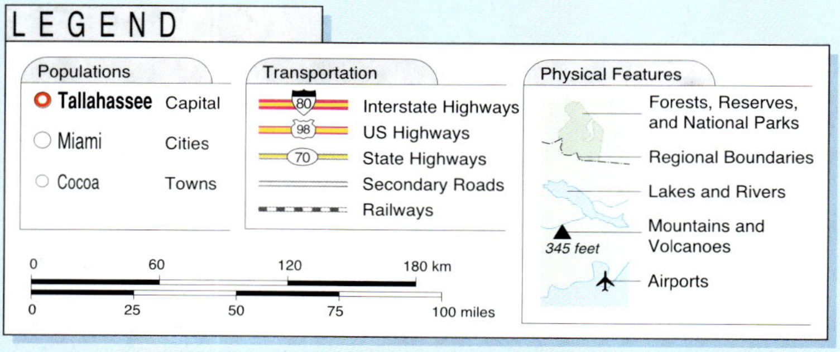

GEORGIA
ATLANTIC
OCEAN
GULF OF
MEXICO
GULF OF
MEXICO
N
Fernandina Beach
Amelia
Island
Jacksonville
Jacksonville Beach
Orange Park
Madison
Live Oak
Lake City
Perry
Starke
Castillo
San Marcos
Saint Augustine
St. Augustine Beach
Alachua
Gainesville
Palatka
Marineland
Suwannee River
Chiefland
Flager Beach
Bunnell
Suwannee
Lake
George
Ormond Beach
Daytona Beach
Ocala
Ocala
National
Forest
Cedar Key
De Land
New Smyrna Beach
Crystal River
Inverness
Wildwood
Eustis
Deltona
Sanford
Leesburg
Winter Park
Mims
Lake
Apopka
Titusville
Brooksville
Withlacoochee
State Forest
Orlando
John F. Kennedy Space Center
Clermont
Walt Disney World
Merritt Island
Cape Canaveral
Dade City
Lake Buena Vista
Kissimmee
Cocoa
Cocoa Beach
New Port Richey
St. Cloud
Satellite Beach
Tarpon Springs
Haines City
Melbourne
Tampa
Lakeland
Winter Haven
Clearwater
Lake
Kissimmee
Indian Rocks Beach
Bartow
Florida's Turnpike (Toll)
Madeira Beach
Lake Wales
St. Petersburg
Frostproof
St. Petersburg Beach
Fort Meade
Pinellas Bayway (Toll)
Sunshine Skyway (Toll)
Avon Park
Vero Beach
Sebring
Holmes Beach
Fort Pierce
Longboat Key
Sarasota
Lake Placid
Arcadia
Venice
North Point
Jupiter Island
Lake
Okeechobee
Englewood
Palm Beach
Gardens
North Palm Beach
Pahokee
Lake Park
Riviera Beach
West Palm Beach
Clewiston
Royal
Palm
Beach
Palm Beach
Belle Glade
Lake Worth
Cape Coral
Fort Myers
Loxahatchee
National
Wildlife Refuge
Boynton Beach
Captiva
Island
Delray Beach
Immokalee
Boca Raton
Sanibel
Island
Fort Myers
Beach
Sawgrass
Expwy (Toll)
Deerfield Beach
Corkscrew Swamp
Sanctuary
Lighthouse Point
Everglades Parkway (Toll)
Pompano Beach
Alligator Alley
Naples
THE EVERGLADES
Fort Lauderdale
Big Cypress
Davie
Hollywood
Isle of Capri
Carrestown
National Resrve
North Miami Beach
Miami Beach
Marco
Island
Everglades City
Sweetwater
Miami
Ten
Thousand
Islands
Pinecrest
Coral Gables
Key Biscane
National Park
Everglades
National Park
Biscaye
Bay
MONROE
Homestead
Florida City
Barnes
Sound
CAPE
SABLE
KEY LARGO
Key Largo
OYSTER
KEYS
Florida
Bay
Intercostal Waterway
Islamorada
Bahai
Honda
State
Park
Long Key
Lower Matecumbe Beach
Marathon
Big Pine
Key Colony Beach
Key West
KEY WEST
FLORIDA KEYS

BEACON
720

TOP SPOTS

Melt into the Miami Scene

GREATER MIAMI IS ONE OF THE WORLD'S ULTIMATE TOURIST DESTINATIONS, with mile after mile of white sand beaches, endless palm trees and other lush tropical vegetation, accommodation that ranges from vast resort hotels to intimate inns, hundreds of restaurants and nightclubs, elegant shops and air-conditioned mega-malls, historic buildings and art deco mansions, museums and art galleries, more than 800 parks and nature areas, and sporting opportunities galore.

The area is the home of many celebrities, from aging heiresses and ageless film stars to sporting greats and pop culture vanguards. A playground for both the rich and the rabble, the city's cosmopolitan nature attracts visitors from around the world as well a steady flow of immigrants, many of them refugees from Latin America and the Caribbean. Which explains why so many street signs are in both English and Spanish.

Cuban exiles, in particular, have had a major impact on the culture, traditions and cuisine of the area. But in the last decade, Miami has become a mosaic of distinct foreign accents, music, food and culture. The more than 30 cities and towns in the 2,000 square miles that make up Greater Miami are an eclectic blend of communities living out their own versions of the American dream (for detailed information on the city, see MIAMI AND ENVIRONS, page 83).

On the streets of Little Havana, the heart of Miami's Cuban community, you can load up on high-octane café Cubano (guaranteed to give you an alert buzz) and other Cuban delicacies like conch fritters or black beans and rice. Music seems to pour out from every open door and window — salsa and samba, and jig and rumba. Older men gather at Domino Park to play dominoes or chess and discuss local politics or foreign affairs, primarily the fall of Cuban leader Fidel Castro. Southwest Eighth Street, the area's main artery, is probably best known for hosting Calle Ocho, the largest block party in the United States. Held in March, the festival features top Latin artists performing free on outdoor stages, where the music and the dancing couples inspire you to feel the rhythm.

Automotive and architectural reminders of the past in Miami Beach's Art deco district.

FOUNTAIN OF YOUTH

Another lively immigrant community that has sprouted in recent years is Little Haiti, where many artists, musicians and entrepreneurs from the French-speaking Caribbean find their first foothold in America. The neighborhood showcases the Caribbean Marketplace, an open-air replica of the Iron Market in Port-au-Prince, Haiti.

Miami is the world's largest cruise ship port, and Miami International Airport handles 28 million passengers a year from around the world, most of whom head for the city's 13 miles (21 km) of tropical beaches.

Greater Miami is also one of the nation's major sporting centers with the NFL's record-breaking Miami Dolphins, the Florida Marlins of Major League Baseball (the 1997 world champions), the fast-breaking Miami Heat of the National Basketball Association, and the National Hockey League's Florida Panthers. There is championship golf, international tennis, grand prix motor racing and a wealth of watersports from windsurfing and scuba to sailing and jetskiing. You can battle with a marlin in the Gulf Stream or spot alligators in the nearby Everglades. Miami really does have something for everyone.

Transcend Time in St. Augustine

WHEN YOU CROSS THE BRIDGE OF LIONS OVER THE MATANZAS RIVER INTO ST. AUGUSTINE, YOU EMBARK ON A JOURNEY THAT TAKES YOU BACK NEARLY 500 YEARS INTO THE AMERICAN PAST. The narrow streets and the clay-tiled roofs of the country's oldest city are a welcome relief from the theme parks and modern-day attractions that abound elsewhere in the state.

The Bridge of Lions, carved from Carrera marble, is the entry way from Anastasia Island to an impeccably-preserved historic city. Founded by the Spanish in 1565 — 42 years before the English colonized Jamestown — St. Augustine is a living museum with 144 blocks of historic buildings listed on the National Register of Historic Places.

After even a single day or a weekend here the visitor will leave with an enriched perception of colonization, warfare and the influence of the wealthy. Men like Henry M. Flagler, who built an empire based on railroads and resort hotels. Ponce De Leon searched for the waters of the Fountain of Youth in these parts, and you can visit the Fountain of Youth Archeological Park to seek your own immortality. But this charming seacoast community can also be relaxing and romantic, which will inevitably refresh the soul, at least.

Horse-drawn carriages clip clop along narrow cobbled streets, red-tiled roofs overhang walled courtyards on St. George Street, and guitar music drifts from Spanish Renaissance Revival style buildings, made from crushed seashells and coral, known as coquina. You can stroll down to the Spanish quarter, meander along the waterfront with its ancient gnarled trees festooned with hanging Spanish moss, or just laze the day away on the miles of nearby white-sanded beaches.

Animated guides lead visitors through the centuries by horse and carriage, trolleys and riverboats, or on walking tours beneath a canopy of large, oak

OPPOSITE: Locals believe this is the site of Ponce de León's legendary Fountain of Youth.
ABOVE: St. Augustine's beautiful buildings span five centuries of history.

trees. One of the most intriguing is Ghostly Walking Tours ☎ (850) 461-1009 TOLL-FREE (888) 461-1009, led by a guide dressed to fit the period, who conjures images and tales of the past while relating the city's significance.

Take in Castillo de San Marcos ☎ (850) 829-6506, built in 1695, and the nation's oldest stone fort, and Fort Matanzas, constructed half a century later, which can only be reached by boat.

The city proudly boasts of having the nation's oldest wooden schoolhouse, the oldest store and the oldest surviving house (1727), as well as other architectural masterpieces, including Henry Flagler's luxurious ninteenth century Ponce de León Hotel, which is now Flagler College, and the Venetian Renaissance Revival Memorial Presbyterian Church.

There is the Lightner Museum with one of the world's most impressive cut glass displays. Attached to the back of the museum are antique shops and a café — housed in what used to be the indoor pool of the Alcazar Hotel. To re-live more of the past, visit the candy-striped Lighthouse Tower and Museum, Spanish Quarter Museum and nearby Fort Mose (established for free slaves) and the first black settlement in North America.

When you have finally had your fill of antiquity, visit America's first reptile theme park, the St. Augustine Alligator and Crocodile Farm ☎ (850) 824-3337, established in 1893, or discover the 24 miles (38 km) of unspoiled beaches on neighboring Anastasia Island (for more on the town see ST. AUGUSTINE, page 148, in THE ATLANTIC COAST)

Trail Gators in The Everglades

CHUCK, THE AIRBOAT DRIVER FROM BILLIE SWAMP SAFARI, parked the airboat in the middle of the swamp on the Seminole Indian Reservation off Interstate 75 (also known as Alligator Alley). He wanted us to see One-Eyed Jack, an impressive 10-foot-long alligator who had taken refuge in this part of the 2200-acre fenced-in area of the Everglades. But as we waited in the afternoon stillness, and Chuck tossed bits of dog food over the edge of our vessel, we were gradually surrounded by smaller gators trying to catch a snack.

Chuck explained the prowess and speed of the alligators, who can leap straight up in the air about six feet or scramble 30–35 miles per hour across dry land — or even faster in the water. Those facts were very disconcerting as the alligators drew closer and closer to the boat. Chuck assured us there was no danger because these were "docile" 'gators, fed nearly every day. Nevertheless, it was an eerie feeling from our vantage point, knowing we were on their turf.

An airboat ride is the quickest way to visit the outlying areas of the Everglades. You can combine your ride with an introduction to South Florida's Native American communities by visiting either the Seminole or Miccosukee Indian reservations.

At the Miccosukee Indian Village off the Tamiami Trail you can also see an "alligator wrestling" show, and either be amazed or dumbfounded by the trainer's bravery in straddling a 'gator, putting its snout underneath his chin and prodding the animal to open its mouth.

Standing in a pit with four or five seemingly indifferent gators, Ron Huff explained the amazing characteristics of alligators, and the history behind the wrestling concept. He casually opened one's mouth to display its 81 teeth and then taunted it with a stick to hear the snap of its killer jaws. Spectators gasped at the sound and the hissing of another alligator being pulled by the tail.

"I have read and studied them," said Ron, who has been doing this for almost two years. "When I go in and play with them, I don't take a lot of chances. I guess I was scared of them at first, but then I learned their range of motion and how close I can stand to

A boardwalk allows visitors to safely explore the Everglades Cypress Swamp Reserve.

them. But every now and then, they do something that reminds you where you need to be."

Doug Shinkel, a ranger at the Everglades Alligator Farm in Florida City, has a teeth imprint on his right shoulder as proof that you have to be careful when handling these reptiles. One of the smaller ones bit him, although fortunately it only broke skin and didn't do any more harm. Visitors are given a chance to hold a baby alligator the size of an iguana and pose for a picture. You can learn more about alligators at the adjacent commercial alligator farm and educational center.

Florida City is also the main jumping off point for Everglades National Park, the largest remaining subtropical wilderness in North America. The reserve covers more than 1.5 million acres (600,000 hectares) and is home to scores of threatened and endangered species of plants, animals and birds. The Everglades is really a vast slow-moving, freshwater river up to 50 miles (80 km) wide and often only a few inches deep, fed by Lake Okeechobee to the north. More than half the park is covered by shallow water, although wading is not a good idea because of the large numbers of poisonous snakes and tens of thousands of alligators, some more than 20 ft (six meters) long.

Much of the vegetation is similar to that found in Cuba and the West Indies. Several species of palms and other tropical and subtropical plants, almost 300 species of birds, and 600 species of fish can be found within the park. It is one of the few areas where the docile manatee, alias the sea cow, is assured a permanent sanctuary, and you can also spot turtles, snakes and on occasions, porpoises.

Everglades City on the Gulf Coast is another popular access point to the park and offers a wide choice of water tours; from sedate glass-bottom craft to air boats that skim across the surface. The National Park Service also has guided boat tours, which leave from the ranger station south of Everglades City. The E. J. Hamilton Observation Tower, on State Road 29, offers panoramas over the Everglades and Ten Thousand Islands; while the Tamiami Trail (State Road 41) runs almost coast to coast along the northern edge of the park, providing a number of access points.

The national park is open year round and apart from the boat trips, there are four marked canoe trails. It is advisable to file your trip with the ranger office before leaving and to report back on your return. There are also a number of well posted scenic drives and conducted tram tours that leave from the Shark Valley entrance. Other trails on that side of the park can be accessed on rented bicycles, as can the Anhinga Trail, which starts at the Royal Palm Visitor Center.

There is a lot to see and do in the Everglades so allow as much time as possible — and don't forget your insect repellent, especially in the summer when the rains hit.

See THE EVERGLADES, page 239 for detailed information on the area.

Capture the Cuban Spirit

WHETHER IT'S THE AROMA OF PERCOLATING CUBAN COFFEE DRIFTING THROUGH THE AIR OUTSIDE THE YBOR CITY STATE MUSEUM, or the smell of tobacco from the hand-rolled cigars in the Tampa Rico cigar company inside Ybor Square, there is no mistaking you are in Tampa's Cuban quarter.

The Cubans brought their cigar-making skills with them when they emigrated in their thousands in the mid-nineteenth century. Bustling with craftsmen who work in close packed houses and small factories, Ybor City has changed little over the decades. There are still cobblestone streets, intricate wrought iron balconies, and Spanish tiles in abundance.

Ybor City is now better known as a dining, shopping, and entertainment district, particularly on weekend evenings when Seventh Avenue is closed off to automobiles and becomes a pedestrian thoroughfare. The atmosphere rings with the sounds of Latin music and the laughter of festive people.

Two local events that have become part of Tampa's urban fabric are Fiesta Day and Guavaween — annual street parties that feature ethnic food and music. Fiesta Day, which celebrates the

district's culturally diverse background, has been going on for more than 50 years. Guavaween, Ybor City's Latin version of Halloween, honors the mythical Mama Guava. Families take to the streets to celebrate during the day, and at night the serious partying begins

The history of the city, now part of Tampa, is told in the Ybor City State Museum, which makes a useful first port of call (see TAMPA, WHAT TO SEE AND DO, page 216 in THE GULF COAST). While there, pick up a map and a self-guided walking tour brochure of the area. On Saturdays, the museum offers an escorted walking tour for a nominal fee. Located on the corner of 9th Avenue and 19th Street, the museum is dedicated to the city's founder, Don Vicente Martinez Ybor. His settlement attracted thousands of immigrants and their special skills; Ybor City quickly established itself as the cigar capital of the world. The rich history of the city is preserved at the museum, once the town bakery, and you can visit the nearby La Casita House Museum, a restored cigar worker's home.

OPPOSITE: Tall masts and skyscrapers jut into the evening sky at Tampa Bay. ABOVE: Cuban expatriates play dominoes in Miami's Little Havana.

The first cigar factory was in Ybor Square ☎ (813) 247-4497, 1901 North 13th Street, on the corner of 8th Avenue and 13th Street, now a shopping mall specializing in antiques and assorted memorabilia. Many of its restaurants reflect the ethnic traditions of the early settlers. The Don Quijote Restaurant specializes in authentic Cuban cuisine. Try the fresh baked Cuban bread at La Segunda Central Bakery ☎ (813) 248-1531, 2512 North 15th Street, which offers a conducted tour of the premises if you ask in good time. There are a number of interesting shops and craft centers along 15th Street, including a glass studio and the Ritz Theater, which now houses a popular nightclub. On 15th and 8th Avenue is El Encanto Cleaners, an Ybor City family business that has survived for three generations.

You can also take an organized tour at El Sol Cigars ☎ (813) 248-5905 WEB SITE www.elsolcigars.com, 1728 East Seventh Avenue, where the traditional methods of hand-rolling are still demonstrated.

Soak up Sultry Tarpon Springs

TARPON SPRINGS CONSIDERS ITSELF "THE SPONGE CAPITAL OF THE WORLD" AND FLORIDA'S "LITTLE GREECE." Located 27 miles northeast of the Tampa/St. Petersburg area, Greek fishermen and sponge divers helped settle the area in 1876. By the 1890s it was a thriving port, and there is still something very Mediterranean about the picturesque sponge dock. The sponge boats are anchored along the quay and the other side of the road is packed with shops selling more sponges than you have ever seen, as well as exquisite Greek restaurants, bakeries, and the imposing Orthodox church.

Most people who visit the town believe that it is on the coast, although it is some way inland on the Anclote River. One highlight for the visitor is to take a boat cruise down the river, past luxury waterside homes, the many islands and secluded beaches to the sea and back.

You can also go out on a sponge boat and watch the divers at work wearing the traditional rubber suit, lead boots, and screw-on helmet with its pipe connected to an air pump on board.

Visit the Saint Nicholas Greek Orthodox Church, built in 1943 as a replica of the Byzantine St. Sophia's in Constantinople (now the Haga Sofia Mosque, in modern-day Istanbul). The Konger Coral Sea Aquarium has a simulated coral reef with marine life in a 100,000 gallon (380,000 liter) tank and tidal pool, and the Spongeorama Exhibit Center traces the history of sponge diving.

The Anclote Keys are three miles (five kilometers) off Tarpon Springs and only accessible by boat. You can be dropped in the morning, spend the day swimming and sunbathing and be picked up in time for dinner.

Visitors flock to this tiny corner of Florida's Gulf Coast each January 6th for the Epiphany Celebration on Spring Bayou. Greek boys dive into the water for a white cross, a tradition that marks the Greek Orthodox observance of the holiday. Later in the day, the sponge docks are crowded with people in traditional costumes dancing to Greek music.

For more information contact the Tarpon Springs Chamber of Commerce ✆ (813) 937-6109 FAX (813) 937-6100 WEB SITE www.tarponsprings.com, at 11 East Orange Street.

At Home with Hemingway

ASK ALMOST ANYONE OF THE 27,000 RESIDENTS OF KEY WEST HOW THEY ENDED UP LIVING IN THE SOUTHERNMOST CITY IN THE CONTINENTAL UNITED STATES, and the response will usually be: "I came here for vacation and I just stayed."

Key West's tropical breezes and the 330 days of sunshine each year might be enough to lure you into staying as well. "Most people just drop here from the rest of the continent," says Pablo McGrail, co-owner of Sebago Water Sports, which offers relaxing sunset catamaran cruises to unwind from a day of sightseeing. McGrail arrived in Key West 18 years ago and now is a local entrepreneur. "They are usually escaping something… either a spouse or the law or maybe both."

While fugitives might find this paradise appealing, eccentrics are the ones most attracted to this incredibly beautiful island, where the waters of the Florida Straits blend in different shades of azure like the swirls in a mood ring.

Key West's unique atmosphere has evolved largely because it's only 90 miles (145 km) from Havana — closer than Miami — and has always had a strong Caribbean influence. The town's relative isolation has long attracted a bohemic lifestyle and laissez-faire attitude. Over the years it has been the home of Spanish conquistadors, pirates, New England

OPPOSITE: Greek boys dive in Tarpon Springs for the white cross to mark the start of Greek Orthodox Epiphany. ABOVE: A bottle-encrusted fence in Key West, one of the islands many eccentricities.

mariners, and European royalty. Today, it has a strong gay population, many artists and writers, and attracts about 1.5 million visitors a year.

Ernest Hemingway lived and wrote here, and it's not difficult to understand why other writers have flocked to this paradise and have been stimulated to greatness. Key West writers have won ten Pulitzer Prizes and more than 100 published authors live full- or part-time on the island. It is still popular with writers, artists and the famous, and celebrity-spotting is an island pastime.

The eclectic architecture is just one of the many pleasing aspects of Key West. Many of the wooden buildings are built in a style referred to as Conch or Bahamian. The town adopted West Indian gingerbread decorations in the 1850s, and it became very fashionable to incorporate elaborate scrollwork on balconies, under eaves, and under gables. Wrought iron railings were also popular, and these features continue to add a special Caribbean charm.

Watching the sunset from Mallory Square on the waterfront is a daily ritual whether you are a visitor or "Conch" as the natives are called. The place comes alive as the sun goes down with street artists, musicians and jugglers out in force to entertain the crowd. People find their perch along the seawall, sitting close to each other in every available space to watch nature's theater — the sun finding its resting place on the watery horizon, which provides a perfect backdrop to the festive atmosphere of the performers.

Before your visit to Key West is complete, include a snorkeling or scuba diving trip to the coral reef that stretches 200 miles underneath the island. Wading in the crystalline waters is a wonderful way to spend a leisurely afternoon, but wear some sort of waterproof shoes or sandals because the ground is rocky. Other sights include the beautifully restored 1812 Audubon House; the Curry Mansion, a Victorian home packed with antiques, rare Tiffany glass and other furnishings; the Old Customs House — now the Museum of History and the Arts; the Wrecker's Museum/The Oldest House; and Ernest Hemingway House and its Museum. When Hemingway and his wife moved in, they built the city's first swimming pool in the spacious grounds, where peacocks and scores of cats roamed around.

Perhaps after touring this vibrant community, you will be inspired to some artistic creativity as well.

Discover Florida's Secret Beaches

FLORIDA HAS MANY OF THE FINEST BEACHES IN THE UNITED STATES but the beaches of the Panhandle remain some of its best kept secrets.

This stretch of coastline from Pensacola, close to the state's border with Alabama, east to Panama City, runs for almost 100 miles (160 km) and contains one sweeping, spectacular sugar-white sand beach after another. Nicknamed the Redneck Riviera, the area residents have no more than a tinge of Southern accents, but their old Southern hospitality is unmistakable.

The unspoiled beaches of Pensacola, Florida's westernmost city, run for 25 miles (40 km) and span two long and narrow barrier islands, which form part of the Gulf Islands National Seashore (see page 207, in THE PANHANDLE, for more on this beautiful area). Much of Pensacola Beach is protected from development, although high rise condos, vacation homes and old time night spots are to be found on Perdido Key.

The Navarre, Fort Walton, and Destin area has 24 miles (38 km) of beaches known as the Emerald Coast because of the brilliant emerald green waters. Navarre was a sleepy fishing village until outsiders discovered its beaches, and now it is one of the fastest growing

OPPOSITE TOP: Hand-in-hand, a sunset stroll along a Gulf Coast beach. BOTTOM: All the wildlife on Sanibel Island is protected, making it one of the world's top bird-watching centers.

communities along this coast. However, the pace of life remains gentle and the beaches unspoiled. The two towns of Fort Walton and Destin are noted for their southern hospitality and excellent fish restaurants. Almost two-thirds of their beaches are protected, and the safe waters make them ideal family vacation destinations. While a surprisingly wide range of land and water-based sporting opportunities are possible in both of these towns, the most popular activities are sunbathing and swimming.

South Walton has 26 miles (42 km) of undisturbed beaches, with Grayton Beach voted the best beach in the continental United States in a recent survey. There are 18 small beach communities in South Walton and no fast-food outlets, amusement parks, or large hotels. The area is popular with families with young children who just want to enjoy mile upon mile of 40 ft (12 m) high sand dunes and crystal clear, warm water.

Panama City Beach is the last and longest stretch of beach along the Panhandle, running for more than 27 miles (43 km). It is rated the number three sports beach in the United States and is noted for its fishing — thus its claim to be the seafood capital of the world. While the beaches attract visitors during the day, there are a wide range of entertainment and activities to keep them amused at other times. This Florida Gulf Coast community has also become popular with the college spring break crowds, and many of their week-long festivities are televised on Music Television programs.

Visit the Friendship Gate

FORT MYERS IS THE MAIN CITY ALONG FLORIDA'S SOUTHWEST COAST, a place that's packed with history, fine old homes and museums. In the mid-1800s there were many Seminole Indians (*seminole* is the Creek word for "free" or "runaway") and runaway slaves in the area. Then in 1865 Fort Myers (formerly Fort Harvie) was reopened — as a Union Fort manned by all-black regiments of former slaves.

Today Fort Myers is called the City of Palms. Running for 15 miles (24 km) through Fort Myers, McGregor Boulevard is lined with towering royal palms, the first 200 of which were imported from Cuba by Thomas Edison. The Edison Estate is one of the city's major attractions, the inventor's winter home for 46 years. The house is on a 14-acre (six hectare) riverfront lot that was built in 1886. It was donated to the city by his widow Mina Miller Edison and opened to the public in 1947. His first light bulbs had such rugged elements that some of the originals are still in use today. The huge banyan tree in the garden was a gift to Edison from industrialist Harvey Firestone. The tree is the largest specimen of banyan in the United States and the aerial roots have a circumference of more than 400 feet (122 m).

The Henry Ford home is next door. Ford and Edison were close friends and there was a gate between the two properties, which is still known as the

Friendship Gate. The city has many other fine historic downtown homes and a rich cultural life. Fort Myers Beach on Estero Island is one of the world's safest beachesn because of its gently sloping shoreline, soft sand and warm, clear waters.

The Fort Myers area is also rich in natural history and an ideal place to launch into a nature vacation. Most of the beaches and parks along the "Shell Coast" remain unspoiled and a prominent conservation effort is being made to preserve natural habitats.

Northeast of the city is the vast wilderness of the Crescent B Ranch, which encompasses 90,000 acres that includes oak hammocks, wetlands and the Telegraph Cypress Swamp. A swamp buggy ride with Babcock Wilderness Adventures ☎ (800) 500-5583 WEB SITE www.babcockwilderness.com, takes you through the far corners of the ranch. Well-informed guides explain the area's history and describe the landscape, which has featured in movies like *Just Cause*. In the winter (the dry season) you can take a guided bicycle ride through the swamps. Other areas where you can explore the vast virgin subtropical vegetation include Matanzas Pass Wilderness Preserve and Calusa Nature Center and Planetarium.

From Fish Tale Marina in Fort Myers Beach, you can board the dolphin encounter tours offered by Calusa Coast Outfitters' ☎ (941) 418-5941 WEB SITE www.calusacoast.com. This is not just a dolphin-watching ride, but an educational experience where you can hear (with the help of marine hydrophones) the chatter of the bottlenose dolphins found in the Estero Bay Aquatic Preserve. Florida native Arden Arrington, who is also a volunteer for the Florida Park Service Environmental Protection, interprets the dolphins' different sounds and actions as they interact with each other and frolic in the wake of a motorboat. Calusa Coast Outfitters also offer the only walking historical/archaeological tour of the Mound Key State Archaeological Site.

Sanibel Island is an idyllic getaway reached by a toll causeway that helps to keep visitors down. The island's beaches are consistently voted among the best in the world, and Sanibel is also world famous for its shells and wildlife. More than 400 different types of shell have been found along its beaches. As the light starts to fade, you can wade through the water with manta rays swimming around your legs and ibis and egrets following you along the sand.

Periwinkle Way is the island's main thoroughfare and on either side, hidden among the lush tropical vegetation, are interesting shops, galleries, and fine restaurants. The best way to get around the island is to rent a bike from one of the many outlets. The Old Schoolhouse Theater, formerly a one-room schoolhouse built in 1894, is now a cozy community theater. The Pirate Playhouse is the island's professional theater, staging major productions and attracting big name stars to this intimate venue where no seat is more than 15 feet (five meters) from the stage.

On both Sanibel and Captiva Islands, the majority of the islands are protected wildlife areas. One of the state's best wildlife spots is the J.N. Ding Darling National Wildlife Refuge, which occupies 5,400 acres (2,160 hectare) on the north side of Sanibel Island. It's named after Pulitzer Prize-winning cartoonist Jay Norwood "Ding" Darling, the first environmentalist to hold a presidential cabinet post (in Franklin Roosevelt's administration). There are driving, walking and cycling trails and you can rent a canoe or kayak and paddle your way along the coast through the tiny offshore mangrove islands. The Sanibel-Captiva Conservation Foundation is another delightful nature center covering 1,100 acres (440 hectare) just south of the island's main road. The Bailey-Matthews Shell Museum is the only dedicated sea shell museum in the United States.

The Columbia restaurant, a renowned tourist haunt since 1905.

Relax in St. Petersburg-Clearwater

THE BEACHES FROM ST. PETERSBURG BEACH TO THE EDGE OF CLEARWATER BEACH ARE STILL NOT OVERSATURATED WITH HIGH-RISE CONDOS, but enough people come to these shores to make this the most popular vacation spot on Florida's gulf coast, attracting more than four million visitors a year — 90 percent of whom say they will return.

The twin cities occupy the Pinellas peninsula, the most densely populated area in all Florida. St. Petersburg is largely a resort city, connected by a series of bridges with Tampa and by causeways to the Holiday Isles to the west. It claims the title "Sun Capital of America", because of a one-time record 768 consecutive days of sunshine. Between 1910 and 1986, the St. Petersburg *Evening Independent* was given away free on days when the sun did not shine. Over the course of the 76 years, the paper was given away free only 295 times, less than four times a year. This resort city boasts palm-lined stree ts, a bustling waterfront and pier, excellent shops and restaurants, and three fine museums — the Museum of Fine Arts, the Salvador Dali Museum and the Great Explorations museum.

Clearwater and Clearwater Beach offer excellent swimming and long stretches of sandy beaches for sunbathing. Many smaller motels are within a few feet of the shore, so you can sit out on the porch or balcony and relax as the sun sets before you in golden tones over the Gulf of Mexico.

Clearwater Marina harbors a bustling sports-fishing fleet. There are all sorts of trips offered from deep-sea fishing, dolphin-spotting and dinner specials to sunset cruises. Concerts and Broadway shows are staged at the Ruth Eckerd Hall, and you can spend an interesting and educational afternoon at the Clearwater Marine Aquarium, a research and rehabilitation facility for marine life. Clearwater Sunset is a nightly open-air celebration staged at Pier 60 featuring magicians, musicians, jugglers and other entertainers who perform as the crowds gather to watch the sunset over the Gulf. Top sights include the reconstructed 1890s Boatyard Village on Fairchild Drive and Largo Heritage Village on 125th Street (see ST. PETERSBURG AND CLEARWATER, page 222 in THE GULF COAST, for detailed information on this area).

Speed Along the Space Coast

THE SPACE COAST IS A DRAMATIC JUXTAPOSITION OF TECHNOLOGICAL WIZARDRY AND OUR ENDURING STRUGGLE TO PROTECT THE ENVIRONMENT. The shoreline from Melbourne to Daytona offers more than a hundred miles of sandy beaches flanked by lagoons and the open Atlantic. But the simmering sands take a back seat to the area's other attractions: America's main base for launching missions into outer space, barrier islands that make up the one of the most important wildlife preserves in the state, and the fast cars of Daytona.

Marvel at the accomplishments of the United States Space Program through exhibits at the John F. Kennedy Space Center. Children and adults with adventure in their blood will get a thrill out of the United States Astronaut Hall of Fame. There you can ride in an enclosed fighter jet simulator, which allows you to experience 4 G-forces with the help of a precisely timed and filmed video from the view of a cockpit. Then there is the Merritt Island National Wildlife Refuge, which is the home of number of endangered species, it is the largest refuge in the United States.

Daytona's reputation is built on its beaches and racing cars. Between 1902 and 1935, it was more famous for speed trials than sunbathing and swimming. During those years, 13 world speed records were set on the sands by motoring aces like Barney Oldfield, Sir Henry Seagrave and Sir Malcolm Campbell, while Louis Chevrolet and Henry Ford used the beach to test their early racing cars.

The racing tradition continues at the Daytona International Speedway, which presents top racing events throughout the year, including the 24 hours race of Daytona in January, the Daytona 500 in February and Bike Week in October, which attracts thousands of bikers from around the world. Daytona USA is a new interactive motorsports attraction allowing visitors the chance to take part in a pit stop, design their own race car, and become a television race commentator.

Cars can be driven along the hard packed sand from the Ormond Beach exit to Ponce de León Inlet in the south for a small charge. Alongside the beach is the bustling promenade, with the palm-lined Boardwalk amusement area near the fishing pier, and a sightseeing tower and sky ride over the Main Street Pier. Offshore is a Mecca for watersports activities from sailing, canoeing, surfing and jet skiing to power boats, scuba and fishing. Daytona Beach is also noted for its museums and year round program of cultural events including world class visiting symphony orchestras at the Peabody Auditorium, the Daytona Playhouse, and a summer season at the Seaside Music Theater.

Rare are the weeks when Daytona is not bustling with crowds in its hundreds of beach-front megaplex hotels. The Las Vegas influence of themed hotels has invaded this part of the Atlantic Coast, sometimes clashing with the sand dunes and the beauty of the ocean.

Plan ahead for any trip to this famous city. The chances are that despite the abundance of hotel rooms, there may not be one when you need it because of a spring break or racing week.

Cars and pedestrians mingle on Daytona's famous beaches.

YOUR CHOICE

The Great Outdoors

Florida has world class beaches, theme parks, and other attractions, like the John F. Kennedy Space Center, but it also offers vast natural beauty that too few visitors take time to enjoy.

In the north there are huge forests with walking and cycle trails and lakes and waterways for canoeing and boating. Plus there is a wealth of wildlife, including the Florida black bear and the endangered Florida panther.

From coast to coast the state has farming and ranching land, with citrus groves and cattle farms and thousands of lakes. Most of these lakes are connected by navigable rivers and waterways, on which it is possible to travel hundreds of miles south to the Everglades and the Atlantic Ocean.

Of course, the Everglades dominate the southern part of the state, and while it is not advisable to go too far in without an experienced guide, there are lots of opportunities to canoe, cycle, and walk by yourself among the lush vegetation and surrounded by exotic wildlife.

Florida has five national parks. The largest and the most famous is the **Everglades** (see MELT INTO THE MIAMI SCENE, page 11, in TOP SPOTS), a naturalist's, walker's, and canoeist's paradise. Even if you do not get out of your car, you can see the most exotic wildlife close up. The various visitors centers and ranger stations have free brochures detailing nature walks and what to see along the way, and you should experience at least one of the trails, which are mostly on boardwalks so you don't get your feet wet.

The other national parks are the **Canaveral National Seashore and Merritt Island**, which runs along the coast by the John F. Kennedy Space Center and is an internationally important wader and wildfowl habitat; the **Fort De Soto Park**, on Tampa Bay, which commemorates De Soto's landing in Florida in May 1539; the mostly underwater **Biscayne National Park** in Miami Bay; and the **Gulf Islands**

OPPOSITE: An anhinga, or snake bird, dries its wings. ABOVE: The shy green heron can be found in marshes throughout the state.

National Seashore, a chain of sandy barrier islands running from Pensacola east towards Panama City.

Florida has 145 state parks and recreation areas, as well as ornamental gardens. Most offer campsites, picnicking facilities, swimming, fishing, hiking trails, nature walks and boat ramps. Many also have distinctive features that make them special — you may be able to watch manatees at close quarters, take a guided tour through caverns, or snorkel among coral and tropical fish. A state park is defined as "an area of regional or statewide significance established to preserve the natural setting, while permitting a full program of compatible recreational activities."

A major advantage of Florida's great outdoors is its utter flatness. Trails may be a little uneven in places, but they are rarely steep, so they are accessible to almost everyone. In areas where the ground is marshy, boardwalks allow easy and dry access. Many trails are also wheelchair accessible. The main disadvantages are that Florida is semi-tropical so insects abound, and it's usually very hot and humid. If you are planning to go hiking or cycling in one of the state parks, use an insect repellent, wear a hat, and carry drinking water.

The other problem is deciding just where to go because the choice is so great. Even if you are vacationing in central Florida be adventurous and travel around, as you can almost always find a motel or hotel room if you need to stay overnight.

There are about 1,744 miles (2,800 km) of hiking trails in Florida, about 120,000 conveniently placed picnic tables along the way, and more than 120,000 campsites in official campgrounds, so backpackers have a lot of options. Florida is still a relatively new state and most settlement has taken place in the last 100 years, so there is still a strong pioneering spirit. Hunting, fishing and camping are very popular.

The best backpacking trails are in the national and state parks and forests, where maps showing trails and campgrounds are available from the ranger stations. The state's longest trail is the 1,300-mile-long (2,094-km) **Florida National Scenic Trail** which runs the length of the state and connects with many other trails along the way.

You can get a good flavor of what this long distance trail is like in **Ocala National Forest**, which covers over 430,000 acres (172,000 hectares). The forest is crisscrossed by hiking, cycling and canoe trails, while the Ocala Trail runs the length of the forest. The 65-mile-long (105 km) Ocala Trail is part of the Scenic Trail, and you should plan to take at least four days to walk it — adding an extra day if you have the time. The paths are good and well posted, but there are lots of distractions along the

way, and a slow pace is advisable because of the heat and humidity. If you rush you will most likely miss much of the wildlife, which includes alligators, black bears, armadillos, raccoons, skunks, porcupines, wild pigs, and the rare Florida panther. There are lots of opportunities to take a swim in the many lakes, or you can rent a canoe for a few hours from one of the many concessions.

As with all the parks, there are always other trails to explore. For instance, in the Ocala National Forest at Alexander Springs you can detour on to the Timucuan Trail, a self-guided interpretive walk explaining the plants used by Native Americans for culinary and medicinal purposes.

Another good day's walk is in the **Lower Wekiva River State Preserve** ☎ (407) 884-2009, Wekiwa Springs State Park, 1800 Wekiwa Circle, Apopka. The entrance is on State Route 46, off Interstate 4 east of Orlando in Sanford. There is a 10-mile (16-km) walk through the reserve to Rock Springs Run and then along the St. Johns River. The spring is formed by several artesian wells, and wilderness camping is allowed. Along the way you may see some black bears, white tailed deer, river otters, alligators, and snakes — the most common of which is the long, black and non-poisonous indigo

Gentle manatees graze in the warm waters of Homosassa Springs.

snake. Because of the fresh water, this area was settled by Native Americans long before the Spanish arrived, and some mounds remain. (Although Native American artifacts are still found, it is an offense to touch or remove them.) From St. Johns River, you can then join another trail which leads into the Wekiva Springs State Park, where there is a family camping area.

The **Tosohatchee Trail** runs through the Tosohatchee State Reserve. Take State Route 50 east through Christmas and then Taylor Creek Road to the reserve entrance. The trail, through stands of slash pine — some of which are more than 250 years old — follows old logging roads in places. There are three wilderness campsites at the end of a three-mile (five-kilometer), 10-mile (16-km) or 25-mile (40-km) hike in. You must telephone the ranger station in advance to reserve a campsite ☎ (407) 568-5893.

Some of the best hiking on Florida's west coast is in the **Withlacoochee State Trail**, where the Florida Trail Association has marked out and maintains a 46-mile (48-km) trail converted railroad track in the Croom area. Florida's state forests are often not as well posted as either state parks or national forests, but they are worth seeking out because they all have well marked trails, are rich in wildlife, and are usually far less frequented. The Croom Wildlife Management Area runs for about 16 miles (26 km) along the Withlacoochee, a Native American word for "long and winding river," and is reached on State Route 50 and Rital Croom Road, which runs just east of Interstate 75. The trail starts at the Tucker Hill Tower just off the Croom Road, where you can pick up a free trail map. The route is divided into three loops for those who do not want to overnight here, but there is a campsite for those who do.

You can get more details about the different state parks and their trails on the Florida Park Service WEB SITE www.dep.state.fl.us/parks. For more detailed information contact the **Department of Environmental Protection Park Information** ☎ (850) 488-9872, Mail Station

No. 535, 3900 Commonwealth Boulevard, Tallahassee. Among the many special places worth visiting are those listed below. If you need more information on particular parks we list the address and telephone number of the local park authorities in each case.

NORTHWEST

Florida Caverns State Park is 60 miles west of Tallahassee and three miles (five kilometers) north of Marianna on State Route 167. The park has a network of caverns with eerie limestone formations and offers guided one-hour tours from the interpretive center. There are campgrounds, nature and hiking trails, swimming, fishing and boating. Park authorities ☎ (850) 482-9598, 3345 Caverns Road, Marianna.

Manatee Springs State Park, six miles (10 km) northwest of Chiefland on State Route 320, has hiking trails and canoe rentals, and a boardwalk where you can see manatees in the water underneath. Manatees make occasional appearances near the mouth of the springs, where

117 million gallons (443 million liters) of crystal clear water flow daily. Park authorities ✆ (352) 493-6072, 11650 Northwest 115th Street, Chiefland

St. George Island State Park, in the mouth of the Apalachicola River, is reached by a toll bridge off US Highway 98, 10 miles (16 km) southeast of Eastpoint. It offers nine miles of the most pristine beaches and shoreline in the state. The oyster industry is based here and it offers good birdwatching with nature trails and observation platforms. Park authorities ✆ (850) 927-2111, 1900 East Gulf Beach Drive, St. George Island.

St. Joseph Peninsula, near Port St. Joe off State Route 30, is noted for its white sand beaches and huge barrier dunes. It is also a major birdwatching area with 210 species recorded in a small area. In the autumn it is one of the best observation points in the eastern United States to spot migrating hawks. In the back of the park there are luxury furnished cabins, as well as a couple of campsites. Park authorities ✆ (850) 227-1237, 8899 Cape San Blas Road, Port St. Joe.

Torreya State Park, the area between Bristol and Greensboro, is mountainous by Florida's standards, with canyons and steep bluffs, some rising 150 ft (46 m) above the Apalachicola River. In the autumn, the surrounding hardwood forests provide one of the best foliage displays in the state. There are nature and hiking trails, guided tours and campfire programs. There are three very different trails that take you either in or around the park. Park authorities ✆ (850) 643-2674, Route 2, Box 70, Greensboro.

Wakulla Springs State Park, on State Route 61, 14 miles South of Tallahassee, is one of the world's largest and deepest freshwater springs. It remains a constant 70-degrees year round. There are glass bottom boat tours, plus hiking and nature trails, wildlife observation boat trips, and overnight accommodation in a 27 room Spanish-style lodge, built in 1937, and featuring marble floors, ornate ceilings and antique furnishings. Park authorities ✆ (850) 224-5950, 550 Wakulla Park Drive, Tallahassee.

NORTHEAST

Ichetuckee Springs, four miles (six km) north of Fort White on Route 2, is a good place for nature watching, hiking and snorkeling. There are nine springs and the average flow of water is about 233 million gallons (845 million liters) a day at a constant temperature of 23°C (73°F). Tubing and snorkeling are now available on the clear river, but the number of visitors are limited to maintain the park. With only about 750 tubers allowed per day, plan on arriving early. Park authorities ✆ (850) 497-2511, Route 2, Box 108, Fort White.

Little Talbot Island State Park, on State Route A1A, 17 miles (27 km) northeast of Jacksonville, is an area of sand dunes and quiet beaches, and an an important nesting site for sea turtles. There are guided walks, and good surf fishing. Park authorities ✆ (850) 251-2320, 11435 Fort George Road East.

O'Leno State Park ✆ (850) 454-1853, Route 2, Box 1010, 20 miles (36 km) south of Lake City on US Highway 441, is a popular camping area, offering hiking, canoeing, horse back riding, guided walks and nature trails. One of its main attractions is the river sink, where a stretch of the Sante Fe River disappears underground for more than three miles (five kilometers) before re-emerging. It is a good place for alligator and turtle spotting. Seventeen cabins are available, but the furniture is sparse with mainly cots and mattresses.

The Suwannee River is the state river and subject of the state anthem, although most people mistakenly refer to it as the Swanee. The first park to become part of the Florida State Parks system, **The Suwannee River State Park**, 13 miles (21 km) north of Live Oak on US Highway 90, has nature and hiking trails, and it is the site of the former town of Columbus. Parts of the old stage road, which ran from Pensacola to Jacksonville in the early 1800s, can still be walked. Park authorities ✆ (850) 362-2746, County Road 132, Live Oak.

Spanish moss festoons these Kissimmee trees.

CENTRAL EAST

Blue Spring State Park is a winter gathering ground for manatees seeking shelter from the colder waters of the nearby St. Johns River. The mammals can be clearly seen from a number of observation platforms over the water, and you can even swim in the spring. There are nature and hiking trails, canoe rentals, boat tours of the St. Johns River, camping areas and vacation cabins (which have air-conditioning and fireplaces).

For hundreds of years this lagoon area of natural springs along the St. Johns river was the home of the Timucuan people. Their staple food was snails gathered from sandbars in the river and the huge mounds of discarded shells can still be seen. In 1766, three years after England acquired Florida from Spain, John Bartram, a British botanist, explored the St. Johns River and landed at Blue Spring. By the middle of the nineteenth century it was at the heart of a large citrus estate with steamships navigating upriver to pick up the fruit. The pilings of the old dock, as well as the restored estate house, can still be seen. Park authorities ☎ (850) 775-3663, 2100 West French Avenue, in Orange City.

Bulow Creek State Park, just north of Ormond Beach on Old Dixie Highway, is famous for the Fairchild Oak, believed to be more than 800 years old and one of the largest oak trees in the United States. This is a 5,000-acre (2,000-hectare) area of coastal hardwood forest, *hammocks* — raised, tree-clad mounds in the swamps, which serve as observation points and campsites — and salt marsh, with hiking and nature trails. Park authorities ☎ (850) 676-4050, 2099 North Beach Street, Ormond Beach.

Hontoon Island, six miles (10 km) west of DeLand, can only be reached by private boat or the free public ferry, which runs from 9 AM to one hour before sundown. However, you can stay overnight in the campground or in one of the six rustic cabins with bunk beds and ceiling fans. The island is interesting because it was a Native American settlement for many centuries. There is a replica of a large owl totem carved more than 600 years ago and some interesting Native American mounds. Park authorities(850) 736-5309, 2309 River Ridge Road, DeLand.

Tomoka State Park, three miles (five km) north of Ormond Beach on North Beach Street, is another ancient Native American settlement, with guided tours from the museum and visitor center. Also, there are nature and hiking trails and canoe rentals. In the late 1700s, the land was granted to Richard Oswald, a wealthy English merchant and statesman, who helped negotiate the accession treaty with England after the American Revolution. You can go boating, canoeing or fishing, but swimming is not permitted. Park authorities ☎ (850) 676-4050, 2099 North Beach Street, Ormond Beach.

CENTRAL

Highlands Hammock State Park, six miles (10 km) west of Sebring on State Route 634, is one of Florida's four original parks and was created when local residents became alarmed at plans to clear the hardwood forests for farmland. There are walking, cycling and horse riding trails, an interpretive center, guided tram-tours, picnic areas and campsites. The winding road is great for cyclists. Park authorities ☎ (941) 386-6094, 5931 Hammock Road, Sebring.

Lake Kissimmee is fifteen miles (24 km) east of Lake Wales, and a long way from Kissimmee City. The park offers a taste of Florida past and present. Observation platforms, hiking, nature and canoe trails allow you to see how the area's environment and wildlife are being managed today, while you can see what life used to be like in a recreated 1876 hunting camp and a cow hunter demonstration. Park authorities ☎ (941) 696-1112, 14248 Camp Mack Road.

CENTRAL WEST

Caladesi Island State Park is reached by ferry from Honeymoon Island and downtown Clearwater. For ferry boat information in Clearwater call ☎ (813) 442-7433 or (813) 734-5263 on Honeymoon Island. Caladesi is one of the few

undisturbed barrier islands in the state. It has nature and hiking trails and offers swimming, fishing and more than two miles (three kilometers) of white sand gulfside beaches, which are rated among the top five beaches in the United States. Much of the island appears the same as it did in the 1500s when the Spanish explored the area. A three-mile nature trail winds through island's interior. Park authorities ((813) 469-5942, No. 1 Causeway Boulevard, Dunedin.

Egmont Key National Wildlife Refuge, southwest of Fort DeSoto Beach, can only be reached by boat. The lighthouse, once the last remaining manned light in the United States, is now automated. The key was used as a camp for captured "Indians" during the Third Seminole War, and was the Union navy base in the Civil War. Now it is a wildlife refuge. Park authorities ((813) 893-2627, 4905 34th Street, South, No. 50000, St. Petersburg.

Homosassa Springs State Wildlife Park, on Fish Bowl Road, combines state park, wildlife park and the Florida Nature Museum, which has a collection of artifacts and fossils found in the region. The 55-feet (17-m) deep springs are the headwater of the Homosassa River, and you can descend into the underwater observatory to view the fish, manatees, and other wildlife. The springs are important because they are home to both freshwater and saltwater fish. There are nature trails and guided boat tours. Now it also serves as a rehabilitation center and refuge for endangered West Indian manatees, which are often injured in boating accidents. There is a fee for educational programs. The park is open 9 AM to 5 PM daily. Park authorities ((352) 628-5343, 4150 South Suncoast Boulevard, Homosassa.

THE SOUTH

Cayo Costa, north of Captiva Island in Pine Island sound, is one of the largest undeveloped barrier islands along the coast and only accessible by boat. Only

Wildflowers can be found in profusion along most of Florida's beaches.

one man lives on the island — the park ranger. Cayo is noted for its wildlife and Native American relics, and there are nature and hiking trails. Both osprey and bald eagles nest on the island, frigate birds are regularly spotted and it has one of the largest brown pelican rookeries in the state. It is also a good place for shell collectors, especially during the winter months. There are no paved roads and only primitive cabins for overnight rentals. Park ranger ☎ (941) 964-0375, Cayo Costa.

Collier-Seminole Park, 17 miles (27 km) south of Naples, on Route 41, is special because it features a tropical hardwood hammock of trees more commonly found in the West Indies and Mexico's Yucatan peninsula than in southwest Florida. It also has an extensive mangrove swamp. There are hiking and nature trails, observation platforms, fishing, swimming and camping. Occasionally you might be able to see the endangered Florida panther. However, the park allows only a limited number of visitors each day. Park authorities ☎ (941) 394-3397, 20200 East Tamiami Trail, Naples.

The **Lovers Key State Recreation Area** is Florida's newest park, a combination of the former Lovers Key and Carl Johnson parks. It has 2.5 miles of white sand beaches, swimming, birdwatching, canoeing and kayaking. As if to add to the lore of the romantic setting, it also has a 100-seat, turn-of-the century beachfront pavilion available for weddings and other special events. Park authorities ☎ (941) 463-4588, 8700 Estero Boulevard, Fort Myers Beach.

For a park like no other, check out **Biscayne National Park**, with 95 percent of its 180,000 acres located underwater. Entrance to the park by car is from the west only, where you take North Canal Drive (Southwest 328th Street). The other way to enter is by boat. There is a fee for docking the boat overnight at Boca Chita Key and Elliott Key. The offshore breezes and protected waters make it an ideal place for windsurfing, and rentals are available. This is also a great place for snorkeling and scuba diving. Park authorities ☎ (305) 230-7275 FAX (305) 230-1120 WEB SITE www.now.gov/bisc, 9700 Southwest 328th Street, Homestead.

THE KEYS

Bahia Honda State Park is a wildlife reserve containing many rare species of plants and birds, such as the white crowned pigeon, great white heron, roseate spoonbill, reddish egret and least tern. The offshore waters offer some of the best tarpon fishing in the state. There are a number of hiking and nature trails, with campground, cabins and swimming in both the Atlantic Ocean and Florida Bay. The teal-colored waters are inviting for swimming or snorkeling. Park authorities ☎ (305) 872-2353, Route 1, MM 37, Bahia Honda Key.

John Pennekamp Coral Reef State Park, on Key Largo at MM 102.5, is the state's only underwater park and the first to be designated in the nation. On land there is an interpretive center, campsite, hiking and nature trails, but it is the water that mainly attracts the visitors. It is the only area of living coral reef in the continental United States, and the park covers 178 sq miles (463 sq km) of reef, seagrass beds and mangrove swamps. You can explore by boat or canoe, snorkel, or scuba. For more information contact the park concession at ☎ (305) 451-1621. An attraction is the 10-foot (3-m) high bronze statue of Christ of the Deep, which stands in 20 ft (6 m) of water in the Atlantic Ocean. It is one of the state's top diving and snorkeling areas. Park authorities ☎ (305) 451-1202, PO Box 487, Key Largo.

Sporting Spree

Florida is in a league of its own when it comes to sporting opportunities. No other state has as many tennis courts, golf courses — more than 1,150 at last count — or as many pleasure boats.

Whether a spectator or a player, the great thing about Florida is that the year-round good weather means you can enjoy your favorite recreation whenever you want. There are also college and amateur sporting events to be enjoyed throughout the state year round. Regional convention and visitors centers can provide a wealth of information about sporting and recreational activities.

TENNIS

If Florida had an official state sport, it would undoubtedly be tennis. It's no accident that the former queen of American tennis, Chris Evert, and younger star Jennifer Capriati are both products of Floridian tennis courts. Courts (both public and private) are everywhere, including at all the larger hotels. Surfaces include clay, grass and hardcourt and many are floodlit. There are tennis hotels and training schools where you can take lessons from the pros, as well as scores of professional and major amateur tournaments. Book your court for early in the morning or late in the afternoon when the sun is less intense. Local recreation departments can give you details on all the courts in your area, or you can contact the **Florida Tennis Association** ☎ (954) 968-3434, 1280 Southwest 36th Street, Pompano Beach, FL 33069.

GOLF

Golf is a close second to tennis as the most popular pastime in Florida, and the state is

OPPOSITE: A pelican waits for a catch on New Cedar Key. ABOVE: The Sunshine State boasts more golf courses than any other region on earth.

world-famous for its links, both public and private, which attract more than a million golfers each year from around the globe. Not only are there splendid public courses in every corner of the state, especially near the more popular resort areas, but most of the private courses admit visitors for a nominal fee. There are even resort courses where you can take a vacation villa or an apartment alongside the fairway and play all day long. Golf passes allow you to play at a number of courses in the area you are staying, and at fees well below those you would normally pay. The **Florida Sports Foundation** ☎ (850) 488-8347, FAX (850) 922-0482 E-MAIL fsf@tdo.infi.net WEB SITE www.flasports.com, 107 West Gaines Street, Tallahassee FL 32399, can provide more details about the wealth of golfing opportunities in the state. Alternatively, you can get in touch with the **Florida State Golf Association** ☎ (941) 921-5695, 5714 Draw Lane, Sarasota, FL 34238.

If you are a golf spectator, you should plan on visiting Florida in February, March, or October — during the major PGA tournaments. In February the Doral Eastern Open is held in Miami, in March the Tournament Players Championship is held in Jacksonville, and in October you have both the Pensacola PGA Open and the Walt Disney World National Team Championship Golf Classic.

FISHING

With 8,000 miles (12,800 km) of tidal coastline, 30,000 lakes, and countless rivers and streams, it is hardly surprising that Florida is a fisherman's — and fisherwoman's — paradise. While no license is required for saltwater fishing, you will need a non-resident's license for freshwater fishing (unless you are under 16). Licenses can be bought from any marina or tackle shop.

There are more than 600 different species of saltwater fish off the Florida coast, and there are almost as many species of boats for charter in every port to take you out to fish for them. For landlubbers, there are many public fishing piers from which you can fish in the ocean

without waiting, there are ample opportunities for shellfishing among Florida's offshore population of crabs, scallops, and lobsters.

Anglers can also try their luck at reeling in a marlin, sailfish or shark on a sportsfishing excursion in the Atlantic Ocean or Gulf of Mexico. There are 24 species of game fish in Florida's lakes and waterways, and state records include a 20-lb (nine-kilogram) largemouth bass, 38.5-lb (17-kg) striped bass, and 40.5-lb (18-kg) carp. Daily bag limits have been imposed for many species to conserve stocks, and an honor system is in place whereby small fish are returned to the water to grow so they can be caught another day.

For a complete guide to fishing in Florida, write to the **Florida Game and Freshwater Fish Commission** ☎ (850) 488-0520 FAX (850) 413-0381 E-MAIL wattenb@mail.state.fl.us WEB SITE www.fcn.state.fl.us/gfc/fishing, 620 South Meridian Street, Tallahassee, FL 32399. The commission's web site contains articles and information that can be downloaded, as well as answers to frequently asked questions about fishing in Florida's waters.

WATERSPORTS

Florida offers endless opportunities for **watersports** of all kinds. There are over 1,000 miles (1,600 km) of beach, more than 7,700 natural lakes of 10 acres (four hectares) or more, as well as 1,700 rivers and waterways navigable by small boats and canoes.

As soon as the sun breaks the horizon, **surfers** are crouched over the boards waiting to catch the first waves of the day, while beneath the sparkling blue waters of the Florida Keys, **snorkelers** explore the only living coral reef in the continental United States.

Scuba divers can explore the more than 4,000 shipwrecks that lie off the coast, and **water-skiing**, **parasailing** and **jetskiing** can also be enjoyed throughout the state.

Boating is a year-round activity in Florida's balmy climate. The state has 8,426 miles (13,481 km) of tidal shoreline, 4,500 sq miles (11,707 sq km) of inland water, and 750,000 registered boats. Any boat over 16 ft (4.9 m) has to be registered with the Florida Department of Natural Resources. Powerboats are more popular than sailboats mostly because they operate better in shallow water and because distances are so great — one of the reasons why Florida is one of the main venues for international power boat racing, including grand prix events. Both sailboats and powerboats can be rented throughout the state, while more sedate house boats are available for cruising some of the larger lakes and waterways.

Canoeing is still one of the best ways to explore the state's hundreds of miles of inland waterways. The great advantage of canoeing is that it enables you to silently explore many areas not accessible on foot, and to see a varied wildlife at close quarters. There is good canoeing throughout the state, but among the best locations are the Blackwater and Suwannee Rivers in the northwest and the Myakka and Peace Rivers near Arcadia. Local canoe operators provide equipment rentals and transportation for visitors. In Kissimmee, only a short distance from Disney World, you can rent a canoe by the main road and within a couple of minutes be in a different world, exploring backwaters where the only sounds are the calls of the birds and the croaking frogs. Canoeing is great fun, especially for families. It takes a few minutes to get the hang of paddling though, and it is best that an adult sits at the back to control the direction of the canoe; otherwise there's a tendency to go round in circles! This also allows grown-ups to keep their eyes on the children in front.

If planning a canoe trip, remember to keep your bearings at all times — it is possible to get disoriented, especially when paddling among mangrove islands. Wear a hat and sunscreen, generously apply insect repellent, and always carry something to drink as it is easy to dehydrate when exercising in the heat.

TEAM SPORTS

There are lots of opportunities to watch a wide range of team sports in Florida, and for non-Americans, the chance to learn something about **baseball**, **basketball** and **American football**. Twenty of the nation's 30 major league baseball teams have spring training camps in Florida where you can watch some of the best players in action. For something a bit different, there is the fast and furious jai alai, reputed to be the world's fastest ball game — the ball reaching speeds of 175 mph (110 kph). Jai alai was introduced to Florida by Cuban immigrants.

The Sunshine State has a home team in every major spectator sport. National Football League (NFL) teams in Miami, Jacksonville and Tampa play from September to December; National Basketball Association (NBA) teams in Miami and Orlando play from October to May; National Hockey League (NHL) teams in Orlando, Fort Lauderdale and Tampa play from October to April; while the Miami-based Florida Marlins and Tampa Bay Devil Rays play during a Major League Baseball season that runs from April to September.

Boating is the best way to explore the Everglades and its rich wildlife.

AUTO RACING

Daytona Beach is home to the world famous Daytona 500 motor race, where racing fans can also enjoy the 24-hour race, a test of endurance and skill. There is also the Grand Prix of Miami, and the FedEx Championship Series Indy-style car race held at the Metro-Dade Motorsports Complex in Homestead.

POLO

Polo is played from mid-November to the end of March at the Palm Beach Polo and Country Club. Prince Charles is a regular guest, as well as at the Royal Palm Polo Club in Boca Raton and the Windsor Polo Club in Vero Beach.

The Open Road

You see it in the distance as you drive down to the southern tip of St. Petersburg, tall and yellow and undulating, like a giant roller coaster ride across Tampa Bay — the **Sunshine Skyway Bridge** — leaping over the water to the mainland north of Bradenton. The route consists of mile after mile of causeway joined by

soaring roadway, which rises to 183 feet (53 m) above the water — high enough to let the largest ocean vessel pass beneath. The 4.1-mile (6.5 km) architectural and engineering marvel was modeled after the Brotonne Bridge that spans the Seine in France, although that one is a little longer — running for almost 15 miles (24 km). If staying in central Florida, the Sunshine Skyway can easily be included as part of a long day trip to the Gulf.

The $1 toll allows you to ascend smoothly to the top. As you descend, the banana-colored cables and spires dance in the rearview mirror. It's hard to keep your eyes focused ahead and not glance back and stare at the image of an art sculpture afloat the water. For those afraid of heights, just keep your eyes on the road ahead, it won't even seem like you are so high. At night the bright structure is flooded with lights, making it an imposing landmark in Tampa Bay.

With the speed limit on most of Florida's major highways at 70 mph (113 kph), it is now possible to get from one place to another a little more quickly, but there is little point in rushing when there is so much to see and do along the way. If you want a glimpse of the real Florida it is better to avoid the Interstate highways and turnpikes and stick to the country roads.

A word of warning: roads and streets often change names or will carry two names for a section. For instance, US Highway 41 going across the state in the southern part by the Everglades is also known as the Tamiami Trail. US Highway 1 is also known as South Dixie Highway. Double-check all directions, because sometimes natives may give you the more scenic route to your destination, as opposed to the most direct.

Florida has a number of other scenic drives; one of the most spectacular is along **State Route A1A**. It runs along the Atlantic Coast north from Daytona Beach for 105 miles (169 km) until the turn off for Fernandina Beach on Amelia Island — Florida's first resort and long before that a notorious haven for pirates and

smugglers. Mile after mile on Highway AIA, which is also known as Atlantic Avenue up and down the coast, you'll find huge stretches of near deserted sandy beach. Stop wherever you want to enjoy the views, laze in the sun, or take a swim.

Almost as spectacular, but generally much busier, is the drive from mainland Florida to Key West. The **Overseas Highway**, or US Highway 1, is the only route through the Keys. It follows the path of the Overseas Railroad, which was completed at huge cost in 1912 and destroyed by a hurricane in 1935. Highway 1 crosses 43 bridges on its 113 mile (182 km) island-hopping route to Key West. Although it is an interstate, for most of its way through the Keys it is only a two-lane highway. It offers wonderful scenery, passing emerald-green lagoons, turquoise seas, gently waving palms and olive-green mangroves. You may see dolphins offshore as well as herons, pelicans, spoonbills and ospreys. Mile markers (MMs) are positioned every mile along the Overseas Highway so that you always know where you are. They indicate the distance between Florida City on the mainland and Key West, and everyone uses them to give directions. If you stop to ask where your hotel is, you will be told it is just before MM 26, and all the brochures and guides use mile markers as locator points. As you leave Florida City the marker bears the number 126, and when you get to the end of the road at the corner of Fleming and Whitehead Streets on Key West, the marker has the number 0. You are at the southernmost point of any road in the Continental United States. The journey between Miami and Key West can be traveled in less than four hours, but the whole idea of visiting the Keys is to slow down, so what's the hurry? Apart from the high season when most accommodations are fully booked, you can usually find a motel and hotel room along the way. If you are staying in central Florida and want to explore it, this makes a good two or three day trip with the bonus of getting to visit Key West.

Other scenic drives include **Bayshore Boulevard**, in Tampa, which offers scenic

OPPOSITE: A custom car in Clearwater. ABOVE: The Sunshine Skyway Bridge is a roller-coaster of a ride.

views of Hillsborough Bay and some of the area's most exclusive homes. The drive allows you to take in Davis Island, one of Tampa's most beautiful neighborhoods, built on three man-made islands constructed in the 1920s.

Indian River Scenic Drive in Fort Pierce follows the river's west shore towards Jensen Beach past native trees, exotic flowers and a rich birdlife. The farming community grew on the site of a United States Army post built in 1838 during the "Indian Wars." The St. Lucie County Historical Museum on Seaway Drive highlights the history of the area — focusing on the Seminole people and the first Spanish colonists. Take time during the drive to stop and cross the footbridge over to Jack Island, a bird and wildlife refuge where you can enjoy a swim and a picnic.

There are a number of scenic drives in the Miami and Miami Beach area, the best of which is along the **Main** and **Ingraham** highways and **Old Cutler Road.** The drive runs south from Coconut Grove and takes in exclusive Coral Gables, then Old Cutler Highway passes Matheson Hammock Park and the Fairchild Tropical Gardens — where the trees form a canopy. It feels like you are slipping into a tunnel at one end and coming out in a tropical paradise on the other.

South Miami Avenue between 15th Road and Dixie Highway, is lined with royal poinciana trees, which are a blaze of red flowers during late May and June. The tree is known locally as the traveler tree — because the flowers arrive in the summer and immediately turn bright red!

Another interesting drive is along **Collins Avenue** in Miami Beach. With its huge hotels and nearby luxurious island homes, the styles range from Spanish Colonial to ultra-modern. While the homes are not open to the public you can drive round and view them from the road. You may not be doing much driving on **Ocean Drive** in South Beach during the afternoons and evenings, especially on weekend. But the views are spectacular, with the ocean to the east and beautiful art deco buildings to the West. From your car, as you cruise along at a two mile-per-hour rate, you have the best seat for great people watching.

The **Tamiami Trail** (US Highway 41) skirts the northern borders of the Everglades National Park. A memorable drive is to take **State Route 9336** that runs to the park's main entrance and then south to Flamingo. Locals tend to speed along the road, just slow down and let them pass. If you rush you will miss so much. As you drive through this area, you will also see signs alerting you to watch out for the rare Florida panther, which may suddenly appear on the road. Apart from the drive itself through the heart of the Everglades, there are a number of walking trails along the road that can be explored. In Flamingo there are restaurants, a variety of wildlife, fishing, and sightseeing boat tours.

In the Panhandle, **US Highway 98** offers a scenic drive along the Gulf of Mexico for almost 100 miles (160 km) from Panama City to Gulf Breeze, just south of Pensacola. The road either follows the

OPPOSITE: The warm waters of Sanibel Island teem with an amazing array of fish. ABOVE: An immature eagle is displayed in the Everglades National Park.

coast or is never far from it, and there are lots of opportunities to find your own near-deserted stretch of beach or explore among the huge dunes. This coastline has some of the highest and most extensive dunes in the southeast, which the onshore winds are constantly changing and re-sculpting. If the winds have been strong, sand does get blown across the road and can be quite deep in places, so always drive carefully.

Backpacking

Even though you might be traveling on a limited budget, you can still enjoy much of what Florida has to offer, particularly the beaches, the natural beauty of the parks and preserves, and the differences in culture from region to region.

One way to keep your journey inexpensive is by sleeping at **campsites**. Most drive-in campgrounds offer a high degree of comfort with toilets, washrooms, laundry facilities, picnic tables and barbecue grills. There are usually electricity and water hook-ups for motor caravans, known as recreational vehicles (RVs) in the United States.

Many of Florida's state and national parks also have wilderness campsites, which are more remote and have few or no facilities. These are true backpacking havens where you have to carry in everything you need, including water, and carry out all evidence of your stay. Primitive camping is usually free, although some parks levy a small charge. The number of sites is usually restricted both on environmental grounds and so that you actually feel you are alone in the wilderness and not surrounded by scores of other campers. If heading for a primitive campsite, let the park visitor center or ranger station know where you are going and how long you plan to be there, and report back on your return so they can cross you off their list and not institute a search party.

State park campsites and facilities are listed at WEB SITE www.dep.state.fl.us /parks, where you can determine which

parks are closest to the area you want to visit and if they suit your needs. Some county parks also allow camping. Another good source for campsite information is the Official Florida Camping Directory at WEB SITE www.floridacamping.com.

KOA Kampgrounds are also good places to stay, such as the **Fiesta Key Resort KOA Kampground and Motel** TOLL-FREE (800) 562-7730, Gulfside at MM 70, Long Key. In Jacksonville, **Huguenot Park** ☎ (850) 251-5355, offers primitive oceanfront camping.

Another low-budget lodging option is staying at local hostels. Not only are they affordable, but they usually offer some kind of discount on popular activities in the area.

For example, **Hostelling International**

Key West ☎ (305) 296-5719 TOLL-FREE (800) 51-HOSTEL, FAX (305) 296-0672, 718 South Street, offers $15 rooms for members (plus tax) and $18 for non-members at. Plus they offer an incredible $18 price for snorkeling trips in the amazingly blue waters off the Keys. Meals are also less than $5 each.

At the **Everglades International Hostel** ☎ (305) 248-1122 TOLL-FREE (800) 372-3874 FAX (305) 245-7622 E-MAIL gladeshostel@hotmail.com WEB SITE www.members.xoom.com/gladeshostel, 20 Southwest Second Avenue, Florida City, you can stay overnight at a gateway to both the Everglades National Park and the Florida Keys. The hostel offers canoe rentals and discounts on diving and snorkeling expeditions in the Keys.

Another incredibly well-situated place is the **Banana Bungalow Beach Hotel and Hostel** ☎ (305) 531-3755 TOLL-FREE (800) 746-7835 FAX (305) 531-3217 WEB SITE www.bananabungalow.com, 2360 Collins Avenue, Miami Beach, which is across the street from the beach and near a tranquil canal. The **Clay Hotel and International Hostel** ☎ (305) 534-2988 TOLL-FREE (800) 379-CLAY FAX (305) 673-0346 WEB SITE www.clayhotel.com, 1438 Washington Avenue, Miami Beach, is two blocks from the beach off 14th street. You will feel somewhat spoiled by the decor of the hotel, which is on the National Registry of Historic Places.

The **St. Petersburg Youth Hostel** ☎ (813) 822-4141, 326 First Avenue North, is located

The Everglades Swamps are threatened by man's encroachment.

at the McCarthy Hotel, which is within walking distance to downtown areas of shopping and dining, including The Pier. A public bus stop is conveniently located in front of the hostel and the Greyhound Bus Station is three blocks away.

Getting from one city to another can be done conveniently and easily on **Greyhound Bus Lines** TOLL-FREE (800) 231-2222. Also **Bus One** ☎ (305) 870-0919 TOLL-FREE (888) 287-1669 FAX (305) 870-0180 WEB SITE www.busone.com, 2601 LeJeune Road, Miami, offers daily non-stop service between Miami and Orlando.

Aside from Florida's bigger cities, most of the motels in the smaller coastal towns are relatively affordable, which should not make exploring the state prohibitive.

Tourist offices can give you the latest information about new attractions, and there is a mass of free information available throughout the state. Look for free magazines such as *Enjoy Florida* and *The Best Read Guide* which not only list all the attractions and current prices and times, but are packed with discount vouchers. Don't ignore these give-away magazines; over the course of a two-week vacation, they can save a family hundreds of dollars off the price of restaurant bills and attraction tickets.

Living It Up

Florida is known for its pleasant, and sometimes maybe too hot, weather, which many take advantage of by going to the beach. But the Sunshine State also offers many opportunities to be pampered at luxury resorts and fine restaurants. The major resort hotels offer their own restaurants, night clubs and floor shows, and there is never a shortage of choice if you want to go out.

For the ritziest of the ritziest, you need only go to Palm Beach, where just looking at the oceanfront mansions is enough to boggle the best of us. The palm-tree lined boulevard that marks the entrance to the island rolls out in front of you like a red carpet. Take a turn or two and you are on Worth Avenue, the shopping and restaurant district that caters to the most discriminating tastes.

The Breakers ☎ (5617) 655-6611 TOLL-FREE (888) 273-2537 FAX (561) 659-8403 WEB SITE www.thebreakers.com, at One South County Road, is one of the most luxurious places to stay. The building itself is too immense to believe. **The Colony** ☎ (561) 655-5430 TOLL-FREE (800) 521-5525 FAX (561) 832-7318 WEB SITE www.thecolonypalmbeach.com, at 155 Hammon Avenue, where the Duke and Duchess of Windsor usually stayed, is another grand old hotel. Another hotel that was built in the same era as the Breakers and recently renovated is the **Brazilian Court Hotel** ☎ (516) 655-7740 TOLL-FREE (800) 552-0335 FAX (561) 655-0801 WEB SITE www.braziliancourt.com, at 301 Australian Avenue in West Palm Beach, where your pets can be spoiled with gourmet pet food ordered from room service.

Meals at these hotel restaurants are exquisite, but for Northern Italian cuisine with authentic Italian ambiance, try **Bice** ☎ (561) 835-1600, 313 1/2 Worth Avenue, Palm Beach.

Generally, the finest dining in central Florida is in the major resort hotels, especially within Walt Disney World. Non-guests are welcome to dine in these restaurants but reservations are essential.

Among the best gourmet restaurants in central Florida are **Park Plaza Gardens** ☎ (407) 645-2475 WEB SITE www .ParkplazaGardens.com, at 319 Park Avenue South, Orlando, where in absolutely delightful surroundings you can enjoy such specialties as flounder *meunière* and shrimp in curry sauce.

A visit to charming St. Augustine, the oldest city in the United States, will be completely satisfying with a stay at the recently renovated **Casa Monica** TOLL-FREE (888) GRAND 123, WEB SITE www.grandthemehotels.com, which opened in the fall of 1999. Situated in the very heart of St. Augustine, the hotel has 138 luxurious rooms and four of the hotel's

Fountains, palms and tropical flowers decorate this Turnberry Isle property.

five towers are offered as one or two-bedroomed suites. A pool, fitness facilities, fine dining, and a piano bar round out its facilities.

In the Greater Miami area there are even more hotels and an even greater choice of restaurants and night spots. When the sun goes down in Miami, the stars really do come out — along with world famous models, musicians, and other celebrities who live nearby. Star spotting is a sport in Miami whether in a dance club, jazz café or more exclusive night spot.

The South Beach's club scene rivals that of New York and Los Angeles; Coconut Grove and Coral Gables offer some of the area's finest — and most expensive — restaurants, while downtown Miami has a vast range of regional and international cuisines to tempt you. For the finest dining, try **Victor's Café** ☎ (305) 445-1313, 2340 Southwest 32nd Avenue, Miami, or **Casa Juancho** ☎ (305) 642-2452, 2436 Southwest 8th Street, Miami, for Cuban cuisine. And for fabulous New World cuisine visit **Norman's** ☎ (305) 446-6767, WEB SITE www.normans.com, 21 Almeria Avenue, in Coral Gables.

If you head over to the Southwest Gulf Coast of Florida, which is decidedly more sedate than Miami or Fort Lauderdale, you can enjoy a more secluded resort experience. The **Sanibel Harbour Resort and Spa** ☎ (941) 466-4000 TOLL-FREE (800) 767-7777 WEB SITE www.sanibel-resort.com, 17260 Harbour Pointe Drive, Fort Myers, offers spa services for individuals and also a children's program for those with families. But if you want to relax away from the kids, babysitters are also available. Fine dining can be enjoyed at the resort's **Chez Le Bear** restaurant, with wonderful Mediterranean cuisine.

For a romantic sunset dinner cruise, board the **Sanibel Harbour Princess**, where you are greeted onto the 100-foot yacht with champagne and hors d'oeuvres. Full-course meals await you, and dolphins jump in the wake to see you sail off into the evening.

If you really want to get away from it all, including Florida, go as far north as you possibly can on the Atlantic Coast to the **Amelia Island Plantation** ☎ (850) 261-6161 TOLL-FREE (800) 874-6878 FAX (850) 277-5945 WEB SITE www.aipfl.com, PO Box 3000, Amelia Island, just north of Jacksonville. The Georgia border is within view of the coast. The 1,350 acres of the Plantation feature 249 oceanfront hotel rooms, fine dining, including Sunday brunch, 54 holes of championship golf, and 23 tennis courts.

Behind the gated entry you feel like you have really entered the south, nestled between the salt marshes of the Intracoastal Waterway and the Atlantic Ocean.

Family Fun

Florida is the ideal destination for children of all ages, with its safe, sandy beaches and warm shallow waters, spacious affordable accommodation, and cheap eating places — and enough attractions to keep even the most active child amused for weeks on end.

Most families head for the theme parks of Central Florida, which can easily swallow up every minute of a two-week vacation. However, remember that there are lots of other things in Florida to keep the kids amused, and many of them are free.

There are, of course, the **beaches**. The Gulf coast generally offers the safest paddling and swimming for young children, as the surf and rip tides can sometimes be a problem on the Atlantic coastline. Most of the popular beaches are patrolled by lifeguards but if you have children, you should always keep an eye on them while they are in or near the water.

It is great to spend time lying in the sun and swimming; however, be especially careful if you have young children. They should wear a sun hat and T-shirt with their swimming suits and be digilent with the sunscreen. A sunscreen

Children and parents get a close-up look at Florida's marine life at this Key West aquarium.

with a protection factor of at least 20 is recommended.

Take time as a family to discover the real Florida. Spend a day walking and picnicking in one of the many state parks and see how many new plants, animals and birds you can spot. Canoeing is another fun and affordable family pastime, and great for younger children. Canoe rentals are available throughout the state, and you can take a canoe out for an hour or two or the whole day provided you take a picnic and drinks with you. The advantage of canoes is that they are silent. As you drift up backwaters, you will see a wide range of wildlife that would normally be frightened away. Again, with canoeing, it is important to wear a hat, sunscreen and insect repellent, and to take drinks to replace the fluids lost through the (even modest) exertion of paddling. It is also vital that young children and non-swimmers wear the life vests that are provided.

You might also like to take the family on one of the hundreds of boat trips available around the state. There is a huge selection from wildlife trips in glass bottom boats up the quiet St. Johns river or through the Everglades, to game fishing trips into the Gulf. For a little more action, rent an air boat, the sort of craft made famous in James Bond's Everglades chases, which zoom across the water. It does take a little while to get the hang of steering.

Cycling can be fun for older kids. Escape to the car-free trails of the state and national parks where you can rent bikes and pedal in safety. There are already 2,000 miles (3,600 km) of bicycle trails in Florida, and the state has embarked on an ambitious program of developing new trails, many following the old railroad tracks.

Many of Florida's cultural and scientific attractions are specially geared for children. There is Tampa's **Florida Aquarium**, where you can peek into the underwater world of sharks through a larger-than-life glass window and feel like they are right next to you.

There is **The Teddy Bear Museum** of Naples ☎ (941) 598-2711, 511 Pine Ridge Road, Naples. In Fort Lauderdale kids will love the **Museum of Discovery & Science** ☎ (954) 467-6637 WEB SITE www.mods.org, 401 Southwest Second Avenue, with its hands-on exhibits that allow you to watch bees at work in a glass-fronted hive, go cave crawling, bend rays of light, and touch a star, among other things. There is also an IMAX cinema with a 55 by 75 ft (17 by 23 m) screen.

In Kissimmee you can pet young farm animals at **Green Meadows Petting Farm** ☎ (407) 846-0770, five miles south of Highway 192 on Poinciana Boulevard, or even milk a cow. Watch lions, elephants and zebras from the safety of your car at West Palm Beach's **Lion Country Safari** ☎ (407) 793-1084 WEB-SITE www.lioncountrysafari.com, where you can drive along eight miles (13 km) of paved roads.

Cultural Kicks

With the exception of St. Augustine, when you talk about historic buildings in Florida you are talking about structures generally dating back 100 or 150 years. It is perhaps one reason why the state protects so fiercely what culture and heritage it has both in its museums and its historic sites.

As well as world class museums in Miami and St. Petersburg, Fort Lauderdale has spent millions of dollars on the **Museum of Art** ☎ (954) 525-5500, at One East Las Olas Boulevard. It has an extraordinary collection of ethnographic art, including pre-Columbian, West African, Oceanic, and Native American art.

Up the Atlantic Coast a little further is a truly unique museum that the whole family will enjoy. The **International Museum of Cartoon Art** ☎ (561) 391-2200 FAX (561) 391-2721, 201 Plaza Real in Boca Raton is the first and only international museum devoted to the collection, preservation, exhibition and study of all types of cartoon art, including animation,

comic books and strips, editorial cartoons, advertising cartoons and greeting cards.

Daytona Beach's **Museum of Arts and Science** ☎ (850) 255-0285, 1040 Museum Boulevard, features multicultural exhibits in arts, science and history.

Of the 13 historical and art museums in the Miami area, the top ones are the **Miami Art Museum** ☎ (305) 375-3000 FAX (305) 375-1725, 101 West Flagler Street, which is one of three facets of the Miami-Dade Cultural Center and features international art.

The **Lowe Art Museum** ☎ (305) 284-3535 FAX (305) 284-2024 WEB SITE www.lowemuseum.org, 1301 Stanford Drive, at the University of Miami in Coral Gables, has permanent exhibits of Italian Renaissance and Native American artifacts.

Miami's many ethnic groups have influenced the arts in South Florida, the **Ballet Espanol Rosita Segovia** ☎ (305) 237-3582 FAX (305) 347-3738, 300 Northeast Second Avenue, is a professional dance company presenting Spanish Flamenco dance. The modern dance company, the **Black Door Ensemble** ☎ (305) 385-8960 FAX (305) 380-0751 are also exciting to watch.

For more current information on cultural events in Miami, check out publications, the *Arts and Culture in Greater Miami and the Beaches* brochure and the quarterly edition, which is a companion, the *Arts & Culture Calendar of Events*. It is available at the theater or entertainment facilities, or call TOLL-FREE (800) 283-2707.

For the world's most comprehensive collection of Salvador Dali art check out the **Salvador Dali Museum** ☎ (727) 822-6270 TOLL-FREE (800) 442-DALI WEB SITE www.daliweb.com, in St. Petersburg. Modern art can be found at the St. Pete's **Museum of Fine Arts** ☎ (813) 896-2667.

On the Gulf Coast, Sarasota has earned a reputation as being a culture hot spot. Start off with the **John and Mable Ringling Museum of Art** ☎ (941) 359-5700

A blacksmith re-creates daily life in Spanish colonial St. Augustine.

or (941) 351-1660, 5401 Bay Shore road, Sarasota. Although owned by the one of the partners of the famous Ringling Brothers Circus, this museum sitting on the waters of Sarasota Bay does not just focus on the circus theme. The art museum inside the complex features 500 years of European Art. There is also a vivid recapturing of what the Roaring Twenties were about.

The **Sarasota Ballet of Florida** ☎ (813) 351-8000, 5555 North Tamiami Trail, can be seen at several venues from the Florida Southern University Center to the Van Wezel and the Sarasota Opera House.

There are also a few slightly more offbeat museums, such as the **John Gorrie State Museum** ☎ (850) 653-9347, PO Box 267, in Apalachicola. Gorrie was the inventor of the first artificial ice machine in 1851, which eventually led to air-conditioning and refrigeration, two essentials for life in Florida. The **Forest Capital**, just south of Perry, is a museum dedicated to the state's forestry industry which, after tourism, remains one of Florida's largest earners. In the grounds you can explore a Cracker homestead, the traditional log cabin built by the first settlers. Early Floridians were known as "crackers" because of the sound their whips made as they drove their oxen carts. In Port St. Joe off US Highway 98, you can also visit the **Constitution Convention,** where the state's constitution was hammered out. St. Joseph was one of Florida's most prosperous towns until hit by a yellow fever outbreak in 1841, which killed or drove away all the residents. The new town of Port St. Joe dates from 1900.

Florida has many historic and archaeological sites, and some have become living museums with costumed guides re-enacting life in bygone times — such as **Fort Clinch State Park** at Fernandina Beach. The fort was built in the mid-1800s and was captured by stealth by the Confederates in 1861 during the Civil War. A year later it was retaken by Union troops. Today, the life of the Union soldier in 1864 is recreated with role-playing soldiers.

The **Natural Bridge Battlefield State Historic Site**, six miles (10 km) east of Woodville, recreates the battle between Union and Confederate forces which took place on March 6, 1865. Union troops had landed south of Tallahassee with the task of disrupting Confederate war supplies and taking the capital. After

12 hours of fighting, the Union troops were forced to withdraw and Tallahassee was the only Confederate state capital east of the Mississippi River not captured. The battle is re-staged on the Sunday closest to March 6.

Kissimmee Cow Camp, at Lake Kissimmee State Park, has something for all the family. It is a recreated 1876 cattle camp, typical of those set up along the route of the annual Florida cattle drive. The scrub cows that can be seen today are directly descended from the Spanish Andalusian cattle. Each spring the cattle would be rounded up and driven to Punta Rassa near Fort Myers, from where they were shipped to Cuba. The cowboy actors show what life was like on a cattle drive more than a century ago.

Fort Foster, at Hillsborough River State Park, six miles (10 km) southwest of Zephyrhills, also has costume-clad, role-playing, musket-carrying rangers re-enacting the lives of soldiers during the "Indian Wars" of the 1830s.

Interesting archaeological sites include **Lake Jackson Mounds** ((850) 562-0042 or (850) 922-6007, just north of Tallahassee, with Native American mounds dating back to AD 1200, and the **Fort George Island State Cultural Site** ((850) 251-2320, 12157 Hecksher Drive, 16 miles (26 km) east of Jacksonville on State Route A1A, an island that has been occupied continuously by humans for more than 5,000 years. Traces of each occupation period have been found. Also at this site, at 65 feet (20 m) Mount Carnelia is the highest point along the Atlantic Coast south of Sandy Hook, New Jersey. The **Crystal River** complex, which is off US Highway 19/98, also has traces of a Native American settlement dating back to 200 BC, including burial mounds, a temple, and hundreds of graves.

There are also a number of state run ornamental gardens such as **Ravine** ((850) 329-3721, at Palatka. The gardens of azaleas and camellias are planted inside a ravine which creates its own micro-climate along the west bank of the St. Johns River. The flowers are in full bloom in March and April. **Washington Oaks** ((850) 446-6780, 6400 North Oceanshore Boulevard, Palm Coast, two miles (three kilometers) south of

OPPOSITE: You don't need to don a wetsuit to go treasure hunting in Florida. ABOVE: At Kissimmee's Gatorland alligators get acquainted with visitors to Miccuosukee Indian Village.

Marineland on the A1A, are formal gardens planted with exotic species, including azalea, camellia and many species of roses. About 100 species of camellia and 50 species of azalea, along with some 160 species of other exotics, can be seen at the **Alfred B. Maclay Gardens** ☎ (850) 487-4556, 3540 Thomasville Road, in Tallahassee, where there are guided tours, nature and hiking trails, and canoe rentals.

Shop Till You Drop

When you pack to go to Florida it is a good idea to include an empty carry-on to bring back vacation purchases. Because of low taxes, intense competition, and millions of free-spending consumers, Florida offers some of the best shopping opportunities in the country. Antique shops, department stores, discount malls, boutiques and flea markets abound. Flea markets come in all shapes and sizes, and most have hundreds of stalls — usually indoors — offering everything from surplus army gear to high fashion, and antiques to the latest CD systems. Some stores even offer their own theme-like thrills. The Fort Lauderdale Swap Shop, for example, features fairground rides and daily circus performances, while Old Town, Kissimmee, offers rides on an antique carousel and Ferris wheel.

While there are few true Florida specialties other than local arts and crafts and bags of citrus fruit (which can be mailed worldwide), there are real bargains to be had — especially for European visitors, because there is no VAT and everything from clothing to cameras, and luggage to lingerie is much cheaper than at home.

My advice here is the same as my advice on eating out: look for what the natives do best, for what you can't get elsewhere. This means, if you are like me, you will come back with a whole suitcase stuffed with cigars and an innocent smile on your face as you pass through Customs. Florida, especially Tampa, is God's gift to budget-conscious cigar-lovers.

It is also God's gift to kitsch-lovers: if you like deliciously vulgar, outrageously colorful, unbelievably silly, totally useless things, you have come to the right place. Outside the souvenir shops, only a relative handful of pink flamingos exist in Florida.

Of the items that you might want to bring back as gifts, the lightest and most beautiful are the seashells you can buy almost anywhere, but especially along the southwest coast. The heaviest and tastiest are the sacks and/or crates of Florida citrus, which any store will be happy to ship back home for you. Florida is also the place to buy any leisure wear that you might need for the beach, as well as any accessories such as suntan oil or beach towels, because the competition to provide these things in a beach-fringed state is so intense that the prices are correspondingly low.

When it comes to things that are typically Floridian, aesthetically appealing, and attractively priced, your best bet is the range of handicrafts still produced by the Seminole. These include colorful hand-sewn garments and wall hangings, leather goods, and turquoise jewelry.

The best bargains, however, if you are coming from outside the United States, are indisputably to be found in the mouth-watering array of electronic gadgetry (well, it makes *my* mouth water). Everything you could possibly need — as well as everything you *couldn't* possibly need — for the home or office, is available here, usually at a fraction of the prices these things sell for overseas. But do remember that American electrical items run on 110 volts; if your home voltage is 220 or 240 volts, you will need an adapter.

Florida's sales tax is another thing that might cause problems. It varies from county to county, but is generally around six percent. This tax does not appear on the price tag, but is automatically added at the check-out counter, which can cause misunderstandings.

Finally, and unfashionably, I would like to put in a good word for the American shopping mall. If you want convenience and quality and value for money, plus a good return on your investment of time and effort, I would direct you to any of the thousands of shopping malls scattered around Florida. They are all — or almost all — open until 9 PM seven days a week, and all are worth a visit, regardless of what you are looking for.

Outlet malls have also become the trendy thing, since here you can find name brands and designer fashions for fractions of what you might pay at the department stores. But often you will pay the same price as in the retail stores or just barely a small discount. Usually these centers are best to visit before a major holiday, because nearly all the stores will offer additional savings.

Short Breaks

No matter where your vacation base is in Florida, you should aim to see as much of the state as possible during your stay. From Orlando and the major central Florida attractions, it is only an hour or so to either Cocoa and the John F. Kennedy Space Center on the Atlantic Coast, or Tampa, Clearwater and St. Petersburg on the Gulf. It is three hours or so north to St. Augustine and an overnight trip if you want to explore the Panhandle. From Orlando, allow just over three hours to drive south to Miami on the Atlantic coast, or Everglades City on the Gulf and the gateway to the Everglades National Park (see Everglades).

Your options don't end there, however. Just north of the Kennedy Space Center is Port Canaveral, one of the country's main cruise ship terminals, and from here you can sail off on a three day mini cruise to the Bahamas. Contact anyone of the following cruise lines for more information on short cruising trips: Canaveral Cruise Lines TOLL-FREE (800) 910-SHIP, Carnival Cruise Line TOLL-FREE (800) 327-7276, Disney Cruise Line TOLL-FREE (800) 951-3532, Norwegian Cruise Line TOLL-FREE (800) 327-7030,

Conch shells and T-shirts are offered as souvenirs at the southernmost point in the continental United States — Key West.

Premier Cruise Line TOLL-FREE (800) DREAM-54 or Royal Caribbean International TOLL-FREE (800) 327-6700.

And if you have visited Florida before, you might decide to fly out from one of the many airports and spend a couple of days in New Orleans, Boston, New York — or whatever strikes your fancy.

As most visitors stay in the central Florida area, either inland in the Orlando region or on the Gulf or Atlantic coasts, the following suggestions are places to visit either as a long day out, or involving an overnight if you want to take your time. Apart from the height of the tourist season (over Christmas and August), you should be able to find a hotel or motel bed, but it is always advisable, for peace of mind, to have made a reservation.

Ocala and Horse Country. Historic, downtown Ocala with its pre- and post-Civil War houses, has a traditional 1800s city square, and is just over an hour from Orlando. Get a self-guided walking tour brochure from the Chamber of Commerce and see the sights, and then explore the surrounding countryside. Ocala is surrounded by horse farms where you can see thoroughbred Arabians, Quarter Horses, Tennessee Walkers, Morgans and many other breeds. Many farms have welcome signs for visitors; keep an eye out.

Gainesville is a two hour drive north of Orlando and deserves a visit for its well preserved historic district. Although most of the properties are little more than 100 years old, more than 700 are protected. There are nineteenth-century Queen Anne-style homes along Northeast Third Street and Third Avenue. On University Avenue there are Italian style houses, and the curbside blocks used to step in and out of horse-drawn carriages can still be seen. There are other historic buildings in the Southeast and Pleasant Street districts and downtown, including the Hippodrome Star Theatre, converted from the old post office, and one of the finest examples of Florida's Beaux Arts Classical style. The University campus also has 19 red-brick buildings built between 1905 and 1939 in the collegiate Gothic style of Yale and Princeton, with intricate tracery, fan vaulted ceilings, and gargoyles.

St. Augustine really deserves a longer visit, as there is too much to see and do here in one day. It is the oldest city in the United States and one of the most delightful, and has many charming bed-and-breakfasts —

where southern hospitality can add to your enjoyment of the town (it is best to book in advance). It is a good two hours drive from Orlando. The fastest route is to take Interstate 4 and then Interstate 95 north until the US Highway 1 or State Route 214 exits, both of which lead into the historic area. The best way to see the city is on foot, but you can catch the tram which runs between all the main sights. The ticket allows you to get on and off as often as you like. There are regular trams throughout the day and you can spend as long as you like in one area before moving on. Opening times and prices vary according to the season, so your first stop should be the Visitors Center on the corner of Castillo Drive and San Marco Avenue, where you can pick up free brochures and maps and watch a 15-minute video to familiarize yourself with the area. Parking is a problem, so park away from the Center and either walk in or catch the tram.

Sights that you must visit include the Castillo de San Marcos National Monument, where park rangers dressed in seventeen century Spanish uniforms re-enact fort life and demonstrate how the old weapons were used. The restored Spanish quarter of St. George Street is also a must. Many buildings have been restored to show how Spanish settlers and soldiers lived 300 years ago, and craftsmen, dressed in period clothing, recreate daily life in the eighteenth century. There are many excellent restaurants in the area. Also take in the Oldest House, the Oldest Store and Oldest Schoolhouse, the Old Jail, the Moorish Zorayda Castle, and the Lightner Museum.

For overnight accommodation try to stay at one of the 25 historic Victorian or Spanish Colonial-style bed-and-breakfast inns, with their gingerbread trim and welcoming hot cider.

Festive Flings

With more than 40 million visitors a year to Florida, every day is a holiday. There are a number of special occasions, both festive and sporting, throughout the year, that are worth looking out for.

JANUARY

Start the New Year off from January 6–9 with the **Epiphany Celebration** in Tarpon Springs, which has been maintained by the Greek Orthodox community. The celebration begins with church services in the morning and moves to the Spring Bayou, where young boys dive in the water for the white cross. Afterwards, food, dancing and merriment can be had at the sponge docks. For more information contact ☎ (813) 937-3540.

In Miami Beach, a seven-block **street festival** is held along Ocean Drive highlighting the city's historic Art Deco district during a three-day weekend in the middle of the month. Call ☎ (305) 672-2014.

FEBRUARY

The **Battle of Oust** was the largest Civil War Battle in Florida and it saved Tallahassee from falling into the hands of Union forces. It is re-enacted every year in Lake City with more than

OPPOSITE: The impressive gardens surrounding the Castillo de San Marcos in St. Augustine. ABOVE: You can pick your own fruit at citrus farms like this one in Lake Wales.

2,000 participants, and is followed by a downtown festival with parades and arts and crafts displays.

Speed Week in Daytona Beach is one of the first events in the North American motor racing calendar and features both road racing and stock car events at the Daytona International Speedway. It begins with the 24 hours of Daytona Race and culminates with the Daytona 500 on the last day. Speed week actually goes for 15 days, in early February. For more information contact: The Official Welcome Center in the main lobby of DAYTONA USA at (850) 253-8669, WEB SITE www.daytonabeach.com, 1801 West International Speedway Boulevard.

It's a good idea to make Tampa your hub for the first two weeks of February, since several important events that celebrate the city's history and people take place.

Enjoy the **Florida State Fair** ✆ (813) 223-1000 TOLL-FREE (800) 345-FAIR WEB SITE www.fl-ag.com/statefair, held from February 4 to 15. It is a festival of food, country and western stars, agricultural exhibits, and a fun fair.

A historical insight to Tampa can be discovered at the **Gasparilla Pirate Fest Weekend** ✆ (813) 251-4500. Gasparilla was Florida's most notorious pirate. He is remembered by a mock pirate invasion, which launches a parade on Bayshore Boulevard, and a huge street party takes place downtown. The fun lasts for two days, usually the first weekend of the month.

In adjoining Ybor City, you can celebrate all day in the festival known as **Fiesta Day** ✆ (813) 248-3712.

A glimpse of African-American history and culture can be gleaned from the **Sistrunk Historical Festival** in Fort Lauderdale. Held along Sistrunk Boulevard, it features food, arts and crafts, and entertainment.

In Fort Myers, they remember the city's most famous resident with the **Edison Festival of Light** — two weeks of events and parades. Contact the Lee Island Coast Visitor and Convention Bureau ✆ (941) 338-3500 TOLL-FREE (800) 237-6444 FAX (941) 334-1106 WEB SITE www.LeeIslandCoast.com, 2180 West First Street, Suite 100, Fort Myers.

A taste of the old Florida can be found at the **Silver Spurs Rodeo** ✆ (407) 847-4052, in Kissimmee. Despite the world-famous attractions nearby, central Florida is still predominantly a farming community producing citrus fruit and raising beef. The Silver Spurs Rodeo is one of the top 25 rodeos in the nation and you can watch professional cowboys competing in events such as bull-riding, steer-wrestling and calf-roping.

MARCH

The nation's largest Hispanic celebration, **Carnaval Miami** — reminiscent of Mardi Gras in Rio de Janeiro — takes place in Miami's Little Havana around March 5-14. The fun culminates in the **Calle Ocho Festival**, a 23-block all night street party featuring food, dance, music, costumed revelers and top Latin entertainers. Call ✆ (305) 644-8888.

Or go back to the Sponge Docks at Tarpon Springs for **Greek Independence Day** on March 21. For information contact the St. Nicholas Greek Orthodox Cathedral at ✆ (727)937-3540.

In Kissimmee, the annual **Bluegrass music** festival is held from March 6–8. Contact ✆ (407) 473-7773.

In New Port Richey, outside the Tampa Bay area, the **Chasco Fiesta** commemorates the celebration of friendship between the native Calusa people and the Spanish colonists. It features sporting events, a coronation ball, a Native American pageant, arts and crafts displays, and food and entertainment.

APRIL

Elgin Airforce Base near Fort Walton Beach, the largest military base in the free world, open its gates — and skies — during the annual **Elgin Air Show**, which features the aerial acrobatics of the famous Thunderbirds display team. Coinciding with the air show is the Fort Walton Beach

Bahamanian dancer at Miami Pasco.

Seafood Festival.

Pensacola has a two-day **jazz festival** that attracts many top performers, and Tallahassee's **Springtime** has grown into a four-week-long celebration of spring with parades, contests, festivals, and arts and crafts displays.

The **Easter Parade** in downtown St. Augustine features horses and carriages, marching bands and floats. The horses wear hats donated by famous people. The parade is held on easter Sunday afternoon. For information call ☎ (850) 829-2992.

Easter Weekend also lures in the surfers to the Cocoa Beach Pier for the annual **Easter Surfing Festival**, which has been going on for 35 years. It's the largest and longest-running beach event in Florida. Call ☎ (800) USA-1969 for details.

Sunfest ☎ (561) 659-5992, in downtown West Palm Beach, has become one of Florida's largest music, art, and water events festivals, while the **Seven mile Bridge Run** in Marathon attracts many runners from around the world. Call ☎ (305) 743-8513.

MAY

Fort Walton Beach hosts the **Hog's Breath Hobie Regatta**. Downtown and riverfront Jacksonville stages **Heritage Days** featuring costume parades, street musicians, and arts and crafts.

Shrimp lovers should head for Fernandina Beach and the Isle of Eight **Shrimp Festival**, a weekend filled with celebrations for the birthplace of the state's shrimping industry. The Greater Daytona Beach **Striking Fish Tournament** is the largest offshore fishing competition on the east coast, with more than 250 boats taking part.

If you are into the NASA space program then you should plan on being at Cape Canaveral at the Kennedy Space Center Visitor Complex for **Space Week**. Contact ☎ (800) USA-1969 for more details.

JUNE

On the first weekend of June, Grand Avenue, the main street through Coconut Grove, is shut off to traffic for the **Miami/Bahamas Goombay Festival**, with food from the islands and music to match. ☎ Call (305) 372-9966.

The **Fiesta of the Five Flags**, a tribute to the five countries that ruled Florida at various times, is held in Pensacola with boat and street parades, music, ethnic festivals, and sandcastle contests. At Destin and Fort Walton Beach, the **Billy Bowlegs Festival** celebrates another of Florida's famous pirates, with 500 boats taking part in an "invasion" of the Emerald Coast. In Orlando, there is the **Florida Film Festival** ☎ (407) 629-1088, which is held mostly at the Enzian theater, featuring more than 100 films, documentaries and shorts from around the world.

JULY

The **Fourth of July** is celebrated in every town and city throughout the state, but Tallahassee has the largest fireworks display. Flagler Beach combines the festivities with the **Miss Flagler County Pageant**, and Daytona Beach celebrates it with motorcar racing, of course, and jazz and country music.

At Key West, **Hemingway Days** ☎ (305) 294-4440, is a week-long festival celebrating the life and work of the author. At Big Pine Key, the **Underwater Music Festival** takes place in mid-July — when divers gather at the Looe Key National Marine Sanctuary to listen to an underwater symphony. The **Caribbean Calypso Carnival** is held at Vinoy Park in St. Petersburg on the third weekend of the month, featuring steel drum bands, Caribbean food and limbo dancing. Call ☎ (813) 821-6164.

AUGUST

Panama City hosts the **Beach Fishing Classic** with lots of prizes for anglers of all ages. Around the first of the month, Miami hosts the annual **Reggae Festival** at the AT&T Amphitheater in Bayfront Park, 401 Biscayne Boulevard in the heart of downtown Miami. Call ☎ (305) 891-2944 for information on the acts performing.

SEPTEMBER

Some of the country's best seafood is available in Pensacola Beach at the **Seafood Festival**, which also features music and arts and crafts.

OCTOBER

The mufflers are revved up loud for Daytona Beach's **Biketoberfest**, which transforms the city into a biker's dream. The motorcycle races and festivities are usually held the third week in October.

Tampa's Ybor City hosts the Latin-Style Halloween known as **Guavaween** on the 30th. There are activities for the family during the day, while at night the Mama Guava Stumble parade makes its way through the quarter. Music stages abound. Call ☎ (813) 242-4828 for more information.

The Celebration gets even more outrageous leading up to Halloween in Key West. Known as **Fantasy Fest**, the 10-day costumed celebration ends on October 31, but reaches a climax with a parade on October 30. For more information call ☎ (305) 296-1817 or their WEB SITE www.warptime.net.

Madeira Beach, near St. Petersburg, has its **John's Pass Seafood Festival**, where major consumption of fish, shrimp and crab occurs. Entertainment and crafts are included in the event that lasts a weekend towards the end of the month. Call ☎ (813) 391-7373 for more details.

While at Destin, known as the World's Luckiest Fishing Village, more than 1,000 competitors from around the world gather for the **Fishing Rodeo** which features inland, shore, offshore and bayou fishing.

Jacksonville is the venue for The World's Greatest Free Jazz Concert.

Naples stages the raucous **Fifth Avenue Oktoberfest**, with live performers, carnival rides, dancers, German bands and food.

NOVEMBER

Pensacola holds its famous **Blue Angels Homecoming Show**, which welcomes the Navy's aerobatics team back after their year attending air shows around the world.

Sarasota has its annual **French Film Festival,** while Greater Fort Lauderdale is the venue for the east coast's largest **film festival**, featuring entries from around the world.

Rodeos are still very popular in the nation's major beef-producing state.

You can try your hand at **sand sculpting** in the annual contest at Fort Myers Beach, while in St. Petersburg, it is **Sunsational Museums Month** with special events showcasing the city's world class museums. For information about combining a hotel package, call ☎ (800) 345-6710.

DECEMBER

Tallahassee stages the month-long **Southern Accents of Winter**. It was the site of the first Christmas celebration in North America. There are **Christmas parades** in many towns and cities. The spectacular parade in St. Augustine is followed by the **Grand Illumination**. Fernandina Beach has a month-long **Victorian Seaside Christmas** with tours of historic homes, ballet, Teddy Bear Teas and New Year's Gala. In Fort Myers the historic winter homes of Thomas Edison and Henry Ford are dressed up for Christmas week.

Miami has the **Orange Bowl Parade** on Biscayne Boulevard on New Year's Eve. Call ☎ (305) 371-4600 for information on reserved seating.

Galloping Gourmet

The four overriding impressions one has of eating in Florida are portions, service, choice and price. Portions, in a word, are huge.

One of the great treats of Florida, especially on the coast, is being able to dine leisurely outside year-round, enjoying both the sea views and the seafood. There is yellowtail and mutton snapper, mullet, pompano, grouper, tiny grunt, "dolphin" (the fish mahi mahi, not the mammal), spiny lobster, oysters, conch, giant pink shrimp, and delicious stone crab all from local waters. They come from the waters off the western side of the state, where the crab fishermen haul in the stone crabs, break off a large claw, and then — as required by law — throw the crab back into the sea, where it will grow another claw to replace the one you're eating. Stone-crab claws are heavenly. Note, however, that during the closed season, mid-October to mid-May, only frozen ones are available.

The wonderful thing about seafood is its versatility in the kitchen. It can be eaten grilled, boiled, baked or sautéed. It is used to make mouth-watering soups, chowders and stews; and lobster and crab are delicious cold and served with a mayonnaise sauce. Conch (pronounced "konk") are highly nutritious, and can be served in a variety of ways. They can be grilled, ground in conch burgers, fried in batter as fritters, or eaten raw in salads.

Southern cooking is represented by dishes such as Southern fried chicken, grits and hushpuppies (deep-fried balls of cornmeal and onion). There is excellent beef, and very tender steaks, which is not surprising as Florida is the nation's second largest beef producer after Texas. Most steaks come in 8-oz and 12-oz sizes, but some restaurants specialize in 16, 32, and even 64-oz steaks!

Most restaurants offer wonderful salad bars and all-inclusive specials which makes eating out both a pleasure and affordable. All-you-can-eat breakfasts, lunches, and dinners are ideal for parents who have growing children with almost endless appetites, and if you want to dine a little early, most restaurants offer "early bird" specials where you have the same menu but at lower prices.

At the very least, you should sample the best of Old Southern, Cuban, and the Florida version of American cooking. Among the dishes from the Old South are southern fried chicken (of course), hush puppies, ham steak, stuffed turkey, catfish, grits (granulated white corn), rice with giblet gravy, okra, collard

OPPOSITE: Exotic fruit drinks at a Key West stand. ABOVE: Enjoying the fruits of the sea.

greens, black-eyed peas, cornbread, and pecan pie. The mainstays of Cuban cuisine are black beans and rice, fried plantains, paella, *arroz con pollo* (chicken with rice), *picadillo* (ground beef with olives and onions in a piquant sauce), and a scrumptious variety of pork dishes. In Miami and elsewhere you can try Cuban-inspired *lechon*, roast pork flavored with garlic and tart oranges, which give the dish a unique flavor. Other dishes include *ropa vieja* made from beef (it translates as "old clothes"). All are usually served with boiled white or yellow rice, flavored with either saffron or bihol, and black beans.

Desserts include "flans," — baked and caramelized custard — guava shells stuffed with cream cheese, and fresh tropical fruits perhaps served with tropical fruit-flavored ice cream. Florida's winter strawberries are particularly succulent. And, of course, there is Key Lime pie, made with condensed or evaporated milk and the juice and minced rind of the piquant Key limes. Florida's official dessert is so sacred to Floridians that it is often the subject of almost theological debates: what sort of lime juice is best, to what temperature should the pie be chilled, should it be served with a meringue or should the eggs be beaten into the pie itself, and so on. Anyway, two things are certain — the pie should be made with Key limes (which are small and yellow, not green), and it should have a graham cracker crust.

Fast-food outlets still account for the vast majority of eating places in Florida and, for a family, they offer a fun and cheap way of eating out. Europeans, in particular, will find that most fast-food outlet prices in Florida are about half those back home.

There are also amazing all-you-can-eat family buffet restaurants where you can help yourself as often as you want. These make great breakfast stops, and the budget-minded can fill up for the day often for just a couple of dollars.

Don't dismiss these eateries as cheap and bad; if they were, they would quickly go out of business in Florida, where competition is intense and standards very high. They are certainly cheap, but they can offer outstanding value for money.

The Sizzlers chain for instance, which is found throughout Florida, offers all-you-can-eat meals throughout the day, and there can be a choice of as many as 100 dishes for lunch and dinner. While you tuck into salad, pasta, fish or meat from the carvery, your children can try anything they want. The meal price includes all the soft drinks you can drink, and a family of four can eat as much as they want for about $25.

Choice really comes into its own if you are self-catering either in a motel room or rented vacation home. The food sections of supermarkets offer a huge variety from exotic fruits and live lobsters to ready-prepared meals. Whether eating in or out, the food is almost always good.

Local specialties include giant Gulf shrimps and Key Lime pie. Fresh produce is jetted in from around the world so there is a wide range of foods to enjoy. There are exotic fruits and juices, such as mango, papaya and carambola, and the freshest of fish and shellfish.

There is probably not much point in raving about Florida's fruit. After all, you have probably been eating it all your life, given that 70 percent of the world's grapefruit and 25 percent of the world's oranges come from Florida. Not to mention the tangerines, lemons, limes, and other citrus fruits, which Florida bestows on the world's dining tables. But it's better there because it's fresher. And citrus is only half the story; the subtropical half includes the most delicious mangoes, papayas, carambolas, lychees, guavas, zapotes, and coconuts.

Stop at a roadside stall and buy a large sack of oranges, grapefruit, lime, or juicy tangelos for just a few dollars. However, don't be tempted to stop and help yourself from a tree by the roadside, it is a felony (for which you can go to prison) to steal fruit in Florida. If traveling around during the winter months, you will almost certainly see huge lorries filled with oranges, bound for the juice factories. The citrus season lasts over the winter and there are many types of fruits to be enjoyed. Growers are always developing new strains of seedless or juicier fruit. Towards the end of the season, look for late fruits

such as Valencia oranges and seedless grapefruit. Even out of season, you should try some of the many citrus products, such as marmalade, orange wine and lemon jelly and candies. Roadside stalls also sell home grown peanuts, boiled or roasted, and pecans. While in the south you can buy locally grown sugar cane and the syrup and molasses made from the sugar.

Another culinary treat is the number of different ethnic cuisines available; from Cuban to Chinese, Caribbean to Italian and German to Japanese. You can try authentic Greek fare in Tarpon Springs, Spanish food in and around St. Augustine, Creole cuisine in the Panhandle, and a Native American dishes such as fry breads and mashed cassava roots in the Everglades.

Two more comments about Florida restaurants. Except for the seriously upmarket eateries, restaurants in Florida tend to be very informal, and they tend to open and close earlier (for all meals) than do restaurants in the rest of the world.

OPPOSITE: Citrus can be shipped worldwide if you want to take a taste of Florida home with you. ABOVE: A giant reptile has a leisurely meal.

Special Interests

LITERARY LOVERS

It's more than just coincidence that so may talented writers have flocked to Key West and then made their mark of greatness. Pulitzer Prize winners abound — perhaps the most famous American writer of the twentieth century was Ernest Hemingway, who arrived in Key West in the 1920s on a tip from fellow writer John Dos Passos. Other poets and playwrights soon followed, including Tennessee Williams. Because of that proud heritage, the writer's community works hard to inspire others.

Now in its 17th year, the **Key West Literary Seminar** brings together some of the most respected novelists to conduct writers' workshops. There are lecture, readings and of course festivities. It is usually held in the second week of January. For more information call ☎ (888) 293-9291.

If you love to read and write, and are ever in the St. Petersburg area, then a trip to **Haslam's Book Store** ☎ (727) 822-8616 WEB SITE www.haslams.com, 2025 Central Avenue, is a must. It is considered Florida's largest book store, with new and used hardbacks and paperbacks. Now in the third and fourth generation of management, the bookstore sells at bargain prices. The 65-year-old business attracts readers of all ages.

CIRCUS, CIRCUS

Sarasota is the birthplace of the world famous Ringling Brothers and the legendary Barnum & Bailey Circuses. As a result, many circus families have made this Gulf Coast town their home. Experienced circus professionals have now created a professional circus school in Sarasota. The National Circus School of Performing Arts is a non-profit organization, hoping to keep the skills and art of the circus alive. For more information call ☎ (941) 924-7054.

WINE

Florida is the birthplace of wine in the United States, as the first grapes were harvested by French Huguenot settlers around 1562. They used the local Muscadine grape, which was able to survive the very hot summers. Today, the **Lakeridge Winery and Vineyards** in Clermont offers the chance to visit one of Florida's only two surviving wineries and sample its products — with grape juice available for children and drivers. The vineyard is undergoing expansion and will eventually cover 110 acres (44 hectares) growing several different grapes from classic varieties to modern experimental blends. The winery is open Monday to Saturday from 10 AM to 6 PM and on Sunday from noon to 6 PM. There is a museum featuring the state's winemaking history, including the boom period in the early 1900s, when more than 2,000 acres (800 hectares) of vines were cultivated in the Clermont area.

The most southerly vineyard in the United States is **Eden Vineyards Winery and Park**, on State Route 80, east of Fort Myers. It produces seven types of wine from American and French hybrid grapes and offers wine tastings and a tram tour.

GHOSTS AND SPOOKS

Being the oldest city in the United States St. Augustine is home to many historic inns and bed-and-breakfasts, quite a few of whom lay claim to having a resident ghost on the premises. In particular the townsfolk of Lake Wales insist that a ghost is responsible for one of the most eerie phenomena occuring in the state.

Follow the signs for **Spook Hill**, off US Highway 17 and at the junction of North Avenue and 5th Street. The idea is to drive a little way up Spook Hill, stop at the mark on the road, put the car in neutral and take your foot off the brake, after making sure there is nothing behind you. In a few seconds the car will start to roll slowly, and when you look out of the rear window, you will be certain that you are going uphill. It is a very eerie illusion which locals will tell you is all because of an old Seminole Chief called Cufcowellax. He is said to have stalked for a month and then slain a huge alligator that had killed many members of his tribe. Ever since, the spirit of the alligator has roamed the hill, responsible for this bizarre occurrence.

Taking A Tour

Both active and leisurely guided tours are possible throughout Florida. You'll find tour companies in all major towns, and along the length of the Florida Keys. Many list a broad range of options, like **Spinning Wheels and Country Roads** ((352) 666-3397 TOLL-FREE (800) 811-6614 WEB SITE www.spinningwheels.com, 518 Colonial Drive, Brooksville, which offers biking, hiking or canoeing on the Withlacochee River. Transportation and lunch are free, and the tours are tailored for all ages and abilities.

For an all-inclusive tour showcasing everything Miami has to offer — from history and cultural-based tours to nature and the Everglades — contact **Adam Productions** ((305) 865-0363 FAX (305) 375-9415, 1177 Kane Concourse, Suite 231 Bay Harbor Islands. In Miami itself, **American Sightseeing Tours** ((305) 688-7700 TOLL-FREE (800) 367-5149 WEB SITE www.sightseeing.com, based at 11077 Northwest 36th Avenue, Miami, also

OPPOSITE: Genuine cowboy boots make good souvenirs. ABOVE: The great blue heron is the largest of Florida's many species of heron.

specializes in customized tours of Miami and South Florida attractions for groups or individuals.

Tampa Tours ☎ (813) 621-6667 FAX (813) 654-3759, PO Box 311623, Tampa, will customize your exploration of the Tampa-St. Petersburg area, including guided day trips and transportation to theme parks, shopping and sporting events.

ECO-TOURISM

Eco-tourism might be a fashionable term these days, but when people are exposed to the beauty of nature and how precariously its future hangs in the balance, they are deeply touched. At least that's what Arden Arrington, of **Calusa Coast Outfitters** in Fort Myers, would like to think.

"Orlando and the theme parks are fine," he says. "But people want more than that. They want an educational experience, and they want to experience our culture, history and see our natural resources. Things are moving towards nature-based and heritage tourism."

Arrington, who volunteers for the Florida Park Service and has been active in Fort Myers preservation legislation, operates educational tours on a pontoon boats in the Estero Bay Marine Estuary. Passengers get to watch for and listen to dolphins with hydrophones (See Top Spots). With the aid of binoculars, you help document sightings of already identified dolphins by their dorsal techniques. Arrington says that people leave with an appreciation for the value of the natural resources and a desire to protect it.

Up the Gulf Coast on Indian Shores is the **Suncoast Seabird Sanctuary** ☎ (813) 391-6211 FAX (813) 399-2923 WEB SITE www.webcoast.com/Seabird, 18328 Gulf Boulevard, where Ralph T. Heath, Jr. hopes visitors end up feeling the same way for birds. In 1971, Heath rescued a wounded bird and nursed it in his backyard. Since then his private non-profit bird hospital has expanded and brings in an average of 15 to 20 new birds daily. Heath offers free tours, where you can see many of Florida's rare birds up close, twice a week.

He also gives lectures, and the sanctuary has exhibits and educational programs to help improve public awareness. The rehabilitated birds are released, but those that cannot safely return to their natural environment remain permanent guests.

With so many parks, lakes and rivers in Florida, it shouldn't be difficult to find an eco-tourist experience. If you head over to the Atlantic Coast near the Merritt Island National Wildlife Refuge and Canaveral National Seashore, you can do a guided kayak nature tour with **Osprey Outfitters** ☎ (407) 267-3535 FAX (407) 268-3933 E-MAIL osprey@gnc.net WEB SITE www.nbbd.com/osprey, 132 South Dixie Avenue, Titusville. One of the better trips is to paddle down

the Haulover Canal around sunset when hundreds of birds fly over the Indian River to return to their home on Merritt Island. You could possibly see manatees and dolphins in the deep canal waters.

These are just a few of the options that will make you understand what protecting our environment means to our future existence.

Cruises

There are so many ocean cruises from Florida ports that the peninsula could almost be considered one giant dock. There are morning cruises and afternoon cruises, sunlight and starlight cruises, half-day and one-day cruises, two-day and two-night cruises, week-long and longer cruises, cruises to the Bahamas and the Virgin Islands, to the West Indies and Mexico, even through the Panama Canal to Los Angeles and San Francisco.

One option for a day or evening cruise is the **Europa Sea Kruz** ☎ (941) 463-5000 TOLL-FREE (800) 688-PLAY. Snug Harbor, 645 San Carlos Boulevard, Fort Myers Beach, a six-hour voyage that includes full meal and live entertainment, as well as casino with slot machines and video poker. You will find similar cruises in many other Florida cities. Check the phone directory for the local casino cruise line.

Abundant tropical vegetation adds to the charm of this Key West resort.

Welcome to Florida

FLORIDA IS BY NO STRETCH OF THE IMAGINATION a land of contrasts. It is a land of spectacular sameness. True, the oldest city in the United States, St. Augustine, is just up the coast from the headquarters of the Space Age, Cape Canaveral; while in the middle of ancient Native American territory is the 28,000-acre (over 11,600-hectare) reservation known as Walt Disney World. And no one has ever mistaken the antebellum Southern charms of Tallahassee for the Latin rhythms of Miami, any more than have the literati of Key West been confused with the glitterati of Palm Beach. And where other states have a generation gap, Florida has a generation chasm — between the young who flock there to live it up, and the retired who migrate there.

Nonetheless, the overall impression is, if not of sameness, then of minor variations on a few major themes. The principal theme, of course, is sunshine: Florida is very aptly nicknamed the Sunshine State. Another theme is flatness: Florida's highest point is only 345 ft (105 m) above sea level. Another is water: quite apart from the vast swampland of the Everglades, Florida has 30,000 lakes and 10,000 miles (16,130 km) of rivers, and of course its 1,350 miles (2,177 km) of coast is lapped by the sea. Now, when you add to this the fact that most of the hotel rooms in the state are distinguishable from one another only by their addresses, the endless beaches are distinguishable only by their names, and most of the roads are distinguishable only by their numbers, you can see why it would be difficult to speak convincingly of Florida as a land of great variety.

Why, then, with all this standardization and uniformity, do more than 40 million people visit Florida annually? Simple: because standardization is highly desirable if the standards are high, because uniformity is a good thing if things are uniformly good. That's Florida's secret. People know exactly what to expect. When you know that the weather will be sunny, and the beaches lovely, and most of the people friendly, and the service efficient, and the accommodation comfortable, and the prices reasonable, then you know why Florida is one of the most popular tourist destination in the world. What you may have difficulty deciding is which part of the state is your favorite, if traveling from the southern tip of the state in Key West to the northwest point of Pensacola.

A day in the Florida Keys, surrounded by everything tropical — from the whiffs of the fruit to the see-through water only feet from the road — will stir your senses enough to forget about rigid schedules, deadlines, and agendas. Key West, where you can watch the sun rise and set over the same waters of the Straits of Florida, might inspire a lax attitude. But it's still alive and thriving with the creativity of an artistic community. You walk away — if you can — inspired by the charm of the Victorian homes and hotels and the serenity of the slow breezes.

Miami, on the other hand, moves at its own pace, an unmistakable Latin and Caribbean sashay. There's no city in the United States quite like it. Miami's political and social history provide the fire that stimulates everything good and bad about this city. Savor the multicultural experience while you are there, and don't get into political discussions with exiles, unless you are prepared to lose.

While South Florida definately has its idiosyncracies, the further north you go the less diversity you will find. Orlando is the exception, but sometimes the fantasy from theme parks and surrounding attractions make it difficult to ascertain how this city defines itself. Is it an entertainment capital for kids or adults? And with all the neon lining International Drive, you are reminded of Las Vegas.

To escape the lights, venture to the sea, either the Gulf of Mexico or the open Atlantic. The Gulf Coast features awakening communities like Naples and Fort Myers, where you can combine nature-based activities with incredible beaches. On the Atlantic side, the towns of the Space Coast are still mostly in a sleepy state, but they are energized by the impact of NASA's Kennedy Space Center. For a sense of why this state exists, a visit to St. Augustine should be included. The oldest city in the United States has plenty of tales to tell within its walls.

If the various parts of the state are defined by population and pace, then northern Florida is almost like a different country. An imaginary line parallels Interstate 10 as it zooms from Jacksonville into the Panhandle, a divide between the Old South and modern Florida. The northern counties are a lot more "Southern Dixie" in attitude and old-fashioned in the way things are done. The accents, which become more of a drawl, are not the only obvious difference.

However, one thing I can predict with absolute certainty: you will find much to enjoy in Florida. In fact, if you can't enjoy yourself in Florida, don't bother to try anywhere else.

OPPOSITE: A street performer amuses the crowd in Mallory Market, Key West. ABOVE: The pier at Naples reaches out into the Gulf of Mexico.

Florida and Its People

OUNTY
XIII
XI

THE HISTORICAL BACKGROUND

It is perhaps appropriate that the world's most visited vacation spot should itself be populated mostly by new arrivals. Only about a third of Florida's nine million inhabitants were actually born there. And none of its inhabitants are descended from the native peoples who had been living there for over 10,000 years before the Europeans arrived in the sixteenth century and began the systematic extermination of the original native population.

Although Columbus claimed the unseen territory for Spain in 1492, the first European actually to lay eyes on Florida was almost certainly the English cartographer John Cabot. He sailed down the east coast of America on behalf of King Henry VII in 1498. The first European to set foot in Florida was the Spanish explorer Juan Ponce de León, who landed near present-day St. Augustine on April 2, 1513. The explorer was looking for the legendary Isle of Bimini, which according to folklore had a miraculous fountain of youth. Having arrived at Easter, he named the new land after Spain's Easter celebration, Pascua Florida, or Feast of Flowers.

Ponce then sailed down the coast, out around the Florida Keys (which he called Los Martires, because they appeared to him like kneeling martyrs in the water), and back up the west coast as far as Charlotte Harbor, near present-day Fort Myers. He returned to Florida in 1521 along with 200 settlers, and attempted to establish a settlement near Charlotte Harbor. However, the local Indians were in no mood to see the white man encroaching on their territory, and they launched a ferocious attack on the settlement, in which Ponce himself was badly wounded. The entire party was forced to withdraw to Cuba, where Ponce died of his wounds.

Seven years later another Spaniard, Pánfilo de Narváez, landed at Tampa Bay with 300 would-be colonists. He led them on a march up to the Panhandle, where they were to rendezvous with his ships after conducting a search for the gold he was certain he would find en route. He found no gold, nor did he find his ships waiting for him. With his party now much reduced by the hostile attentions of the Indians they had encountered on their march, they decided to build their own boats and set sail for Mexico. They never arrived.

Undeterred by the fate of his two predecessors, Hernando de Soto sailed from Cuba in 1539 with 600 troops. They landed on Tampa Bay and marched northwards, more or less in the footsteps of Pánfilo de Narváez, searching for the same gold treasure that the Spanish were convinced was there somewhere. When he didn't find it, he just kept going and kept looking. He died on the banks of the Mississippi River three years later.

In 1559 the conquistador Don Tristán de Luna arrived with 1,500 men at Pensacola Bay, where he attempted to establish a colony. After two years of struggle, he gave up and went home.

Ironically, it was the French who were indirectly responsible for the first Spanish success at colonization in Florida. In 1562, Jean Ribault explored the mouth of the St. Johns River and claimed the area for France. Within two years there was a colony of 300 Huguenots living there in the newly-built Fort Caroline. Not amused by the presence of these French squatters — and Protestant ones at that — on their territory, the Spanish dispatched a former smuggler, Pedro Menéndez de Avilés, to found a settlement nearby and to deal with the French. He accomplished both tasks.

Landing south of Fort Caroline on August 28, 1565, the feast day of San Augustin, Menéndez named his new settlement in honor of the saint, and then led his men northward to sort out the French. Unfortunately for the little Huguenot community, Jean Ribault had the same idea regarding the Spanish. He had set sail with his men to destroy the fledgling settlement of St. Augustine. Thus Menéndez found Fort Caroline virtually undefended and captured it easily, killing everyone except the women and children. Meanwhile, Ribault's force had run into a storm at sea and were shipwrecked well before they could reach St. Augustine. The spot where Menéndez later found the survivors is known to this day as Matanzas — Spanish for "killings" — for he took no prisoners.

A replica of the *HMS Bounty* moored at Miami.

For the rest of the century the Spanish labored feverishly to consolidate and expand their hold on the peninsula. A chain of forts was established, along with a network of Franciscan missions to convert the native inhabitants. Although Sir Francis Drake succeeded in burning down St. Augustine in 1586, two years before he defeated the Spanish Armada, niether the English nor the French challenged Spain's colonial supremacy in Florida throughout the seventeenth century. At the same time, native resistance to Spanish domination was crumbling rapidly.

Those who weren't killed by Spanish firepower succumbed to the European diseases brought by the Spanish — smallpox, diphtheria, and syphilis — while others were taken into slavery for the plantations in the West Indies. Thus, for over a century the Spanish were the acknowledged overlords of Florida.

However, by 1700 there were signs that Spain's grip on Florida was slipping. To the north, English colonies were proliferating — and flourishing. To the west, LaSalle had claimed the entire Mississippi River valley for France. Then the War of the Spanish Succession in 1702 brought English troops into Florida. Along with the help of the Creek native population, the English overran most of Spain's military outposts in the north and destroyed almost all Spanish missions. Then the French captured Pensacola in 1719. Although they handed it back soon afterwards, purely to keep it out of English hands, it was over for Spain.

Finally, in 1763, after France's defeat in the French and Indian Wars left England as the undisputed master of the American continent, Spain ceded Florida to England in exchange for Havana, which the English had captured. By this time all of the native inhabitants had vanished, to be replaced by renegade Creeks from neighboring territories to the north and west. They were called Seminoles, from the Spanish words for renegades or runaways, *cimarrones*. The situation went well at first between the English and the Seminoles. The English cultivated them as trading partners instead of exterminating them as savages. But England's ambitious plans for developing Florida had to be put on hold as the rebellion in the 13 colonies to the north approached revolution.

If the British colonial presence in Florida was brief — two decades, from 1763 to 1783 — it was also benign, as indicated by the fact that Florida did not join in the American Revolution, and indeed provided a haven for prominent English Tories fleeing the war. But when the war was lost, Britain traded Florida back to Spain in 1783 in exchange for the Bahamas.

In the years following the War of Independence, citizens of the newly-sovereign United States of America began to develop a keen and acquisitive interest in this Spanish-owned territory dangling below the infant nation. The Seminoles were still loyal to their British landlords, and mistrustful of the intentions of the Americans who were buying up land in big chunks all around them. The Seminoles became violent nuisances to the new settlers — so much so that in 1817 Andrew Jackson led a small army into northern Florida to punish the "Indians". This became known as the First Seminole War. Apart from teaching them an unhappy lesson, it taught the Spaniards that they were manifestly incapable of protecting their territory. They sold Florida to the United States in 1821.

Andrew Jackson — an obvious choice — was created military governor of the newly annexed territory. Less obviously, Tallahassee was created its capital. This choice came about because the British had divided the territory for administrative purposes into East Florida and West Florida, with capitals in St. Augustine and Pensacola respectively, and the two settlements had rival claims to be the capital of a united Florida. To settle the issue, the territorial legislature came up with a novel solution. One man was dispatched from St. Augustine to Pensacola, and another man was dispatched from Pensacola to St. Augustine. Wherever they met would be the new capital. They met in the forest at Tallahassee.

As the influx of new settlers from the north increased, the resistance of the Seminoles stiffened. As a result, Congress passed the Removal Law of 1830, which required that all "Indians" be moved to the Arkansas Territory west of the Mississippi. Again the Seminoles resisted, and when Seminole warriors ambushed and wiped out a detachment of 139 United States troops under Major Francis Dade near Tampa in 1835. This gave President Andrew Jackson just the excuse he needed to go in and get rid of the Seminoles once and for all. But yet again the white man had underestimated the fighting spirit and determination of the red men. The Second Seminole War lasted for seven bloody years, even though the Seminoles' brilliant chief Osceola had been captured in 1837, while negotiating with the United States commander under a flag of truce.

In 1842, most of the surviving Seminoles were removed along the Trail of Tears to what is now Oklahoma. Even then, several hundred refused to capitulate, escaping into the Everglades where they and their descendants remained defiantly independent until the United States finally signed a treaty with them in 1934.

In 1845 Florida joined the Union as the twenty-seventh state, with a population of about 80,000, of which almost half were black slaves and almost none were Naive Americans.

Not surprisingly, given the state's geography and plantation economy, Florida sided with the Confederacy during the Civil War. Largely given to the state's historical vulnerability to outside occupation, no major battles were fought there as the Union forces marched in and captured all the strategic spots without too much difficulty. The period of Reconstruction was also less traumatic than in other southern states. Thanks to a wealthy Philadelphia industrialist named Hamilton Disston, who in 1881 was persuaded to buy four million acres (1.5 million hectares) of south-central Florida swampland for $1 million, which erased the state's debt burden in one stroke.

The next few years saw several developments which would put Florida firmly on the road to becoming, a century later,

the world's premier vacation playground. First, the American Medical Association declared St. Petersburg to be the healthiest spot in the United States. Then the youngish inventor Thomas Edison forsook New Jersey for Fort Myers, where he built an estate with America's first modern swimming pool. Then along came Henry Bradley Plant, a Connecticut Yankee who built the Atlantic Coastline Railroad from Richmond, Virginia to Tampa. The single greatest attraction was Plant's Tampa Bay Hotel, a phantasmagorical hostelry stretching for a quarter of a mile (four-tenths of a kilometer) under mina-

OPPOSITE: A typical sight in Pensacola's historic Seville Quarter. ABOVE: The Old Capitol in Tallahassee, now a museum.

rets, cupolas, and domes. Simultaneously, Henry Morrison Flagler, a retired Standard Oil executive, was building his Florida East Coast Railroad down the other side of the peninsula. He laid his tracks to St. Augustine, and then to Ormond Beach, and then to Palm Beach, and then to the little hamlet of Miami, and then, eventually, by way of a series of arched bridges, over the ocean and the Florida Keys to Key West. At every important stop along the way Flagler left behind at least one stunning hotel to accommodate the people his railway was

transporting down from the north: the Ponce de León and the Alcazar in St. Augustine, the Ormond in Ormond Beach, the Royal Poinciana in Palm Beach, and the Royal Palm in Miami. In the course of his triumphal march to the southernmost tip of the United States, Flagler also created two future cities: Palm Beach and Miami.

In 1912, the year before Flagler died, a millionaire from Indianapolis, Carl Fisher, discovered a barrier sandbar in Biscayne Bay, where he bought a large tract of land and then added to it with the help of a dredge. A few hotels and golf courses and tennis courts later, Miami Beach was in business. To the south of Miami George Merrick created Coral Gables, the nation's first fully planned city, while up the coast the eccentric architect Addison Mizner was putting up mansions in Palm Beach and buying up scrubland which was to become Boca Raton. At the same time, swampland in the Everglades was being drained to create rich farmland.

All of this activity led to a spectacular land boom in the early 1920s. People poured into the state from all over the country to get a piece of the action. As prices spiraled wildly upward, con-men sold the same parcels of land over and over. Others bought and resold land on the same day. Many bought unseen land, only to discover later that the land was under water. As a result of this feeding frenzy, by 1925 two and a half million people had invested in Florida land. But the following year the bottom fell out of what had come to be known as the "surreal estate market".

The boom was bound to go bust in any case, but its collapse was hastened by the fact that the railways simply couldn't handle the enormous demand for building materials, and many builders went bankrupt as a consequence. Then one of the boats bringing materials to Miami capsized, blocking Miami's harbor and bankrupting more builders. The final blow, literally, came on September 17, 1926, when a savage hurricane blew into Miami, damaging over half the buildings and leveling nearby developments. The party was now over, and three years later when the stock market crash brought on the Great Depression, the lights were turned out.

They flickered back on again during World War II, when the United States military decided to take advantage of Florida's climate and use it as a year-round training ground. Not only did this give thousands of young soldiers their first tantalizing glimpse of this sunlit, sub-tropical land, but it also produced corollary benefits such as a much-improved system of roads and airports, which made it possible for growers to ship their produce all over the country. Equally importantly for the state's economy, military research led to the development of coolants that were to give Florida efficient air conditioning for its sweltering summers as well as a means of creating frozen concentrates out of its vast citrus crops. The war was definitely good for Florida.

So was the land bust of 1926, because when people and prosperity began to return to Florida in the post-war years, the lessons of 1926 were remembered. Property transactions were regulated, developments controlled, subdivisions properly planned. Consequently, Florida is still enjoying the remarkable growth that was launched at roughly the same time as the first rocket from Cape Canaveral in 1950.

Perhaps no other American city has experienced such massive growth over the last century as Miami. The South Florida metropolis started to take on a distinctly Latin flavor with the first wave of Cuban immigrants, who were seeking exile after Fidel Castro took control of Cuba in the revolution of 1959. Over the next two decades, more than half a million Cubans poured into Miami establishing their homes away from home and the community of Little Havana, which is still a thriving symbol of Cuban influence in South Florida. Many of the early Cuban exiles, who were from the professional class, used their entrepreneurial spirit to forge Greater Miami into the unofficial Capital of Latin America. The 1980s brought another wave of Cuban refugees, known as Marielitos because Castro released a majority of prisoners from the Mariel Prison and allowed them to flee on rafts and overcrowded boats to inundate South Florida's shores. Miami wasn't prepared for this flood of immigrants and nearly burst at the seams, an erruption of ethnic tension and crime plagued many neighborhoods.

Within a few years, Miami became the entry point for many other refugees – political, economical, social – seeking freedom from neighboring Caribbean and Latin American countries. Miami's melting pot finally boiled over when political tensions flaring in the latter part of the decade. By the 1990s, tensions had cooled down, and just as the Cubans left their imprint on the patchwork quilt that makes up modern Miami, the other groups have woven their own cultures into the urban fabric. Today, Miami is an international and cosmopolitan city, with both the good and bad that goes with it. There is more tolerance for racial and ethnic differences than in the past and the city now moves to the beat of many different native tongues, from Spanish to Portuguese to French or Creole. No other city in Florida has that kind of diversity.

On the Gulf Coast, the Tampa Bay area is undergoing its own population explosion, and resembles what Miami looked like 15 years ago. It could be that Florida soon might well have international hubs on both coasts. And let us not forget Orlando in the center of the state. A landscape once dominated by orange groves has evolved into endless housing developments that stretch Orlando's city limits farther and farther. With so many tourist attractions and theme parks, Orlando always has jobs, a fact which attracts those new to the United States and in search of their share of the American Dream. The rest of the state is also growing, but not nearly as fast. Although Jacksonville is the emerging city as the century comes to an end, it still moves at the pace of the Old South, given its proximity to the Georgia border. The state's increasingly diverse population has not pushed its way that far north yet.

There are those who think that this growth has been achieved in part at the expense of the environment, that too little attention has been paid to the natural beauty that made

OPPOSITE: Sunset in Panhandle. ABOVE : The Panhandle town of Seaside.

the state so attractive in the first place. Others point to the paradox that the state's glorious climate is starting to become a financial burden: by luring so many retirees away from less hospitable climes, it ensures that the costs of health care and programs for the elderly will have to grow as well.

As of now, these are mere sunspots on the sun that shines on Florida.

GEOGRAPHY AND CLIMATE

At first glance, it would seem rather pointless to write about Florida's geography and climate. After all, there must be very few travelers anywhere in the world who couldn't find Florida on a map or who wouldn't know what sort of weather they could expect to find when they got there. Nonetheless, there are aspects of Florida's geographical and climatic conditions that may still come as a surprise to the visitor.

By United States standards the state is not very large — less than 60,000 sq miles (97,000 sq km), about the size of England and Wales combined. Nor is it topographically very diverse. Most of Florida is either swampland or former swampland surrounded by coastal plains. Offshore these plains continue to surface intermittently as islands, sand bars, or coral reefs. At its edges, where Florida rejoins the sea whence it emerged some 20 million years ago, the beaches do not vary significantly in either texture or appeal. Along the northern Atlantic coast they tend to be broad and the sand is tightly packed; along the southern Atlantic coast they are still broad but softer; along the Gulf Coast they are narrower and softer still, and strewn with shells in the south; in the Panhandle, from Pensacola to Panama City, the beaches are sugary, almost powdery, both in color and consistency.

Within these sandy margins, there are over 300 species of trees, over 400 species and subspecies of birds, and at least 80 different land mammals. Florida's official state tree is the wonderful sabal palm, which can be found almost everywhere in the state, but in different regions its pre-eminence is challenged variously by pines, cypresses, magnolias, and live oaks. And of course there are the vast citrus groves in the central and south-central parts of the state.

Of Florida's permanent bird population, the most spectacular inland (and usually swampland) residents are the ibises, egrets, herons, ospreys, cormorants, cardinals, roseate spoonbills and flamingos. Along the shoreline you will find a somewhat less exotic array of sandpipers, terns, and pelicans. Then there are ducks and geese, who just like wintering in Florida.

The most interesting mammals are, sadly but predictably, also the rarest: gray foxes, black bears, pumas, and wildcats. However, there is one mammal that is both very interesting and very common: the friendly dolphin, which can often be seen near the beach or beside your boat. Other familiar figures in the landscape, markedly less friendly, include those huge, waddling handbags called alligators (or, by Floridians, just 'gators).

Although Florida was named for the Easter Feast of Flowers in Spain, it could just as appropriately have been named for the feast of flowers which it offers its beholders. This is especially true in the spring, when the bougainvillea, poincianas, orchid trees, geraniums, azaleas, trumpet vines, and tiger lilies conspire to incite a riot of color.

The climate — well, you already know about the climate or you wouldn't want to know about everything else. Other than the occasional hurricane and freak winter storm, it's sunny year round, with temperatures in most places ranging from fairly warm to very warm. In mid-winter in the northern parts of the state it sometimes, but rarely, plunges to 50°F (10°C); otherwise the thermometer tends to hover around 60°F (15°C). You add degrees as you move south: it can easily be 75°F (24°C) in Key West in January.

In the summer, it's correspondingly warmer in different parts of the state. But — and here's the good news — not all that much warmer. It seldom reaches 95°F anywhere, and all the coastal areas are naturally air conditioned by ocean breezes. (Every interior space untouched by the ocean breezes has been air conditioned by man.) And more good news: the waters around Florida, thanks partly to the Gulf Stream, are agreeably warm even in winter.

The bad news? You have to dial "H" to get the latest scoop on Humidity and Hurricanes. Neither, however, constitutes a serious inconvenience. Humidity can be avoided by staying indoors or in the water around midday in summer; hurricanes can't be avoided if you happen to be directly in their path. Usually you have enough warning to get out of danger and seek shelter. Hurricane evacuation routes out of places like the Florida Keys are clearly marked. However, if you wait too long, you could be sitting in bumper-to-bumper traffic trying to escape the islands as the first effects of the storm hit. Pay close attention to National Weather Service warnings. And if instructed to evacuate, you should.

Fortunately, hurricanes are relatively infrequent, even in the hurricane season (late July to mid-November) and their arrival is announced well in advance by the news media. Moreover, the buildings are built to withstand high winds (as in California, where they are built to withstand earthquakes).

Basically, though, if you take the right steps to prepare, there is little in Florida that can come between you and the sea and the sun, and a great time.

Sunset, soft sand, and serenity on the beach at Seaside, Florida.

AmeriFirst

Miami and Environs

MIAMI AND MIAMI BEACH
NORLAND
NORTH MIAMI BEACH
OPA-LOCKA
NORTH MIAMI
HIALEAH
MIAMI SPRINGS
WEST MIAMI
MIAMI
WESTWOOD LAKES
COCONUT GROVE
SOUTH MIAMI
KENDALL
CORAL GABLES
MIAMI BEACH
Country Club of Miami
Florida's Turnpike (toll)
Palmetto Expressway
Miami Gardens Drive
North Miami Beach Boulevard
West Dixie Highway
N.E. 135th Street
N.W. 27nd Avenue
N.W. 22nd Avenue
N.E. 6th Avenue
Biscayne Boulevard
Biscayne Park
Miami Shores
Indian Creek Village
Collins Avenue
Sunny
Haulover Beach Park
Bal Harb
Surfsi
Okeechobee Road
Hialeah Speedway (Auto Racing)
Hialeah Park (Horse Racing)
N.W. 79th Street
79th Street
J.F. Kennedy Causeway
Harbor Island
Treasure Island
North Bay Village
Intercoastal Waterway
Morningside Park
Alton Road
Arthur Godfrey
Curtis Parkway
S.W. 87th Avenue
Miami International Airport
Poinciana Boulevard
Dolphin Expressway (toll)
Sunset Islands
Venetian Islands
Venetian Causeway (toll)
Dade Boulevard
Holocaust Memorial
Collins Park
Convention Center
Ocean Drive
Ocean Front Auditorium
Dade County Museum
Orange Bowl Stadium
West Flager Street
Flagler Street
Miami Art Museum
Dodge Island Causeway
Bayfront Park
Port of Miami
Fisher Island
S.W. 8th Street
Coral Way
Brickell Avenue
Miracle Mile
S.W. 27th Avenue
Museum of Science and Planetarium
Vizcaya
David Kennedy Park
Rickenbacker Causeway
Virginia Key
Planet Ocean
Seaquarium
Virginia Beach
Bitmore Golf Course
40th Street
Bird Road
South Bay Shore Drive
South Dixie Highway
Crandon Park
S. Dade Expressway (toll)
University of Miami
Sunset Drive
Main Highway
Snapper Creek Expressway
Key Biscayne
N. Kendall Drive
Ingraham Highway
Biscayne Bay
ATLANTIC OCEAN
Matheson Hammock Park
Fairchild Tropical Garden
Parrot Jungle
Bill Baggs State Recreation Area
Cape Florida Lighthouse
Howard Drive
Old Cutler Road
Palmetto Golf Course
Biscayne National Park
0 1 2 3 miles
0 1 2 3 4 5 km
N

ON JULY 28, 1890 THE SMALL FISHING and farming community of Miami, with a population of 343 people, was incorporated as a city. By 1920 the population had grown to 30,000, and Miami's development as a major resort was well under way. Nowadays, nearly two million people live in the 26 municipalities that make up the Greater Miami area. These municipalities include Miami Beach, with its Art Deco hotels and miles of sand; the South Pacific-like Virginia Key and Key Biscayne islands below Miami Beach; Coral Gables, colloquially known as the Miami Riviera because of its Mediterranean-style buildings and High Society contingent; Coconut Grove, which is noted for the quality of its shops and its nightlife; and Little Havana, west of the downtown area, the city's Cuban district. Greater Miami now contains 2,040 sq miles (3,284 sq km) of land — of which 1,423 acres (58 hectares) are public beaches along a 15-mile (24-km) stretch of coast between Key Biscayne and Bal Harbour — and 354 sq miles (570 sq km) of water.

The area's ethnic mix is 36 percent white, 18 percent black, and 46 percent Hispanic. The majority of the Hispanics are of Cuban origin, but there are also considerable numbers originally from Panama, Colombia, El Salvador, and Nicaragua, as well as some 150,000 French-speaking Haitians. The influx of foreigners into Miami has given rise to the sobriquet "America's Casablanca," as some of the immigrants are political or economic refugees, particularly those from Latin American countries and the Caribbean.

Despite the tensions involved in such a racial mixture, and despite its (largely undeserved) reputation for crime and vice, the Miami area has recently been judged the twentieth most desirable place to live in the United States among the 333 cities surveyed in Rand McNally's *Places Rated Almanac*. The almanac ranks cities according to the level of crime and the quality of such things as health care, the environment, public transportation, education, recreation, the arts, and the climate. By these criteria, Miami ranks among the best cities in the country.

The Miami International Airport is the second busiest in the nation, handling up to 850 flights a day. The Port of Miami is indisputably the cruise ship capital of the world, welcoming over two and a half million cruise passengers every year. But the crucial number — the number that attracts all these numbers of people — is 76°F (24°C). That's the average annual temperature in the Greater Miami area.

MIAMI

BACKGROUND

The first American settler in the area was a Carolina planter named Richard Fitzpatrick, who in 1826 brought a group of slaves to work the land on the banks of the Miami River. Fitzpatrick's Miami holdings were inherited by his nephew, William English, in 1842, the same year in which the Second Seminole War came to an end. English saw clearly the place's potential and began drawing up plans for a village by the mouth of the Miami River. He decided to call the new settlement Miami, a corruption of the Tequesta word *mayaime*, meaning "very large," which is what the Tequesta tribe once called Lake Okeechobee to the northwest.

Through newspapers in the state's northern cities, English advertised lots for sale at $1 each. Reassured that the Seminoles were no longer a threat, small but growing numbers of people were lured south by the bargain offer. Homesteads were established and the community grew steadily until 1855, when the Third Seminole War broke out.

During the Civil War the Miami area became a refuge for spies, deserters and blockade runners, but the actual battles were confined to the northern part of the state. New settlers arrived after the war, and the area's growth resumed: agricultural communities were established at Lemon City, Coconut Grove, Buena Vista and Little River, while a merchant named William Brickell set up a trading post near the mouth of the Miami River, which did a lively trade with the local Indians.

The "Mother of Miami" (so called because she is said to have "conceived" the city), a wealthy widow by the name of Julia Tuttle, arrived in 1875. She set herself up in

William English's old house and over the next 15 years became the area's most important landowner. She was persistent in her efforts to persuade Henry Flagler to extend his Florida East Coast Railroad to Miami, and even tried to tempt him with an offer of 300 acres (120 hectares) of land free, but to no avail. In 1895, however, freak weather conditions came to Mrs. Tuttle's aid. That was the year of the Great Freeze, which wiped out 90 percent of the state's citrus crop but left the Miami area relatively untouched.

The effects of the Great Freeze cut Flagler's railway profits and severely damaged the image of his resorts on the coasts to the north. Seeing her chance, Mrs. Tuttle sent a bouquet of Miami orange blossoms to Flagler as a little reminder that the Miami area had a climate dependable enough to produce citrus crops all year round. Flagler got the point, and his railway reached Miami the following year in 1896. Developers soon followed, building hotels and condominiums, and Flagler himself further invested in the new city by putting up the Royal Palm Hotel.

The real estate boom quickly accelerated and by 1910 the population had grown to 5,000, including some very rich people who had built some very fancy houses along Brickell Avenue overlooking Biscayne Bay. James Deering's elaborate Villa Vizcaya, still ogled by tourists today, was probably the most impressive of these private palaces. By 1920 the planter John S. Collins and his partner, the businessman and speedway mogul Carl Fisher, had bought up most of the almost 1,600 acres (640 hectares) of mangrove island just off the coast, drained it, and developed it into Miami Beach. The decade of the Twenties was a major boom period for Miami: in the winter season of 1924–25, 300,000 tourists visited the city, and the population swelled to 100,000. In 1926, however, the boom came to an abrupt end and the financiers and developers who had fueled the boom rapidly began divesting.

Still, the development continued at a modest pace through the Depression years. George Merrick established Coral Gables as one of the most exclusive suburbs in the area, and Glenn H. Curtiss made Hialeah and

Miami Springs into popular resort centers for winter vacationers. In Miami Beach, marvelous Art Deco hotels rose from the sands. In the 1937–38 winter season, more than 800,000 tourists came to Miami. The city expanded relentlessly to accommodate the ever-increasing numbers of visitors and new residents, until — like Los Angeles on the other coast — it became difficult to decide where the city stopped and the rest of the state began.

After the Cuban revolution in 1959, Miami began receiving waves of refugees: more than half a million over the following years. The Cubans added a whole new dimension to the appearance and the sociocultural character of the city. Miami's architecture, food, music, politics, media, and of

course, language were all profoundly affected by the new arrivals. They also brought considerable entrepreneurial skills with them, reinforcing the city's economic base and helping to establish it as one of America's most important financial centers. In addition to the hundreds of banks and insurance companies in Miami, many multinational corporations have their Latin American headquarters in the city because of its unrivaled airline connections to the Caribbean and South America.

Like all big cities, Miami has its problems. But I think it's fair to say that there are few cities in the world that wouldn't willingly swap their problems for Miami's — especially if the climate and charm were part of the deal.

General Information

Comprehensive information on hotels, transportation, sporting events, and special attractions in the Miami area can be obtained from the **Greater Miami Convention and Visitors Bureau** ✆ (305) 539-3063 or 539-3034 TOLL-FREE (800) 283-2707 FAX (305) 539-3113 WEB SITE www.miamiandbeaches.com, 701 Brickell Avenue Suite 2700, Miami. For more detailed information on where to stay, contact the **Greater Miami and the Beaches Hotel Association** ✆ (305) 531-3553 TOLL-FREE (800) SEE-MIAMI FAX (305) 531-8954 WEB SITE www.gmbha.org, 407 Lincoln Road, Suite 10G, Miami Beach.

Downtown Miami's bold skyline reflects its status as one of America's most important financial centers.

For specific information on the most popular tourist areas, contact one or more of the following chambers of commerce: **Miami Beach Chamber of Commerce** ☎ (305) 672-1270 FAX (305) 538-4336 WEB SITE www.sobe.com/miamibeachchamber, 1920 Meridian Avenue, Miami Beach; the **Key Biscayne Chamber of Commerce** ☎ (305) 361-5207, 95 West McIntire, Key Biscayne; the **Coconut Grove Chamber of Commerce** ☎ (305) 444-7270, 2820 McFarland Road, Coconut Grove; the **Coral Gables Chamber of Commerce** ☎ (305) 446-1657, 50 Aragon

Avenue, Coral Gables; the **South Miami Chamber of Commerce** ☎ (305) 238-7192, 6410 Southwest 80th Street, South Miami; and the **Bal Harbour Chamber of Commerce** ☎ (305) 573-5177, 655 96th Street, Bal Harbour.

If you still need more information, you can drop by the visitors centers located at **Aventura Mall** ☎ (305) 935-3836, 19501 Biscayne Boulevard or **Bayside Marketplace** ☎ (305) 539-8070, 401 Biscayne Boulevard for free brochures and maps. The Sears stores in Coral Gables, Miami International Mall, and Westland Mall also have information centers.

To get around town, you can take a taxi for about $1.75 per mile. Two recommended companies are **Flamingo Taxi** ☎ (305) 885-7000 FAX (305) 754-4600, 198 Northwest 79 Street and **Metro Taxi** ☎ (305) 888-8888 FAX (305) 947-0371, 1995 Northeast 142 Street.

Metrorail ☎ (305) 638-6700, a 21-mile elevated rail system, runs from downtown Miami to as far south as Kendall and west to Hialeah. Rides cost $1.25 each way.

Water taxis ☎ (954) 467-6677 FAX (954) 728-8417 WEB SITE www.watertaxi.com, which depart from hotels, restaurants and marinas, carry from 27 to 49 passengers.

For medical emergencies, **Mercy Hospital** ☎ (305) 854-4400 FAX (305) 285-2971 WEB SITE www.mercymiami.com, 3663 South Miami Avenue, Coconut Grove, offers international patient services and a physician referral number ☎ (305) 285-2929.

Most dental emergencies can be handled at the **Beach Dental Center** ☎ (305) 532-3300 FAX (305) 267-4568, 1370 Washington Avenue No. 201, Miami Beach.

WHAT TO SEE AND DO

There are so many things to see in Miami that the best approach is to take one area at a time. A good place to start is downtown, the commercial and business center of the city. Here you will find the **Miami Art Museum** ☎ (305) 375-3000 FAX (305) 375-1725, 101 West Flagler Street, where the focus is on art of the Western Hemisphere since World War II. The museum is one of three components of the Miami-Dade Cultural Center.

The history of the region is brought into focus at the **Historical Museum of Southern Florida** ☎ (305) 375-1492 FAX (305) 375-1609 WEB SITE www.historical-museum.org, in the same complex. Displays illuminate the lifestyles and culture of both the Indians and nineteenth-century settlers; a photography and film exhibition shows how Miami emerged as a major city.

Those who are more enthralled by modern technology should head for the **Miami Museum of Science and Space Transit Planetarium** ☎ (305) 854-424 or 854-4242 FAX (305) 285-5801 WEB SITE www.miamisci.org, 3280 South Miami Avenue. It has over 140 hands-on exhibits examining the natural sciences, biology, and human anatomy. There are also live scientific experiments, displays of advanced computer technology, and an Animal Exploratorium with a collection of rare natural history specimens. The Planetarium has a dome 65 ft (20 m) high which houses astronomy and laser shows, and the Weintraub Observatory for evening star

ABOVE: The *Heritage of Miami* under full sail passes a cruise liner in Biscayne Bay. OPPOSITE: Getting around, Miami style.

gazing. The museum is open from 10 AM to 6 PM daily, with separate late openings at weekends for the observatory.

Another popular downtown attraction is the **Vizcaya Museum and Gardens** ☎ (305) 250-9133 FAX (305) 285-2004, 3251 South Miami Avenue, where antiques, paintings, and Oriental decorations adorn the interior of James Deering's 34-room Italian Renaissance villa. The European-style formal gardens and fountains surrounding the villa are among the most beautiful in the country. Opening hours are daily from 9:30 AM to 5 PM.

On the southern tip of Virginia Key is the **Bill Baggs Cape Florida State Recreation Area** ☎ (305) 361-5811, 1200 South Crandon Boulevard, which has nature trails and beaches in addition to the oldest structure in south Florida, the 95 ft (30 m) high **Cape Florida Lighthouse**. You can climb to the top of the lighthouse and enjoy the view over Biscayne Bay and the Atlantic beyond.

Back on the mainland is the bayside community of Coconut Grove, a haven for hippies during the sixties, but now home to an altogether more sophisticated set who enjoy the

exclusive shops, French-style cafés, and trendy nightlife. Sights in "The Grove" include **Silver Bluff**, a fascinating rock formation dating back thousands of years. You'll find it on Bay Boulevard between Crystal View and Emathia Streets. The **Barnacle State Historic Site** ☎ (305) 448-9445, 3485 Main Highway, is a tranquil five-acre (two-hectare) estate with one of the region's oldest houses (1870) where you can see authentic period furniture and historical photographs.

To reach **Virginia Key** and **Key Biscayne** take Rickenbacker Causeway across Biscayne Bay. There are parks and beaches on both keys, with swimming and sporting facilities, and you can also see pockets of old mangrove swamp of the type that once covered Miami Beach. The first thing to see on Virginia Key is the **Miami Seaquarium** ☎ (305) 361-5705 FAX (305) 361-6077 WEB SITE www.miamiseaquarium.com, 400 Rickenbacker Causeway, home to a performing killer whale called Lolita, as well as Flipper the porpoise, veteran of films and a television series. There are regular dolphin shows, a shark pool, sea lions, and thousands of other sea creatures in dozens of aquariums. The Seaquarium is open from 9:30 AM to 6:30 PM daily.

A few miles farther down the coast is Coral Gables, known as the "Miami Riviera" because of its Mediterranean-style architecture and well-heeled inhabitants. For a good example of the architecture, visit the **Coral Gables Merrick House** ☎ (305) 460-5361,

907 Coral Way, a coral rock structure built at the turn of the century as a home for George Merrick, the founder of the community. The **Venetian Pool** ☎ (305) 460-5356, 2701 DeSoto Boulevard, is a lagoon carved out of rock, with caves, stone bridges, and waterfalls. Set in the middle of a large mansion, the pool is a delightful place to laze away an afternoon.

The **Fairchild Tropical Garden** ☎ (305) 667-1651 FAX (305) 661-8953 WEB SITE www.ftg.org, 10901 Old Cutler Road, is one of the nation's largest tropical botanical gardens, with hourly train rides through its 83 acres (33 hectares) of exotic flora. The plant house contains rare specimens and a miniature rainforest. The gardens are open daily from 9:30 AM to 4:30 PM. At the **Lowe Art Museum** ☎ (305) 284-3535 FAX (305) 284-2024 WEB SITE www.lowemuseum.org, 1301 Stanford Drive, Coral Gables, at the University of Miami, there are several El Greco paintings among the fine Kress collection of Renaissance and Baroque art.

Continuing down the coast from Coral Gables, you come to the area of Greater Miami known as South Dade County, which has some of the most popular tourist attractions in the region. The largest cageless facility in the nation, **Miami Metrozoo** ☎ (305) 251-0400 FAX (305) 378-6381, 12400 Southwest 152nd Street, features very rare and beautiful white Bengal tigers, koalas, and over 300 exotic birds in a free-flight aviary. The animals live in natural habitats separated from the public by moats. Opening hours are from 9:30 AM to 5:30 PM daily. More exotic birds can be seen at **Parrot Jungle and Gardens** ☎ (305) 666-7834 FAX (305) 661-2230 WEB SITE www.parrotjungle.com, 11000 Southwest 57th Avenue, where the birds fly around a sub-tropical jungle. You can feed them or pose for a picture. Open daily from 9:30 AM. Humans are the ones locked in while the animals run free at **Monkey Jungle** ☎ (305) 235-1611 FAX (305) 235-4253, 14805 Southwest 216th Street. A unique colony of apes and monkeys live semi-wild in a natural tropical habitat. There are also daily shows featuring performing chimps. This primate enclave can be visited daily from 9:30 AM to 5 PM.

Weeks Air Museum ☎ (305) 233-5197 WEB SITE www.weeksairmuseum.com, 14710 Southwest 128th Street, is an increasingly popular attraction, housing 35 immaculate civilian and military aircraft dating

OPPOSITE: Villa Vizcaya, John Deering's Italian Renaissance villa, and ABOVE its sculptured stone barge.

from the earliest days of aviation. There are also exhibits and photographs depicting aviation history. The museum is open daily from 10 AM to 5 PM.

Gold Coast Railroad Museum ☎ (305) 253-0063, 12450 Southwest 152nd Street, has historic trains on display and features a ride around the museum grounds in a steam locomotive on the weekends. Open daily from 10 AM to 3 PM.

Numerous cruise lines offer a wide variety of cruises from the Port of Miami, the most popular being the half-day cruises, evening dinner cruises, and full-day cruises to Bimini and the Bahamas. The prices are reasonable, ranging from $50+ for half-day cruises to $100+ for full-day cruises. Contact **Costa Cruise Line** ☎ (305) 358-7325 TOLL-FREE (800) 462-6782 FAX (305) 375-0676 WEB SITE www.costacruises.com, 80 Southwest Eighth Street, Miami.

A couple of gambling casino cruises that take you out in the evenings are **Casino Miami** ☎ (305) 577-7775 FAX (305) 577-0128 WEB SITE www.florida-concierge.com/miamicasino, located at Dupont Plaza on the Miami River, and **Casino Princesa** ☎ (305) 579-5825 FAX (305) 379-5522, located near the Hard Rock Café at Bayside Marketplace.

With so much water around Miami, sightseeing cruises can be a very rewarding introduction to the area. Try **Miami River Historical Jungle Tours** ☎ (305) 579-8687 FAX (305) 579-1074, 300 Biscayne Boulevard Way Suite 720, Miami, or **Flyer Catamaran Excursions** ☎ (305) 361-3611, 4400 Rickenbacker Causeway, Miami.

Sports

Football fans can watch the **Miami Dolphins** of the NFL play between September and January at Pro Player Stadium ☎ (954) 452-7000 WEB SITE www.pwr.com/dolphins, 2269 Northwest 199th Street, Miami. For ticket information dial ☎ (305) 620-2578. The **Miami Heat** basketball team ☎ (954) 835-7000 WEB SITE www.heat.com, of the NBA plays from October to April at the Miami Arena ☎ (305) 577-4328, 721 Northwest First Avenue, Miami. By early in the 21st century the Heat will play at a new arena in downtown Miami. Miami's most recent World Champions are the **Florida Marlins** ☎ (305) 626-7400 WEB SITE www.flamarlins.com, who won the 1997 Major League Baseball World Series and also play at Pro Player Stadium. For ticket information call ☎ (305) 930-4487. The baseball season runs from April to early October. The newest kid on the sports block is the

Miami Fusion ☎ (888) FUSION4, of Major League Soccer. They play at Lockhart Stadium in Fort Lauderdale.

For college sports fans, the **University of Miami Hurricanes** ☎ (305) 284-2263 WEB SITE www.miami.edu/athletics, Coral Gables, field men's and women's teams in a variety of sports from football to basketball to track played in the collegiate season that runs from September through June.

Horse racing takes place in the lovely surroundings of **Hialeah Park** ☎ (305) 885-8000, 105 East 21st Street, Hialeah, which has a French Mediterranean-style clubhouse and grandstand. There is a Metrorail station in the grounds of the track. Florida has been a thoroughbred racing center for more than 50 years. Two other famous racetracks are: **Calder Race Course** ☎ (3050 625-1311 FAX (305) 623-9084 WEB SITE www.calderracecourse.com, 21001 Northwest 27th Avenue, Miami, and **Gulfstream Park** ☎ (954) 454-7000 FAX (954) 457-6192 WEB SITE www.gulfstreampark.com, 901 South Federal Highway, Hallandale. Calder is located next to Pro Player Stadium and features daily racing with full-card simulcasting. Gulfstream is also set in lush tropical surroundings. Racing season is January-March.

Jai alai enthusiasts can see the sport played at the **Miami Jai Alai Fronton** ☎ (305) 633-6400 FAX (305) 633-4386 WEB SITE www.fla-gaming.com, 3500 Northwest 37th Avenue, Miami. It's open year round and it's legal to bet on the games.

You can always see many of the world's top tennis players in action at the annual **Lipton Championships** ☎ (305) 446-2200 TOLL-FREE (800) 725-5472 FAX (305) 446-9080 WEB SITE www.lipton.com, 150 Alhambra Circle Suite 825, Coral Gables, which features the world's top men and women players competing prize money totaling $4.5 million. The tournament is held in March at the Crandon Park Tennis Center ☎ (305) 365-2300, 7300 Crandon Boulevard, Key Biscayne.

For those who want to play rather than watch sports, there are 34 public golf courses in the Greater Miami area, including the **Fontainebleau Golf Club** ☎ (305) 221-5181 FAX (305) 221-3265, 9603 Fontainebleau Boulevard, Miami; the **Golf Club of Miami** ☎ (305) 829-4700 FAX (305) 829-8457, 6801 Northwest 186th Street; the **Crandon Golf Course** ☎ (305) 361-9129 FAX (305) 361-1062, 6700 Crandon Boulevard, Key Biscayne, the **Biltmore Golf Club** ☎ (305) 460-5366 FAX (305) 460-5315, 1210 Anastasia Avenue, Coral Gables; and the **Palmetto Golf Course** ☎ (305) 238-2922 FAX (305) 233-7840 WEB SITE www.metro-dade.com/parks, 9300 Southwest 152nd Street in South Dade County.

Tennis players are also well catered for in the Miami area. There are 11 public tennis centers including the **Biltmore Tennis Center** ☎ (305) 460-5360, at 1210 Anastasia Avenue in Coral Gables, which has ten hard courts, and the **Tennis Center at Crandon Park** ☎ (305) 365-2300, Key Biscayne, which has 17 hard courts. More information on tennis facilities in and around Miami can be obtained from the **City of Miami Parks and Recreation Department** ☎ (305) 416-1313 FAX (305) 416-2154, 444 Southwest Second Avenue, Miami, or the **Miami-Dade Park and Recreation Department** ☎ (305) 755-7800 FAX (305) 755-7857 WEB SITE www.co-miami-dade.fl.us/parks, 275 Northwest Second Street, Miami.

OPPOSITE: Some inhabitants of Parrot Jungle greet a visitor. ABOVE: The Bayfront Park in downtown Miami.

There is, as you might expect, terrific fishing in the waters off Miami. To arrange a fishing trip, contact **Mark the Shark Charters** ☎ (305) 759-5297 FAX (305) 375-0597, 1633 North Bayshore Drive, Miami at the Biscayne Bay Marriott Marina. Sailing boats can be rented from **Biscayne America Company-Sail Miami** ☎ (305) 857-9000 FAX (305) 274-0069, Dinner Key Marina, Coconut Grove, where you can also rent powerboats and scuba diving equipment. Diving charters (and lessons) which go to various offshore reefs can be arranged through **Diver's Paradise** ☎ (305) 361-3483, 4000 Crandon Boulevard, Key Biscayne, which also rents equipment. Jet skis and other water sports equipment are available from **Water Sports** ☎ (305) 932-8445 FAX (305) 944-0195 WEB SITE www.members.aol.com/dd1wtps, 17875 Collins Avenue, Miami Beach.

Shopping

For the widest range of choices in North Miami go to the **Aventura Mall** ☎ (305) 935-1110 FAX (305) 935-9360, WEB SITE www.shopaventuramall.com, 19501 Biscayne Boulevard, Aventura, which contains several major department stores and more than 250 shops selling just about everything you could possibly want. Another impressive shopping plaza is the **Bayside Marketplace** ☎ (305) 577-3344 FAX (305) 577-0306 WEB SITE www.baysidemarketplace.com, 401 Biscayne Boulevard, downtown Miami. It is an open-air complex with brick walkways lined with tropical trees and plants; its 100 shops specialize in women's fashions, jewelry, gifts, African and Oriental arts and crafts, and personalized souvenirs. In Little Havana you can find Cuban arts and crafts shops along the colorful **Southwest Eighth Street** between Route 95 West and 35th Street. For more upmarket shopping go to the **Streets of Mayfair** ☎ (305) 448-1700 fax (305) 448-1541 WEB SITE www.streetsofmayfair.com, 2911 Grand Avenue, Coconut Grove, or **The Shops at Sunset Place** ☎ (305) 663-9110 FAX (305) 663-6619, 5701 Sunset Drive, South Miami. The latter boasts South Florida's first NikeTown and the first IMAX theater, as well as FAO Schwartz and Z Gallerie. More designer shops can be found at the **Miracle mile** between Douglas Road and Lejeune Road in Coral Gables and **Paseos** ☎ (305) 444-8890 FAX (305) 447-9177, WEB SITE www.paseos.com, a futuristic shopping mall at 3301 Coral Way, in Miami.

Nightlife

There are many cultural events to illuminate the Miami night. For a comprehensive listing you should consult the Arts Section of the *Sunday Miami Herald* and the weekly *Miami New Times* newspapers. Most of the major events are staged at the **Gusman Center for the Performing Arts** ☎ (305) 374-2444 FAX (305) 374-0303, 25 Southeast Second Avenue, Miami, hosts the **Miami Film Festival** every February. At the **Lincoln Theater** ☎ (305) 673-3330 FAX (305) 673-6749, 541 Lincoln Road, Miami Beach, you can see the **New World Symphony** ☎ (305) 673-3330 FAX (305) 673-6749.

Opera lovers will tell you that the **Florida Grand Opera** ☎ (305) 476-1234 FAX (305) 476-9292 is the area's oldest and most revered cultural institution, and regularly attracts the likes of Pavarotti and Domingo. The **Dade County Auditorium** ☎ (305) 547-5414 fax (305) 541-7782, 2901 West Flagler Street, Miami is home to the **Florida Philharmonic Orchestra** ☎ (305) 476-1234 FAX (305) 476-9292 and the **Miami City Ballet** ☎ (305) 532-4880 FAX (305) 532-2726. The **Florida Shakespeare Theatre** ☎ (305) 445-1119 FAX (305) 445-8645, 1200 Anastasia Avenue, Coral Gables presents innovative productions and Florida premieres of Tony-Award winning plays.

Teatro Avante ☎ (305) 445-8877 FAX (305) 445-1301, 235 Alcazar Avenue, Coral Gables, produces the annual International Hispanic Theatre Festival and classical Spanish language plays. The **Coconut Grove Playhouse** ☎ (305) 442-2662 FAX (305) 444-6437, 3500 Main Highway, Coconut Grove, presents world, national and regional premieres in the classic-style theater.

The liveliest popular nightlife in the region occurs in downtown Miami, Little Havana, and Coconut Grove. **Tobacco Road** ☎ (305) 374-1198, 626 South Miami Avenue, downtown Miami, is one of the city's oldest watering holes and features live blues bands. **Firehouse Four** ☎ (305) 371-3473,

Palms and ponds decorate this golf course.

1000 South Miami Avenue, which is exactly what the name implies, has a different sound every night of the week. Sometimes its a live Latin band, other nights its a one-man-blues show.

All the action in Little Havana is along Southwest Eighth Street. At No. 3850 is **La Taberna** ☎ (305) 448-9323, where there is a piano bar on Monday through Friday and live acts the other days. At N 2212, vintage Cuban musical film clips accompany the sounds of the live music at **Café Nostalgia** ☎ (305) 541-2631.

For salsa lovers, **Club Mystique** ☎ (305) 265-3900, 5101 Blue Lagoon Drive, at the Miami Airport Hilton, attracts the hottest salsa artists on Friday or Saturday nights.

In Coconut Grove, several lively clubs can be found in the Coco Walk complex or The Shops at Mayfair. One hot club that mixes it up between house music, funk, and hip-hop is **Club 609** ☎ (305) 444-6092, 3342 Virginia Street, Coconut Grove. It features at least three dance floors and an open patio area to sit and cool off. **Club St. Croix** ☎ (305) 446-4999, 3015 Grand Avenue, on the top level of Coco Walk, has an equal array of sounds throughout the week.

The **Hungry Sailor** ☎ (305) 444-9359, at 3064 1/2 Grand Avenue, is an English-style pub serving food, wine, and beer along with its jazz, reggae, and folk music.

For a more mellow, but very hip scene in Coral Gables, check out **The Globe Café and Bar** ☎ (305) 445-3355, 377 Alhambra Circle, where live jazz is played on Saturday nights, house music on Fridays, and live blues on Mondays. You can also enjoy a wonderful grilled chicken and gorgonzola pizza or drop by for the Guava Cheesecake dessert.

WHERE TO STAY

Lodging in Miami can be quite expensive, but the city also features some of Florida's most pampering places to stay, hotels that are well worth the expense.

Luxury

It's a short taxi ride from the airport to the **Doral Golf Resort and Spa** ☎ (305) 592-2000 TOLL-FREE (800) 71-DORAL FAX (305) 591-6670 WEB SITE www.doralgolf.com, 4400 Northwest 87th Avenue, Miami. The Doral is one of the largest golf resorts in the world, with five championship courses in its 2,500-acre (1,000-hectare) grounds. You can attend the Jim McLean Golf School, and there are 15 tennis courts. Other exceptional facilities include the four-story Doral Spa, complete with steam rooms, saunas, Turkish baths, and gyms, and the 24-stable Doral Equestrian Center, which offers riding lessons. If you are still stuck for something to do, the hotel provides a regular shuttle service to the beach. Near the Bayside Marketplace downtown is the **Hotel Inter-Continental Miami** ☎ (305) 577-1000 TOLL-FREE (800) 327-3005 FAX (305) 372-4440 WEB SITE www.interconti.com, 100 Chopin Plaza, a 34-story triangular building with 645 attractive rooms and suites, a theater, and a rooftop recreation area with tennis and racquetball courts, a swimming pool, gardens and a jogging trail. In the hotel's lobby it is hard to miss the 70-ton sculpture by Henry Moore.

Downtown luxury can also be found at the **Wyndham Hotel Miami** ☎ (305) 374-0000 TOLL-FREE (800) 2-WYNDHAM FAX (305) 374-0020, 1601 Biscayne Boulevard, sits above the Omni International Mall and has been newly renovated. Many of the rooms have stunning views of the Miami skyline and Biscayne Bay. Over on Key Biscayne is the **Sonesta Beach Resort** ☎ (305) 361-2021 TOLL-FREE (800) SONESTA FAX (305) 361-2082 WEB SITE www.sonesta.com, a popular hotel with families because it has a comprehensive program of activities for children. All the rooms and suites have balconies overlooking the island or the Atlantic, and the 28 villas on the grounds are fully self contained with private swimming pools.

Two of the best hotels in the area can be found in Coconut Grove. The glamorous and extremely non-budget **Mayfair House** ((305) 441-0000 TOLL-FREE (800) 433-4555 WEB SITE www.hotelbook.com/live/welcome/2137#top, 3000 Florida Avenue, has its own shopping mall with designer boutiques, nine restaurants, and a central atrium with fountains and plants. The hotel's 181 suites have Japanese hot tubs or Jacuzzis, and the rooftop facilities include a swimming pool and a solarium. Newspapers come with breakfast, and complimentary caviar is served in the Tiffany Bar. The elegant **Grand Bay Hotel** ((305) 858-9600 TOLL-FREE (800) 327-2788 FAX (305) 858-1532 WEB SITE www.miami.vcn.net/grandbay, 2669 South Bayshore Drive, Coconut Grove, has English and French suites with baby grand pianos, and in every room new arrivals are greeted with flowers and complimentary champagne. The service is splendid, and you can arrange golf, tennis, or sailing through a very helpful concierge. The hotel's Grand Café is one of the best restaurants in Miami.

The Moorish castle-like **Westin Biltmore Hotel** ((305) 445-1926 TOLL-FREE (800) 727-1926 FAX (305) 913-3152 WEB SITE www.biltmorehotel.com, 1200 Anastasia Drive in Coral Gables is a National Historic Landmark, and has large rooms with antique furnishings and vaulted ceilings adorned with frescoes. This very romantic setting includes beautiful grounds featuring a golf course, tennis courts, and an enormous and extravagent swimming pool.

Mid-range

Moderately priced and near the airport, the **Hotel Sofitel Miami** ((305) 264-4888 TOLL-FREE (800) 258-4888 FAX (305) 261-7871, 5800 Blue Lagoon Drive, offers a sauna, tennis courts, continental breakfasts, and soundproof rooms. The **Everglades Hotel** ((305) 379-5461 TOLL-FREE (800) 327-5700 FAX (305) 577-8445 WEB SITE www.miamigate.com/everglades, 244 Biscayne Boulevard in downtown, has very comfortable, very modern rooms, while the rooftop has a swimming pool and a bar. Also downtown near the Bayside shops is the **Biscayne Bay Marriott Hotel and Marina** ((305) 374-3900 FAX (305) 375-0597, 1633 North Bayshore Drive, where the marina has boating, fishing, and windsurfing facilities; the other amenities include five restaurants, a games room, and free in-room movies.

The huge swimming pool ABOVE in the Moorish castle setting of the Biltmore Hotel in Coral Gables and OPPOSITE its interior.

In Coral Gables the best mid-range priced hotel is the **Hotel Place St. Michel** ☎ (305) 444-1666 TOLL-FREE (800) 848-HOTEL FAX (305) 529-0074 WEB SITE www.hotelplacestmichel.com, 162 Alcazar Avenue. Recently renovated, every room is tastefully appointed, including European antiques. As well as the complimentary continental breakfasts, the hotel's French restaurant is of a very high-quality, as is the service throughout the hotel. One of the top hotels centrally located between the business and retail districts in the Gables is the **Omni Colonnade Hotel** ☎ (305) 441-2600 TOLL-FREE (800) THE-OMNI FAX (305) 445-3929, 180 Aragon Avenue, Coral Gables. The **Holiday Inn Coral Gables – Business District** ☎ (305) 443-2301 FAX (305) 446-6827, 2051 LeJeune Road, is one of the most convenient locations to stay and within walking distance to fine dining and entertainment. It has everything you need, and for a good price.

Inexpensive

Coral Gables also has a few budget-priced motels that are located closer to the University of Miami. The **Riviera Court Motel** ☎ (305) 665-3528 TOLL-FREE (800) 368-8602, 5100 Riviera Drive, sits on the Coral Gables Waterway and is within minutes to great shopping areas like Dadeland Mall and Miracle mile.

The **Budget Inn** ☎ (305) 871-1777 TOLL-FREE (800) 4-BUDGET FAX (305) 871-8080 WEB SITE www.budgetel.com, 3501 Northwest LeJeune Road, Miami Springs, has large rooms for a reasonable price.

The **Royalton Hotel** ☎ (305) 374-7451 TOLL-FREE (800) 972-8436 FAX (305) 358-5842, 131 Southeast First Street, Miami, is conveniently located close to downtown shopping and convention facilities.

Close to the airport is the **Miami Airport Fairfield Inn South** ☎ (305) 643-0055 TOLL-FREE (800) 228-9290 FAX (305) 649-3997, which has complimentary breakfast and airport shuttle service.

WHERE TO EAT

Expensive

Le Pavillion ☎ (305) 577-1000, 100 Chopin Plaza at the Hotel Inter-Continental Miami, should offer a map with its menu: the specialties include Key West tuna, Carolina pheasant, Texan cactus, Wyoming rabbit, and Hawaiian sweet onions. **Chef Allen's** ☎ (305) 935-2900, 19088 Northeast 29th Avenue, Aventura, has adapted Caribbean influences to perfect new world cuisine. Their specialty is the yellowtail fish smothered in coconut milk and curry sauce.

Southwest Eighth Street in Little Havana has two (among many) distinguished restaurants. **Casa Juancho** ☎ (305) 642-2452, WEB SITE www.casajuancho.com, 2436 Southwest Eighth Street, is a Spanish restaurant which serves immense portions of food, including roast suckling pig. A few doors away at No. 2499 is **El Bodegon de Castilla** ☎ (305) 649-0863, specializes in Spanish cooking — mostly Castillian, obviously, but some Catalan and specializes in seafood.

In Coconut Grove I would strongly recommend eating at the **Mayfair Grill** ☎ (305) 441-0000, in the Mayfair House Hotel, 3000 Florida Avenue. The star attraction on the menu — I'm not joking — is the grilled buffalo. In Coral Gables, try the popular **Christy's** ☎ (305) 446-1400 FAX (305) 446-3257, 3101 Ponce De Leon Boulevard, but get there early because there is always a line for the tasty Midwestern beef and prime steaks. Broiled lamb chops and marinated filet mignon are also wonderfully accompanied by a hefty Caesar salad. If your in the mood to eat a lot try **Porcao** ☎ (305) 373-2777 WEB SITE www.porcaousa.com, 801 South Bayshore Drive in the Four Ambassadors lobby, where you can sample everything on the Brazilian style feast of salads and meat. Everything from lamb to pork and chicken are grilled, skewered or cooked to order.

Moderate

For authentic Nicaraguan food, you should go to **El Novillo** ☎ (305) 284-8417, 6830 Bird Road, South Miami. The restaurant has a surprisingly tasty pepper steak in cream sauce and excellent desserts. For Spanish food try **Las Tapas** ☎ (305) 372-2737, 401 Biscayne Boulevard, downtown Miami at the Bayside Marketplace waterfront. The house specialty is of course *tapas*, which can easily and infinitely be expanded into a wonderful main course.

For Cuban seafood I would single out **La Esquina de Tejas** ☎ (305) 545-0337, 101 Southwest 12th Avenue, for their delicious black bean dishes. And for New Miami Cuban style dishes check out **Victor's Café** ☎ (305) 445-1513, 2340 Southwest 32nd Avenue, Miami.

In Coconut Grove, **Monty's Stone Crab Seafood House** ☎ (305) 858-1431 WEB SITE www.montysstonecrab.com, 2550 South Bayshore Drive, is a big local favorite, with its outdoor raw bar overlooking a marina, and its reggae and calypso bands playing on the weekend.

In Coral Gables, devotees of Thai food are grateful for the presence of **Bangkok, Bangkok** ☎ (305) 444-2397, 157 Giralda Avenue, where everything from the spring rolls to the house combination plate known as Special Earth, Wind and Fire and the plum wine leave a delectable memory. You can absorb the entire experience by eating Thai style — sitting on cushions and leaving your shoes by the door.

Fans of Indian food sing the praises of the **House of India** ☎ (305) 444-2348, 22 Merrick Way, off Coral Way at Southwest 37th Avenue in Coral Gables.

La Palma Ristorante and Bar ☎ (305) 445-8777, 116 Alhambra Circle, is in the historic La Palma building and presents tratorria-style cuisine in a charming patio for relaxing al fresco dining. The restaurant features a changing selection of hot and cold plates in the daily lunch buffet.

Take a scenic drive to the Gables by the Sea area, where you can dine by the beach at **Red Fish Grill** ☎ (305) 668-8788, 9610 Old Cutler Road in the Matheson Hammock Park. The seafood, from the crabcakes to the sautéed snapper, is recommended.

Inexpensive

In North Miami, **Sara's of North Miami** ☎ (305) 891-3312, 2214 Northeast 123rd Street, serves Middle Eastern and home-cooked Jewish food. The challah, falafels and hummus are excellent.

Two of my favorite Italian restaurants in Miami give you great meals for a great deal. **The Pasta Factory** ☎ (305) 261-3889, 5733 Southwest Eighth Street, has plenty of choice with homemade pasta dishes that you know are fresh — because you can see the pasta being churned from machines and stuffed by the cooks in a center room of the restaurant. If you have room for more, you can always order a second or half-portion of your dish.

But for genuinely inexpensive, genuinely tasty meals, your best bet is simply to walk up and down Southwest Eighth Street in Little Havana: you will be amazed (and tantalized) by the number and range of budget-priced eateries.

Two quality Cuban eateries with fast service in a casual atmosphere are **La Carreta** ☎ (305) 444-7501, 3632 Southwest Eight Street, Miami (also in West Dade and Key Biscayne), and **Latin American Cafeteria** ☎ (305) 381-7774, 401 Biscayne Boulevard at Bayside Marketplace. Latin American eateries are also at more than half a dozen locations scattered around Miami.

If you're looking for an old-fashioned experience try **Picnics at Allen's Drug Store** ☎ (305) 665-6964, 4000 Red Road, where you can eat home-cooking style fried chicken and malts in the ambiance of a 50s diner, where the jukebox and the waitstaff take you back to that era.

Shorty's Bar-B-Q ☎ (305) 670-7732 9200 South Dixie Highway, has been a legend for about 50 years in this South Miami neighborhood. The smell of the hickory-smoked ribs and chicken will grab you as you drive by or sit in traffic on US Highway 1.

How to Get There

More than 80 national and international airlines fly into **Miami International Airport** ☎ (305) 876-7000 WEB SITE www.miami-airport.com, which is only six miles (9.5 km) west of downtown. It is the second airport in the United States for international passenger traffic. Numerous taxi and limousine companies serve the airport as well as **SuperShuttle** ☎ (305) 871-2000 FAX (305) 871-8475 WEB SITE www.supershuttle.com, which offers door-to-door transportation to and from the airport. A taxi takes about 20 minutes to reach the middle of Miami, and charges about $18. Call (305) 375-2460 with any questions, comments, or complaints about taxi service. There is also a Metrobus ☎ (305) 638-6700, station at the airport, which operates a shuttle downtown that is much less expensive.

If you are traveling from the north by car you have several options: Interstate 95 and Route 1 come directly down the coast, and Florida's Turnpike goes through central Florida and Orlando on its way to the southeast. Route A1A, ocean-skirting and island-hopping, is the slow and scenic way to approach Miami from the north. From the west you will take Interstate-75 also known as "Alligator Alley".

The **Port of Miami** ((305) 371-7678 WEB SITE www.metro-dade.com/portofmiami, is the nautical entrance to the city known as the cruise capital of the world.

The most important thing for first time visitors to remember is to look for the orange sun on a blue background sign. Follow the sun and it will take you to primary routes from the airport to all popular tourist destinations.

MIAMI BEACH

Miami Beach is a narrow strip of land a little over seven miles (11 km) long and only a mile (1.6 km) wide at its widest point. It is separated from mainland Miami by Biscayne Bay, and connected to it by three causeways. It probably has more hotels than any other comparable patch of land in the world, and in a few blocks at the southern end of the island it has the largest concentration of Art Deco buildings in America. And then there is the beach itself, running along the entire eastern side of the island. Not only that, but it is getting bigger all the time, recently a dredging operation pumped offshore sand on to the island to create a strip of beach over 300 ft (91 m) wide.

South Beach, as the Art Deco District is also known, has become a haven for models and celebrities to hang out. Their presence adds to the already fascinatingly colorful landscape along Ocean Drive. The further north you go along Highway AIA, the more family-oriented the beach becomes and the taller the hotels are that line the shore. No matter where you decide to spend the day, night, or week, Miami Beach has enough diversity to keep anyone happy.

BACKGROUND

In 1912, Miami Beach was an offshore mangrove and palmetto swamp inhabited mostly by crocodiles. The only inhabitant to note was a horticulturist named John S. Collins, who had bought some land there and established an avocado and citrus plantation. He founded the Miami Beach Improvement Company in 1912, initiated land sales on the island and began the construction of a bridge to the mainland.

Collins ran out of money the following year, in 1913, and the unfinished bridge became known as "Collins' Folly". Undaunted, Collins set up a partnership with Carl Fisher, who, in exchange for large areas of land on the island, injected much-needed

capital into the company, enabling the bridge to be completed and further development to be launched. Fisher cleared the swamps from his land and created new acreage by draining the shallow bays. What slowly emerged was a tropical island with a wide swath of beach, which Fisher and Collins immediately recognized as a potential resort. They spurred the development of the island into the Twenties, building shopping plazas, hotels, golf courses, and tennis courts.

Elderly people came here to retire, while vacationers began to arrive by the thousands. Then, in the Thirties, after the worst of the Depression was over, a new building boom began at the southern end of the island. Pastel, geometric, streamlined buildings started to appear: Art Deco had arrived with a vengeance. Today over 100 Art Deco houses and hotels are to be seen in what is one of the most architecturally striking pockets in the country. Since the 1930s, the story of Miami Beach has been one of steady growth and development into one of the leading resorts in America, as hordes of tourists swarm in to enjoy the beaches and the winter sun. At the same time, more and more northerners are choosing to retire there, while from the south, Latin Americans continue to arrive and to do their part in the island's growth.

Seven miles (11 km) of beach, the winter sun, and a lot of enterprise transformed a former mangrove and palmetto swamp into Miami Beach, one of America's leading resorts.

General Information

The **Miami Beach Chamber of Commerce** ☎ (305) 672-1270 FAX (305) 538-4336, 1920 Meridian Avenue, Miami Beach has maps and can point you to areas of interest. For 24-hour information on hotels contact the **Greater Miami and the Beaches Hotel Association** ☎ (305) 531-3553 TOLL-FREE (800) SEE-MIAMI FAX (305) 531-8954 WEB SITE www.gmbha.miami.fl.us, 407 Lincoln Road, Suite 10G, Miami Beach.

What to See and Do

Undoubtedly the main sight in Miami Beach is the **Art Deco District**, a square mile of historic architecture which runs from a block north of Sixth Street (between Lummus Park and the beach) to the southern tip of the island. Each of the curved, multicolored buildings has its own unique character. If you would like to learn more about them, get in touch with the **Miami Design Preservation League** ☎ (305) 672-2014 FAX (305) 672-4319, 1001 Ocean Drive at the Art Deco Welcome Center, which organizes walking, biking or in-line skating tours of the district.

Three of the largest and most impressive Art Deco hotels in Miami Beach are on **Collins Avenue**, which is more or less the spine of the island. The Delano, the National, and the Ritz Plaza resemble, respectively, a spaceship, a balloon, and a submarine. The most impressive hotel is the majestic **Fontainebleau Hilton**, set among tropical vegetation, lagoons, and waterfalls, with a huge, wonderful mural on one of its exterior walls.

The island's oldest museum is the **Bass Museum of Art** ☎ (305) 673-7530 FAX (305) 673-7062, 2121 Park Avenue, which has Renaissance, Baroque, Rococo, and modern works in its collection, including interesting works by Rubens and Toulouse-Lautrec. The museum is open from 10 AM to 5 PM Tuesday through Saturday and from 1 PM to 5 PM on Sunday; admission is $5 for adults and $3 for children, seniors, and students. Florida International University's **Wolfsonian Museum** ☎ (305) 531-1001 FAX (305) 531-2133, 1001 Washington Avenue, is the latest addition to the beach art scene. The collection and adjacent study center has more than 70,000 objects, crafted between 1885 and 1945, that celebrate the design and architectural arts. Displays include glass, furniture and metalwork.

For a more historical perspective, visit the **Holocaust Memorial** ☎ (305) 538-1663 FAX (305) 538-2423, 1933-1945 Meridian Avenue, Miami Beach, a monument created for the six million Jewish victims of Nazi terrorism. A wall surrounding the monument chronicles the horrors of the concentration camps through a photographic mural. Guided tours are available and admission is free.

To understand the impact of the Jewish community on Miami Beach, it is well worth stopping by the **Ziff Jewish Museum of Florida: Home of MOSAIC** ☎ (305) 672-5044 FAX (305) 672-5933 WEB SITE www.jewishmuseum.com, 301 Washington Avenue, Miami Beach. Inside the restored synagogue, built in 1936, is a time-line wall of Jewish history, as well as the permanent exhibit of MOSAIC, Jewish Life in Florida.

For free and lively entertainment stroll along the **Boardwalk** which runs beside the beach from 21st Street to 46th Street. Different parts of the beach seem to have developed distinct personalities. The strand around **21st Street**, for example, has been colonized by young people and couples with small children; the beach at **35th Street** attracts a quieter, older group, and many of its beachfront hotel bars are open to the public; around **46th Street** you get the Very Important Tourists from the Fontainebleau and other top hotels; while up at **53rd Street** and **64th Street** you will find probably the quietest beaches on the island.

Sports

A couple of the best public golf courses on Miami Beach are the **Bayshore Golf Course** ☎ (305) 532-3350 FAX (305) 532-3840, 2301 Alton Road, and the **Haulover Golf Course** ☎ (305) 947-3525 FAX (305) 948-2802, 10800 Collins Avenue, North Miami Beach. Tennis players flock to **Flamingo Park** ☎ (305) 673-7761, 1000 12th Street on the corner of Michigan Avenue and 12th Street, where there are

Art Deco buildings in Miami Beach.

BEACON
720

17 public courts open from 9 AM to 9 PM; there are also public courts at **North Shore Tennis Center** ☎ (305) 673-7754, No. 350 73rd Street. **The City of Miami Beach Recreation, Culture and Parks Department** ☎ (305) 673-7730 FAX (305) 673-7725 WEB SITE www.ci.miamibeach.fl.us, manages these two major tennis facilities and can provide further information on golf and tennis facilities in the area.

If you are keen on deep-sea fishing, all sorts of cruises (from a few hours to a few days or weeks) can be chartered from the

Kelly Fishing Fleet ☎ (305) 945-3801 FAX (305) 757-2870, 10800 Collins Avenue at the Haulover Marina. Also try **Reward Fishing Fleet** ☎ (305) 372-9470 FAX (305) 534-8188 WEB SITE www.worldwidefishing.com.htm, 300 Alton Road, Miami Beach Marina.

Scuba equipment rental, instruction, and chartered excursions are available from **South Beach Divers** ☎ (305) 531-6110 FAX (305) 531-0511 WEB SITE www.southbeachdivers.com, 6850 Washington Avenue. If boating appeals to you, rent a vessel from **Schooner Eagle** ☎ (305) 531-4037 TOLL-FREE (800) 593-7245, Miami Beach, and cruise Biscayne Bay or the adjoining canals. Larger boats can be rented from **Carrousel Yacht-Great Bay Yacht Charters** ☎ (305) 530-9700 TOLL-FREE (800) 950-5336 FAX (305) 539-5108, 1717 North Bayshore Drive, Suite 2500 Miami, at the Fontainebleau Hilton Marina. The best place for **surfing** is Haulover Beach at the north end of the island, but you shouldn't expect a major surfing experience as the area is not famed for its waves. Lately, though, Haulover Park has become known as a nudist beach.

Shopping

The best selection of specialty shops for expensive tastes is **Bal Harbour** ☎ (305) 866-0311 WEB SITE www.balharbourshops.com, 9700 Collins Avenue, an airy tropical setting of shops with waterfalls and ceiling fans. It houses Florida's largest Neiman Marcus and Saks Fifth Avenue. For antiques, arts and crafts, and galleries — or interior decorating ideas — try the **Lincoln Road Shopping District** on Lincoln Road between Collins Avenue and Michigan Avenue. The 12-block pedestrian-only thoroughfare has more than 170 specialty shops and on Sundays features a traditional farmer's market with exotic fruits and vegetables, as well as gourmet treats. If looking for antiques or other unique art pieces, walk over to **Espanola Way**, a narrow street of pink Mediterranean-style buildings it's also great for taking pictures.

On Collins and Washington avenues, as well as on Ocean Drive in South Beach, you will also find the latest designer fashions at places like Hugo Boss, Armani Exchange and Versace.

Nightlife

Most of the after-dark action in Miami Beach takes place in the Art Deco district. The later it is, the better the party gets and it usually lasts until sunrise. The choices seem endless, but here are a few starting places. At super-trendy **Penrod's** ✆ (305) 538-1111, One Ocean Drive, you can choose from various dance floors offering reggae, jazz, and rock music. The beach is only a few feet away if you want to dance in the sand.

Latin music lovers have several choices including **Club Tropigala** ✆ (305) 672-7469, 4441 Collins Avenue, in the Fontainebleau Hilton Resort and Towers, which offers floor shows on Sundays and Wednesdays and live music other nights. Anyone passing by **Mango's Tropical Café and Hotel** ✆ (305) 673-4422, 900 Ocean Drive, will be mesmerized by the beautiful people dancing on the bar. Scantily-clad women and finely-sculpted men perform salsa and merengue dances to throbbing Latin rhythms. The live music makes it a happening place on any night of the week.

Another attractive night spot is the **Van Dyke Café** ✆ (305) 534-3600, 846 Lincoln Road, which features live jazz every night. An eclectic mix of dance music pulses from the DJs at the **Living Room at the Strand** ✆ (305) 532-2340, 671 Washington Avenue, where the trendy people also hang out.

At the **Irish House Bar** ✆ (305) 672-9626, 1430 Alton Road, a place full of character as well as characters, the odd song is played on the elderly jukebox, but the patrons mainly shoot pool and drink beer.

WHERE TO STAY

Miami Beach offers many choices of accommodation, depending on the kind of experience you want to have. The South Beach area has many small European-style hotels, located on the famous strip along Ocean Drive or just a block away on Collins Avenue, but still within a heartbeat of the pulsing entertainment and nightlife on the beach.

For a more lavish experience, try the larger resort hotels whose backyards are huge pools and decks that spill onto the white sand beaches.

Luxury

There are 18 acres (seven hectares) of beautifully landscaped grounds surrounding the famous **Fontainebleau Hilton Resort and Towers** ✆ (305) 538-2000 TOLL-FREE (800) 548-8886 FAX (305) 531-9274 WEB SITE www.fountainebleauhilton.com, 4441 Collins Avenue, Miami Beach, which also has 300 feet (91 m) of its own beach, seven tennis courts, several swimming pools and waterfalls, a giant spa with mineral baths, saunas, and Jacuzzis, not to mention 1,206 splendidly appointed rooms. There is also a specially supervised program for children. The luxury suites at the **Alexander Hotel** ✆ (305) 865-6500 TOLL-FREE (800) 327-6121 FAX (305) 341-6554, 5225 Collins Avenue, are elegantly furnished, and each one has a private balcony overlooking the ocean and the hotel's 600 feet (183 m) of beach. Then there is the quirky and delightful old **Eden Roc Resort and Spa** ✆ (305) 531-0000 TOLL-FREE (800) 327-8337 FAX (305) 674-5537 WEB SITE www.edenrocresort.com, 4525 Collins Avenue, with its 1950s furnishings, its New York deli with Israeli music, and its marvelous ocean-view restaurant. My favorite is the **Hotel Cavalier** ✆ (305) 604-5000 TOLL-FREE (800) OUTPOST FAX (305) 531-5543 WEB SITE www.islandlife.com, 1320 Ocean Drive, Miami Beach, in the Art Deco district. This oceanfront classic from 1936 was redone in 1996 and is a purely joyful experience. Also owned by the Island Outpost group, **The Tides** ✆ (305) 604-5000 TOLL-FREE (800) OUT-POST FAX (305) 672-6288 WEB SITE www.islandpost.com, 1220 Ocean Drive, is the crown jewel of the collection from this hotel group. It's an all-suite hotel with amazing views from the tallest building on Ocean Drive.

Mid-range

Although most of the hotels in the Art Deco district are as highly priced as they are highly desirable, there are some notable exceptions. Two of which are a few doors down from

Golf is played year round in Florida's temperate climate.

each other and owned by the same group are: the **Chesterfield Hotel** (305) 531-5831 TOLL-FREE (800) 244-6023 FAX (305) 672-4900 WEB SITE www.southbeachgroup.com, 855 Collins Avenue and the **Lily Guest House Hotel** (305) 535-9900 FAX (305) 535-0077 WEB SITE www.decoweb-com/lily/, 835 Collins Avenue. Both are located only one block from the beach and all the action on Ocean Drive, but are far enough away to enjoy a more peaceful stay. The Chesterfield has standard rooms and the well-known Safari Bar and Café in the lobby. The Lily Guesthouse gives you the comforts of being at your own private bed-and-breakfast, with 18 wooden-floored studios or suites. You can also enjoy a private sun deck.

Another good South Beach find is the **Park Central Hotel** (305) 538-1611 TOLL-FREE (800) 727-5236 FAX (305) 534-7520 WEB SITE www.theparkcentral.com, 640 Ocean Drive, which has a ceiling fan in each room.

Away from the Art Deco district and heading north towards Sunny Isles Beach is the **Monaco Oceanfront Resort** (305) 932-2100 TOLL-FREE (800) 227-9006 FAX (305) 931-5519, 17501 Collins Avenue, which has lots of bamboo and tropical plants, as well as water sports facilities and 400 feet (122 m) of beach. **Chateau by the Sea** (305) 931-8800 TOLL-FREE (800) 327-0691 FAX (305) 931-6194, 19115 Collins Avenue, has a country flavor to it.

Inexpensive

The family-run **Beachcomber Hotel** (305) 531-3755 TOLL-FREE (888) 305-4683 FAX (305) 673-3609 E-MAIL beach-comber@travelbase.com WEB SITE www.BeachcomberHotel.com, 1340 Collins Avenue, was renovated in 1937, and offers clean and comfortable rooms in the Art Deco district, and a very friendly atmosphere. I would also recommend the **Bayliss Guest House** (305) 531-3755 FAX (305) 673-8609 E-MAIL bayliss@travelbase.com, WEB SITE www.thebayliss.com, 500 14th Street, Miami Beach, which is owned by the same company, and has affordable self-contained units with kitchens for self-catering. The pretty **Beach Plaza Hotel** (305) 531-6421 TOLL-FREE (800) 395-9940 FAX (305) 534-0341 WEB SITE www.beachplazahotel.com, 1401 Collins Avenue, is conveniently located close to shopping and restaurants.

The inexpensive **Banana Bungalow Beach Hotel and Hostel** (305) 538-1951 TOLL-FREE (800) 746-7835 FAX (305) 531-3217 WEB SITE www.bananabungalow.com, 2360 Collins Avenue, has a tropical bungalow decor and is located by a relaxing canal.

WHERE TO EAT

Expensive

If you are going to pay a lot of money for your dinner, you might as well have it at **The Forge** (305) 538-8533, at 432 41st Street, Miami Beach, one of the nation's best continental restaurants, which now has a decor — chandeliers and stained glass and antiques — to match its rich menu and even richer wine list.

In Bal Harbour, you will find the Argentine steakhouse, **Al Carbon** (305) 868-2518, 9701 Collins Avenue, in the Sheraton Bal Harbour Beach Resort, where they serve a medley of steaks with Mediterranean spices and accompaning live music. The empanadas are also a pleasant treat.

One South Beach area restaurant well worth a visit is **Joe's Stone Crab** (305) 673-0365 WEB SITE www.joesstonecrab.com, 11 Washington Avenue, where the specialty is obvious (although for me the real specialty is their Key Lime pie). This place has become so famous the lines start forming before dinner time. Expect a long wait, but you won't be disappointed. **Yuca** (305) 532-9822 WEB SITE www.yuca.com, 501 Lincoln Road, is classified as new Miami Cuban cuisine. The specialties are variations on traditional Cuban food, like sweet plantain stuffed with dried cured beef. The coconut-curry rice is also wonderful.

Moderate

Two Italian restaurants in the Art Deco district that have delighted people for many years are: **Tiramesu** (305) 532-4538 WEB SITE www.winnet.net/tiramesu, 721 Lincoln Road, and **Gino's Italian Restaurant** (305) 532-6426, 1906 Collins Avenue. Tiramesu moved from Ocean Drive and has now added meat and fish mains to its menu. It offers three sizes of plates for each meal, including the family size that is served with a ladle.

A well-known Cantonese restaurant in this area is **Christine Lee's** ☎ (305) 947-1717, 17082 Collins Avenue, North Miami Beach, has 35 years experience. A favorite dish is the shrimp with lobster sauce.

El Rancho Grande Mexican Restaurant ☎ (305) 673-0480, 1626 Pennsylvania Avenue, Miami Beach, is the closest thing to Mexican food in this eclectic collage of restaurants off Lincoln Road, with excellent guacamole, enchiladas, and taquitos, and perfect margaritas. For authentic Panamanian food go to **La Mola Restaurant** ☎ (305) 531-3503 WEB SITE ww.hotelbook.com, 1825 Collins Avenue in the Riande Continental Miami Beach Hotel.

Inexpensive

If you have finished a hard day's tanning on the beach near the Art Deco district, you can eat well and cheaply at **The Palace** ☎ (305) 531-9077, 1200 Ocean Drive. It is anything but palatial, being a 1950s-style diner, but it *is* a treat. The **News Café** ☎ (305) 538-NEWS, WEB SITE wwwnewscafe.com, 800 Ocean Drive, is a bit more sophisticated, or at least tries to be, but is of equally good value. The beautiful people hang out at the indoor/outdoor café, which is open 24 hours. If you are feeling a little piggish, but still want good quality with your quantity, the best place in town is probably **Wolfie's Gourmet Deli Restaurant** ☎ (305) 538-6626, 2038 Collins Avenue. Another good place for a healthy meal and some real, old-fashioned, chicken soup is **San Loco** ☎ (305) 538-3009, 235 14th street, Miami Beach.

How to Get There

First you have to get to Miami (see earlier section). Seven causeways link Miami and Miami Beach. Take the Broad Causeway to the Bay Harbour Islands and over to Bal Harbour, the John F. Kennedy Causeway to northern Miami Beach, the Julia Tuttle Causeway (Interstate 95) to central Miami Beach, and the MacArthur Causeway (Interstate 395) to southern Miami Beach.

Shopping malls like this one in Miami are often open round the clock.

The Gold Coast

DRIVING ALONG THE 60-MILE (97-KM) STRETCH OF coastline known as the "Gold Coast", where glittering resorts confront the ocean across golden sandy beaches, it is hard to believe that less than a century ago this was mosquito-infested swampland.

Indeed, the only mark left on the Gold Coast by earlier centuries is the name itself. It derives from the most lucrative business enterprise to occupy the inhabitants of this area in the nineteenth century: salvaging gold from the frequent shipwrecks offered up by Mother Nature on the rocks offshore. These salvage operations, known as "wrecking," proved to be so profitable that the wreckers are said to have taken not just to praying for shipwrecks but to praying for particular *kinds* of shipwrecks according to the demands of the market at any given time. And when Mother Nature failed to oblige, they were even known to indulge in a little do-it-yourself shipwreck-making, by luring passing vessels onto the rocks.

Wrecking largely died out towards the end of the century, with the advent of more sophisticated maritime navigational equipment and the arrival of Henry Flagler's Florida East Coast Railroad. Now it became the turn of the land to supply the riches. Flagler himself started the new gold rush in 1894 by erecting the enormous Royal Poinciana Hotel in Palm Beach, to which he enticed some of the richest families in America. The hotel, since demolished, had 1,150 rooms and a staff of 1,400. Two years later he built The Breakers in Palm Beach, which burned down twice but which now, in its third incarnation, stands as one of the most famous hotels in the world. That same year, 1896, Flagler extended his railway to Fort Lauderdale, and in 1902 built himself his own 55-room marble mansion in Palm Beach. Thus, by the turn of the century, the ground had been prepared for this once-inhospitable bit of coast to become one of the most popular and celebrated resort areas in the world.

Among the first to see the possibilities here was the flamboyant architect Addison Mizner, who arrived a few years later and decided that what the place needed was a lot of pastel stucco buildings, designed by him. Whether it needed them or not, it got them as well as many more by other architects trying to imitate his style. That style has been variously described as "Italianate," "Pseudo-Spanish," "Mediterranean Revival," "Spanish-Moorish" and, my favorite, "Bastard Spanish-Moorish-Romanesque-Gothic-Renaissance Bull-Market Damn-the-Expense" style. Mizner's *chef d'œuvre* was the Cloister Inn in Boca Raton, now the Boca Raton Hotel and Club, a wonderful pink confection that remains one of the most expensive hotels ever built. To this palace Mizner lured as many of the rich and famous as he could attract, and they in turn attracted the multitudes. As Mizner had predicted, "Get the big snobs, and the little ones will follow."

Meanwhile, to the south, in Fort Lauderdale another visionary was doing his part to add luster to the Gold Coast. Charles Rodes, a property developer from West Virginia, suddenly came up with the "Venetian Solution" to the problem of what to do with all that swampland: he began dredging a series of finger canals that converted sodden, useless land into prime waterfront real estate. As a result, today the *soi-disant* "Venice of America" has almost 200 miles (322 km) of inland waterways to go along with its seven miles (11 km) of beautiful beach.

By the 1920s the allure of the Gold Coast had set off a feeding frenzy among property speculators, developers, investors, builders, prospective retirees, and would-be winter migrants from the north. There followed a land boom of incredible proportions, over 2,000 people a day were arriving to stake their claim to a little bit of paradise. For most of them, however, that paradise was lost in 1926 when the boom abruptly collapsed.

For the next two decades, through the years of the Depression and the Second World War, some of the shine left the Gold Coast (though none of the sunshine: there are 3,000 hours of it every year, with an average annual temperature of 75°F, or 24°C). Then paradise was regained after the war, and for the second half of this century it has been an irresistible magnet for countless millions of pleasure-seekers.

The Atlantic horizon, in a latticework frame.

FORT LAUDERDALE

Although sunny by disposition as well as by climate, Fort Lauderdale has long had an image problem. For decades it had to put up with being called Fort Liquordale, a sobriquet it earned during Prohibition when its bars and night clubs were awash in illicit alcohol smuggled in from the Bahamas. Then, in 1960, the old image was given a new twist in the film *Where the Boys Are*, which depicted the place as America's party headquarters for college students on their spring break. Although the new image had only a fractional basis in reality, the film succeeded in creating the phenomenon it was ostensibly portraying, so that for many years afterwards Fort Lauderdale was visited annually by migratory swarms of fun-seeking college students. Now, to the manifest relief of the natives, most of the Eastertime action seems to have shifted north to Daytona Beach.

BACKGROUND

Fort Lauderdale's early history has vanished as completely as the fort which Major William Lauderdale built near the mouth of the New River in 1838 to protect settlers from attack by the Seminoles. What is known is that the first settler, Charles Lewis, arrived in 1793 and established a plantation by the New River. Exactly 100 years later another settler, Frank Stranahan, arrived and established a trading post for doing business with the Indians, as well as a general store and a ferry system. When he married a few years later, Stranahan converted the general store into a residence, which has since been restored and is open to visitors.

Although the arrival of Flagler's railway in 1896 opened up the area to accelerated settlement, there were still fewer than 200 residents when Fort Lauderdale was incorporated in 1911. It was not until the land boom of the Twenties that the city's spectacular growth began in earnest. Today, with upwards of 30,000 pleasure craft roaming its rivers and canals, and untold thousands of bodies from all over the world glistening on its beaches. The ghosts of

Henry Flagler and Charles Rodes must be blinking in wonder.

GENERAL INFORMATION

The **Greater Fort Lauderdale Convention and Visitors Bureau** ☎ (954) 765-4466 TOLL-FREE 800-227-8669 FAX (954) 765-4467, WEB SITE www.sunny.org, is at 1850 Eller Drive, Suite 303, Fort Lauderdale, FL 33301. The **Greater Fort Lauderdale Chamber of Commerce** ☎ (954) 462-6000, is at 512 Northeast Third Avenue, Fort Lauderdale, FL 33301. If you are looking for accommodation, the **Greater Fort Lauderdale Lodging and Hospitality Association** ☎ (954) 832-9477, 2190 South East 17th Street, Suite 301, Fort Lauderdale, FL 33316, can be of help.

For international or domestic flight information, call the **Fort Lauderdale/Hollywood International Airport** ☎ (954) 359-1200. The **Yellow Cabs** number is ☎ (954) 565-5400, and in case of a **medical emergency**, call Physicians Referral ☎ (954) 355-4888.

Wearing big smiles: a bikini contest in Fort Lauderdale.

WHAT TO SEE AND DO

It is not often that the most entertaining means of seeing the sights are themselves major tourist attractions, but this happens to be the case in Fort Lauderdale, where the 550- and 180-passenger *Jungle Queen I* and *Jungle Queen II* **paddlewheel riverboats** cruise the waters in and around the city.

The Jungle Queen ☎ (305) 462-5596 EMAIL jungle@bellsouth.net, WEB SITE www.introweb.com/junglequeen, has two three-hour cruises daily, at 10 AM and 2 PM, leaving from the Bahia Mar Yachting Center, 801 Seabreeze Boulevard. The cruise includes a stop at Indian Village, where you can see rare birds, monkeys, and alligator wrestling. In the evening there is a four-hour dinner cruise, which leaves Bahia Mar at 7 PM and features a vaudeville revue and other entertainment. The dinner, served on an exotic island in the New River, is an all-you-can-eat affair of barbecued ribs, chicken, and shrimp.

For sightseeing on your own by water your best bet is to call up **Water Taxi** ☎ (954) 467-6677 WEB SITE www.watertaxi.com, 651 Seabreeze Boulevard. They will deliver you up or down the river and Intracoastal Waterway to hotels, restaurants, cultural events or shopping areas.

The best way to see Fort Lauderdale by land is on **South Florida Trolly Tours** ☎ (954) 946-7320. The trip is narrated and you can board and re-board at any of the stops along the route, which covers hotels, restaurants, historic sites and cultural attractions. The trolley also stops at most Water Taxi locations.

For a romantic evening tour of the city, **Royal Horsedrawn Carriages** ☎ (954) 971-9320 can be found at the Carriage Stand at Southeast Eighth Avenue and Las Olas Boulevard on Wednesdays to Sundays from 7 PM.

A unique perspective of South Florida can be had by taking a helicopter sightseeing tour. **Heliflight** ☎ (954) 771-6969, 2675 Northwest 56th Street, offers tours lasting from 15 minutes to an hour.

Among the sights particularly worth seeing I would put the **Museum of Discovery and Science** ☎ (954) 467-6637 WEB SITE www.mods.org, 401 Southwest Second Avenue, at the top of the list. This is a science and nature museum with hands-on exhibits that allow you to watch bees at work in a glass-fronted hive, go cave crawling, bend rays of light, and touch a star, among many other things. Children love it. There is also an IMAX cinema with a 55-by-75 ft (17-by-23 m) screen.

Also well worth a visit is the city's multimillion-dollar **Museum of Art** ☎ (954) 525-5500, at One East Las Olas Boulevard. It has an extraordinary collection of ethnographic art, including pre-Columbian, West African, Oceanic, and American India and its Dutch and Flemish collections are quite good as well. The museum stays open late on Fridays, and is closed on Sunday mornings and Mondays.

The **Stranahan House** ☎ (954) 524-4736, Fort Lauderdale's oldest remaining structure, is where Frank Stranahan traded with the local native Americans and sold to the settlers at the turn of the century, before he converted it into a home. It has been lovingly and immaculately restored to its pre-World War I condition, and is open to the public on Wednesday through Saturday from 10 AM to 4 PM, and on Sundays from 1 PM to 4 PM. The house is just off Las Olas Boulevard at the New River tunnel.

Another historic estate worth a visit is the **Bonnet House** ☎ (954) 563-5393 FAX (954) 561-4174 WEB SITE www.bonnethouse.com. Built in 1926, this exclusive beachfront property was the winter residence of artists Frederic and Evelyn Bartlett and is open Wednesday through Friday from 10 AM to 1:30 PM, Saturdays and Sundays noon to 2:30 PM and closed on Mondays, Tuesdays and holidays.

To get an idea (but only an idea) of how some of the local Native Americans once lived, visit the **Seminole Okalee Indian Village Museum** ☎ (954) 792-1213 WEB SITE www.seminoletribe.com, 5845 South State Road Seven. The Seminole community here now support themselves by selling arts and craft and running **Hollywood Seminole Gaming** ☎ (954) 961-3220 at 4150 North State Road Seven.

Butterfly World ☎ (954) 977-4400, in Tradewinds Park, 3600 West Sample Road, is home to over 150 species of butterflies and features a screened-in tropical rain forest where thousands of exotic "flying flowers" flutter by. **Flamingo Gardens and Wray Botanical Gardens** ☎ (954) 473-2955, at 3750 Flamingo Road, features a jungle tram ride, crocodiles, alligators, monkeys, tropical birds, a petting zoo and, of course, pink flamingos.

Improbable as it may seem, Fort Lauderdale is one of the best places to see and savor the Wild West as it really (more or less) was. The suburban community of **Davie** has turned itself into an authentic cow town, complete with cowboys and cowgirls. On weekend nights, a rodeo is held at the **Bergeron Rodeo Grounds** ☎ (954) 384-7075, at Orange Drive and Davie Road.

Sports

Baseball fans should know that the **Baltimore Orioles** hold their spring training here from February to March, during which they play exhibition games at Fort Lauderdale Stadium ☎ (305) 776-1921, 5301 Northwest 12th Avenue, while soccer fans can watch the **Fusion** major league soccer team play from March to October at Lockhart Stadium ☎ (954) 717-2200, 5201 Northwest 12th Avenue.

If you like more fast-paced action, combined with legal betting, you can see **jai alai**, at Dania Jai Alai ☎ (305) 949-2424 FAX (954) 920-9095, 301 East Dania Boulevard, from late June until mid-April.

Golf enthusiasts will be pleased to learn that there are no less than five dozen (yes, *dozen*) golf courses in the Fort Lauderdale area. There are 11 public courses within the city limits of Fort Lauderdale alone, not to mention the many private courses that welcome non-members. Among the most attractive and challenging courses are the American Golfers Club ☎ (954) 564-8760, near the beach at 3850 North Federal Highway, the Bonaventure course ☎ (888) 650-4653, at 200 Bonaventure Boulevard, and the Deer Creek Golf and Tennis Club ☎ (954) 421-5550, at 2801 Deer Creek Country Club Boulevard, Deerfield Beach.

Scuba diving and snorkeling can be enjoyed at more than 80 different dive sites along the coastal strip stretching about 12 miles (19 km) in each direction north and south of Fort Lauderdale. These include coral reefs, sunken wrecks, and ships that were deliberately scuttled to create artificial reefs. Among the many stores offering classes in diving and daily diving trips, as well as scuba and snorkeling equipment, are The Scuba School ☎ (954) 566-6344, 3331 East Oakland Park Boulevard; Force E ☎ (954) 943-3483 WEB SITE www.force-e.com, at 2160 West Oakland Park Boulevard, and Pro Dive ☎ (954) 761-3413 E-MAIL prodive @icanect.net, 515 Seabreeze Boulevard.

Fishing expeditions can be arranged through Sport Fishing Charters ☎ (954) 627-6357 or Fishing Headquarters Big Game ☎ (954) 527-3460, 301 Seabreeze Boulevard (954) 527-3460.

Speed boat rides are on offer at Speed Boat Adventures ☎ (954) 779-7660, 301 Seabreeze Boulevard, where Captains "Crazy" Gregg Newell and Buddy Street host the thrills. Parasail, waverunner and sailboat rentals are also available, or you can rent **Waverunners** at Evolution Water Sports ☎ (954) 788-5333 FAX (954) 788-5744, 3701 Northwest Pompano Beach. They can also teach you how to wakeboard and waterski.

Shopping

For maximum choice you should head for the **Galleria** ☎ (954) 564-1015, a huge shopping

Consuming is conspicuous along Worth Avenue in Palm Beach. OVERLEAF: A Fort Lauderdale welcome for yachts on the Round-the-World race.

TRASH

mall that has over 150 stores and restaurants, including five department stores, at 2414 East Sunrise Boulevard, only a few blocks from the ocean.

For maximum chic, palm-lined **Las Olas Boulevard** boasts an infinite variety of handsome (and occasionally offbeat) boutiques. At the other end of the shopping spectrum, the **Festival Flea Market Mall** WEB SITE www.festivalfleamarket.com, hosts over 850 merchants selling brand-name merchandise at below-outlet prices at 2900 West Sample Road, Pompano Beach. While **Fort Lauderdale Swap Shop** TOLL-FREE (800) 345-7920, on Sunrise Boulevard, offers 75 acres (30 hectares) of garage sales, farmers markets and international bazaars, as well as a free circus and carnival rides. Adventure sport enthusiasts should head straight for the **Outdoor World Bass Pro Shop** ✆ (954) 929-7710, 200 Gulfstream Way in Dania. This is an enormous store featuring a 39,000-sq-ft (3,600-sq-m) aquarium, four-story waterfall, full-scale log cabin, fish restaurant, museum, archery and rifle ranges.

Nightlife

Still one of the "in" places to go in Fort Lauderdale, **Shooter's** ✆ (954) 566-2855 www shooterscafe.com, is at 3031 Northeast 32nd Avenue, is. Don't worry if you can't get in, because another hot spot called **Bootlegger** ✆ (954) 563-4337 WEB SITE www.bootlegger1.com, is right next door.

Jazz fans won't want to miss **O'Hara's Pub and Jazz Cafe** ✆ (954) 524-1764, along Las Olas Boulevard, which features live jazz and blues seven nights a week and twice on Sundays. Other Las Olas Boulevard venues include **Mangos Restaurant** ✆ (954) 523-9001, which transforms each evening into a nightclub with live R&B, soul and classic rock, as well as **Cathode Ray** ✆ (954) 462-8611, a gay nightspot which plays the hottest dance music seven nights a week. If you like country-and-western music, **Desperado's Nightclub** ✆ (954) 463-2855, at 2520 South Miami Road, features national and local acts with free dance lessons and mechanical bull rides.

If you want a good laugh, **Uncle Funny's** ✆ (954) 474-5653 FAX (954) 370-6930, at 9160 State Road 84, is a great place to catch top comedy acts from HBO and the Comedy Channel on Wednesdays through Sundays.

Those who would prefer to be entertained by the sights rather than the sounds of the night should ascend to the **Pier Top Lounge** ✆ (954) 525-6666, which rotates above the 17-story Hyatt Regency Pier 66 Resort and Marina at 2301 Southeast 17th Street.

Beach Place, along Fort Lauderdale's new beachfront at 17 South Atlantic Boulevard, offers 100,000 sq ft (9,300 sq m) of shopping, dining and entertainment. Nighttime entertainment at Beach Place includes **Howl at the Moon** ✆ (954) 522-7553, a sing-along bar featuring dueling pianos, and **Sloppy Joe's** ✆ (954) 522-7553 with its Caribbean style live music.

If you're in the mood for a quick shot, **Adobe Gila's** features 60 different types of tequila. Or if you want to sample a real Fort Lauderdale tourist tradition, drop in the **Mai Kai Polynesian Restaurant and Dinner Show** ✆ (954) 563-3272 TOLL-FREE (800) 262-4524, at 3599 North Federal Highway for a Polynesian show that has been running for the past 35 years.

For something more towards the cultural, the **Broward Center for the Performing Arts** ✆ (954) 462-0222 FAX (954) 468-3282,

201 Southwest Fifth Avenue, offers Broadway shows, concerts and performances by the Florida Philharmonic Orchestra, Florida Opera and Miami City Ballet.

WHERE TO STAY

Luxury

What do you call a hotel with 1,100 ft (335 m) of beach frontage, 8,000 sq ft (2,438 sq m) of free-form swimming pool (with a waterfall), five restaurants and five tennis courts, three boutiques and three lounges? You call it the **Marriott's Harbor Beach Resort** ((954) 525-4000 TOLL-FREE (800) 222-6543 FAX (954) 766-6193 E-MAIL mhbrbc@bellsouth.net, at 3030 Holiday Drive.

The **Radisson Bahia Mar Resort and Yachting Center** ((954) 627-63063 TOLL-FREE (800) 531-2478 FAX (954) 524-6912, at 801 Seabreeze Boulevard, also boasts some impressive numbers: a 40-acre (16-hectare) yacht basin, a 350-slip marina, and small fleet of charter fishing boats — but only (sigh) four tennis courts.

The **Hyatt Regency Pier 66 Hotel and Marina** ((954) 728-3540 TOLL-FREE (800) 334-5774 FAX (954) 728-3551 WEB SITE www.hyatt.com, at 2301 Southeast 17th Street, was Fort Lauderdale's first luxury high-rise hotel, and is still one of the area's very finest, with a beautiful 142-slip marina and excellant facilities for water sports, which are rivaled only by Bahia Mar.

Away from the beach — indeed, away from it all — is the **Wyndham Resort and Spa** ((954) 389-3300 TOLL-FREE (800) 225-5331 FAX (954) 384-0563, 17 miles (27 km) west of Fort Lauderdale at 250 Racquet Club Road. Set in 1,250 acres (506 hectares), it has four restaurants, five swimming pools, 24 tennis courts, two 18-hole golf courses, a 160-seat amphitheater, a bowling alley, a roller-skating rink, riding stables, and a massive spa.

Perhaps the most charming hotel in Fort Lauderdale — certainly the one with the most charming and solicitous staff — is the **Riverside Hotel** ((954) 467-0671 TOLL-FREE (800) 325-3280 FAX (954) 462-2148 E-MAIL RiversideHotel@worldnet.att.net, at 620 East Las Olas Boulevard. More Southern Comfortable than nouveau ritzy, it is in the heart of the city's most fashionable shopping area, with a swimming pool and gardens in the back beside the picturesque New River.

OPPOSITE: College students take advantage of Fort Lauderdale's balmy climate for a relaxing spring break. ABOVE: Seaside promenade at sunset.

Mid-range

Some might argue that the **Lago Mar Hotel** ✆ (954) 523-6511 TOLL-FREE (800) 524-6627 FAX (954) 524-6627 E-MAIL Reservations @lagomar.com, at 1700 Southeast Ocean Lane, belongs in the above category, but for what you get it is definitely not expensive. And what you get, most of all, is the peace and quiet that comes from being on the exclusive south end of the beach, far from the madding crowds. The hotel has a lagoon on one side and the Atlantic on the other, with two swimming pools, four tennis courts, and a putting green in between.

Banyan Marina Apartments ✆ (954) 524-4430 FAX (954) 764-4870 TOLL-FREE (800) 524-4431 E-MAIL info@banyanmarina.com WEB-SITE www.banyanmarina.com, at 111 Isle of Venice, offers accommodation ranging from motel rooms to two-bedroom apartments for stays of one night to a few months. Situated in a quiet neighborhood on one of the inter-coastal islands, this comfortable complex features dock space for eight yachts, a large swimming pool, and amenities including washer/dryer and full kitchen.

The **Holiday Inn Express-Fort Lauderdale North** ✆ (954) 566-4301 TOLL-FREE (800) 465-4329 FAX (954) 565-1472 is at 3355 North Federal Highway and is just one of about a dozen hotels run by this chain in the area.

Inexpensive

There is a stretch of North Birch Road, just two blocks away from the beach, that has dozens of inexpensive motels, with pools, side-by-side. Two of the nicest of these are the **Sea View Resort Motel** ✆ (954) 564-3151 TOLL-FREE (800) 356-2326 FAX (954) 561-9147, at 550 North Birch Road, and the **Sea Chateau** ✆ (954) 566-8331 TOLL-FREE (800) 726-3732 FAX (954) 564-2411, at 555 North Birch Road.

WHERE TO EAT

Expensive

Eat City Grill ✆ (954) 565-5569 at 505 North Atlantic Boulevard, on revitalized Fort Lauderdale Beach, offers imaginative regional South Florida dishes with Caribbean, Asian and Southwestern flavors.

The **Left Bank** ✆ (954) 462-5376, despite its name, is more American than Parisian, and more romantic than bohemian. Anyway, the owner-chef Jean-Pierre Brehier has created a superb restaurant, at 214 South Federal Highway. The cuisine leans more toward the nouvelle, and is memorably delicious. **La Coquille** ✆ (305) 467-3030, at 1619 East Sunrise Boulevard, is an enchanting little bistro run by Jean and Hélène Bert.

If you have a hankering for the very best in seafood, head straight for the **15th Street Fisheries** ✆ (954) 763-2777 at 1900 Southeast 15th Street. With views overlooking the Intra-coastal and dock space for those arriving by boat, this restaurant serves up an unusually wide selection of glorious seafood from all over the world. **Jackson's Four Fifty** ✆ (954) 522-4450 at 450 East Las Olas Boulevard is an upscale, yet understated, supper club with a menu that spans prime steaks and chops, seafood and made-to-order dessert soufflés.

Moderate

Louis Flemati's **Café de Paris** ✆ (954) 467-2900 FAX ((54) 467-2308, at 715 East Las Olas Boulevard, is deservedly popular with the locals, as much for its cheery atmosphere (which includes musicians) as for its tasty food.

Look out for the deco-inspired exterior of **Blue Moon Fish Co** ✆ (954) 267-9888, a moderately price eatery with a contemporary American menu — don't miss the gospel brunch on Sundays. Located at 4405 West Tradewinds Avenue, Lauderdale By-The-Sea.

Casablanca Cafe ✆ (954) 764-3500 at the corner of Alhambra and A1A, is situated inside a beautifully restored historical home with a delightful ocean side setting. Chef Erick Martin creates continental cuisine with a blend of cultures.

Purportedly not a board has been altered on the island shanty, **Cap's Place** ✆ (954) 941-0418, since the likes of FDR and Churchill dined there during World War II. Park your car and hop on a commuter boat for a short cruise to the restaurant at Cap's Dock, 2765 Northeast Court, Lighthouse Point. House specialties include juicy broiled seafood accompanied with fresh heart of palm salad.

The palms of Palm Beach.

Inexpensive

If it's something meaty and spicy you're after, try **Ernie's Bar-B-Que** ((954) 523-8636, at 1843 South Federal Highway. But however good the meat dishes are, you must try Ernie's famous conch chowder.

If you're a devotee of Tex-Mex food, you can't do better than **Carlos and Pepe's 17th Street Cantina** ((954) 467-7192, at 1302 Southeast 17th Street. Celestial food at bargain-basement prices. A word of warning, however: I'm not the first person to discover the cantina. So unless you go early, you could have a bit of a wait at the bar.

Try My Thai ((954) 926-5585 serves authentic Thai dishes at an intimate eatery at 2003 Harrison Street, in Hollywood. The Decor includes a collection of neckties on the walls. For theme-eating while you shop at the enormous Sawgrass Mills outlet mall, try **Rainforest Cafe** ((954) 851-1015, 12801 Sunrise Boulevard, in Sunrise. Here you dine in a tropical rainforest amid live and animated wildlife and special effects.

HOW TO GET THERE

The sprawling Fort Lauderdale/Hollywood International Airport is served by a large number of national and international airlines, and all the major car-hire companies have desks here. The airport is only 20 minutes from the city center. Nonetheless, many people still prefer to fly into Miami, which is about an hour's drive to the south.

Approaching Fort Lauderdale by car from the north or south, drivers can take the Florida Turnpike (a tollway), Interstate 95, Route 1 (also known as the Federal Highway), or Route A1A, which snakes slowly and scenically along the coast. The main road from the west is Route 84, a tollway also known as the Everglades Parkway or, more colloquially, Alligator Alley.

PALM BEACH AND BOCA RATON

In a sense, Palm Beach is a mirage, because its special appeal is very much in the eye of the beholder. To some, it is an oasis of taste and style, a chic enclave for the upper classes, an island paradise for the mega-wealthy. To others though, it is a 12-mile-long (19-km) shrine to vulgarity and excess, an offshore game reserve where cash-laden social climbers and penniless aristocrats can prey on each other in peace. That globetrotting chronicler of high society, Taki, has called it, rather harshly, "a Gulag for the rich, the last refuge of the lifted, a Mecca for the monosyllabic."

To be honest, there is some merit to both views. But whichever view you take, there is no denying that the place is special, if not unique. Where else would you find flocks of (specially imported) parrots where you would normally find pigeons, or find an artificial reef offshore anchored by a Rolls Royce and a yacht, or find a city ordinance banning outdoor clotheslines because they are unsightly? Exactly.

BACKGROUND

During the 'Twenties Palm Beach became the place where anybody who was Anybody went for the winter season. Mansions sprouted among the palms. West Palm Beach was created, on the mainland, across from the island, by Flagler "for my help" — the army of servants required to staff the hotels and private homes. Since automobiles were prohibited as disturbers of peace, the gliterrati were ferried to and from by blacks in wicker rickshaws known as "Afromobiles". Palm Beach became the ultimate Fantasy Island for The Haves. Today its social cachet may have been diluted somewhat by the infiltration of certain high-decibel, high-visibility parvenus, but it nonetheless remains a wonderful example of the happiness that money can buy.

GENERAL INFORMATION

The **Palm Beach County Convention and Visitors Bureau** ☎ (561) 471-3995 FAX (561) 471-3990 WEB-SITE www.palmbeachfl.com, is at 1555 Palm Lakes Boulevard, Suite 204, West Palm Beach, FL 33401. Their tourist information center ☎ (561) 575-4636 is at 8020 Indiantown Road in Jupiter. The **Business Development Board of Palm Beach** County ☎ (561) 835-1008 TOLL-FREE (800) 226-0028 is at 222 Lakeview Avenue, Suite 120, West Palm Beach, FL 33401. The **Jupiter-Tequesta-Juno Beach Chamber of Commerce** ☎ (561) 746-7111 is located at 800 North US Highway One. The **Boca Raton Chamber of Commerce** ☎ (407) 395-4433, is at 1800 North Route 1, Boca Raton.

For flight information, call **Palm Beach International Airport** ☎ (561) 471-7400, or for a cab try **Yellow Cabs** ☎ (561) 689-2222.

WHAT TO SEE AND DO

Mansion-gazing is by far the most popular form of sightseeing in Palm Beach, and the best way to gaze at the mansions is from the water. Narrated sightseeing cruises go every day from Steamboat Landing — as do luncheon, cocktail, and dinner cruises with live entertainment. Among the best is the **Star of Palm Beach** ☎ (407) 848-7827, Steamboat Landing, 900 East Blue Heron Boulevard, Riviera Beach, FL 33404.

Among the mansions themselves, the two most noteworthy are **Mar-A-Lago** ☎ (561) 832-2600 at 1100 South Ocean Boulevard, the 118-room Moorish extravaganza built for cereal heiress Marjorie Merriweather Post in the Twenties and now owned by Donald Trump, and the 55-room marble palace built by Henry Flagler in 1902, which was originally called Whitehall but is now the **Henry M. Flagler Museum** ☎ (561) 655-2833. As the Trump mansion is not open to the public, and only its 75-ft (23-m) tower is clearly visible from the road, the visitor's time is better spent inspecting Mr. Flagler's palatial edifice on Coconut Row. There are seven kinds of rare marble in the foyer alone, and each guest bedroom is decorated in the style of a different period in world history. Parked outside the mansion is Flagler's private railway car.

Considering that most of the expensive art in Palm Beach is in private homes, the **Norton Gallery of Art** ☎ (561) 832-5194, at 1451 South Olive Avenue in West Palm Beach, has a surprisingly impressive collection, particularly of the French Impressionists and of twentieth-century American art. It also has a delightful outdoor sculpture garden. It is closed on Mondays.

A truly unique collection that the whole family will enjoy is the **International Museum of Cartoon Art** ☎ (561) 391-2200 FAX (561) 391-2721, at 201 Plaza Real in Boca Raton. It's the first and only international museum devoted to the collection, preservation, exhibition and study of all genres of cartoon art, including animation, comic books and strips, editorial cartoons, advertising cartoons and greeting card art.

Exterior and interior views of the Henry M. Flagler Museum.

Animal lovers and people traveling with children will want to visit the **Palm Beach Zoo at Dreher Park** ☎ (561) 547-9453 or (561) 533-0887 WEB SITE www.palmbeachzoo.org, at 1301 Summit Boulevard in West Palm Beach. The zoo's 23 acres (nine hectares) are home to 400 animals from Australia, South and Central America, Asia, and the United States.

About 15 miles (24 km) farther west on Southern Boulevard is the 500-acre (200-hectare) **Lion Country Safari** ☎ (407) 793-1084 WEB SITE wwwlioncountrysafari.com, where you can drive along eight miles (13 km) of paved roads past African lions, elephants, zebras, giraffes, white rhinos, antelopes, and chimpanzees, to name only a few of the animals that roam free. There is also a petting zoo as well as a number of free rides, games, and boat cruises. If you don't have a car, or drive a convertible, you can rent a car for the duration of your visit. Worth noting, too, is the excellent campground next to the park ☎ (561) 793-9797.

The **South Florida Science Museum** ☎ (561) 832-1988WEB SITE wwwsfsm.org, at 4801 Dreher Trail North, West Palm Beach has dozens of hands-on exhibits to keep hands of all ages busy. Nearby are aquariums and the **Aldrin Planetarium**.

At the **Palm Beach Maritime Museum** ☎ (561) 863-9305 or (561) 842-7606, on historic Peanut Island, you can tour the command post and atomic shelter built to protect President Kennedy in the 1960s, a restored New England-style home that once housed a United States Coast Guard station, and an exhibit documenting the sinking of the battleship *Maine*. Transportation is by ferry from Currie Park in West Palm Beach.

Sports

Two major league baseball teams hold their spring training in West Palm Beach, the **Montreal Expos** and **St Louis Cardinals**. They play exhibition games at Municipal Stadium ☎ (407) 684-6801, Lakes Boulevard and Congress Avenue. You can watch **jai alai** from January until the middle of May at the Palm Beach Jai Alai Fronton ☎ (407) 844-2444, 1415 West 45th Street, West Palm Beach.

Polo players in Boca Raton.

3
BROOKFIEL
1
BROOKFIEL

The spectator sport most closely associated with Palm Beach is **polo**. Polo is played from early November until late April, at the Palm Beach Polo and Country Club ☎ (561) 798-7000, 13198 Forest Hill Boulevard, Wellington, the Royal Palm Polo and Sports Club ☎ (561) 994-1876, 6300 Clint Moore Road, Boca Raton, and the Gulfstream Polo Ground ☎ (561) 965-2057 at 4550 Polo Club Road, Lake Worth.

With over 145 **golf courses** in the area, golfers have plenty of choice. An especially beautiful course is Emerald Dunes ☎ (561)

684-4653 at 2100 Emerald Dunes Drive, West Palm Beach. **Tennis** players too will find no shortage of courts, many of them free. The Jupiter Bay Racquet Club ☎ (561) 744-9424 is at 353 South US Highway 1, The Lake Park Recreation Tennis Club ☎ (561) 881-8038 is at Kelsey Park, 535 Park Avenue and the North Palm Beach Tennis Club ☎ (561) 626-6515 is at 951 US Highway 1.

There are countless opportunities for **scuba diving** and **snorkeling** along this coast. In North Palm Beach try Aquashop ☎ (561) 848-9042, 505 Northlake Boulevard. In West Palm Beach, the Scuba Club ☎ (561) 844-2466, 4708 Poinsettia Avenue, has been around since 1972 and in Boynton Beach contact TNT Dive Charters ☎ (561) 762-7668 at 115 Southwest 25th Avenue. For general information, call the Palm Beach County Diving Association ☎ (561) 691-5808.

A day of family **boating** fun can be had at the Jupiter Outdoor Center ☎ (561) 747-9666 FAX (561) 747-3469 WEB SITE www.jupiteroutdoorcenter.com, at 18095 North Highway A1A in Jupiter, where you can rent kayaks, paddleboats or electric boats to explore the Loxahatchee River or bicycles for exploring nearby parks. Guided historical, birding and ecological tours leave from Burt Reynold's Farm ☎ (561) 747-5390.

Shopping

If you know anything about Palm Beach, then you already know about **Worth Avenue** ☎ (561) 659-6909. It's to Palm Beach what Fifth Avenue is to New York.

Although Worth is only three blocks long, with the Atlantic at one end and Lake Worth at the other, the street is home to over 250 stores and boutiques, ranging from Saks Fifth Avenue to Chanel. Take a walk along the various "vias" behind the avenue and you'll discover beautiful sculptured gardens, galleries and small, interesting shops. Look out for the metal sculptures of kids on Via Gucci and visit artist **Ronni Pastorini** in her studio on Via Mizner.

As the renaïssance of downtown West Palm Beach continues, a **Fine Arts District** is emerging, bordered on the east by the Professional Arts Building on South Dixie Highway and on the west by the Eaton Gallery. The **Professional Arts Building** alone offers more than 10 galleries with high-quality works in a variety of media. **Soho Arts** ☎ (561) 833-2787 at 312 South Dixie Highway has traditional art as well as experimental processes. **Galleria Chiaro Scuro** ☎ (561) 832-5151, 316 South Dixie Highway specializes in photography.

Golf enthusiasts will find all the clubs and accessories they can dream of at the **Palm Beach Golf Center** ☎ (561) 842-7100 E-MAIL info@palmbeachgolfcenter.com, 7100 North Military Trail, Palm Beach Gardens.

Nightlife

Not surprisingly, most Palm Beach nightlife revolves around private entertaining. But there are some interesting night spots.

Ta-Boo ☎ (561) 835-3500, a fashionable supper club at 221 Worth Avenue, has a DJ playing dance music on Friday and Saturday nights throughout the year. For a more casual evening, at the other end of the nightlife spectrum, **Boston's on the Beach** ☎ (561) 278-3364 has live music nightly at 40 South Ocean Boulevard. **Panama Hatties** ☎ (561) 627-1545, Palm Beach Gardens, has live reggae music to accompany seafood and continental dishes.

The ever-popular **Waterway Cafe** ☎ (561) 694-1700, 2300 PGA Boulevard, serves up live jazz and R&B in a casual waterfront setting right on the Intracoastal. Country music fans shouldn't pass up a visit to **Country Nights** ☎ (561) 689-7625, 4833 Okeechobee Boulevard, West Palm Beach, which offers karaoke on Mondays and free dance lessons Monday to Friday.

On Thursday nights, **Clementis Street** ☎ (561) 659-8007 comes alive with live music, arts and crafts displays and food vendors.

The **Kravis Center for the Performing Arts** ☎ (561) 832-7469 TOLL-FREE (800) 572-8471 WEB SITE www.kravis.org, 701 Okeechobee Boulevard, hosts "finer" dance, drama, and music events.

One Palm Beach institution you shouldn't pass up is a martini at the **Leopard Room** in the Chesterfied Hotel ☎ (561) 659-5800, 363 Coconut Row. Words can't describe the exotic playfulness of the animal decor.

Boca Raton also has a lot to offer after dark. The **Royal Palm Dinner Theater** TOLL-FREE (800) 841-6765, at 303 Southeast Mizner Boulevard Golfview Drive, presents Broadway musicals, with occasional guest stars, throughout the year. The **Caldwell Theatre Company** ☎ (561) 241-7432, Levitz Plaza, 7873 North Federal Highway offers up professional productions year-round. The professional ballet company **Boca Ballet** ☎ (561) 995-0708, performs at 5620-B North Federal Highway.

Club Boca ☎ (561) 368-3333, 7000 West Palmetto Park Road, is strictly for night owls, staying open until 5 AM with a combination of live music and DJs catering to the whim of the crowd. On any given evening you can catch reggae, ska, punk, rock, or industrial music.

WHERE TO STAY

Luxury

Hotels don't get much more luxurious than the twin-towered Italianate palace known

OPPOSITE: The Breakers, a Palm Beach landmark since the turn of the century. ABOVE: Worth Avenue.

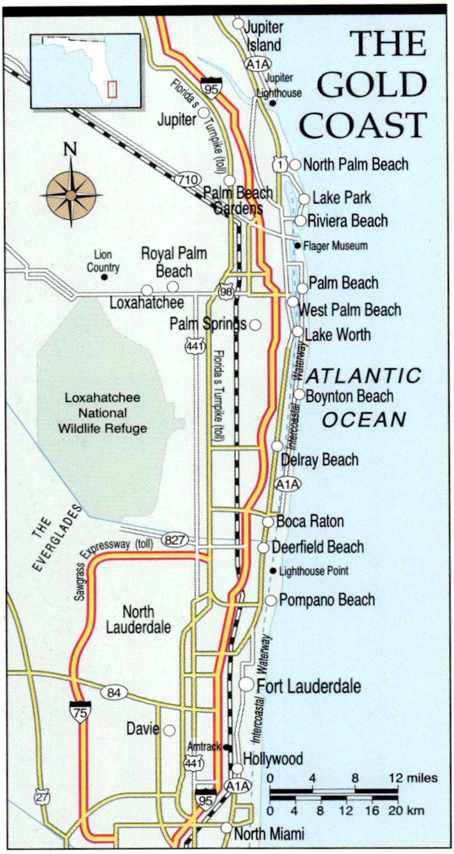

as **The Breakers** ☏ (5617) 655-6611 TOLL-FREE (888) 273-2537 FAX (561) 659-8403 WEB SITE www.thebreakers.com, One South County Road. Modeled on the Villa Medici in Florence, The Breakers was rebuilt in 1926 following extensive damage caused by two fires. Ever since its renaissance, it has served as the unofficial community center for Palm Beach's glitterati — all the while retaining its well deserved reputation for graceful formality. In addition to almost half a mile (800 m) of beachfront, the hotel has 14 tennis courts, two 18-hole golf courses, and a newly opened 20,000-sq-ft (1,800-sq-m) indoor/outdoor spa.

Matching — some would say surpassing — The Breakers in upper-crustiness is **The Colony** ☏ (561) 655-5430 TOLL-FREE (800) 521-5525 FAX (561) 832-7318 WEB SITE www.thecolonypalmbeach.com, at 155 Hammon Avenue, where the Duke and Duchess of Windsor normally stayed, and where John Lennon famously didn't (having been turned away on grounds of scruffiness). Although the hotel's *look* is distinctly, but tastefully, Floridian, it *feels* European: the service is excellent and impeccably understated — just right. Locals describe The Colony admiringly as "a hundred rooms and a reputation."

One might think that the above hotels would be impossible acts to follow, but the **Brazilian Court Hotel** ☏ (516) 655-7740 TOLL-FREE (800) 552-0335 FAX (561) 655-0801 WEB SITE www.brazilaincourt.com, at 301 Australian Avenue in West Palm Beach, is right up there with them. Built in the same year as The Breakers and recently renovated, it too combines the best of New and Old World hospitality, but this hotel is particularly welcoming to guests with pets, and even has a special pet menu, with each main course accompanied by a bottle of "designer" water.

The fourth member of this dazzling quartet is the **Boca Raton Resort and Club** ☏ (561) 395-3000 TOLL-FREE (800) 327-0101 WEB SITE www.bocaresort.com, at 501 East Camino Real in Boca Raton, also built in 1926. Originally named the Cloister Inn, this was undoubtedly Addison Mizner's masterpiece. It has since expanded outwards and upwards (only 100 of the hotel's 963 rooms are in the original building), and now includes five swimming pools, an extensive tennis and fitness center, two golf courses, a 23-slip marina, seven restaurants, and a half mile (800 m) of beach.

For those who want to be pampered but are traveling with children, the **Ritz Carlton, Palm Beach** ☏ (561) 533-6000 TOLL-FREE (800) 241-3333 FAX (561) 540-4949 WEB SITE www.ritzcarlton.com, is a good choice. Located on the southern tip of Palm Beach Island, this attractive Mediterranean-style resort offers all the usual luxury amenities plus an extensive kids' program.

Another good hotel for children is the **Radisson Palm Beach Shores Resort** ☏ (561) 863-4000 TOLL-FREE (800) 333-3333 FAX (561) 845-3245 WEB SITE www.palmbeachshoresresort.com, at 181 Ocean Avenue, Singer Island. The two-room suites can comfortably hold an entire family and the hotel offers a comprehensive youth program.

Don't let the name fool you — **Disney's Vero Beach Resort** ((561) 234-2000 WEB SITE www.dvc-resorts.com, is a full two hours from Disneyworld, on the Vero Beach coast at 9250 Island Grove Terrace. This friendly family-style resort offers a touch of old Florida, with a choice of spacious studios and comfortable family villas as well as conventional suites.

Mid-range

Towards the top of the middle range is the **Howard Johnson Motor Lodge** ((561) 582-2581 TOLL-FREE (800) 654-2000 FAX (561) 582-7189, at 2870 South Ocean Boulevard in Palm Beach. The service here is outstanding, and it is conveniently located close to shops and the beach.

Nearby, and much more charming, is the **Beachcomber Apartment Motel** ((561) 585-4648 TOLL-FREE (800) 833-7122 FAX (561) 547-9438, at 3024 South Ocean Boulevard. A very reasonably priced motel for this part of the world, the Beachcomber comes complete with a great beachfront location and a salt-water swimming pool.

In Palm Beach Shores, the very lovely **Sailfish Marina and Resort** ((561) 844-1724 TOLL-FREE (800) 446-4577 FAX (561) 848-9684 E-MAIL sailfish@sailfishmarina.com WEB SITE www.sailfishmarina.com, at 98 Lake Drive incorporates a pretty marina, a decent-sized swimming pool and a shaded outdoor barbecue grill area.

Incongruous but striking "Italianate" buildings in downtown Palm Beach.

Inexpensive

If you don't mind staying a little inland, the **Sunland Motel** ✆ (561) 996-2817 FAX (561) 992-5273, at 1080 South Main Street in Belle Glade is an excellent value. Other budget places I would recommend are the **Breezeway Motel** ✆ (561) 582-0882, 2001 North Dixie Highway in Lake Worth, and the **Okeechobee Inn** ✆ (561) 996-6517 FAX (561) 996-6517, at 265 North US Highway 27 in South Bay.

WHERE TO EAT

Expensive

Like the Casa Vecchia in Fort Lauderdale, **La Vielle Maison** ✆ (561) 391-6701, at 770 East Palmetto Park Road in Boca Raton is another old house restored and refurbished by the redoubtable Leonce Picot and Al Kocab. An elegant, two-story, artifact-filled honeycomb of alcoves and intimate spaces, the restaurant specializes in wonderfully imaginative French Provincial cuisine.

Also in Boca Raton is **Maxwell's Chophouse** ✆ (561) 347-7077, 501 East Palmetto Park Boulevard, which offers top-quality steaks aged on the premises, as well as chops, grilled fish and huge Maine lobsters in a comfortable New Orleans setting with dark wood, brick and wrought iron.

For Northern Italian cuisine with authentic Italian ambiance, try **Bice** ✆ (561) 835-1600, 313 1/2 Worth Avenue, Palm Beach. By contrast, **The Dining Room** ✆ (516) 655-7740, which graces the Brazilian Court Hotel, celebrates many different cuisines, often in arresting new combinations. This is the place to go if you want to experience true luxury, in the meals as much as the decor.

Moderate

It's probably a waste of space to recommend **Chuck & Harold's Café** ✆ (561) 659-1440, at 207 Royal Poinciana Way in Palm Beach, because most of the natives you meet will do it for me. For celebrity-spotting at all hours of the day or night, as well as for an amazing array of dishes in a splendid setting, plus live (and lively) music at night, you won't do any better than this.

Another local favorite is **Panama Hattie's** ✆ (561) 471-2255, at 361 A1A Beach Boulevard in Palm Beach Gardens, which offers a glorious ocean view together with steamed seafood pots, prime rib and the best burgers in town.

For excellent pizza, pasta and veal prepared with traditional family recipes, stop by **No Anchovies** ✆ (561) 684-0040 at 1901 Palm Lakes in West Palm Beach. For really good seafood at a reasonable price in picturesque surroundings on the Intracoastal Waterway, it's got to be **Charley's Crab** ✆ (561) 744-4710, 1000 North US Highway 1, Jupiter.

Inexpensive

Hamburger Heaven ✆ (561) 655-5277, at 314 South County Road in Palm Beach, serves heavenly hamburgers; while **Duffyís** ✆ (561) 743-4405, 185 East Indiantown Road, is a great place to have a beer and a bite.

In Lake Worth, **John G's** ✆ (561) 585-9860, 10 Ocean Boulevard, is a popular place for breakfast and its fish and chips lunch specials. **Toojay's** ✆ (561) 241-5903, at Polo Shops, 5030 Champion Boulevard, Boca Raton is the best deli around with sumptuous soups and sandwiches. **Pineapple Grill** ✆ (561) 265-1368, 800 Pail Trail, Delray Beach, serves up American food which reflects various ethnic and regional differences as well as contemporary folk music on weekends until midnight.

HOW TO GET THERE

Although Palm Beach International Airport is only minutes away from Palm Beach itself, the Fort Lauderdale airport is served by many more airlines and flights.

The principal north-south roads into Palm Beach and Boca Raton are the same as for Fort Lauderdale. The main road from the west is Route 98, which becomes Southern Boulevard as it approaches Palm Beach.

Facing the Atlantic: beach huts stand sentinel.

UNITED STATES
NASA
UNITED STATES

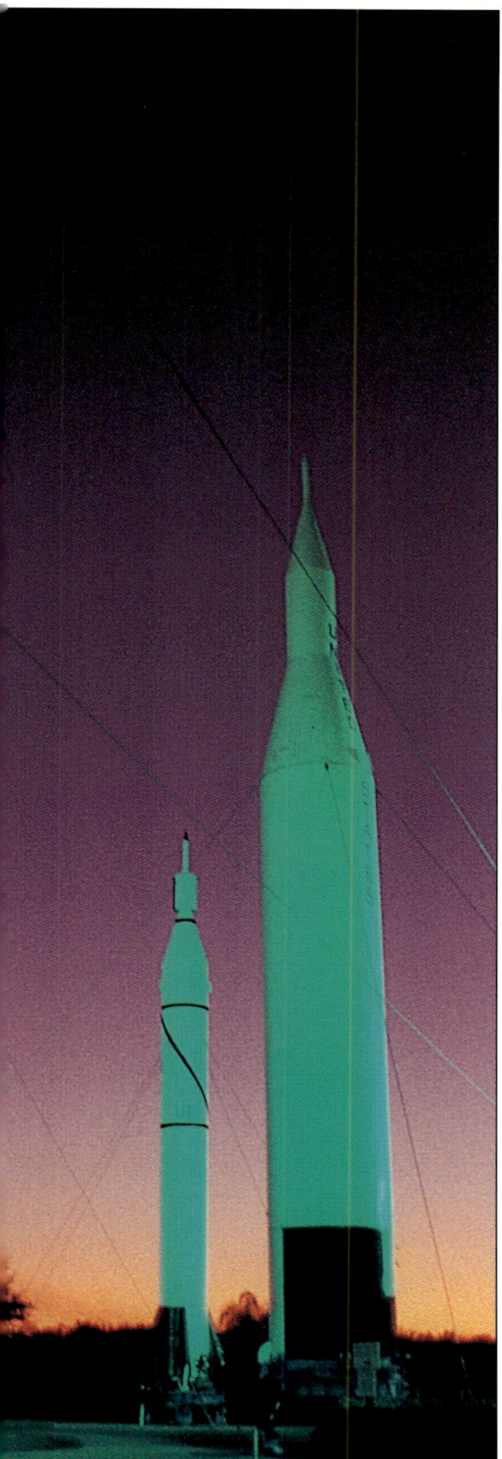

The Atlantic Coast

STRETCHING FOR OVER 300 MILES (480 KM) FROM Palm Beach to the Georgia state line, Florida's Atlantic coast has attractions ranging from the oldest city in the country — St. Augustine — to the extremely high-tech marvels at the Kennedy Space Center on Merritt Island near Cape Canaveral.

Following in the wake of Columbus, the Spanish explorer Ponce de León led an expedition across the Atlantic in 1513 to try to discover the "Fountain of Youth" waters, rumored to exist somewhere near present-day St. Augustine. Ponce de León may not have found the fountain, but is remembered today in St. Augustine's Fountain of Youth Discovery Park.

By 1562 a small expeditionary force of French Huguenots had settled at what was to become Fort Caroline near the mouth of the St. Johns River, around which Jacksonville now stands. Responding to this challenge, King Philip II of Spain sent Pedro Menéndez de Avilés to Florida with orders to drive the French out of the northeast and establish a garrison town on the coast. At the end of August 1565, Menéndez spotted a strategic point overlooking a bay and some days later landed there. Thus began the long history of St. Augustine. Wasting no time, Menéndez marched against Fort Caroline and routed the garrison, and then destroyed what remained of the French forces on his way back to St. Augustine.

Although this confirmed Spain as the dominant power in the region, it by no means assured Spanish control. Indeed, Fort Caroline was retaken only two years later, and Amelia Island, just above Jacksonville, has seen no fewer than eight flags raised above it since 1562. The whole area was tossed around between the Spanish, French, and English for a few centuries, and Mexico even laid claim to it for a brief period before the Union wrenched it away from the Confederacy.

In the years following the end of the Civil War, the coast began to prosper from the north downwards. Jacksonville rose to prominence as a port, and the arrival of Henry Flagler's Florida East Coast Railroad in the 1880s secured the city's position as the state's shipping and industrial center. As his railway crept further south Flagler dotted the coastline with luxury hotels to cater to the expensive tastes of the wealthy northerners who began wintering in Florida. Resort towns soon developed to accommodate the increasing flow of tourists to the region. However, not all of the new arrivals were tourists: it was the now-famous climate that attracted NASA to Florida's Atlantic coast in the 1960s.

THE SPACE COAST

Every year more than 2.5 million people visit the **John F. Kennedy Space Center** visitor complex, and many of them plan their stay to coincide with the launch of a spacecraft. Although the Space Center remains the main attraction, the 72-mile stretch of Atlantic shore offers options from surfing and fishing to exploring more than 250 square miles of protected wildlife refuges and parks, where one can see such endangered species as the Western Indian manatee and the Southern bald eagle.

The Space Coast, which encompasses the cities of Titusville, Cocoa Beach, Melbourne and Palm Bay, is the closest beach to Orlando and a great escape at an affordable price.

BACKGROUND

Ais and Timucuan tribes were the original inhabitants of the Cape area. The name "Canaveral" is derived from a Timucuan word meaning cane, a hollow reed that grew abundantly on the Atlantic Coast of Florida. To this day, large areas of the region remain a wilderness of mosquito-infested swamp, savannah, and rugged coastline. In fact, most of Merritt Island is a national wildlife refuge; of the 140,000 acres (56,000 hectares) of the island owned by NASA, only seven percent has been developed for the space program. The rest is an extension of the wildlife refuge — a fact that NASA, is keen to emphasize. Old tribal burial mounds have also been left untouched and lie next to the bunkers and buildings of the Space Center.

Hard on the heels of the Soviet Union's *Sputnik*, America's first satellite, *Explorer I*, was launched from Cape Canaveral on January 31, 1958. The National Aeronautics and

A Saturn 5 rocket; one of the many on exhibit at the John F. Kennedy Space Center.

Space Administration (NASA) was created the following year, originally operating from the Cape itself but moving over to Merritt Island in 1964. By 1968, the Apollo program was well under way, and it came to fruition on July 20, 1969 with Neil Armstrong's first step on the moon. Such local towns as Cocoa Beach (which is opposite Cape Canaveral, unlike the town of Cocoa which is on the mainland across Indian River) were transformed by the influx of scientists, technicians, and workers from the Space Center.

GENERAL INFORMATION

For more information on Space Coast attractions contact the **Space Coast Office of Tourism** ☎ (407) 633-2110 TOLL-FREE 1-800-USA-1969 WEB SITE www.space-coast.com, 8810 Astronaut Boulevard, Suite 102.

The offices of the **Cocoa Beach Area Chamber of Commerce** ☎ (407) 459-2200 FAX (407) 459-2232 E-MAIL chamber1@iu.net WEB SITE www.cocoabeachchamber.com, 400 Fortenberry Road, Merritt Island, are also a helpful place to get maps and more information, or call for tourist information on ☎ (407) 455-1309.

In case of a medical emergency, Cape Canaveral Hospital is located at 701 Cocoa Beach Causeway and can be reached at ☎ (407) 799-7111.

If you would like to be among the many international visitors who come to the Space Coast for a launch, call the Kennedy Space Center for flight schedules and visitor services at ☎ (407) 867-4636 or (407) 452-2121 TOLL-FREE IN FLORIDA (800) 572-4636 WEB SITE www.kscvisitor.com — recorded launch information is updated daily. A limited number of launch viewing opportunity tickets are sold on a first-come first-serve basis at the ticket pavilion in the main entrance of the visitor complex. These passes, which cost about $10 per person, allow you to take a bus to a viewing site approximately six miles from the launch pad.

Good vantage points outside the Space Center include Route 1 in Titusville and Highway AIA in Cape Canaveral, the Cocoa Beach Pier or any of the 72-miles of beach along the coast. Just park and watch the launch The United States Space Walk of Fame, a waterfront terrace on the edge of the Indian River, is also a great observation area.

WHAT TO SEE AND DO

The John F. Kennedy Space Center Visitor Complex features a replica of the shuttle Explorer, a rocket garden where spacecraft from the early days of space exploration are exhibited, and an astronaut memorial. These three areas (and the parking lot) are free to enter. The Visitor Complex is located off State Road 405, NASA Parkway. Use State Road 3

on Merritt Island if you are approaching from Merritt Island or Cocoa Beach. From Interstate 95, use exit 78 northbound or exit 79 southbound.

But to understand and appreciate the accomplishments of the United States space program, a guided bus tour is highly recommended. Comfortable air-conditioned tour buses take visitors to any of three destinations and allow them to explore at their leisure. One can begin at the Apollo/ Saturn V Center, home of an enormous 363-foot (110-m) authentic Saturn V rocket, which was once used to transport astronauts to the moon. There is an actual moon rock on display and a multimedia reenactment of the first lunar landing. The latest attraction on the tour is **Launch Complex 39**, a 60-foot (18-m) observation tower that has a 360-degree view of Launch Pad 39A.

Then take the bus to the **International Space Station Center**, where visitors cross an elevated walkway to a viewing gallery to witness the processing of a space station module. The module will be sent into orbit to attach to the International Space Station already being constructed 240 miles above the Earth.

If you want to be transported to another space experience, try either of the two IMAX Theaters, with five-story-high screens that show three different films about the space shuttle and space exploration.

After the Space Center you can come back down to earth with a driving tour through **Merritt Island National Wildlife Refuge** ☎ (407) 861-0667, which wraps around the Kennedy Space Center. You can guide yourself along the **Black Point Wildlife Drive** by entering the refuge via County Road 402, off Route 1 in Titusville. Bird-watchers will be particularly excited by the more than 310 species that inhabit the area including black rails, phalaropes and yellow-breasted chats.

Nature-lovers can also see the largest sea turtle nesting area in the United States at **Spessard Holland Park**. Sightings are most frequent between May and August when loggerheads, green seas, and leatherbacks lay around 600 eggs along the shore.

If you really want to get away from it all, take a half-hour airboat ride up the **St. Johns River** and get a close-up look at alligators hanging out on the riverbank. The boat leaves from **Lone Cabbage Fish Camp** ☎ (407) 632-4199, at Route 520, six miles (10 km) west of Interstate 95, Cocoa. Another airboat ride service is **Camp Holly Fishing** ☎ (407) 723-2179.

Of course, alligators and bald eagles can just as easily be spotted alongside the road as the buses take guests from one attraction to another in the Kennedy Space Center. A keen guide or bus driver will be sure to point them out.

Located at 6225 Vectorspace Boulevard, the **United States Astronaut Hall of Fame** is just 15 minutes west from the entrance to the Kennedy Space Center ☎ (407) 269-6100. WEB SITE www.astronauts.org. Relive the daring accomplishments of the first 44 United States astronauts as you see their stories unfold, and walk through a timeline of the early days of American space exploration. Many of the astronauts' personal artifacts — including their military academy uniforms, letters and pictures — are on display. Interactive recordings from the astronauts answer questions about their experiences, everything from using the toilet in space to whether they believe in extra-terrestrials. This is not just a museum. Guests can experience the rigors and stresses of astronaut training on

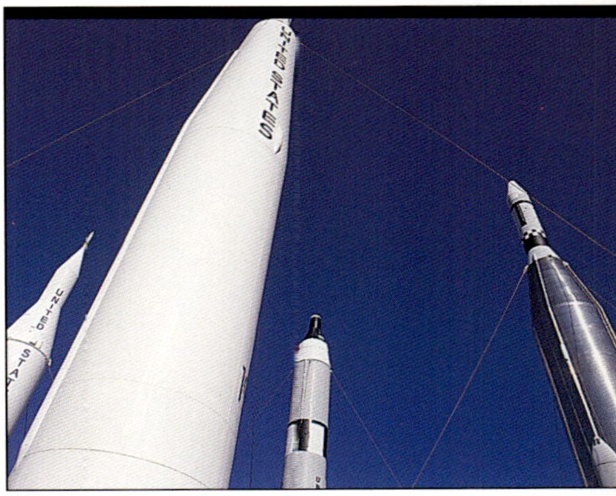

several motion-based and virtual reality flight simulators designed to make you feel the forces of gravity. These rides give you a basis for comparison to see if you could handle space flight. Most people would not make it past the G-force simulator because of motion sickness.

United States Space Camp Florida, where registered participants — usually school-age children — learn about astronaut training, is housed in the Astronaut Hall of Fame facility. At times you might be able to catch a seminar in session or a class graduation.

Other space attractions worth visiting include the **Astronaut Memorial Planetarium and Observatory** ☎ (407) 634-3732 in Cocoa and the **Airforce Space and Missile Museum** ☎ (407) 853-3245 in Cape Canaveral.

Port Canaveral is the second largest multi-day Cruise Passenger Port in the United States with cruise lines such as *Premier*,

OPPOSITE AND ABOVE: Two views of the Rocket Garden at the John F. Kennedy Space Center.

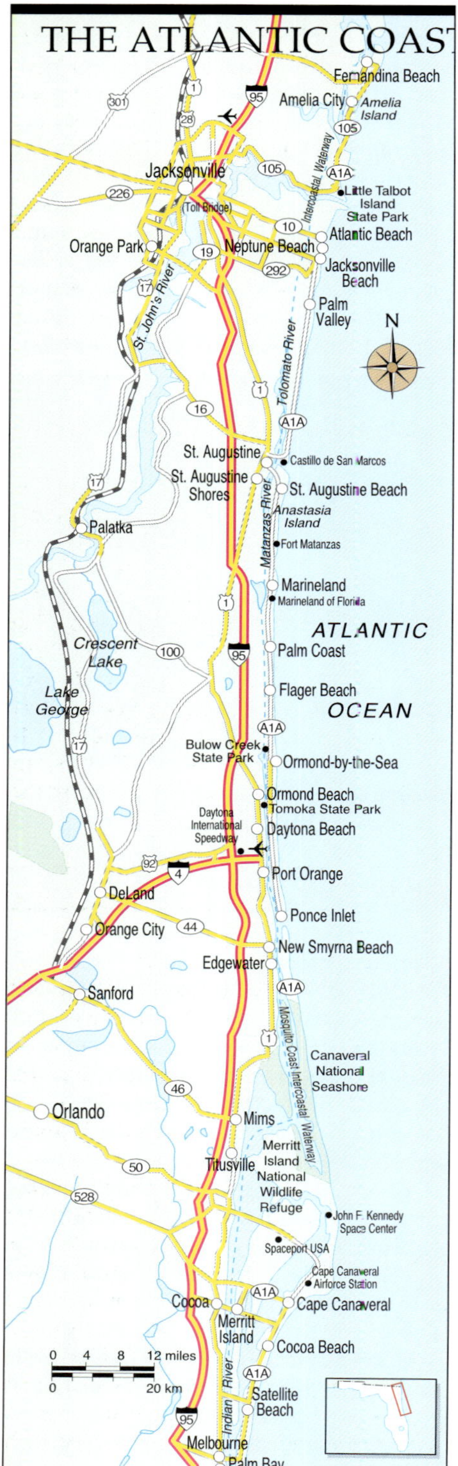

Carnival, *Cape Canaveral* and *Disney* departing to the Caribbean. The second Disney ship, *Disney Wonder*, will be in operation by the end of 1999. You can also try a gambling cruise offered by **Sterling Casino Lines** ☎ (407) 784-8558 TOLL-FREE 1-888-81-LUCKY (58259), 180 Jetty Drive, Cape Canaveral, for a five-hour gaming experience.

Sports

Sebastian Inlet State Recreation Area, Palm Bay, has become the top surfing destination in Florida because of its natural jetties and crashing waves. For more information contact ☎ (407) 984-4852. Other surfer favorites are Playalinda and Cocoa Beach. Each April, the annual Easter Surfing Festival is held.

For the best bass fishing in Florida discover **Stick Marsh**, where you can panfish for crappie, bluegill and large mouth bass at Farm 13. The area has more than 30 marinas and three fishing piers where one can catch flounder, Spanish mackerel, pompano and snook. Deep sea charters are available where anglers can try for dolphin, grouper, sailfish and marlin.

Speaking of marlin, baseball enthusiasts can catch the **Florida Marlins** during spring training (February) at the Space Coast Stadium in Melbourne ☎ (407) 633-9200. From March to September, the Marlins' Class A franchise team, the Brevard City Manatees, play at the 7,600-seat stadium.

Shopping

The best shopping in the area is at Cocoa Village in downtown Cocoa. Over 50 shops offer a variety of goods in an Old World market atmosphere that retains the charm and sense of ease that so many modern malls have lost. **Village Outfitters** ☎ (407) 633-7245, WEB SITE www.villageoutfitters.com, 113 Brevard Avenue, has a good selection of outdoors clothing and gear. At **Handwerk Haus** ☎ (407) 631-6367, 401 Brevard Avenue, you will find a collection of beautifully-crafted stuffed animals and rag dolls. At **United Spacecoast Crafters Co-op** ☎ (407) 632-6553 E-MAIL crafters@cocoavillage.com, 410 Brevard Avenue, you can find unique gifts produced by 28 crafters, from notecards to wheel thrown pottery. Cocoa Beach reputedly has the world's largest surf shop,

The Atlantic Coast

the **Ron Jon Surf Shop** ☎ (407) 799-8888 WEB SITE www.ronjons.com, 4151 North Route A1A. The neon-lit, megaplex theater structure with sand sculptures on the outside sells and rents everything you might need in or on the water and it never closes.

Nightlife

Gregory's Upstairs ☎ (407) 799-2557, WEB SITE www.gregoryonthebeach.com, 900 North Atlantic Avenue, Route A1A, Cocoa Beach, is located above Gregory's Steak and Seafood Grille. It features Groucho's Comedy Club with a new show each night and Latin night on Saturdays. **Coconuts on the Beach** ☎ (407) 784-1422 WEB SITE www.coconutsonthebeach.com, 2 Minutemen Causeway on Cocoa Beach, features nightly entertainment and food served until 1 AM. At **Dino's Jazz Piano Bar** ☎ (407) 799-4677, 520 Causeway, Cocoa Beach, one can happily waste some after-dark hours in a relaxed atmosphere listening to good jazz and blues. For a taste of local flavor, visit **Johnathan's Pub** ☎ (407) 783-9368, 140 North Brevard Avenue, Cocoa Beach, where freshly squeezed juice drinks are served.

WHERE TO STAY

Accommodation along the Space Coast is said to be among the most affordable on Florida's Atlantic Coast.

Luxury

There are no surprises about the **Cocoa Beach Hilton Oceanfront** ☎ (407) 799-0003 TOLL-FREE (800) 345-6565 FAX (407) 799-0344 1550 North Route A1A, Cocoa Beach. The facilities are typical of the Hilton chain, and many of its 300+ rooms overlook the sea. If you are lucky (or clever) enough to be there at the right time, you can witness space launches from the second-floor rooms at the **Inn at Cocoa Beach** ☎ (407) 799-3460, 4300 Ocean Beach Boulevard, Cocoa Beach, a beautifully preserved residence, which manages to combine luxury with a cozy atmosphere. **Radisson Resort at the Port** ☎ (407) 784-0000 TOLL-FREE (800) 333-3333 FAX (407) 784-3737 WEB SITE www.radisson.com/capecanaveralfl, 8701 Astronaut Boulevard, Cape Canaveral, is closely located to the port for a day excursion or two and three-night cruises.

Mid-range

The **Ramada Oceanfront Resort Hotel** ☎ (407) 777-7200 TOLL-FREE (800) 345-1782 FAX (407) 777-7200, 1035 State Road AIA, Satellite Beach has its own private beach to revel on. **South Beach Inn** ☎ (407) 784-3333 TOLL-FREE (800) 54MOTEL WEB SITE www.southbeachinn.com, 1701 South Atlantic Avenue, Cocoa Beach, welcomes pets and is ideal for families. Self-contained apartments are very well-equipped at **Surf Studio Beach Resort** ☎ (305) 783-7100, 1801 South Atlantic Avenue, Cocoa Beach, which has 11 moderately priced units and personal, friendly service.

Inexpensive

The family-owned **Sea Aire Motel** ☎ (407) 783-2461 TOLL-FREE 1-800-319-9637 FAX (407) 783-2461 E-MAIL garcar@aol.com WEB SITE www.L-N.com/SEAAIRE/, 181 North Atlantic Avenue, Cocoa Beach, offers fully-equipped oceanfront appartments. The property has a covered BBQ pavilion where you can enjoy an outdoor meal with family in front of the ocean. Another good budget choice is the **Ocean Suite Hotel** ☎ (407) 784-4343 TOLL-FREE (800) 367-1223, 5500 Ocean Beach Boulevard, Cocoa Beach, next to the Cocoa Beach Pier.

WHERE TO EAT

Expensive

The elegant **Black Tulip** ☎ (407) 631-1133 WEB SITE www.blacktulip.com, 207 Brevard Avenue, is probably the most fashionable restaurant in Cocoa Village. The emphasise is on the starters and they are particularly delicious — including crab cakes served on Kaiser rolls, and artichoke hearts in mustard sauce. The beef, poultry, and seafood mains are a little less interesting, but still very good. **Rusty's Seafood and Oyster Bar** ☎ (407) 783-2041, at Two South Route A1A in Cocoa Beach, has a big reputation and even bigger menu, on which you will find such culinary curiosities as bear meat and chocolate-covered ants. Their crab and lobster are deservedly celebrated locally, but my favorite dish was the freshwater salmon — batter-dipped and fried, and served with toasted almonds.

Moderate

The **Dixie Crossroads** ✆ (407) 268-5000, 1475 Garden Street, Titusville, is a large, family-oriented restaurant specializing in — what else? — seafood. Hint: try the smoked mullet. For a meal before or after your visit to the Space Center you could do well to drop in at the **Kountry Kitchen** ✆ (407) 459-3457, 1115 North Courtenay Parkway, Merritt Island, which serves up hearty bacon-and-egg breakfasts and mountainous dinners. At **Café Margaux** ✆ (407) 639-8343 FAX (407) 639-8355 E-MAIL margaux@margaux.com WEB SITE www.margaux.com, you can delight in creative French cooking with the house specialty crepes, or crab cakes in mango chutney mayonnaise during a quiet lunch in the courtyard.

Inexpensive

Roberto's Little Havana Restaurant ✆ (407) 784-1868, 26 North Orlando Avenue, Cocoa Beach, serves excellent down-home Cuban cooking, including a very garlicky, but good, sautéed shrimp plate.

The **Peking Garden** ✆ (407) 459-2999, 155 East Route 520, Merritt Island, serves excellent Chinese food. But if your priority is treating the kids, let me recommend the **Village Ice Cream and Sandwich Shop** ✆ (407) 632-2311, 120 Harrison Street, Cocoa Village.

HOW TO GET THERE

The **Melbourne International Airport** ✆ (407) 723-6227, about 30 miles (48 km), south of Cape Canaveral, is regularly served by Delta and Spirit Airlines. The major car rental companies have offices in the area.

The three north-south routes to the Space Coast are the same three as for the entire eastern Florida coast: Interstate 95, Route 1, and Route A1A.

DAYTONA

Daytona and Ormond Beach, a few miles to the north of Cape Canaveral, emerged from the great Florida Sun Rush at the end of the nineteenth century as two of the resorts most favored by prosperous northerners.

Daytona Beach, where the speed limit is now a stately 10 mph (16 kph).

FRIES
TRAFFIC LANES
SPEED LIMIT 10

The expanse of hard-packed, white beach between the two resorts must surely be the only beach in the world that owes its fame to being driven upon. It all began at the turn of the century when motoring enthusiasts R.E. Olds and Alexander Winton — watched by their friend Henry Ford from his rocker on the verandah of the Ormond Hotel — raced their cars down the beach in what has become known as America's first drag race.

Now, Daytona Beach is considered a world center of motor racing. The city boasts the Daytona International Speedway and the headquarters of NASCAR, the governing body of the United States stock-car racing association, as well as an ideal climate for year-round testing of race cars of all types.

Daytona Beach has also been popularized by reveling college students on their annual spring break vacations. Between racing events and spring break, it seems like there is never a dull moment in this area of Florida's Atlantic Coast.

The eight communities of the Daytona Beach area are on either side of the peninsula, separated from the mainland by the Halifax River. Daytona Beach and Ormond Beach are located on both the mainland and beachside.

Ponce Inlet at the south end of the peninsula is famous for its fresh seafood (served at restaurants along the marina) and 100-year-old Ponce Inlet Lighthouse.

BACKGROUND

By extending his Florida East Coast Railroad to the area in the late 1880s, Henry Flagler laid the tracks that property developers and winter-weary northerners were soon to travel on in their thousands. Flagler enlarged his own hotel empire by buying and renovating a venerable hostelry in Ormond Beach, the Ormond Hotel. John D. Rockefeller also established a winter residence in Ormond Beach, The Casements, where he spent much of his later life.

The resorts continued to develop and to attract the rich in increasing numbers. Organized racing began in 1904 with an event called the Winter Speed Carnival, which drew speed merchants and their society financiers from all over the world to the Daytona and Ormond beaches. In 1928 Malcolm Campbell, a slightly dotty and speed-obsessed English millionaire, arrived at Daytona with a car powered by nothing less than an aircraft engine. He patiently waited for the surf to create a sufficiently flat beach, then accelerated across it at a record speed of 207 mph (333 kph). He subsequently raised this record to 276 mph (444 kph) on the beach at Daytona.

They no longer race on the beach, but Daytona's love affair with machines and speed continues with stock-car racing and the speedway. The speed limit on the beach these days is 10 mph (16 kph), which is strictly enforced, and the fastest thing you'll see is a surfer riding the waves.

GENERAL INFORMATION

The best place to begin planning your trip is the **Daytona Beach Area Convention and Visitors Bureau** ☎ (850) 255-0415 TOLL-FREE (800) 854-1234 fax (850) 255-5478, WEB SITE www.daytonabeach.com, 126 East. Orange Avenue, Daytona Beach. This visitor's bureau has current information and helpful phone attendants. The web site also gives you access to an interactive planner to maximize your stay.

Once you arrive, you can stop by the **Official Visitors Welcome Center** ☎ (850) 253-8669, 1801 West. International Speedway Boulevard, Daytona Beach, located in the **Daytona USA** lobby, to pick up brochures and other information.

The small **Ormond Beach Chamber of Commerce** ☎ (850) 677-3454, is at 165 West Granada Street.

For tourist information on other cities in Volusia County, contact the **New Smyrna Beach Chamber of Commerce** ☎ (850) 428-2449 TOLL-FREE (800) 541-9621 or the **DeLand/West Volusia Chamber of Commerce** ☎ (850) 734-4331 TOLL-FREE (800) 749-4350.

Memorial Hospital ☎ (850) 676-6000, handles medical emergencies in the area. For taxi cab service ☎ (850) 255-5555. **Votran Bus Lines** ☎ (850) 761-7700 offers bus routes and trolley service.

WHAT TO SEE AND DO

Year after year, the beach lures many from near and far. Two things make the strand unique. It's big — 23 miles (37 km) long and 500 ft (152 m) wide at low tide, and you can drive on it. But remember, no faster than 10 mph (16 kph).

Vehicles are permitted between Ormond Beach and Ponce de León Inlet. Stick to the main track, avoid the water, and heed the warning signs about soft or unsafe areas of the beach.

Beach driving and parking are restricted in several zones that are clearly marked for the conservation and protection of Loggerhead Sea Turtle nesting areas. From April 15 to October 31, turtles emerge from the surf at night to lay their eggs in nests they dig in the sand. In the span of two months, the eggs hatch and baby turtles crawl out to the sea. To protect this cycle, night driving and lighting from beachfront properties is prohibited. Outside of this May to October period, beach driving is allowed from sunrise to sunset. Beach access fees are $5 per vehicle per day.

Contact the **Volusia County Beach Hotline** for the most current information on beach conditions, driving and activities. For the Daytona Beach area ☎ (850) 239-SURF; New Smyrna Beach area ☎ (850) 423-3330; West Volusia ☎ (850) 822-5000.

Speed demons and those who enjoy the sound of powerful thundering engines are in heaven in Daytona. From January onwards there are eight weekends of racing at the **Daytona International Speedway** ☎ (850) 254-2700 WEB SITE www.daytonausa.com, 1801 West International Speedway Boulevard, Daytona Beach. Racing begins with the famous 24 Hours at Daytona Race Track and includes the Daytona 500 Winston Cup race in mid-February. The track gives way to the Daytona Motorcycle Classic the first week of March, and the racing season culminates with the Pepsi 400 during the Fourth of July weekend. During the off season, visitors can tour the facilities on an open-air tram and get an up close look at the high-banked two-and-a-half-mile tri-oval course.

Daytona USA ☎ (850) 947-6800 WEB SITE www.daytonausa.com, 1801 West International Speedway Boulevard, is located just outside of the Speedway's fourth turn. It offers racing fans an interactive experience where you can design your own car, take part in a pit stop and learn more about the history of racing in the Daytona Beach area.

A snake-like bridge lights the way to Daytona Beach.

Classic car buffs will appreciate the collection at **Mark Martin's Klassix Auto Museum** ☎ (850) 252-3800, 2909 West International Speedway Boulevard, Daytona Beach. The classic cars define the role of the automobile in American history.

The **Museum of Arts and Sciences** ☎ (850) 255-0285, 1040 Museum Boulevard, Daytona Beach, houses one of the world's finest collections of Cuban art and sculpture. The main attraction of the science collection is a pleistocene giant ground sloth, which weighed in at five tons and was 13 feet tall.

In neighboring Ormond Beach you can visit John D. Rockefeller's former winter house, **The Casements** ☎ (850) 676-3216, WEB SITE www.ormondbeach.com/the casements, 25 Riverside Drive. The house is now a cultural center exhibiting Hungarian and Italian artifacts and American art. Admission is free, although donations are accepted.

A recent addition to Daytona's museum circuit is the **African American and Caribbean American Museum of Art** ☎ (850) 736-4004, 325 South Clara Street, DeLand. The museum, established in 1994, contains more than 150 pieces of African and Caribbean art in the permanent gallery.

If you want to get an idea of how the Timucuans used to live, visit **Tomoka State Park** ☎ (850) 676-4050, 2099 North Beach Street, Ormond Beach. The park's **Fred Dana Marsh Museum and Visitor Center** ☎ (850) 676-4045, has exhibits showing the history of the ancient Timucuan village of Nocoroco.

You can cruise the waters of the Halifax River on a number of different boats depending on what type of activity you desire. On A Tiny Cruise Line ☎ (850) 226-2343, WEB SITE www.visitdaytona.com/tinycruise, 425 South Beach Street, Halifax Harbor in Daytona Beach, you can choose from four narrated tours aboard the 1890's-style Fantail Launch. The Sun Cruz Casino ☎ (850) 322-9000 TOLL-FREE (800) 373-DICE WEB SITE www.suncruzcasino.com, 4884 Front Street, Ponce Inlet, is a three-deck, 160-foot passenger ship with a full Las Vegas-style casino.

Sports

Golf Daytona Beach ☎ (850) 239-7065 TOLL-FREE (800) 881-7065 E-MAIL golf@totcom.com WEB SITE www.golf-daytona.com, is a program that offers golf and hotel accommodations packages for visitors at discount rates and even free golf during certain times of the year. If you stay at one of the participating lodges for two or more consecutive nights you can play one free round of golf each day at one of 14 participating courses.

Guests pay only for cart fees, but your tee time must be after midday. Daytona Beach is also home to the **Ladies Professional Golf Association International** ☎ (850) 274-LPGA, 300 Champions Drive, Daytona Beach. The city has two public links – the Champions course with five sets of tees and the newly opened Legends Course.

Three other recommended courses are: **River Bend Golf Club,** 730 Airport Road, Ormond Beach; **Indigo Lakes** ☎ (850) 254-3607, 312 Indigo Drive, Daytona Beach, and **Daytona Beach Golf Course** ☎ (850) 258-3119, 600 Wilder Boulevard, Daytona Beach. There are also other hotels not in this program which offer golf packages as well.

Tennis players have eight great choices. The **City Island Courts** ☎ (850) 239-6627 has six hard courts, while the **Ormond Beach Racquet Club** ☎ (850) 676-3285 has eight clay courts.

For anglers, the choices are plenty. Deep sea fishing charters leaving daily from Ponce Inlet. You can also try surf fishing along the coast and pier fishing at the Main Street Pier. If you head west towards DeLand, you can do some freshwater fishing on the St. John's River.

Daytona is home to the Chicago Cubs' Class A affiliate baseball team, the Daytona Cubs, who play at the historic **Jackie Robinson Ballpark** ☎ (850) 257-3172, off East Orange Avenue, Daytona Beach.

At the **Daytona Beach Kennel Club** ☎ (850) 252-6484, 2201 West International Speedway, Daytona Beach, you can watch and wager on live greyhound racing year round.

Shopping

Along four blocks of palm-lined Beach Street in downtown Daytona Beach you can find anything from jewelry to candy to magic stores. Stop in at Angell & Phelps Chocolate Factory ☎ (850) 252-6531, 154 South Beach Street, Daytona Beach to see mouth-watering chocolate made in front of you. For all kinds of gift baskets and a collection of angels and Boyd's Bears check out Absolute Favorites Collections ☎ (888) 255-7690 WEB SITE www.visitdaytona.com/absolutefavorites, 214 South Beach Street, Daytona Beach. Motorcycle afficionados will be amazed by the largest Harley dealer in the United States, Daytona Harley-Davidson ☎ (850) 253-BIKE, 290 North Beach Street. Not only can you find new and used bikes, but the complete line of Harley leather attire.

Bargain hunters will be fascinated by the Daytona Flea and Farmers Market ☎ (850) 253-3330, WEB SITE www.volusia.com/daytonafleamarket, an air-conditioned antique mall with 1,000 covered booths. However, it's only open Friday, Saturday and Sunday.

Nightlife

The **Oyster Pub** ☎ (850) 255-6348, 555 Seabreeze Avenue, Daytona Beach, is where the locals hang out to enjoy the sports bar atmosphere. Just down the street is **Razzle's** ☎ (850) 257-6236, 611 Seabreeze Boulevard, Daytona Beach, with its loud, high-energy dance music. For live blues and jazz try **The Bank and Blues Club** ☎ (850) 254-9272, South Wild Olive Avenue, Daytona Beach. Country music fans will appreciate **The Neon Moon & Concert Hall** ☎ (850) 788-2506, 2400 South Ridgewood Avenue, South Daytona. Located in the former location of the Daytona Opry, the hall hosts weekend concerts by national country music acts like Charlie Daniels, Doug Stone, Lonestar and others.

An evening activity for the family to enjoy is **Teauila's Hawaiian Luau Feast** at the Top of the Surf Supper Club in the Ramada Oceanfront Resort ☎ (850) 672-3770 TOLL-FREE (800) 654-6216, 2700 North Atlantic Avenue, Daytona Beach. This nightly dinner performance features Polynesian dances and comedy.

WHERE TO STAY

As one of the world's most famous beach areas, this 23-mile stretch of Atlantic shore is lined with an array of places to stay. The large hotel chains have developed high-rise resorts for that extra special touch while staying on the beach. But you can also choose from many theme-inspired hotels reminiscent of a Las Vegas experience, or smaller clean and quiet privately-owned motels. The annual hotel occupancy is about 60 percent with an average rate of $72 a night. But with so many annual special events — from race

The pier at Daytona Beach.

weekends to spring break — bookings and deposits are often required in advance. Rates are usually higher during these periods.

LUXURY

The **Daytona Beach Hilton** ☎ (850) 767-7350 TOLL-FREE (800) 221-2424 FAX (850) 760-3651, 2637 South Atlantic Avenue, Daytona Beach Shores, is 11 stories high but has the feel of a beach cottage overlooking the Atlantic Ocean. There's a games room for children, a swimming pool, and two restaurants — one where you can sit by the open French doors and enjoy the sea breezes as you dine. The Adam's Mark Daytona Beach Resort ☎ (850) 254-8200 TOLL-FREE (800) 444-ADAM (2326) FAX (850) 253-0275, 100 North Atlantic Avenue, Daytona Beach, is an enormous deluxe oceanfront resort with 437 rooms and cabanas. For a more secluded retreat try **The Villa Bed & Breakfast** ☎ (850) 248-2020 FAX (850) 248-2020 E-MAIL jim@thevillabb.com WEB SITE www.thevillabb.com, 801 North Peninsula Drive, Daytona Beach. The 17-room historic Spanish mansion is convenient to the beach and all attractions but far enough away from the crowds.

Mid-range

Perry's Ocean Edge Hotel ☎ (850) 255-0581 TOLL-FREE (800) 447-0002 FAX (850) 258-7315 E-MAIL relax@perrysoceanedge.com WEB SITE www.perrysoceanedge.com 2209 South Atlantic Avenue, Daytona Beach Shores, is a world of its own with oceanfront rooms, enclosed garden rooms, or rooms overlooking the solarium swimming pool, whirlpool, and solar-heated spa. Along this main road you will find quite a selection of medium-sized hotels with well-appointed rooms and swimming pools, all very conveniently located close to the beach. Among the nicest of them all is **Treasure Island Inn** ☎ (850) 255-8371 TOLL-FREE (800) 543-5070 FAX (850) 255-4984 E-MAIL oceans11@n-jcenter.com WEB SITE www.daytonahotels.com, 2025 South Atlantic Avenue, Daytona Beach Shores, which looks like a pirate landed on this tropical shore, but is very comfortable. Another excellent hotel on this strip is the renovated family resort **Inn on the Beach** ☎ (850) 255-0921 TOLL-FREE (800) 874-0975 FAX (850) 255-3849 E-MAIL res@innonthebeach.com WEB SITE www.innonthebeach.com, 1615 South Atlantic Avenue, Daytona Beach, with a putting green and a shuffleboard court.

Nautilus Inn ☎ (850) 254-8600 TOLL-FREE 1-800-245-0560, 1515 South Atlantic Avenue, Daytona Beach, has very handsome rooms, each with its own balcony, and a beachfront location — and is still moderately priced. Meanwhile, the smaller **Beach Quarters Resort** ☎ (850) 767-3119 TOLL-FREE (800) 332-3119 FAX (850) 767-0883, 3711 South Atlantic Avenue, Daytona Beach Shores, features lively Caribbean decorated one-and two-bed-

room oceanfront suites. All have the luxuries of home, including two TVs and VCRs, while the two-bedroom penthouse has a washer and dryer and a Jacuzzi bathtub.

Inexpensive

On the higher end for the budget-minded traveler, but well worth the few extra dollars, is **Old Salty's Inn** ☎ (850) 252-8090 TOLL-FREE (800) 417-1466 fax (850) 441-5977.WEB SITE www.visitdaytona.com/oldsaltys, 1921 South Atlantic Avenue, Daytona Beach Shores. A nautical paradise with clever Gilligan's Island decorations, the 20-unit oceanfront lodging offers free beach bikes, weekly hot dog roasts, and morning coffee and cookies. A friendly welcome also awaits guests at the **Del Aire Motel** ((850) 252-2563, 744 North Atlantic Avenue, Daytona Beach, right on the beach.

But if you want a less crowded beach experience try going away from Daytona Beach towards Ormond. You can stay at the all-new **Symphony Beach Club** ((850) 672-7373 TOLL-FREE (800) 822-7399 FAX (850) 673-1174 E-MAIL sbclub@bellsouth.net WEB SITE www.visitdaytona.com/symphony, 453 South Atlantic Avenue, Ormond Beach.

WHERE TO EAT

Expensive

The **St. Regis Hotel Restaurant and Patio Bar** ((850) 252-8743, 509 Seabreeze Boulevard, Daytona Beach, has one of the most elegant dining rooms in Daytona, and includes a lively piano bar. The menu is classic French. **La Crêpe en Haut** ((850) 673-1999, 142 East Granada Boulevard, Ormond Beach, on the upper floor of a courtyard mall next door to the Birthplace of Speed Museum, is renowned for its crêpes and sweetbreads, but it also has some superb steaks. Reservations are recommended. For a romantic sunset view on the river try the **Old Florida Club** ((850) 322-9185 fax (850) 767-7483, 4899 Front Street, Ponce Inlet, where the favorites are a pecan-crusted chicken and roasted prime rib.

Moderate

At **Aunt Catfish's on the River** ((850) 767-4768, 4009 Halifax Drive, Daytona Beach, you can have your catfish cooked in any of a number of "down-south" ways: garlicky, Cajun-style, fried, or blackened. Aunt Jim Galbreath also has a specialty called "Florida Cracker" — a concoction of chicken, crab fritters, catfish fingerlings, shrimp, and coleslaw. Four miles (six and a half kilometers) west of Route AIA on Route 92, **Gene's Steak House** ((850) 255-2059, 3674 US Highway 92, has been in operation since 1948 and offers seven different kinds of prime steak cooked over hickory coals.

Seven miles (11 km) south of Daytona on Route A1A is the small village of Ponce de León Inlet, where you will find the **Inlet Harbor Marina and Restaurant** ((850) 767-5590 WEB SITE www.inletharbor.com, 133 Inlet Harbor, Ponce Inlet. The Caribbean atmosphere on a 1,000-foot (300 m) riverwalk specializes in fresh jumbo shrimp lightly fried in a secret recipe. The tomato-based fish chowder is also quite popular. Also to be found in Ponce de León Inlet, at Timmon's Fish Camp, is **Down the Hatch** ((850) 761-4831, 4894 Front Street, Ponce Inlet, which has its own fleet of boats bringing in shrimp and the daily catch from the ocean. The restaurant is now in its third generation of family ownership on the landing.

Inexpensive

Looking for a healthy breakfast or lunch? Try **The Dancing Avocado Kitchen** ((850) 947-2022, 110 South Beach Street, in historic downtown Daytona Beach, which specializes in vegetarian and health-conscious cuisine. Vegetarian pizza served on a whole-wheat flat pita bread, garden burgers, and salads are popular items. The smoothies come in tropical fruit or mocha flavors.

The **Lost Island Restaurant** within the Castaways Beach Resort ((850) 254-8480 E-MAIL Castaway@america.com WEB SITE www.visitdaytona.com/lostisland, features a breakfast and lunch menu that averages $5. **Hog Heaven Real Pit Bar-B-Q** ((850) 257-1212, 37 North Atlantic Avenue, Daytona Beach, has family prices on slow-cooked baby back ribs.

HOW TO GET THERE

Daytona Beach International Airport ((850) 248-8069 WEB SITE www.volusia.org/airport, is one mile from the intersection of Interstate 4 and Interstate 95 and is served by a number of major airlines.

If you're coming to Daytona Beach by car, the two major interstate roads 4 and 95 intersect here. US Highways 1 and 92, as well as Highway A1A (Atlantic Avenue) also lead to this coastal beach and racing Mecca. Amtrak train provides service to nearby DeLand.

If you're flying into Orlando, which is about an hour and a half west of Daytona, a number of regularly scheduled buses or

Bronze cannon detail at the Castillo de San Marcos in St. Augustine.

other transportation companies will drop you off at the Daytona Beach International Airport. **Daytona-Orlando Transit (DOTS)** ((850) 257-5411 has the details.

ST. AUGUSTINE

The juxtaposition of the old and the new is one of the most striking features of St. Augustine. Some of the nation's oldest buildings and churches stand next to modern shopping malls, bars, and restaurants. The city also presents a pleasing blend of large houses with walled courtyards, balconies overhanging winding lanes, and wide tree-lined avenues. Much of the old city is built of *coquina*, a material consisting of seashells embedded in a lime mortar, which adds to its distinctive appearance. Near the old city gate is the massive fortress, Castillo de San Marcos, built over a period of 70 years by the Spanish, which often served as a refuge for the towns people during a siege. Nowadays, the only invaders are the hordes of tourists who have come to appreciate the charms of this lovely city.

BACKGROUND

St. Augustine was founded on September 8, 1565 — 42 years before the British established Jamestown in Virginia — by the Spanish admiral and ex-smuggler Pedro Menéndez de Avilés. He named the colony after San Augustin, having first sighted the coast on August 28, the saint's feast day. The town was intended to be Spain's principal military base along Florida's northeast coast. Nine wooden fortresses were built, all of which succumbed to hostile forces (one of them being a British squadron led by Sir Francis Drake) or to the elements, before construction of the Castillo de San Marcos commenced in 1672. The final touches were put to the castle in 1756.

During the eighteenth century the city was controlled in turn by the English, French, and Spanish (all of whom left their architectural marks on the place). It endured many sieges before being ceded — along with the rest of Florida — to the United States by Spain in 1821. After the Civil War the city began to flourish as a commercial seaport for the nearby plantations, and the arrival of Henry Flagler's railway in the early 1880s brought trainloads of rich tourists from the north into town. Flagler built the luxurious Ponce de León and Alcazar hotels to accommodate them, and used the city as the base to push his railway-and-hotel empire south along the length of Florida's east coast.

GENERAL INFORMATION

The **St. Augustine Chamber of Commerce** ((850) 829-5681, is at One Riberia Street,

St. Augustine, FL 32084, while the **Ponte Vedra Chamber of Commerce** ((850) 285-0666 is at 500 A1A North, Pointer Vedra Beach. The **St. Johns County Visitors & Convention Bureau** ((850) 829-1711 FAX (850) 829-6149 E-MAIL vcb@aug.com, is at 88 Riberia Street, Suite 250, St. Augustine, FL 32084.

For maps, brochures and other tourist collateral, visit the **St. Augustine Beach Visitors Center** ((850) 825-1000 is at 350 A1A Beach Boulevard, St Augustine Beach.

WHAT TO SEE AND DO

St. Augustine is dense with sightseeing attractions, especially in the labyrinthine streets of the old town. A tour in a horse-drawn carriage is a pleasant way of seeing the city: **Colee's Carriages** ☎ (850) 829-2391 or (850) 797-7095 FAX (850) 829-6658, leave from the Bayfront near the Old Fort. Alternatively, you can take one of the red **Sightseeing Trains** ☎ (850) 829-6545 TOLL-FREE (800) 226-6545 E-MAIL trains@aug.com WEB SITE www .redtrains.com, from 170 San Marco Avenue, for a narrated tour that allows you to disembark at any point along the route and rejoin a later train. The trains run every 15 minutes. **St Augustine Trollys** ☎ (850) 829-3800 TOLL-FREE (800) 397-4071, starts from 167 San Marco Avenue on a similar seven-mile narrated tour.

Tours are also available by water. Try **Scenic Cruise** ☎ (850)824-1806 TOLL-FREE (800) 542-8316 FAX (850) 826-0897 E-MAIL scenic @aug.com, 4125 Coastal Highway, which offers morning, afternoon and twilight narrated cruises. With so many old buildings around, you can rest assured that there are also ghost tours available. Guides in period dress lead **Ghostly Walking Tours** at dusk daily. Call ☎ (850) 461-1009 TOLL-FREE (888) 461-1009, for information and reservations.

You can also conduct your own walking tour. A good place to start is the passage beneath the **Old City Gate** which leads to the **Castillo de San Marcos**, a Spanish castle that remained unconquered throughout its military history. For the price of admission you will receive a guided tour through exhibits that re-create the castle's history, but the view from the ramparts is in itself worth the price. Opening times are 8:45 AM to 4:45 PM daily.

Facing the castle, and centered around St. George's Street, is **San Augustin Antiguo**, a historic district where the lifestyle and environment of an eighteenth-century Spanish colonial town have been re-created. Crafts and activities are demonstrated by costumed artisans. The quarter contains some of the oldest buildings in America, including the **Oldest Wooden Schoolhouse** at 14 St. George Street, which dates from 1778 and is the oldest wooden building in the city. The conditions of an eighteenth-century classroom have been re-created inside.

Dating from 1723, the **Oldest House** ☎ (850) 824-0192 WEB SITE www.oldcity.com/ oldhouse, at 14 Francis Street is the oldest house in the city. The Spanish, French, and British refurbishments that have taken place over the centuries can be seen room-by-room in both the decor and the furnishings. The house is open from 9 AM to 5 PM daily.

Construction of the Castillo de San Marcos began in 1672 and was finally completed in 1756.
OVERLEAF: St. Augustine's Bridge of Lions at night.

16 13
16
18

The **Catholic Basilica Cathedral** ☎ (850) 824-2806, in Treasury Street, can be toured daily, and has the oldest parish records in the country. Ponce de León once searched for magic waters in this area, but you should have less trouble finding the **Fountain of Youth Archaeological Park** ☎ (850) 829-3168 TOLL-FREE (800) 356-8222 at 11 Magnolia Avenue, which features a planetarium, space globe, re-created Seminole village, and a fountain. It's open from 9 AM to 5 PM daily.

One of Florida's best collections of antiques, decorative arts, crafts, and musical instruments can be seen at the **Lightner Museum** ☎ (850) 824-2874, in the City Hall complex at King Street and Cordova Street. If you can handle another dose of antiquity, the **Oldest Store Museum** ☎ (850) 829-9729, at Four Artillery Lane, is home to thousands of gloriously useless items of the kind which people have always bought from stores and then thrown in the attic, where they are found years later by great-grandchildren and donated to museums.

The **Spanish Quarter Museum** ☎ (850) 825-6830, recalls the daily life of the early colonists and is at 33 St. George's Street. The **St. Augustine Lighthouse and Museum** ☎ (850) 829-0745, is on the site of Florida's first lighthouse at 81 Lighthouse Avenue.

To have a look at some of the state's most unhurried reptiles, visit the **St. Augustine Alligator and Crocodile Farm** ☎ (850) 824-3337, South Route A1A.

Three state parks show off the natural beauty of the St. Augustine area: the 1,700 acre (690 hectare), bird-rich **Anastasia State Recreation Area** on Anastasia Island, **Faver-Dykes State Park** on the southern tip of St. Johns County, with 752 forested acres, and **Guana River State Park** in Ponte Vedra Beach — a 2,200-acre (900-hectare) preserve with an ancient Spanish well and Native American shell bluffs.

3-D World ☎ (850) 824-1220, on the corner of San Marco Avenue and Castillo Drive, offers 3-D vision-and-motion rides with full surround sound, as well as motion simulator rides. **Potter' Wax Museum** ☎ (850) 829-9056, 17 King Street, was the first wax museum in the United States and has received much acclaim for the authenticity and costuming of its more than 170 models.

If you are feeling thirsty, **St. Augustine San Sebastian Winery** ☎ (850) 826-1594, 157 King Street, offers free sampling in addition to a tour. And if you get a hankering for something sweet, visit the **Whetstone Chocolate Factory** ☎ (850) 825-1700, 2 Coke Road, for a free self-guided tour and chocolate sampling.

Shopping

The **Fiesta Mall** on 1 King Street has insinuated itself very successfully into its old Spanish surroundings despite being home to the trendiest boutiques in town.

The traditionally produced crafts in **San Augustin Antiguo** are all for sale. **City Gate Crafts** at No. 1 St. George Street has a range of tapestries, leather goods, and silver as finely crafted as anything in the old town. The best antiques around can be found at the **Lightner Antique Mall**, King and Granada streets, behind the Lightner Museum. The mall is in the (now drained) swimming pool of Henry Flagler's old Alcazar Hotel and has stalls like **Second Time Around** ☎ (850) 825-4982, which sells estate jewelry, Orientalia, and Fabergé pieces.

A new-age bookstore worth visiting is **Dream Street** ☎ (850) 824-8536 at 64 Hypolita Street. If your pulse quickens at the thought of discounts, drive to **The Outlet Center** ☎ (850) 825-1555, off exit 95 South on Interstate 95.

Nightlife

Spanish food followed by Spanish music and dancing is the forté of **El Caballero** ☎ (850) 824-2096, in the Fiesta Mall. The town's British influence can be seen at the **White Lion** ☎ (850) 829-2388, 20 Cuna Street, where the ale flows copiously during the "Lion's Roar Happy Hour." The **Conch House Marina Lounge** ☎ (850) 829-8646 WEB SITE www.conch-house.com, 57 Comares Avenue, is a quieter place by the river where the notes of a single guitar fill the air.

Sports

One of the best **golf courses** in the area is at the Radisson Ponce de León Golf and Conference Resort ☎ (850) 829-5314 TOLL-FREE (888) 829-5314 WEB SITE www.radison.com/staugustinefl, on Route 1 North. But there is also the newly acclaimed "The Slammer and the Squire" par-72 championship course at the World Golf Village TOLL-FREE (800) 948-4746 WEB SITE www.wgv.com, 21 World Golf Place, eight miles northwest of St Augustine. After your round of golf, be sure to visit their 75,000-sq-ft World Golf Hall of Fame with more than 70 separate exhibits that combine historic artifacts with the very latest in interactive technology.

The ATP Tour International Headquarters Resort ☎ (850) 285-6400, at 200 ATP Tours Boulevard in Pont Vedra has 42 **tennis courts** with 19 championship surfaced courts including red clay, grass, and cushioned hard courts. In St. Augustine there are nine public tennis courts available at four different municipal sites. For additional information contact the city's recreation department ☎ (850) 471-6616.

Fishing is a popular sport in this area, whether it be just off the end of St. Johns County, Lighthouse, or Vilano Beach piers,

or on a chartered fishing tour. For the latter try Kami J light tackle fishing tours with Captain Dennis Goldstein ☎ (850) 825-1971 PAGER (850) 825-5997.

Sailing cruises on the *Voyager* ☎ (850) 377-9292 leave from the downtown Municipal Marina in St. Augustine, while **powerboats, jet skis** and **sailboats** can be rented from Raging Water Sports ☎ (850) 829-5001 at the Conch House Marina Resort, 57 Comares Avenue.

If you are a bit of a daredevil you an **fly in World War II planes**, take a sightseeing

OPPOSITE: Seeing the sights of St. Augustine in a horse-drawn carriage. ABOVE: The Bridge of Lions, St. Augustine leads visitors to some of the oldest buildings in the nation.

flight, or even take flying lessons at North American Top-Gun ☎ (850) 823-3505 TOLL-FREE (800) 257-1636 WEB SITE www.natg.com at 270 Estrella Avenue.

WHERE TO STAY

Luxury

The **Casa de Solana** ☎ (850) 824-3555 FAX (850) 824-3316 WEB SITE www.old city.com/solana/solana2.html, at 21 Aviles Street, overlooks Matanzas Bay and has four rooms furnished with local antiques that come complete with complimentary chocolate and a decanter of sherry.

A landmark of America's oldest city, which has recently been renovated as a hotel, is the **Casa Monica** TOLL-FREE (888) 472-6312, WEB SITE www.grandthemehotels.com. Situated in the very heart of St Augustine, the hotel has 138 luxurious rooms, with four of the hotel's five towers offered as one or two-bedroomed suites. A pool, fitness equipment, fine dining and a piano bar round out its facilities.

Westcott House Inn ☎ (850) 824-4301 TOLL-FREE (800) 513-9814 WEB SITE www.westcotthouse.com, at 146 Avenida Menéndez, is an elegant Victorian building dating from the 1880s, and its eight guest rooms have exquisite European and Oriental furnishings along with a complimentary bottle of wine for each new arrival.

Villas on the Bay ☎ (850) 826-0575 FAX (850) 826-1892 WEB SITE www.thevillas.com at 105 Marine Street offers nine one- and two-bedroom villas on the Intracoastal Waterway furnished with antiques and Jacuzzis, hammocks and private decks.

World Golf Village Resort Hotel ☎ (850) 940-8000 TOLL-FREE (888)446-5301, 500 South Legacy Trail, six miles west of St. Augustine, is the lodging centerpiece of the World Golf Village and offers 300 guest rooms around a lush 10-story atrium.

Mid-range

In the heart of the old town the **Victorian House Inn** ☎ (850) 824-5214 FAX (9040 824-5214 WEB SITE www.oldcity.com.victorian, 11 Cadiz Street, has been transformed from a derelict boarding house into a quaint hotel, tastefully furnished and decorated.

Casa de la Paz ☎ (850) 829-2915 TOLL-FREE (800) 929-2915 WEB SITE www.casadelapaz.com, at 22 Avenida Menéndez, is a Mediterranean-style hotel with a stucco exterior and walled courtyard. There is also the nice touch of a cozy and well-stocked library.

One of the few hotels in St. Augustine that has its own swimming pool is the **Kenwood Inn** ☎ (850) 824-2116 FAX (850) 824-1689 WEB SITE www.oldcity.com/kenwood, at 38 Marine Street, which also has a lovely patio shaded by a large pecan tree. Care and imagination have gone

into the interior design, so that the rooms are decorated according to different "themes" — English, maritime, honeymoon, and so on.

Also in the old town, with ten comfortable, high-ceilinged rooms, plus a small pond in an attractive courtyard, is the **St. Francis Inn** ☎ (850) 824-6068 TOLL-FREE (800) 824-6062 FAX (850) 810-5525 WEB SITE www.stfrancisinn.com, at 279 St. George Street.

The **Conch House Marina Resort** ☎ (850) 829-8646 TOLL-FREE (800) 940-6256 FAX (850) 829-5414 WEB SITE www.oldcity.com/conchhouse, at 57 Comares Avenue, is a hotel

OPPOSITE: The interior of St. Augustine's oldest house, dating from 1723. ABOVE: The Spanish façade of St. Augustine

with its own fishing pier and a 100+ slip marina. It has two restaurants, outside beach bars, and a cocktail lounge built on pilings near the shore.

Inexpensive

The paintings of bullfights might put you off a bit, but otherwise the rooms at the **Monson Bayfront Inn** ☎ (850) 829-2277, 32 Avenida Menéndez, are very comfortable — and some come with a kitchen.

The **Anastasia Inn** ☎ (850) 825-2879 FAX (850) 825-2724 E-MAIL astasiain@aol.com is more aesthetically pleasing than your regular roadside inn and offers good value, with fridge, microwave, and coffeemaker.

WHERE TO EAT

Expensive

The Columbia ☎ (850) 824-3341, at 98 St. George Street, offers delicious Spanish cuisine, including an especially tasty *paella Valenciana*, accompanied by Spanish guitar music.

The German-Swiss Sinatsch family have a wildly eclectic but lovingly prepared array of dishes on their menu at **Le Pavillon** ☎ (850) 824-6202 WEB SITE www.lepav.com, 45 San Marco Avenue.

The Raintree ☎ (850) 824-7211 WEB SITE www.raintreerestaurant.com, at 102 San Marco Avenue, is best known locally for its vast stock of beers and wines, but it also deserves mentioning that they cook the most basic food very well indeed.

Moderate

Conch chowder is the house specialty at **Conch House** ☎ (850) 829-8646, by the ocean at 57 Comares Avenue. For uncomplicated wholesome cooking, go to **Monk's Vineyard** ☎ (850) 824-5888 WEB SITE www.monksvineyard.com, at 56 St. George Street. For "urban cuisine" try the **Gypsy Cab Company** ☎ (850) 824-8244 WEB SITE www.gypsycab.com, at 828 Anastasia Boulevard.

Salt Water Cowboys ☎ (850) 471-2332, 299 Dondanville Road in St. Augustine Beach is a turn of the century fish camp surrounded by saltwater marshes that specializes in oysters and exotic dishes like alligator tail, cooter and frogs legs, as well as favorites like ribs, chicken and seafood.

Inexpensive

A variety of dishes from the Spanish speaking Caribbean are ready to be savored at **Cafe Latino** ☎ (850) 824-2187 at Lighthouse Plaza, 900-J Anastasia Boulevard.

Healthy cuisine, including truly great smoothies, can be had at the **Manatee Cafe** ☎ (850) 826-0210, 179-A San Marco Avenue, while those looking for good hamburgers, salads, and seafood sandwiches will be happy to find themselves at **World Famous Oasis** ☎ (850) 471-3424 WEB SITE www.worldfamousoasis.com, 4000 Route A1A and Ocean Trace Road. There is also live entertainment here plus 24 beers on tap with five satellite stations and 18 televisions for allround sports viewing.

How to Get There

The nearest airport is Jacksonville International. The principal road from the west is Route 207.

JACKSONVILLE

Embracing 840 sq miles (2,177 sq km) on either side of the mouth of the St. Johns River, Jacksonville is the state's largest city (and one of the largest, in area, in America). It is also Florida's financial center. Amelia Island, with its 13 miles (21 km) of beach, and Fernandina Beach lie just to the north of Jacksonville, providing a quiet retreat from the city.

Background

In 1564, a French garrison was established at Fort Caroline, by the mouth of the St. Johns River. However, during the following year it fell to Spanish forces from St. Augustine. Like St. Augustine, Jacksonville was controlled by different European powers for the next two and a half centuries, until Andrew Jackson marched into the city in 1821 as the first American territorial governor of Florida — hence the name Jacksonville. The city assumed prominence during the Civil War as a strategic port, and later for the export of the citrus produce of the hinterland. The arrival of the Florida East Coast Railroad

Eventide and endless tide.

in 1883 ensured that the city became the principal industrial and shipping center of Florida.

GENERAL INFORMATION

The **Jacksonville Chamber of Commerce** ☎ (850) 366-6600, is at 3 Independent Drive, Jacksonville, FL 32202. The **Amelia Island-Fernandina Beach Chamber of Commerce** ☎ (850) 261-3248, at 102 Centre Street, Fernandina Beach, FL 32034, the **Jacksonville and the Beaches Convention and Visitors Bureau** ☎ (850) 798-9111 WEB SITE www.jaxcvb.com, at 201 East Adams Street, and the **Downtown Visitor Center** (no phone) is at Jacksonville Landing, 1 Independent Drive.

Jacksonville has an **International Airport** ☎ (904) 741-4920, and for a **taxi** call either Checker Cabs ☎ (904) 645-5466, or Gator City Taxi ☎ (904) 355-8294.

WHAT TO SEE AND DO

For a quick overview of what Jacksonville has to offer, **Ped-L-Taxi** ☎ (850) 354-3557 421 West Church Street, Downtown, proposes human-powered modern day rickshaw rides. Sightseeing tours along the St. Johns River are best arranged through **River Cruises, Inc.** ☎ (850) 396-2333, while **East Coast Transportation** TOLL-FREE (800) 829-7433 offers a wide array of packaged and customized tours.

Jacksonville has some of the finest art museums in Florida, including the **Jacksonville Museum of Contemporary Art** ☎ (850) 398-8336, 4160 Boulevard Center Drive, which houses the latest trends in the art world. Permanent collections include works by Sam Gilliam and Ed Paschke. The world's largest collection of Meissen porcelain can be seen at the **Cummer Gallery of Art and Gardens** ☎ (850) 356-6857, 829 Riverside Avenue, has a good collection of Western art from 2000 BC. In addition, the formal gardens along the St. Johns River are a delight.

The **Museum of Science and History** ☎ (850) 396-7062, at 1025 Museum Circle, houses permanent and temporary exhibits, along with multimedia shows daily in the planetarium. The **Museum of Southern History** ☎ (850) 388-3574, 4304 Herschel Street, Riverside, preserves the lifestyle and culture of the Antebellum South through displays and artifacts.

A replica of the bastion established by the French in 1564, can be seen at the **Fort Caroline National Memorial** ☎ (850) 641-7155, 12713 Fort Caroline Road, Arlington. Open daily from 9 AM to 5 PM; free of charge. To complete your historical overview, visit the **Kingsley Plantation** ☎ (850) 251-3537, at 11676 Palmetto Avenue on Fort George Island, from where Zephaniah Kingsley ran a worldwide slave trade and lived with his wife — an African princess. Open daily 9 AM to 5 PM. Admission is free.

There are many wonderful parks in the Jacksonville area for hiking, biking, picnicking and even camping. Some offer guided tours, including **Fort Clinch State Park** ☎ (850) 277-7274, 2601 Atlantic Avenue, Fernandina Beach; **Talbot Islands Geo-park** ☎ (850) 251-2323 at 12157 Heckscher Drive, north of the mouth of St. Johns River; **Timucuan Ecological and Historic Preserve** ☎ (850) 641-7155, 12713 Fort Caroline Road, Arlington; and the ocean side **Kathryn Abbey Hanna Park** ☎ (850) 249-4700, 500 Wonderwood Drive, Mayport.

Jacksonville Zoo ☎ (850) 757-4463, at 8605 Zoo Road, half a mile (800 m) east of Heckscher Drive, is a wonderful place for children. It mostly dispenses with cages, employing moats to separate watcher and watched, and also features elephant rides. Alternatively, **Adventure Landing** ☎ (850) 771-2803, on Beach Boulevard, Jacksonville Beach, features go-karts, laser tag, mini golf and other family entertainment.

You can stroll along the **Riverwalk** on the south bank of the St. John's River, then cross the Main Street Bridge to **Jacksonville Landing** where the street life includes musicians, buskers, shops, bars, and cafés.

Beer lovers flock to the **Budweiser Brewery Tour** ☎ (850) 751-8118 at 111 Busch Driver, Northside, for a sneak peak at a century-old beer brewing process. The tour also includes modern-day filling and packaging lines. All this can be thirsty work, so after the tour you are invited to enjoy complimentary tastings in the hospitality room.

Sports

Golfers will be challenged by the links at the Golf Club of Jacksonville ☎ (850) 779-0800, 10440 Tournament Lane, or the Jacksonville Beach Golf Club ☎ (850) 247-6184, 605 Penman Road, Jacksonville Beach. On Amelia Island the City of Fernandina Golf Course ☎ (850) 261-7804 TOLL-FREE (800) 646-5997 at 2800 Bill Melton Road, Fernandina Beach, welcomes visiting players. Amelia Island Plantation ☎ (850)261-6161 TOLL-FREE (800) 874-6878 FAX (850)277-5945, is a resort that has been recognized by *Golf* magazine as one of the country's best golf resorts, offering three courses to guests. Or if you want to have it all arranged before you arrive, Florida's First Coast of Golf TOLL-FREE (888) 859-8334 offers golf packages, with 26 hotels and 22 golf courses to choose from.

Tennis players should ring the city's recreation department ☎ (850) 633-2540, for information about the various municipal courts in Jacksonville.

Football fans can see the Jacksonville Jaguars play home games at the Alltel Stadium, 1 Stadium Place, Midtown Jacksonville.

There is no better way to explore the waterways and beautiful islands near Fernandina Beach than by **kayak**. Kayak Amelia ☎ (850) 321-0697, lets you go on your own (lessons available) or offers guided tours. Inshore and offshore **sport fishing** from Amelia Island is offered by Hot Ticket Charters ☎ (850) 321-1668.

You can join a guided tour on **horseback** from Sea Horse Stable ☎ (850) 261-4878, 7500 First Coast Highway, Amelia Island, and go galloping along the beach. After the ride, take a stroll among the new-Gothic and Victorian architecture of Fernandina Beach, Amelia Island's main village.

Greyhound racing ☎ (850) 646-0001, is held at the Jacksonville Kennel Club, 1440 North McDuff Avenue, Westside.

Shopping

There are over 65 medium-sized shops, catering to almost every taste, at **Jacksonville Landing** ☎ (850) 353-1188, 2 Independent Drive, on the north bank of the St. Johns River. It is a festival marketplace on two levels, with a number of cafés and restaurants to take a break from all the shopping. **Worth Antiques Gallery** ☎ (850) 249-6000, 1316 Beach Boulevard is Jacksonville's largest antique plaza. On Amelia Island, Fernandina Beach's **Center Street** is the main artery of the shopping district.

Nightlife

Bukkets ☎ (850) 246-7701, 222 Front Drive is an oyster bar where the locals hang out for nighttime music and lively chatter, while **Sterlings Cafe** ☎ (850) 387-0700, 3551 St. Johns Avenue, Avondale has a late-night piano bar with good martinis and a range of cognacs, or stop in for coffee and deserts.

Lynch's Irish Pub ☎ (850) 249-5181 at 514 North First Street, Jacksonville Beach, has 33 draught beers on tap, live entertainment, and a midweek happy hour — which stretches from 11 AM to 8 PM. The **Alhambra Dinner Theatre** ☎ (850) 641-1212 WEB SITE www.alhambradinnertheatre.com, at 1200 Beach Boulevard, Southside has a buffet dinner before performances. Shows run from Tuesdays to Sundays with matinees on Saturdays and Sundays.

WHERE TO STAY

Luxury

The resort complex **Amelia Island Plantation** ☎ (850) 261-6161 TOLL-FREE (800) 342-6841 WEB SITE www.aipfl.com, on Amelia Island, Route A1A, is a small town in itself. Accommodation ranges from rooms in the Amelia Inn and Beach Club to villas on the grounds. There are on-site shops, bars and restaurants, and the resort's leisure facilities include three golf courses, an eight-acre (3.2-hectare) tennis enclave, 23 swimming pools, fishing lagoons and miles of walking and biking paths, not to forget the miles of pristine beach. The resort also has an extensive children's program.

The elegant **Ritz Carlton** ☎ (850) 277-1100 TOLL-FREE (800) 241-3333 FAX (850) 261-9064 WEB SITE www.ritzcarlton.com, is also on Amelia Island, at 4750 Amelia Island Parkway. Located on a mile and a half of beachfront, the resort has indoor and outdoor pools, spas, tennis courts, and a fitness and recreation center. Shops, restaurants, and

OVERLEAF: The mighty Castillo de San Marcos was never conquered.

nightly live entertainment make the Ritz more than just a home away from home.

Also on Amelia Island is the charming **Elizabeth Pointe Lodge** ☎ (850) 277-4851 TOLL-FREE (800) 440-0554 WEB SITE www.ElizabethPointeLodge.com, 98 South Fletcher, which was built on the oceanfront in the 1890s. The lodge is Nantucket shingle-style, and is decorated with an abundance of personal effects from the period. There are rocking chairs on the porches, where lemonade is served each afternoon.

The **Omini Hotel** ☎ (850) 355-6664 TOLL-FREE (800) 843-6664, at 245 Water Street, is one of the best hotels in town, within minutes of the business district and steps away from the Jacksonville riverfront.

Mid-range

The inviting **Bailey House** ☎ (850) 261-5390 TOLL-FREE (800) 251-5390 WEB SITE www.bailey-house.com, is at 28 South Seventh Street in Fernandina Beach, where its Victorian gables, porches, and towers greet the eye. The interior tastefully maintains an Old World feel, with antiques and lace curtains gracing spacious rooms.

Every room has a view of the beach at **Sea Turtle Inn** ☎ (850) 249-7402 TOLL-FREE (800) 874-6000 WEB SITE www.seaturtle.com, 1 Ocean Boulevard, Jacksonville Beach. The hotel has a well-equipped games room and an excellent restaurant.

If you would like a room with a 360 degree view, you can rent one on a daily or weekly basis at **The Lighthouse** ☎ (850) 261-4148, 748 Route A1A, Fernandina Beach.

Katie's Light ☎ (850) 277-4851 TOLL-FREE (800) 440-0554, 614 South Fletcher, Amelia Island, is a replica of a Chesapeake Bay lighthouse, and appeared in the movie "Pippi Longstocking". This charming oceanfront house has three bedrooms and can sleep eight, which makes it moderately-priced accommodation for a large group.

Inexpensive

Inexpensive lodging is relatively difficult to find in this area, but a few chain hotels offer perfectly comfortable accommodation. Try **Comfort Inn Mayport** ☎ (850) 249-0313, 2401 Mayport Road, Atlantic Beach, **Red Roof Inn Airport** ☎ (850) 741-4488, 14701 Airport Entrance Road, or **EconoLodge** ☎ (850) 737-1690, 5221 University Boulevard West.

WHERE TO EAT

Expensive

Beach Street Grill ☎ (850) 277-3662, 801 Beech Street, Amelia Island, offers a progressive menu with such delights as salmon with port or citrus baked mahi mahi, as well as daily blackboard specials of fresh local seafood seasoned with cut herbs and homemade sauces, all served in old world homely surroundings.

In the heart of Fernandina's Historic District, **Le Clos** ☎ (850) 261-8100, 20 South Second Street, on Amelia Island, serves Provencale dishes by candlelight in a charming and intimate 1906 cottage setting.

Giovanni's ☎ (850) 249-7787, has been offering fine Italian dining for almost thirty years at 1161 Beach Boulevard, while you'll enjoy American and European cuisine at the elegant yet comfortable **Sterling's Cafe** ☎ (850) 387-0700, 3551 St. Johns Avenue. The **Wine Cellar** ☎ (850) 398-8989, at 1314 Prudential Drive, Jacksonville, is worth a visit for its game alone.

Moderate

For Caribbean cuisine in a vibrant tropical setting, you must try **Manatee Rays** ☎ (850) 241-3138 WEB SITE www.jaxbeach.com/manatee/ray, where seafood, steak, and chicken are prepared with imagination and a lot of coconut. House specialties include shrimp and lobster crepes and black-and-white sesame tuna.

If you like deep-fried chicken gizzards with sautéed peppers and onions you will be happy at the all-American **Homestead** ☎ (850) 249-5240, 1721 Beach Boulevard, Jacksonville Beach, where you can find other, less demanding, dishes as well. Steak-lovers are advised to try the **1878 Steak House** ☎ (850) 261-4049, at 12 North Second Street in Fernandina Beach.

Crawdaddy's ☎ (850) 396-3546, at 1643 Prudential Drive, Jacksonville, includes alligator and traditional Cajun food on its menu while **Island Grille** ☎ (850) 241-1881, 981 North First Street, Jacksonville Beach, serves continental seafood with an island

theme, with salmon tiki as a house specialty. **Brett's** ☎ (850) 261-2660, at One South Front Street, Fernandina Beach, offers a menu of typical Southern fare with amazing views of the Intracoastal waterway.

Inexpensive

Very generous portions of Oriental pork, beef, and chicken are served at **Chiang's Mongolian Bar-B-Q** ☎ (850) 241-3075, 1504 North Route A1A, Jacksonville Beach.

The Seafood Kitchen ☎ (850) 491-4914, 18 North Second Street, Fernandina Beach, is a great place to get inexpensive seafood, like soft-shell-crab sandwiches and barbecued shrimp, in a quaint blue and yellow trimmed house. The nearby **Amelia Island Gourmet Coffee Company** ☎ (850) 321-2111 offers up delicious deli sandwiches, pastries and ice cream.

In Neptune Beach, don't miss out on the chicken wings, cooked cajun, jerk, terriyaki or buffalo style, at **Papa Joe's Grill and Bar** ☎ (850) 246-6406, 100 First Street.

HOW TO GET THERE

Most national and many international airlines have regular flights into Jacksonville International Airport.

The principal north-south roads are Interstate 95 and Routes 1 and A1A, while the main highway from the west is Interstate 10.

Two perfect ways to end another glorious day in St. Augustine; with a cold drink on a pier cafe, or sailing into the sunset.

Central Florida

EVIDENCE THAT FLORIDA WAS ONCE COVERED by the sea runs from north of Ocala south to Sebring, above Spring Lake, in the form of a limestone ridge which was once a prehistoric coral reef. This ridge is the backbone of the Florida peninsula and rises to about 330 ft (100 m) above sea level. Many of the hillsides along the ridge are lined with citrus groves, while the plains to either side form the state's vegetable garden. In the north, in the hills of Ocala, grass and corrals signify that this is horse country: while in the south, around the old cowboy town of Kissimmee, are the sandy scrublands of cattle country.

The agricultural plains are fed by the pellucid waters of thousands of springs, rivers, and lakes. The waters of Ocklawaha River, which runs through the Ocala National Forest, and the chain of lakes created by it are particularly beautiful, which makes fishing and boating even more enjoyable than usual. The Ocala National Forest, the largest sandy pine forest in the world, is understandably very popular with riders, campers, and seasonal hunters.

Oh yes, there's also Walt Disney World.

BACKGROUND

Early settlers, known as "crackers" (derived from the crack of the cattle whips they used to drive cattle), were tough and industrious people who worked a living from the land, and herded the same breed of cattle that the Spanish had introduced to the region in the sixteenth century. The citrus and cattle industries established by the crackers became the foundation of the region's economy, ensuring that Orlando grew to become one of the state's most important commercial centers. The farmers and ranchers of the region lived alongside the warlike Seminole natives. A band of them massacred 139 United States soldiers on December 28, 1835, igniting the bloody and bitter Second Seminole War. It is generally accepted that Orlando derives its name from one Orlando Reeves, a soldier who was killed fighting the Seminoles.

The coming of the steamboat encouraged tourism and greatly boosted the economy of central Florida, while the arrival of the railroads in the 1880s added further impetus to the area's development. Then, in 1971, something happened. Walt Disney World opened 20 miles (32 km) south of Orlando at Lake Buena Vista, and suddenly central Florida was the most popular vacation destination in the world.

WALT DISNEY WORLD

The Disney people chose the Orlando area as the site for their Eastern United States theme park because of the availability of flat land at reasonable (cheap) prices, good transportation facilities, and a year-round sunny climate. Eventually, after much surreptitious wheeling and dealing, Disney's agents slowly but surely acquired 28,000 acres (11,336 hectares) — that's 42 sq miles (67 sq km), an area twice the size of Manhattan — because Walt Disney wanted enough space to build a wholly self-contained and self-servicing complex. Disney died in 1966, three years before work started on the site. The first visitor walked through the gates in the summer of 1971; by 1985 another 250 million had walked through, making it easily the greatest tourist attraction in the world.

There was a month-long celebration in 1982 for the opening of **Epcot Center**, a futuristic showcase extension to the park. "Epcot" stands for Experimental Prototype Community of Tomorrow, and was Walt Disney's own brainchild: he envisioned a self-governing community existing alongside the theme parks. The final result worked out more or less as Mr. Disney had planned it: the Walt Disney World Vacation Kingdom (to give it its full name) is known in the Florida statute books as the Reedy Creek Improvement District, which is the legal governing body of the entire Disney complex, with powers to enforce building codes, construct roads, and supervise the election of mayors to the district's two towns, Bay Lake and Lake Buena Vista.

A third theme park, **Disney MGM Studios**, showcases all the glamour, technical wizardry and artistry associated with the silver screen.

The Magic Kingdom gives a surrealistic quality to the Disney World skyline.

The latest theme park, **Disney's Animal Kingdom**, was opened in April 1998 and features safaris, encounters with dinosaurs and musical stage shows. If it wasn't for the Disney characters wondering around, you might almost believe that you've been transported to a genuine African game reserve. Just a year after its opening, Disney unveiled a new "land" at Animal Kingdom based on Asian wildlife, part of a property-wide expansion campaign which is the largest in the 27-year history of Walt Disney World Resort.

So, at the time of writing, the 30,500-acre (12,300-hectare) Walt Disney World resort now comprises four theme parks, three water adventure parks, 27 resort hotels, six golf courses, the Disney Institute, the Wedding Pavilion, the Wide World of Sports Complex, and Downtown Disney.

The facilities and services of this utopian kingdom are indeed highly advanced: Disneyland has the first fully electronic telephone system in the world, a land transport system based on an elevated, noiseless, and computerized monorail, and boasts — Mr. Ripley would have loved this — a fleet of over 400 ships, from steamboats to submarines, making it the fifth largest navy in the world.

GENERAL INFORMATION

For all inquiries about Disney attractions and services in the Orlando area contact **Walt Disney World Guest Information** ((407) 824-4321 WEB SITE www.disneyworld.com, Box 10040, Lake Buena Vista, FL 32830-0040.

Try to arrive at Disney World before 9 AM as the place becomes packed very quickly. Follow the signs either to the Magic Kingdom, Epcot Center, MGM Studios or Animal Kingdom. Be sure to remember the name of your parking lot and line number. Trams take visitors from the lots to the Ticket and Transportation Center (TTC), where you buy tickets for entry to the parks.

It's almost impossible to see everything in all the parks on the same day. They are just too huge and too far apart. Try to set aside two days for each park and another week if you don't want to miss the outlying attractions of the complex. The Disney website also includes many links to testimonies from previous visitors and articles from Family.com on the best way to enjoy the park.

To avoid the worst crowds, visit the Magic Kingdom, MGM Studios and Animal Kingdom in the afternoon — or, better yet, in the evening — and Epcot in the morning, working your way back to the entrance gates from the more distant attractions. But be prepared to wait in lines whenever you go.

There are reports that Disney is considering giving visitors reservations for rides, which means that if you arrive at the ride at the correct time, you won't have to suffer the traditional one- to two-hour waits at top attractions. Until then, a good way to avoid the worst lines at popular rides is boarding during the daily parades.

Disney World opens at 9 AM year round (although they often let you in early). The one exception is Animal Kingdom which opens at 8 AM. In the summer months, closing hours range from 7 PM to midnight (earlier in the winter months). Peak times are Christmas through New Year and all major United States holidays. Late August is the summer's quietest period. The periods with the least crowds over the last few years have been the first two weeks of February and the first two weeks of December.

Tickets

All tickets and passports can be bought from the Ticket and Transportation Center; tickets can also be bought at the Orlando International Airport, many hotels in the area and at kiosks around Orlando or you can order them before you travel by contacting Walt Disney World's **Admissions Office** ☎ (407) 824-4321 WEB SITE www.disneyworld.com, Box 10040, Lake Buena Vista, FL 32830-0040. Tickets can als be ordered online at the above web site.

Mail-order tickets take about five weeks to arrive. All prices are subject to variation but can be confirmed by Walt Disney World Information at ☎ (407) 934-7639.

Transportation

Transport is both varied and efficient. The monorail operates daily from 7:30 AM to 11 PM from the Transportation and Ticket Center (TTC), all other modes of transport depart to the various attractions. All buses are color-coded according to their destination. If you prefer to travel around by water, Disney's ferries and launches also leave from TTC.

Maps are available from Guest Relations at City Hall in the Magic Kingdom; Innovations East, Epcot Center; Hollywood Boulevard in MGM; and just left of the entrance in Animal Kingdom. Otherwise you can download a map from the web site.

WHAT TO SEE AND DO

The Magic Kingdom

This truly magic park features more than 40 major adventures spread across 107-acres (43-hectares) including restaurants, shops

and seven theme areas: Adventureland, Liberty Square, Frontierland, Main Street, Fantasyland, Tomorrowland and Mickey's Toontown Fair.

A monorail or ferry boat takes you from TTC to the gates of the Magic Kingdom in a few minutes. You walk through the front gates into the **Town Square** which contains the City Hall, information center, lost-and-found office, and a railway station from which you can take a 15-minute train journey around the park. The square is a lively place with stalls, Dixieland bands, and Disney characters to welcome you.

Stretching away from the Town Square is **Main Street**, a bustling thoroughfare lined with arcades, ice cream parlors, cinemas, shops, cafés, and restaurants with turn-of-the-century façades. Disney characters parade down the street every day at 3 PM; and from 9 PM to 11 PM there's the **IllumiNations Parade** of giant floats.

The Disney World elevated monorail speeds past Space Mountain OPPOSITE to Epcot Center and Spaceship Earth ABOVE.

At the end of Main Street you cross a small bridge over a moat to the 18-story **Cinderella's Castle**. The castle is at the heart of the Magic Kingdom; from here you can take any of the routes leading to the various other "Lands".

Adventureland is one of the most crowded in the kingdom. Top attractions are the **Pirates of the Caribbean**, which, among other buccaneering experiences, takes you through a cannon battle; the **Swiss Family Robinson Treehouse**, a labyrinthine concrete structure offering great views of the park; and the **Jungle Cruise**, which manages to go down the Nile and up the Amazon in one 10-minute journey.

Frontierland takes you back to the Wild West with attractions like **Big Thunder Mountain Railroad**, a hair-raising runaway-train ride through a mine, and the **Country Bear Jamboree** with its singing, cavorting, audio-animatronic bears. For relative peace try **Tom Sawyer Island**, which can be reached by taking a raft.

The fourth "Land" is **Liberty Square**, it features Colonial and American history. Adults and older children will enjoy the **Hall of Presidents**, with animated figures of the nation's bygone leaders delivering famous speeches, and a 15-minute movie charting the history of the American Constitution. Slightly more attention-getting is the popular **Haunted House** and the riverboat that takes you past scenes depicting the Old West.

Fantasyland is particularly popular with children. The attractions include a replica of Captain Nemo's submarine from *20,000 Leagues Under the Sea*, a trek through a forest to meet Snow White and the Seven Dwarfs, and Cinderella's Golden Carousel.

Disney's various fairytale and cartoon characters wander the streets of Fantasyland at frequent intervals. Another popular attraction in this part of the park is **Small World**, a boat journey through a dream world of dolls representing the global village in songs. The adventures of everyone's favorite bear come to life in the summer, when guests can join Pooh and friends for a magical journey through a storybook page and into the Hundred acre Wood in the **Many Adventures of Winnie the Pooh,** which replaces Mr. Toad's Wild Ride.

The **Space Mountain** roller-coaster in **Tomorrowland** is heart-stopping (children under three cannot go on it and those under seven must be accompanied by an adult).

ABOVE TO OPPOSITE BOTTOM: The Moroccan, English, French, and Chinese pavilions at Epcot Center.

The newest attraction in the area is **Buzz Lightyear's Space Ranger Spin,** where guests join forces with Buzz to defend the Earth's supply of batteries from the evil Emperor Zurg.

The colorful buildings and streetscapes at **Mickey's Toontown Fair** look like something straight from a cartoon, which makes it popular with the younger kids. Besides frequent appearances by characters such as Mickey and Minnie and Pluto, the area offers a tot-sized thrill ride called **Gadget's Go Coaster**, an interactive wacky ride on **Roger Rabbit's Car Toon Spin**, and **Donald's Boat,** where wannabe sailors climb a rope ladder and help to steer this double-decker houseboat.

The Epcot Center

The **Experimental Prototype Community of Tomorrow** (Epcot) is an education-oriented complex about twice the size of the Magic Kingdom, with two distinct areas

— **Future World** and **World Showcase** — separated by a lagoon.

It's best to explore World Showcase in the morning and Future World later in the day to beat the crowds. You enter the Epcot Center beneath **Spaceship Earth** (a 17-story spherical structure; 180 ft or 55 m at its highest point) where you can pick up a guide to both areas at **Earth Station**. Future World starts at Spaceship Earth, and World Showcase can be reached by taking the sidewalk which skirts the lagoon.

Future World focuses on discovery and scientific achievements while World Showcase is a collection of eleven national pavilions with displays, films and exhibits on each country's art, culture and lifestyles.

New at Epcot is **Test Track,** the longest and fastest attraction in Disney history. Nearly a mile in length and reaching speeds of 65 mph, this ride immerses guests in an automobile testing ground including a wildly-out-of-control brake test and hairpin turns.

Disney MGM Studios

This park is a working movie, television, radio and animation studio as well as a theme park. At the center of the park, inside a replica of the famous Chinese Theater of Hollywood, **The Great Movie Ride** takes you on a 20-minute train journey through Hollywood history and brings you face-to-face-with the big stars, in audio-animatronics form.

The **Backstage Studio Tour** takes you behind the scenes of a working motion

picture and TV studio to see the costumes, props and backlot. You also discover how moviemakers create floods, earthquakes and gigantic fires during a terrifying excursion through Catastrophe Canyon.

Magic of Disney Animation depicts Disney artists at work on animated features and reveals TV production techniques used in such movies as *Honey, I Shrunk the Kids*. Jim Henson's Muppet Vision 3-D introduces the *Muppet Show* characters.

Among new attractions is the **Rock 'n' Roller Coaster** which features an original soundtrack that blasts into each ride vehicle as they progress through a cutting-edge, high-speed adventure. Shows on offer include "The Hunchback of Notre Dame: A Musical Adventure," and "Fantasmic!", a nighttime spectacle of lights, lasers, fireworks and water animation, plus the daily *Mulan* parade.

The studio is next to Epcot Center off Buena Vista Drive.

Animal Kingdom

Five hundred acres (202 hectares) of Central Florida farmland have been transformed into green savannahs and rainforest here, home to more than a thousand exotic animals and four million trees and shrubs.

The park's centerpiece is the 14-story **Tree of Life**, carved with images of 300 animals. There is also a re-creation of a colonial East African town and an old-fashioned train called the **Wildlife Express**. Another highlight is the **Kilimanjoro Safari**, a 20-minute adventure ride in open-sided trucks, during which time you are very likely to see elephants, giraffes, zebras and maybe even a lion. For the very best animal sightings, plan to go early in the morning or late in the afternoon.

Thrill rides include **Countdown to Extinction**, where you ride a Time Rover back 65 million years to the days of the dinosaurs. Shows include the Broadway caliber "Festival of the Lion King" and "Journey into Jungle Book," both of which employ part-human, part-puppet casts. "It's Tough to be a Bug" is a 3-D show, similar to Epcot's "Honey I Shrunk the Audience." Twice daily there is a **March of the Animals parade** through Safari Village.

Asia, the newest area within Disney's Animal Kingdom, features **Kali River Rapids**, where guests are launched on a 12-person raft into the turbulent Chakranadi River for a wild and wet ride. The **Maharajah Jungle Trek** is a fascinating walking journey through a tropical rainforest environment, and **Flight of Wonder** is a humorous show that looks at the beauty and diversity of birds.

Other Attractions

Blizzard Beach Water Park ☎ (407) 824-4321, is a water park fashioned after a ski resort with runs down 120-ft (40-m) Mt. Gushmore into a tropical lagoon. It's situated next to Disney's new All-Star Resorts. Suitable for older kids.

Water Country USA ☎ (407) 824-4322, is

a popular family spot in summer with families with medium intensity thrills. It features a 56-acre (23-hectare) water playground with the world's largest wave pool.

Typhoon Lagoon TOLL-FREE (800) 423-8368, is Florida's largest water park. The grounds has both shady and open sunny areas and features **Aquazoid**, a sci-fi fantasy ride.

Sports

Golf is a big deal at Disneyworld, with 99 holes spread across six courses. Osprey Ridge and Eagle Pines are highly acclaimed courses created by Tom Fazio and Pete Dye. More information can be obtained from ☎ (407) 939-653, while golf vacations can be arranged through your travel agent or by calling ☎ (407) 934-7639. Non-golfers can tee off at a wacky miniature course called **Winter Summerland**.

More than 30 sports from aerobics to wrestling are offered at **Disney's Wild World of Sport Complex**. The center is designed to accommodate professional-caliber training and competition, tournaments, and vacation fitness activities. The complex is the spring training home for the Atlanta Braves of Major League Baseball, site of the United States men's clay-court tennis championships, and the training and development site of the Harlem Globetrotters basketball team. It also boasts the world's only permanent **NFL Experience**, an interactive football playground which

The Swan Hotel runs a free ferry service to Disney World.

allows fans to test their speed, passing, and field goal kicking ability.

The **Richard Petty Driving Experience** allows guests to get into the driver's seat of an authentic stock car for high speed thrills at the World Speedway.

Disney World also features tennis courts; jogging paths; horseback riding; biking; pools and lakes for swimming, boating, parasailing, water skiing and fishing; and a wedding pavilion for those who want to take the ultimate plunge.

Shopping

Shops seem to appear at every corner in the Disney World theme parks. If you have any money left, visit the **Marketplace** in Downtown Disney, recently remodeled with more than two dozen stores — including the planet's largest collection of Disney character merchandise at World of Disney. The mall offers free delivery from any shop to guests staying in the resort. The prices, however, are high; bargain hunters are better off shopping in Orlando.

Nightlife

In Downtown Disney, the new **Cirque du Soleil** show "La Nouba" features circus acts and street entertainment with 72 artists from around the world. **The House of Blues**, also in Downtown Disney, West Side, has live concerts, a Gospel Brunch and Mississippi Delta soul food. If you're in the mood for a movie, Florida's largest selection is showing at the **AMC 24 Theatres Complex**.

Pleasure Island is a six-acre nightclub theme park near the Marketplace that features seven nightclubs; including the **BET Soundstage Club**, a 5,000 sq ft waterfront club featuring live jazz, R&B, soul and hip hop as well as programming from Black Entertainment Television network. **Wildhorse Saloon** presents live country music, dance, and entertainment as well as barbecue meals. Burgers, salads and pasta top the menu at the 400-seat **Planet Hollywood**. Check out Pleasure Island's **West End Stage** for life performances by big-name music acts.

Disney's Boardwalk, near Epcot, offers a wide variety of nighttime entertainment. **Atlantic Dance** is a place for music, dancing and romancing with live swing music and free dance lessons Sunday through Thursday. Sports video entertainment and sports news rule at **ESPN Club**. **Jellyrolls** offers spontaneous interaction between guest and performers on dueling pianos. Buskers perform around the Boardwalk every night.

Hotels in the Disney resort and the cities in surrounding areas also have a wide array of nightlife opportunities.

WHERE TO STAY

Walt Disney World and environs offers a truly vast selection of hotels to chose from. Your first decision is whether to stay inside or outside the Disney resort grounds. The main advantages of being in the grounds are that you are close to all the things you want to see, with free use of the quick and efficient internal transportation. Moreover, on-site guests receive a guest identification card which allows them to charge anything at Disney World (except in the Magic Kingdom) to their hotel room. And guests are also offered discounted tickets and early entrance into the theme parks.

Your second decision will be whether to stay in one of the hotels owned by Disney World, most of these hotels overlook Bay

Lake next to the Magic Kingdom, or to stay in one of the independently owned hotels within the grounds at Lake Buena Vista in the Walt Disney World Village. These hotels are further away from the main attractions, but most run a shuttle service to and from the theme parks. Some of the hotels in the village have self-catering facilities and there is a supermarket in the shopping complex nearby.

If you need help making these decisions, call **Walt Disney Central Reservation Office** ☎ (407) 934-7639 WEB SITE www.wdw.reservations.disney.go.com, Box 10100, Lake Buena Vista, FL 32830, for a free Disney World accommodation videotape. To reserve a room in any on-site hotels contact the Central Reservation Office as far in advance as possible.

The reservation office can also arrange all-inclusive packages, with admission tickets, car rentals, and hotel reservations inside or outside the Disney World grounds.,

Don't expect bargains at on-site hotels, whether Disney-owned or not.

Disney Hotels

All of the hotels mentioned below should be contacted through the central reservation office mentioned above.

The **Yacht Club** and **Beach Club** are elegant (and expensive) resorts located at Epcot's back door. For ambiance think quaint New England seaside cottages and grand hotels of the 1870s. Shared amenities include a water area with whirlpools, slides and hot springs.

Disney's Boardwalk Inn has 378 rooms and aims to be reminiscent of the traditional bed-and-breakfast inns found along the United States mid-Atlantic coast.

The 644 roomed **Polynesian Village** tries to re-create the atmosphere of a South Pacific island, with a miniature "rainforest" in the lobby consisting of palm trees and sundry exotic plants. The accommodation is in 11 three-story "longhouses". Most of the rooms have balconies and some overlook the Magic Kingdom. The hotel has its own beach and marina where you can rent canoes and boats for sailing, fishing, and water-skiing on the lake.

The 1,053-room **Contemporary Hotel** has the monorail running straight through its lobby. This 15-story, ultra-modern hotel is constructed mainly of glass. Facilities include two swimming pools, health club

OPPOSITE: The Floridian Hotel at Disney World. ABOVE: Surely you joust: the Middle Ages live in Kissimmee, at the Medieval Times Restaurant.

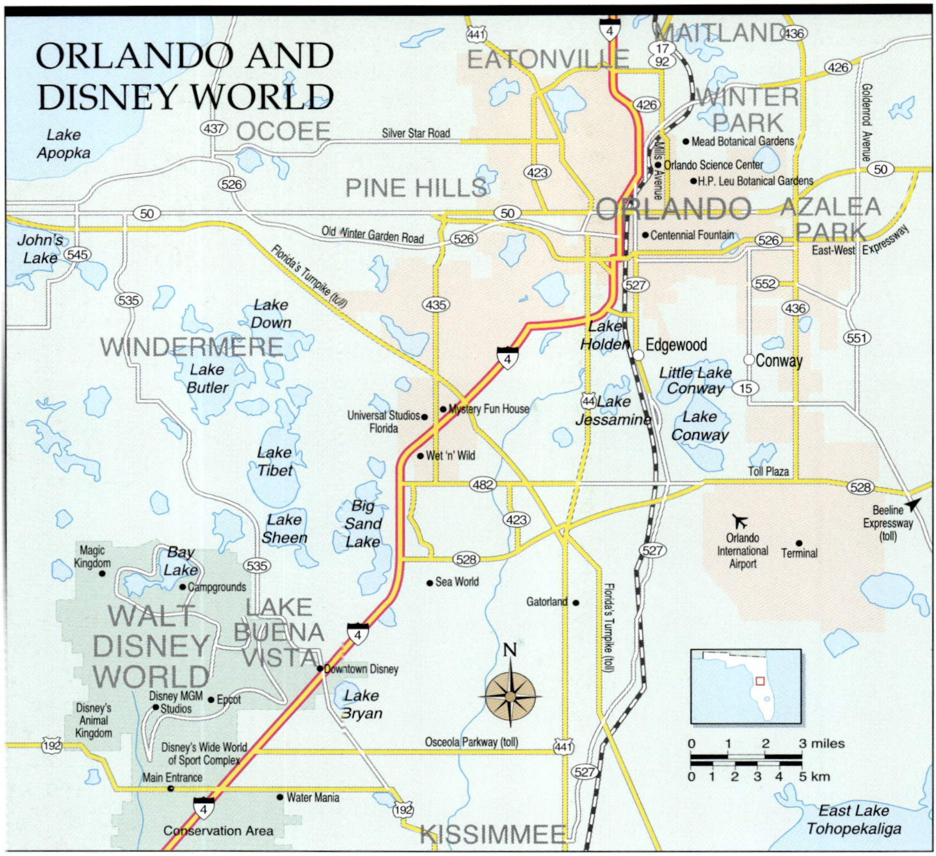

and sauna, and penthouse lounge with dancing and entertainment every night. The hotel is next to Bay Lake.

The massive (1,900 rooms) **Coronado Springs Resort** offers Spanish-style roofs and adobe walls, a five-story Mayan pyramid in the center of a family fun pool, plus 95,000 sq ft (9,000 sq m) of convention space.

The smallest of the medium priced hotels, the **Port Orleans**, offers Southern charm with a Mardi Gras-themed pool.

The least expensive Disney hotels (rooms for under $100) are the three "All-Star" resorts — the **All-Star Movies Resort**, the **All-Star Music Resort**, and the **All-Star Sports Resort**. Amenities are pretty basic and the rooms are small but adequate if you don't plan on spending much time indoors.

Disney Institute offers adults and families accommodation with a choice of stimulating instruction in subjects like photography, cooking, animation, and gardening.

You can also opt to camp in one of the 784 sites at **Disney's Fort Wilderness Campground** ☎ (407) 939 2267 WEB SITE www.disneyworld.com, next to Bay Lake in the Disney World grounds. You can rent self-contained trailers that accommodate four to six people, bring your own trailer, or simply pitch a tent. There are two "trading posts" in the campground, and recreational facilities include canoeing, riding, and Disney film shows.

Independent Hotels

Buena Vista Palace ☎ (407) 827-2727 TOLL-FREE (800) 327-2990 FAX (407) 827-6034 WEB SITE www.bvp-resort.com, 1900 Lake Buena Vista Drive, Lake Buena Vista, is a 27-story, 841-room hotel which cost $93 million to build. Many of its modern, spacious rooms overlook Epcot Center. Facilities include swimming pools, tennis courts, games room, and several bars and restaurants, including

Arthur's 27, a splendid top-floor eatery offering great views of Disney World.

The **Hilton Hotel** ☎ (407) 827-4000 TOLL-FREE (800) 782-4414 FAX (407) 827-6369 WEB SITE www.hilton.com, at 1751 Hotel Plaza Boulevard, Lake Buena Vista, has very confortable rooms with the latest in electronic technology, with all sorts of devices that control the central heating, the air conditioning, and the television. The service is excellent.

At the Colonial-style **Grosvenor Resort** ☎ (407) 828-4444 TOLL-FREE (800) 624-4109 FAX (407) 827-6369 WEB SITE www.grosvenorresort.com, 1850 Hotel Plaza Boulevard, Lake Buena Vista, all the rooms are handsomely decorated and each has its own VCR (you can rent movies from the hotel). There are two swimming pools, basketball, and volleyball courts, and a children's playground.

Other luxury hotels include the **Hotel Royal Plaza** ☎ (407) 828-2828 TOLL-FREE (800) 248-7890 FAX (407) 827-6338 WEB SITE www.royalplaza.com, at 1905 Hotel Plaza Boulevard; and the **Doubletree Guest Suites** ☎ (407) 934-1000 TOLL-FREE (800) 222-8733 FAX (407) 934-1015 WEB SITE www.doubletreehotels.com, at 2305 Hotel Plaza Boulevard, which offers one-and two-bedroom suites with kitchen facilities, a living and dining area, a sofa bed and two televisions.

Hotels Outside Disney World

Two areas close to Disney World offer a wide selection of accommodation: the Maingate area, east off of Interstate 4 just above Disney World's northern entrance; and the Route 192 Corridor between Disney World and Kissimmee.

Expensive

Hyatt Orlando ☎ (407) 396-1234 TOLL-FREE (800) 223-1234, 6375 West Irlo Bronson Memorial Highway, has a surprising sense of seclusion even though it's located off busy Highway 192. The 922 rooms are arranged in four buildings, each with its own pool and whirlpool. Located five minutes from Disneyworld.

The **Doubletree Orlando Resort and Conference Center** ☎ (407) 396-1400 TOLL-FREE (800) 239-6478, 3011 Maingate Lane, is less than a mile from the park and offers pool, restaurants, gym, washer/dryers, and even in-room Playstations to use while you wait for your wash.

Mid-range

Moderately priced accomodation in the Disney World area includes the **Days Inn Orlando Lakeside** ☎ (407) 351-1900 TOLL-FREE (800) 777-3297 fax k(407) 363-1749 WEB SITE www.thhotels.com, 7335 Sand Lake Road; the **Sheraton World** ☎ (407) 352-1100 TOLL-FREE (800) 325-3535 fax (407) 352-3679, 6515 International Drive; **Courtyard by Marriott Maingate** ☎ (407) 396-4000 TOLL-FREE (800) 568-3352, 7675 Irlo Bronson Memorial Highway; and the **Holiday Inn Nikki Bird Resort** ☎ (407) 396-7300 TOLL-FREE (800) 206-2747, 7300 Irlo Bronson Memorial Highway.

Inexpensive

There are dozens of budget motels to choose from here; including the **Knight's Inn Orlando Maingate West** ☎ (407) 396-4200 TOLL-FREE (800) 944-0062 FAX (407) 396-8838, 7475 West Irlo Bronson Highway; the **Quality Inn Plaza** ☎ (407) 996-8585 TOLL-FREE (800) 999-8585, 9000 International Drive; **Comfort Inn Maingate** ☎ (407) 396-7500 TOLL-FREE (800) 223-1628, 7571 West Irlo Bronson; **Days Inn Maingate West** ☎ (407) 396-1000 TOLL-FREE (800) 327-9173, 7980 West US Highway 192; and the **Apollo Inn** ☎ (407) 846-0646 TOLL-FREE (800) 999-2765, 670 East Vine Street.

WHERE TO EAT

There are literally hundreds of dining possibilities in Disney World and the surrounding area. For reservations at Disney restaurants call ☎ (407) 939-3463.

At World Showcase in Epcot you can sample just about all the major cuisines of the world, including Chinese at Lotus Blossom Cafe and Nine Dragons Restaurants; French at Boulangerie Patisserie and Les Chefs de France; German at Biergarten and Sommerfest; Japanese at Tempura Kiku, Teppanyaki Dining Room, and Yakitori House; Mexican at San Angel Inn and Cantina de San Angel; or Norwegian at Kringla Bakeri Og Kafe and Restaurant Akershus.

Another good cluster of restaurants is along the Boardwalk. Here you'll find the moderately priced Spoodles, which offers up imaginative Mediterranean specialties from Spain, France, North Africa, Greece, and Italy. The Flying Fish Cafe is an expensive steak and seafood restaurant with open-kitchen seating. More reasonable "pub grub" can be found at the Big River Grille or Brewing Works, which also brews five specialty beers on-site.

Other restaurants to note include **Fulton's Crab House** ☎ (407) 828-8996, 1670 Buena Vista Drive in Downtown Disney Pleasure Island. Inside a replica turn-of-the-century riverboat, this 19,000-sq-ft (180-sq-m) restaurant has six separate dining rooms serving up signature seafood recipes including seven types of crab. The same owners also run **Portobello Yacht Club** ☎ (407) 934-8888, 1650 Buena Vista Drive, a casual restaurant with innovative contemporary regional Italian cuisine with an emphasis on Tuscan dishes.

Latin singing sensation Gloria Estefan and husband Emilio have joined forces to create **Bongos Cuban Cafe** in Downtown Disney, West Side. With 16,000 sq ft (150 sq m) of indoor and outdoor dining area, the restaurant is housed in a wacky Art-Deco building dominated by a two-story adobe pineapple. The spicy ethic menu was created by Quintin and Carmen Lario from the popular Larios on the Beach restaurant in Miami's South Beach.

Also in Downtown Disney, West Side, is **Planet Hollywood** ☎ (407) 827-7827, 1506 East Buena Vista Drive, another outlet of the prolific chain owned by Arnold Schwarzenegger, Sylvester Stallone and other Hollywood stars. In the same area you'll find the **Wolfgang Puck Café** offering their famous wood-fired pizzas, pasta dishes and fresh salads.

A new entry to the area's themed restaurants is the **Rainforest Cafe** ☎ (407) 939-3463, in Downtown Disney Marketplace, where you're greeted by an animated gorilla and a 65-ft volcano with cascading waterfalls and lush vegetation. The menu features pastas, salads, and sandwiches, and the brownies and sundaes are a sure-fire hit with kids of any age.

How to Get There

No problem. Many international airlines and over 30 national carriers serve Orlando International Airport. Delta, TOLL-FREE (800) 221-1212, also offers package tours to Disney World.

For those traveling by car, the Interstate 4 approaches Disney World from the west and northeast (Tampa and Daytona), and goes by the entrance to Disney World. From the northwest or the Gold Coast, you approach on Florida's Turnpike (a tollway) and join Interstate 4 at Junction 75. If you are traveling from the south, take Route 27 as far as Junction 54, where you join the Interstate 4.

GREATER ORLANDO

The Greater Orlando area, with a population approaching one million, is one of the most rapidly expanding metropolises in America. The growth of the city, and its transformation into a business and tourist center, is largely due to the proximity of Walt Disney World. However, the city does have its own character and attractions distinct from those of Disney World.

Background

United States soldiers became the first non-native inhabitants of the area in 1838, when Fort Gatlin was established as a military outpost to keep the local Seminoles in check. By 1875, the Seminoles had been subdued, increasing numbers of settlers were coming into the area, and the slowly growing community around the fort had been named Orlando. The city's early economy was based on citrus produce and cattle, although the exceptionally cold weather during 1884 and 1885 wiped out many of the citrus groves in the area. The local farmers, ever resourceful, turned to cereals and vegetables as replacement crops.

By the 1880s, the railroad had reached Central Florida, bringing tourists who were attracted to the waters and springs of the region. Orlando was a favorite base for these visitors, whose custom further boosted the city's economy. In those days, Orlando could offer only a handful of hotels for visitors to choose from, but the city has steadily grown and prospered over the years and there are now some 60,000 hotel rooms in the Greater Orlando area.

GENERAL INFORMATION

The **Orlando Regional Chamber of Commerce** ☎ (407) 425-1234 FAX (407) 839-5020, can be contacted at PO Box 1234, Orlando, Fl 32802-1234. The **Greater Orlando Tourist Information Center** ☎ (407) 425-0412, is at 8445 International Drive, Orlando, FL 32819, where you can pick up a complimentary copy of the guidebook, *Discover Orlando*. The **Orlando-Orange County Convention and Visitors Bureau** TOLL-FREE (800) 643-4492, is at 6700 Forum Drive, Suite 100, Orlando, FL 32821.

For flight information call **Orlando International Airport** ☎ (407) 825-2001.

WHAT TO SEE AND DO

Although Disney World might be the "king of the hill" the Orlando area features dozens of other worthwhile attractions — a greater concentration of tourist activities than any other place in the United States.

To save a little on the high entrance fees, look into the **Orlando FlexTicket**, which gives unlimited admission to Sea World, Universal Studios, Wet 'n' Wild, and Busch Gardens of Tampa Bay.

The "Tourist Trail", along Route 192 west from Disney World, includes **Old Town** ☎ (407) 396-1964, 5770 West Route 192 in Kissimmee. Old Town is home to a variety of Old-World-style shops, restaurants and live entertainment. Next-door, real thrillseekers can free-fall (wearing a safety harness) in a hang-gliding/skydiving combination ride at **Skycoaster** ☎ (407) 903-1150, 6805 Visitor's Circle.

At **Jungleland Zoo** ☎ (407) 396-1012, 4580 West Route 192, Kissimmee, visitors can see more than 100 species of exotic and endangered wildlife. See more "gators" and gator wrestling at **Gatorland** ☎ (407) 855-5496 TOLL-FREE (800) 393-5297 WEB SITE www.gatorland.com, at 14501 South Orange Blossom Trail.

Fantasy of Flight ☎ (941) 984-3500 WEB SITE www.fantasyofflight.com, on highway Interstate 4 at exit 21, between Orlando and Tampa, houses the world's largest private collection of vintage military aircraft that served in wars, plus aerial combat simulations and a flight in a 115-ft-tall gas powered balloon.

Splendid China ☎ (407) 396-7111 TOLL-FREE (800) 244-6226 WEB SITE www.floridasplendidchina.com, a 76 acre attraction at 3000 Splendid China Boulevard, Kissimmee, is home to over 60 replicas (full scale and miniature) of China's best known scenic, historic and cultural sites. It also has shows, shops and restaurants.

A killer whale rises to the occasion at Orlando's Sea World.

Just east of Disneyworld on Highway 192 there is **Water Mania** ☎ (407) 396-2626 TOLL-FREE (800) 527-3092 WEB SITE www.watermania-florida.com, with slides, rides, wavepools and a body-board/surf simulator.

More attractions are grouped around International Drive in southwest Orlando. The best of these is **Sea World** ☎ (407) 351-3600 WEB SITE www.seaworld.com, 7007 Sea World Drive, the world's most popular marine life adventure park (with more than

75 million visitors since its opening) with 200 acres (80 hectares) of shows, rides, and exhibits for entertainment and educational purposes.

Among Sea World's attractions are killer whale, dolphin, and sea lion shows, plus a nerve-testing walk through an acrylic tunnel that passes through a shark-infested tank. "Cirque de la Mar" combines acrobatics, modern dance, music and special effects for a nontraditional circus, while the "Intensity Water Ski Show" features amazing water stunts. In the evenings, "Shamu Rocks America" spotlights trainers and killer whales performing rock'n'roll numbers, while "Mystic Knights" has pyrotechnics, laser shows, and flying dragons to entertain even the oldest kid.

Wild Arctic is a thrill ride and exhibit featuring animals of the frozen north. Educational programs include the self-explanatory Dolphin Interaction Program, the Polar Expedition Tour, and the Trainer for a Day Program where guests can shadow Sea World trainers. **Shamu's Happy Harbor** is a three-acre playground for kids. There are also gardens and restaurants. Sea World is open from 9 AM to 7 PM daily.

For those of you who just can't handle the crowds, Sea World has opened **Discovery Cove** ☎ (877) 434-7268 WEB SITE www.discoverycove.com. The Cove is a reservations only, limited entry, tropical theme park featuring up-close and one-on-one encounters with dolphins and other exotic marine animals. But you are going to have to pay dearly for this experience.

Other attractions in the Orlando area include the **Mystery Fun House** ☎ (407) 351-3356, 5767 Major Boulevard, an entertainment center with haunting effects; and **Skull Kingdom** ☎ (407) 354-1564 WEB SITE www.skullkingdom.com, 5933 American Way, which intertwines live performers, robotics and special effects to offer a haunted castle full of fun and fright.

Wet 'n' Wild ☎ (407) 351-1800 TOLL-FREE (800) 992-9453 WEB SITE www.wetnwild.com, at 6200 International Drive, is a 25-acre (10-hectare) waterpark with wave machines and huge water slides. **Malibu Grand Prix** ☎ (407) 351-7093 FAX (407) 363-9133 at 5363 American Way, offers self-drive, three quarter scale Indy-style race cars on a three-quarter-mile track. Your time is clocked and displayed on a lighted scoreboard. MGP also offers miniature golf, baseball batting cages, and video games.

Jungle Adventures ☎ (407) 568-1354 WEB SITE www.jungleadventures.com, 26205 East Highway 50 at Christmas, offers wildlife shows and a "cruise" through alligator country. **Muvico Pointe 21 Theaters/IMAX Theater** ☎ (407) 926-6843 WEB SITE www.muvico.com, 9101 International Drive, Suite 2100, has IMAX shows and 20 regular theaters. On the corner of Church Street and Orange Avenue is a 25-room, haunted house attraction called **Terror on Church Street** ☎ (407) 649-3327, 135 Orange Avenue. If that doesn't get your

adrenaline pumping, pop into **Skyventure** ☎ (407) 903-1150, 6805 Visitor's Circle, for a 120 mph (180 kph) free fall in a wind tunnel with video enhancements.

Among attractions in the downtown area are the manicured grounds of **Lake Eola Park** off Orange Avenue, which retains the serene atmosphere of old Orlando. Watch out for the spectacular **Centennial Fountain**, especially at night, when water and light combine to dazzling effect.

Just north of the downtown area is the **Orlando Science Center** ☎ (407) 514-2000 TOLL-FREE (888) 672-4386, at 777 East Princeton Street, which takes a practical approach to teaching science. A computer will analyze your risk of a heart attack, and another machine will convert your bodily energy into electricity. You can even experience for yourself the journey taken by a particle of food traveling through the human body.

The **Orange County Historical Museum** ☎ (407) 897-6350 WEB SITE www.icflorida .communities.com, 812 East Rollins Street, offers a look back at the people and events that have shaped Central Florida, while the **Orlando Museum of Art** ☎ (407) 896-4231 WEB SITE www.omart.org, has American, and African art collections in a picturesque park setting.

Universal Studios Escape ☎ (407) 363-8000 TOLL-FREE (888) 837-2273 WEB SITE www .universalstudios.com, 1000 Universal Studios Plaza, now considers itself as the

The silent beauty of Lake Kissimmee State Park.

world's most technologically advanced theme park with the opening of its newest zone — **Islands of Adventure**. Among the highlights is "Dueling Dragons," the world's first racing roller-coasters, where riders come within one foot of each other as they speed along the tracks at close to 60 mph (90 kph). Another new roller-coaster called "The Incredible Hulk" utilizes a booster thrust system to hurl riders upward with G-force power equivalent to a F-16 fighter jet, before plunging ten stories in wild zigzags, with a complete weightless inversion 110 ft (33 meters) from the ground. "The Amazing Adventures of Spider-Man" assimilates 3-D, live action and "roving motion base simulator" for an epic battle that includes a 400 ft (121 meters) sensory free-fall, while "Dudley Do-Right Ripsaw Falls" sends riders plummeting 75 ft (23 meters) beneath the surface of the water. Attractions for the little ones include "Seuss Landing" and "Toon Lagoon."

Also new is the 30 acre **Universal Studios CityWalk** which features themed restaurants, nightclubs, concert venue, shops, hotels and a 20-screen, 5,000-seat movie megaplex. The first of the five planned hotels (Portofino Bay Hotel) was recently opened, and The Hard Rock Hotel is scheduled for a fall 2000 opening.

Not to forget its origins, the park also includes expanded film and television production facilities. **Universal Studios** offer more than 40 rides, shows and realistic backlot sets where famous scenes in cinematic history are recreated for visitors. Latest attractions include "Twister... Ride it Out," five-stories of menacing, swirling, tornado fury that includes power lines showering sparks and buildings threatening to topple. "Terminator 2 3-D" puts you smack in the middle of the action through a 3-D film, live action stunt work, and special effects, while "Back to the Future... The Ride" takes time travelers on a wild chase from the Ice Age to 2015. Shows include "Beetlejuice's Graveyard Revue," "The Blues Brothers in Chicago Bound" and "The Dynamite Nights Stuntacular." The Universal parks are open 9 AM to 6 or 7 PM daily.

Orlando offers several ways of escaping the teeming crowds of the theme parks such as **Scenic Boat Tours** ☎ (407) 644-4056, which depart from 312 East Morse Boulevard in Winter Park, North Orlando, on a one-hour tour of the area's canals and lakes through countryside. Alternatively, you can go up and away with **Orange Blossom Balloons** ☎ (407) 239-7677 FAX (407) 239-7632 E-MAIL orangeblossomballoons@juno.com. The sunrise voyage starts off from the parking lot of the Days Inn on Highway 192 West. If the weather is right, you'll embark on a peaceful journey across Central Florida and then back to the hotel for a buffet breakfast. Champagne is served right after the flight.

Southeast of Orlando, at 3702 Big Bass Road in Kissimmee, you,ll find **Boggy Creek Airboat Rides** ☎ (407) 344-9550 WEB SITE www.bcairboats.com. This back country tour starts at a leisurely pace looking for wildlife and finishes up with a race through the marshlands.

Five miles south on Highway 192 is the **Green Meadows Petting Farm** ☎ (407) 846-0770, where you can get up close and personal to over 300 farm animals and even milk a cow if you're so inclined.

Sports

Fans can see the **Orlando Magic** of the NBA and the city's WNBA franchise in games at the Orlando Arena ☎ (407) 896-2442 TOLL-FREE (800) 338-0005 WEB SITE, 1 Magic Place. The **Orlando Solar Bears** ☎ (407) 872-7825 TOLL-FREE (800) 338-0005 WEB SITE wwwsolarbears.theihl.com professional ice hockey team plays home games at the same venue.

If you want to learn to play golf like Arnold Palmer, maybe you should attend the **Arnold Palmer Golf Academy** ☎ (407) 876-5362 TOLL-FREE (800) 523-5362 WEB SITE www.apga.com, 9000 Bay Hill Boulevard.

Orlando's premier links are found at the **Cypress Creek Country Club** ☎ (407) 351-3151 at 5353 Vineyard Road in Orlando has been an Orlando institution for almost 30 years. **Advanced Tee Times USA** ☎ (904) 439-0001 TOLL-FREE (800) 374-8633 WEB SITE www.teetimesusa.com, provides a central reservation service and discounted, all-inclusive golf packages. Didn't think to bring your clubs? **The Flying Golf Club**

((941) 472-1557 TOLL-FREE (888) 367-3342 WEB SITE www.forefgc.com, will rent with delivery and pick-up.

Water sports enthusiasts can rent canoes, airboats and motorboats from **U-Drive Airboat Rentals** ((407) 847-3672, at 4266 West Vine Street, Kissimmee, or take lessons in water-skiing and rent jet skis at **Buena Vista Water Sports** ((407) 239-6939 WEB SITE www.bvwatersports.com, 13245 Lake Bryan Drive. **The Dive Station** ((407) 843-3483 TOLL-FREE (800) 282-3328, 3465 Edgewater Drive, provides scuba instruction from beginner to advanced levels.

World Bowling Center ((407) 352-2695 is a state-of-the-art bowling complex with computerized score-keeping.

Just minutes south of Highway 192, is **Horse World** ((407) 847-4343, where you can horseback ride through 750 acres (303 hectares) of beautiful woods.

You'll have to drive a fair distance from downtown, but you can also ice skate in the Orlando area at **The Ice Factory** ((407) 933-4259 WEB SITE www.icefactory.com, 2221 Partin Settlement Road, Kissimmee. Or work out some of your aggression and stress at **Paintball World** ((407) 396-4199 WEB SITE www.paintball-world.com, 2701 Holiday Trail, Kissimmee.

For some fast-paced gambling action visit the **Orlando-Seminole Jai Alai** ((407) 339-6221 on State Road 436 at 17-92; or **Seminole Greyhound Park** ((407) 699-4510, 2000 Seminola Boulevard, Casselberry.

Bicycle tours are available on 1950's style bikes north of Orlando from **Winter Park Bicycle Tour** ((407) 875-2200 at 1000 Winderley Place, Maitland.

There are **rodeos** each Friday night at the Kissimmee Sports Arena ((407) 933-0020 WEB SITE www.kasrodeo.com, 1010 Suhis Lane, Kissimmee.

Shopping

The fashion-conscious tend to make tracks to the upmarket **Park Avenue** ((407) 644-8281 WEB SITE www.winterparkcc.org, in Winter Park, North Orlando, lined with stylish boutiques, art galleries and antique shops.

Florida Mall ((407) 851-6255 WEB SITE www.go2florida.com/sponsor/floridamall, at 8001 South Orange Blossom Trail, near International Drive, Orlando, offers a wide selection of merchandise in over 160 shops.

Antique shoppers should head for the **Orlando Antique District Merchants Association** ((407) 895-6111 at 1913 North Orange Avenue, where you'll find 30 shops, a mall, two mini-malls and seven restaurants.

Bargain hunters do not need to look further than **Shop America** ((407) 354-0126 at the north end of International Drive, where there are over 170 factory outlets; or try **Flea World** ((407) 330-1792 which has 1700 concessions under one roof at 4311 Highway 17-92 in Sanford.

Nightlife

Orlando offers a number of dinner theaters for the whole family to enjoy (although the evening's biggest mystery could be that so-called meal on your dinner plate).

Sleuth's Mystery Dinner Show ((407) 363-1985 TOLL-FREE (800) 393-1985 WEB SITE www.sleuths.com, 7508 Universal Boulevard, is very entertaining. But be warned: guest participation is expected.

Holding over 1000 guests, **Medieval Times** ((407) 396-1518 TOLL-FREE (800) 229-8300 WEB SITE www.medievaltimes.com, 4510 Irlo Bronson Memorial Highway, offers spectacular pageantry and high decibels when everyone is cheering for their favorite knight. The food isn't great, so if you're a gourmet, eat beforehand.

Other dinner theaters in the area include **Arabian Knights** ((407) 239-9223, TOLL-FREE (800) 553-6116; **King Henry's Feast** ((4070 351-5151 TOLL-FREE (800) 883-8181; **Capone's Dinner and Show** ((407) 397-2378; and **Wild Bill's Wild West Dinner Extravaganza** ((407) 351-5151 TOLL-FREE (800) 883-8181.

Peter Scott's ((407) 834-4477 WEB SITE www.peterscott's.com, 1811 West State Road 434 in Longwood, is a New York-style supper club that puts on an elegant evening of dancing, entertainment, and good food.

Church Street Station ((407) 422-2434, at 129 West Church Street is a vibrant night spot in downtown Orlando which offers a great variety of entertainment, including vaudeville acts at **Rosie O'Grady's**, live country western bands at the **Cheyenne Saloon and Opera House**, and Rock'n'Roll

OAKLEY
BROS. INC.
LAKE WALES, FLA.
LICENSED CITRUS FRUIT DEALER
3300
OAKLEY
BROS. INC.
DADE CITY, FLA.
LICENSED CITRUS FRUIT DEALER
3268
3268

at **Orchid Garden**. Seafood is the order of the day at **Crackers Restaurant**, while Cuban sandwiches are what to order at the **Cuban Cafe**. There's also a lively disco, **Phileas Phogg's Dance Club**, where you can boogie until 2 AM.

The Cactus Club ☎ (407) 894-3041, 1300 North Mills Avenue, is an upscale gay club that welcomes a mixed adult clientele. There is a daily happy hour from 3 PM to 8 PM, and a buffet is served on Fridays. Open 3 PM to 2 am daily.

Movie lovers are in for an absolute treat at the **Enzian Theater & Cafe** ☎ (407) 629-0054 WEB SITE www.enzian.org, a nonprofit cinema and restaurant, which serves delicious food and shows American independent and foreign movies.

Orlando boasts three live professional theater series — MainStage, Family Classics, and SecondStage — with year-round performances at the **Civic Theatre of Central Florida** ☎ (407) 896-7365.

Opera buffs should call the **Orlando Opera Company** ☎ (407) 426-1700 to see what performances are upcoming, while details about ballet can be had from the **Southern Ballet Theatre** ☎ (407) 426-1728 both at 1111 North Orange Avenue.

A one-stop information source for all cultural events in the area is **United Arts of Central Florida** ☎ (407) 425-0277.

WHERE TO STAY

The hotels along the "Route 192 Corridor" and those around International Drive are all within half an hour's drive of Orlando. For more information about the city's seemingly endless list of hotels contact the Greater Orlando Tourist Information Center or the Orlando/Orange County Convention and Visitors Bureau. Here is a small selection of the hotels in the area:

Luxury

The **Park Plaza Hotel** ☎ (407) 647-1072 TOLL-FREE (800) 228-7220, in Orlando's exclusive Winter Park suburb at 307 Park Avenue South, is an especially welcoming hotel with a genuine Southern feel. The 29 handsome rooms all feature flower-bedecked balconies overlooking stylish Park Avenue.

Four suites at the **Colonial Plaza Inn** ☎ (407) 894-2741 FAX (407) 896-7913 WEB SITE www.harleyhotels.com, 2801 East Colonial Drive, Orlando, come with their own small swimming pools. But all the hotel's guests can enjoy the Jacuzzi facilities.

Meadow Marsh (407) 656-2064 TOLL-FREE (888) 656-2064, 940 Tildenville School Road, Winter Garden, is a wonderfully serene Victorian bed and breakfast, 14 miles west of Downtown Orlando. Rooms include ornate open fireplaces, whirlpools, and six-foot-long claw-footed tubs.

The **Peabody Orlando** ☎ (407) 352-4000 TOLL-FREE (800) 732-2639 FAX (407) 351-0073, 9801 International Drive, situated in the heart of the action at International Plaza, has 891 rooms and offers all the first-class amenities you would expect, including three restaurants, athletic club, game room, pool and tennis courts.

Star Island Resort and Country Club ☎ (407) 396-8300 TOLL-FREE (800) 493-8604, 5000 Avenue of the Star in Kissimmee, is a Mediterranean-styled resort and celebrity spa with three-bedroom luxury villas, each with its own whirlpool spa. Vic Braden's Tennis College is located here and guests can enjoy water sports activities on Lake Cecile.

Half an hour northwest of Orlando is the **Mission Inn** ☎ (352) 324-3101 FAX (352) 324-2636, 10400 Country Road 48, Howley-in-the-Hills. It may be a little out of the way, but for golf and tennis enthusiasts, this is the center of the earth. This family-owned resort also offers three restaurants, biking and swimming pool as well as fishing and sailing on Lake Harris

Mid-range

The friendly, family-run **Langford Hotel** ☎ (407) 644-3400 TOLL-FREE (800) 203-2581 fax (407) 628-1952 WEB SITE www.langfordresort.com, 300 East New England Avenue in Winter Park, is one of the best value-for-money hotels in town, considering the extensive facilities, which include a courtyard swimming pool, Jacuzzi, and sauna, and the Empire Room restaurant with its excellent food and live musical entertainment.

Emblematic of the Sunshine State, an orange juice cannery in central Florida.

In downtown Orlando, the **Harley Hotel** ☎ (407) 841-3220 TOLL-FREE (800) 321-2323, at 151 East Washington Street, sits on a beautiful spot next to Lake Eola Park. The Harley has a nostalgic feel that borders on the humorous at times — like the rickety escalator adjacent to the front desk.

Perri House ☎ (407) 876-4830 TOLL-FREE (800) 780-4830 WEB SITE www.perihouse.com, 10417 Centurion Court, Lake Buena Vista, offers bed-and-breakfast lodging in a private and rustic country estate which doubles as a bird sanctuary and wildlife preserve. Pool, spa, library and eight bedrooms.

Set on 97 acres (39 hectares) of lakefront, **Westgate Lakes Resort** ☎ (407) 345-0000 TOLL-FREE (888) 808 7410 WEB SITE www iloveorlando.com, 10,000 Turkey Lake Road, may seem expensive at first glance, but when you factor in that villas can sleep up to 16 guests, the cost per head is very reasonable. Full kitchens available and there's a restaurant (with delivery service) on the property. Amenities include pools, spas, tennis, playgrounds, children's program and water sports. The nearby **Westgate Vacation Villas** ☎ (407) 239-0510, 2770 Old Lake Wilson Road, offers one- and two-bedroom villas that sleep up to ten people.

Another huge compound with all the facilities you could think of is **Vistana Resort** ☎ (407) 239-3100 TOLL-FREE (800) 877-8787 WEB SITE www.vistana.com, which is situated at 8800 Vistana Centre Drive.

Inexpensive

Good budget bets in and around Orlando include the **Apollo Inn** ☎ (407) 846-0675 TOLL-FREE (800) 999-2765 E-MAIL apolloinn @travelbase.com, 670 East Vine Street, Kissimmee, which has in-room microwaves and refrigerators, pool and laundry facilities; **Red Roof Inn** ☎ (407) 352-1507 TOLL-FREE (800) 843-7663 FAX (407) 352-5550; and **Quality Inn Plaza** ☎ (407) 345-8585 TOLL-FREE (800) 999-8585, 900 International Drive.

The **Orlando/Kissimmee Resort** ☎ (407) 396-8282, 4840 West Irlo Bronson Highway, Kissimmee, is a member of Hostelling International. All rooms are air-conditioned, with en-suite bathrooms and a maximum of six beds. Private rooms are available.

For those who prefer to sleep under the stars, **Thousand Trails' Orlando Camping Preserve** TOLL-FREE (800) 723-1217 WEB SITE www.1000trails.com, 2112 US Highway 27 South in Clermont offers campsites in tranquil wooded grounds.

WHERE TO EAT

Expensive

The most romantic ambiance, and some of the best seafood in town, can be found at **Park Plaza Gardens** ☎ (407) 645-2475 WEB SITE www.ParkplazaGardens.com, 319 Park Avenue South, Orlando. In absolutely delightful surroundings you can enjoy such specialties as flounder meunière and shrimp in curry sauce.

Another elegant garden setting is **Ran-Getsu** ☎ (407) 354-0044, 8400 International Drive, Orlando, a Japanese restaurant that overlooks a Japanese garden and koi pond. The menu features such innovations as tofu steak and *atarashii ryori* (Japanese nouvelle cuisine) as well as more traditional fare.

Christini's ☎ (407) 345-8770, 7600 Dr. Phillips Boulevard in the Marketplace Shopping Center, Orlando, is a highly-regarded Italian restaurant with strolling musicians. The menu offers carpaccio from Piedmonte, rack of lamb from Sardinia and perfect homemade pasta.

Maison & Jardin ☎ (407) 862-4410 WEB SITE www.maison-jardin.com, 430 Wymore Road, South of Interstate 4 and S.R. 436 at Altamonte Springs, is housed in a Mediterranean villa on five landscaped acres, (two hectares) secluded by majestic oaks. The fare is Continental and American with main choices like roast Moscovy duckling with raspberry and cassis sauce; beef medallions topped with stilton cheese, black peppercorn sauce and Cognac; and crabmeat-stuffed red snapper, wrapped in puff pastry. There are over 800 different wine selections.

Moderate

For traditional French cuisine at very reasonable prices your best bet is **Le Coq au Vin** ☎ (407) 851-6980, at 4800 South Orange Avenue, Orlando, where Louis and Magdalena Perotte have created an excellent menu and a charming atmosphere.

Italian favorites such as *ravioli al funghetto* and *zuppa di pesce* rule the roost at **Cafe D'Antonio** ☎ (407) 566-2233, 691 Front Street, Suite 110, Celebration. Vegetarian and non-vegetarian *thali* can be enjoyed at **Punjab** ☎ (407) 352-7887, 7451 International Drive.

Larry's Cedar River Seafood & Oyster Bar ☎ (407) 858-0525 WEB SITE www.cedarriver.com, 7101 South Orange Blossom Trail, offers hometown seafood direct from the docks, including such favorites as peel 'n' eat shrimp, crab cakes, and tasty clam chowder.

The Old Southern-style **Lulu's Bait Shack** ☎ (407) 351-9595, 9101 International Drive, Suite 2220, serves up spicy Cajun food with lots of fun thrown in.

Inexpensive

At **Chamberlin Market & Cafe** ☎ (407) 352-2130, 7600 Dr. Philips Boulevard, you can fill up at the hot food bar or the salad bar, or order soups, sandwiches, and vegetarian specialties. All this can be washed down with a delicious fruit smoothie.

Pebbles Restaurant ☎ (407) 827-1111, 12551 State Road 535, offers up good food at reasonable prices. **The Greek Place** ☎ (407) 352-6930, in the Mercado Shopping Village, 8445 International Drive, Orlando, serves decent Greek fast food. **Friday's Front Row Sports Grill** ☎ (407) 363-1414, 8126 International Drive, is a sport theme restaurant with lots of televisions and interactive games room. All-American menu.

OTHER ATTRACTIONS IN CENTRAL FLORIDA

SOUTH OF ORLANDO

Take Route 540 to Winter Haven and the legendary **Cypress Gardens** ☎ (941) 324-2111 WEB SITE www.cypressgardens.com, a 223 acre (89 hectare) park with beautifully-tended botanical gardens, zoological park and miniature railway. You can also see the **Great American Ski Show**, which features water-skiing, powerboat racing, and water-ski jumping. The gardens are open daily from 9 am to 6 PM.

The Green Barn ☎ (407) 847-3559, Overstreet Ranch, 1800 Mac Overstreet Road,

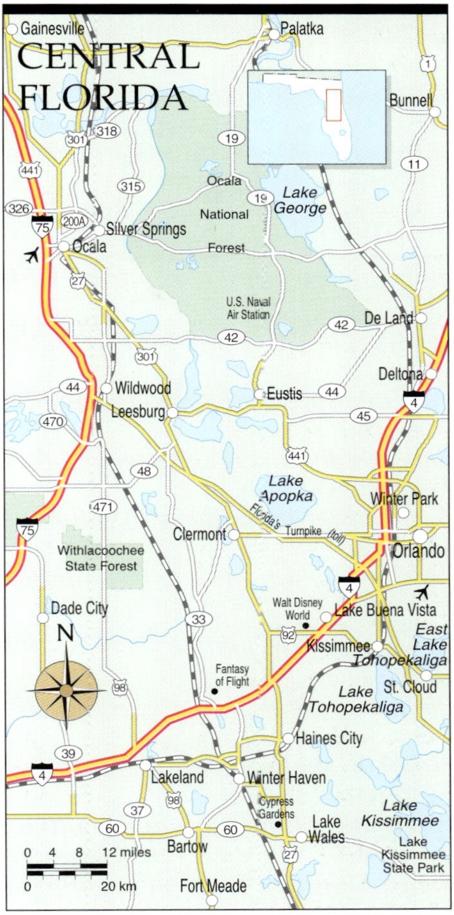

Kissimmee, allows city slickers to experience a working cattle ranch. Barbecues, hay rides, and ranch tours.

For somewhat more natural surroundings, head even farther south down Route 27 to **Bok Tower Gardens** ☎ (813) 676-1408 WEB SITE www.boktower.org, 1151 Tower Boulevard, near Lake Wales. A Gothic tower 200 ft (61 m) high, with a 57-bell carillon, is surrounded by 123 acres (49 hectares) of tranquil gardens and nature trails. Classical music recitals are performed in the gardens on selected summer evenings. Open daily from 8 AM to 5 PM.

If you prefer something wilder, head east out of Lake Wales to **Lake Kissimmee State Park** ☎ (941) 696-1112, 14248 Camp Mack Road, which has excellent fishing, hiking trails, and also features rodeos. The park has several campsites.

The **Lake Wales Area Chamber of Commerce** ☎ (941) 676-3445 FAX (941) 676-3446 E-MAIL lwacc@worldnet.att.net, is situated at 340 West Central Avenue, Lake Wales, FL 33859. Contact the **Haines City Chamber of Commerce** ☎ (941) 422-3751, at PO Box 986, Haines City, FL 33844.

NORTH OF ORLANDO

About 20 miles (32 km) northeast of Orlando on Interstate 4 is the town of Sanford, where you can join a catamaran evening cruise with cocktails, dinner and dancing run by **River Romance** ☎ (407) 321-5091 WEB SITE www.rivershipromance, at 433 North Palmetto Avenue.

Also in Sanford is **Katie's Wekiva River Landing** ☎ (407) 628-1482 WEB SITE www.ktland.com, which offers canoe and kayak trips on the Wekiva River as well as camping and RV sites and furnished log cabins rentals on the river's edge.

Just north of Sanford is the **Central Florida Zoological Park** ☎ (407) 323-4450, 3755 North West Highway 17-92, Lake Monroe, which houses over 400 exotic animals and has picnic areas set in the woods.

50 miles (80 km) northwest of Orlando on Route 441 is the town of Ocala, well known for its Victorian architecture, but better known as the state's racehorse center and home to some of the nation's best thoroughbreds. Many horse farms in the hills surrounding Ocala welcome visitors, including **Bonnie Heath Farm** ☎ (352) 873-3030 FAX (352) 873-3479, 4450 Southwest College Road.

The varied and interesting collection at the **Appleton Museum of Art** ☎ (352) 236-7100 FAX (352) 236-7137, 4333 East Silver Springs Boulevard, Ocala, includes Persian, Oriental, Peruvian and Mexican artifacts.

East of town, **Ocala National Forest**, (see YOUR CHOICE, page 28) embraces more than 300,000 acres (120,000 hectares) of unspoiled woodland, springs, rivers and lakes, bisected by a scenic drive known as the **Backwoods Trail**. Recreational activities include canoeing, hiking, hunting, fishing and tubing (a revived craze among collegians which involves floating downstream on inner tubes). Maps of the forest, as well as information on campgrounds and picnic sites, can be obtained from the USDA Forest Service ☎ (904) 625-2520, 227 North Bronough Street, Suite 4061, Tallahassee, FL 32301.

Ocala Forest is also home to the state's oldest attraction, **Silver Springs** ☎ (352) 236-2121 TOLL-FREE (800) 234-7458 FAX (352) 236-1732, which became a leisure park in the 1890s. These limestone artesian springs are the world's largest, beautifully clear and teeming with fish life, as the glass-bottom tour boats will demonstrate. The springs are east of Ocala 5656 East Silver Springs Boulevard, and are open from 9 AM to 5:30 PM daily (hours extended in the summer).

For further information on this area contact the **Ocala/Marion County Chamber of Commerce** ☎ (352) 629-8051 FAX (352) 629-7651, 110 East Silver Springs Boulevard, Ocala, FL 34470.

ABOVE: A wood stork, one of the rare visitors to Central Florida. OPPOSITE: The Bok Tower at Lake Wales.

The Panhandle

FIRST-TIME VISITORS TO FLORIDA'S PANHANDLE ARE invariably surprised by the diversity of its attractions. There is the state's sophisticated capital city, Tallahassee, and there are all the small towns that have not yet Gone With The Wind; there are the rich resort spots such as Fort Walton Beach and Destin, and the quaint old fishing villages on the marshy coastline between the mouths of the Suwannee and St. Marks rivers. There are crystalline streams flowing through pine and oak forests southwest of Tallahassee, and there are miles of deserted white sand beaches married to the azure Gulf waters west of Panama City. The Panhandle has all this to offer, plus inhabitants who are as welcoming and hospitable.

After the Civil War, the east and west coasts of Florida were transformed by commercial enterprises and by tourism, but the Panhandle remained relatively undeveloped, which could help explain why the region has so successfully retained its distinctive characteristics. The only substantial commercial activity in the region after the Civil War was in the ports, which thrived on the business of sending out wood and forest products to the peninsula's developing east and west coast cities. But for the most part the Panhandle was, and remained until the middle of this century, a region of sharecroppers and tenant farmers working a meager living from the land. As many of these people had come from Alabama and Georgia, they gave the Panhandle a Deep South character not found in other parts of Florida.

Many people only see the Panhandle from the inside of a car, as they hurry to the warmer climate and more loudly trumpeted attractions further south. But it would be well worth your while to get off the beaten Interstate tracks and take the time to explore this often overlooked, but very charming, region of Florida.

TALLAHASSEE

Like the entire region, Tallahassee is an interesting blend. It is the capital city of Florida, it is the most important commercial city in the Panhandle, it is home to two universities, Florida State and Florida A&M, and it has an historic district dating from the early nineteenth century.

BACKGROUND

When Spain ceded Florida to the United States in 1821, the territory's two most important cities were Pensacola and St. Augustine. In 1823, the legislature of the territory, recognizing the need for one capital, proposed that it be established midway between Pensacola and St. Augustine Thereupon two delegates set out, one from each city; they met in the foothills of the Appalachians and named the site Tallahassee (a Siminole word meaning "old town").

From the 1830s, Tallahassee was the distribution center for cotton grown in Florida and the Deep South, and its commercial prominence in the region was secured when the state's first railway was built linking the town to the coast at St. Marks. During the Civil War the town was fiercely Confederate, and the defeat of Union troops at the nearby battle of Olustee ensured that Tallahassee remained the only town east of the Mississippi not to be taken by the Union. Since then, the state's center of gravity has moved steadily southward towards Miami, but Tallahassee still remains the home of Florida's government.

GENERAL INFORMATION

The **Tallahassee Area Convention and Visitors Bureau** ☎ (850) 413-9200 TOLL-FREE (800) 628-2866 FAX (850) 487-4621 WEB SITE www.co.leon.fl.us/visitors/index.htm, is at 200 West College Avenue, Suite 200, Tallahassee, FL 32301.

If you would rather stay in the countryside around Tallahassee, contact the Convention and Visitors Bureau ☎ (850) 681-9200, at 200 West College Avenue, Suite 210, Tallahassee, FL 32301. The **Tallahassee Area Visitor Information Center** ☎ (850) 413-9200, is at 106 East Jefferson Street, downtown, across from City Hall

WHAT TO SEE AND DO

The modern **Florida Capitol** ☎ (850) 413-9200 and the **Old Capitol** ☎ (850) 487-1902 (which dates from 1845) stand next to each other

Between palm and flag: lining up the putt.

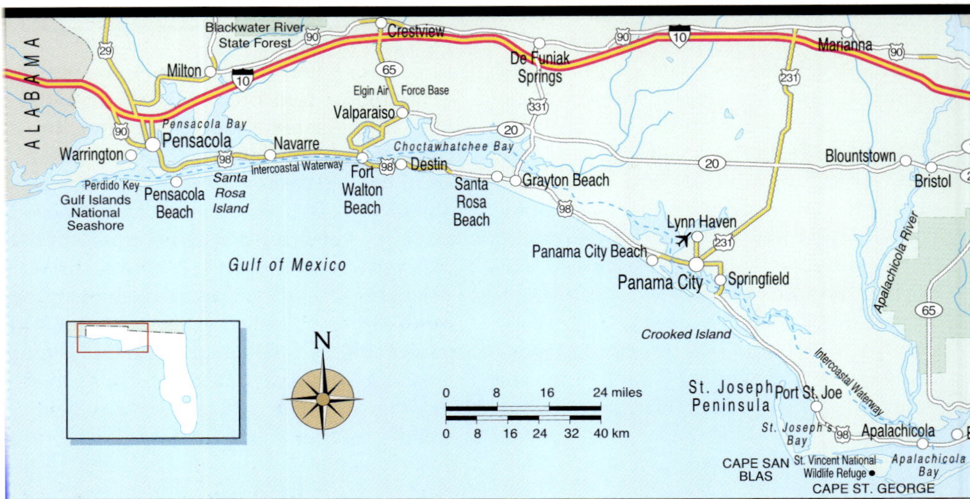

on South Monroe Street. You can tour the new building on weekdays from 8 AM to 5 PM and on weekends from 9 AM to 3 PM; there is a wonderful view of the city from the Florida Capitol's dome. The Old Capitol is now home to exhibits tracing Florida's political history and is open daily to visitors, on weekdays from 9 AM to 4:30 PM, Saturdays from 10 AM to 4:30 PM, and on Sundays from noon to 4:30 PM.

Across from the Old Capitol Museum is the **Florida Vietnam Veteran's Memorial**, which features a 40 ft (12 m) United States flag suspended between granite towers bearing the names of Floridian soldiers who lost their lives in Vietnam.

The **Governor's Mansion** ☎ (850) 488-4661, 700 North Adams Street, is patterned after Andrew Jackson's home, and features antique furnishings and gifts from foreign dignitaries. Open for tours from March to May.

The state's oldest commercial building is now the **Union Bank Museum** ☎ (850) 487-3803, on South Carolina Street and Apalachee Parkway, which houses a display of old state currency. For a look at the city's antebellum houses and buildings, stroll around the **historic district** along Park and Calhoun streets.

Four blocks farther west is the **Museum of Florida History** ☎ (850) 488-1484, in the R.A. Gray Building, 500 South Bronough Street, home to a collection of historic artifacts and relics evoking the state's past; admission is free. The **Tallahassee Museum of History and Natural Science** ☎ (850) 575-8684 WEB SITE www.tallahasseemuseum.org, at 3945 Museum Drive, is a 52 acre (21 hectare) park which includes an 1880's farm with demonstrations of the trades of the blacksmith, sheep-shearer and weaver. Open 9 AM to 5 PM Monday to Saturday, and 12:30 PM to 5 PM on Sunday. **Knott House Museum** ☎ (850) 922-2459, 301 East Park Avenue, is also called "The House that Rhymes." Back in the 1920s, the owner wrote and attached poems to the house's Victorian era furnishings. Tours on the hour.

The **Black Archives Research Center and Museum** ☎ (850) 599-3020, at the Historic Carnegie Library/FAMU Campus, off Martin Luther King Boulevard and Gamble Street, has an extensive collection of African-American artifacts and more than half a million historical documents.

The **Odyssey Science Center** ☎ (850) 671-5001, Kleman Plaza, South Duval Street, features interactive hands-on displays.

Bradley's Country Store ☎ (850) 893-1647, Centerville Road, is a family-owned concern that sells world-renowned homemade sausages and Southern goods. It's also on the National Register of Historic Places. Group tours are available.

Guided walking tours of the downtown area are offered by **Historic Tallahassee Walking Tours** ☎ (850) 509-4199 WEB SITE www.christopher.org/tallahassee/tours. Tours depart from Capitol West Plaza. **Tours With a Southern Accent** ☎ (850) 513-1000,

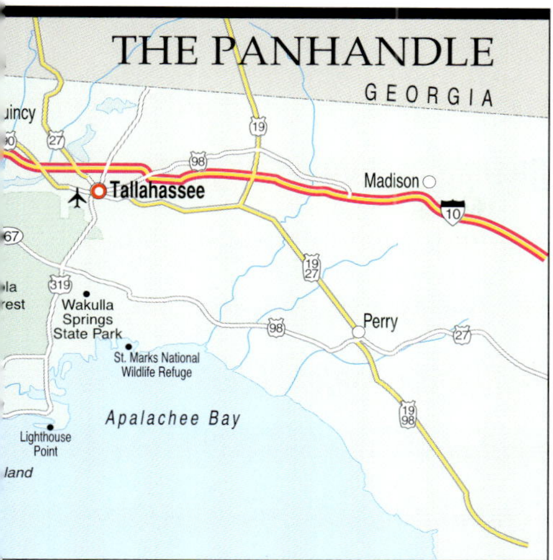

at the corner of Monroe and Brevard streets, offer a variety of walking and riding tours, or free self-guided walking and driving tour maps are available from the **Tallahassee Area Visitor Information Center** ☾ (850) 413-9200, at 106 East Jefferson Street, which is downtown, across from City Hall.

Just to the north of the city is **Lake Jackson Mounds State Archaeological Site** ☾ (850) 922-6007, off Route 27 at 3600 Indian Mounds Road, where excavations reveal evidence of an Indian ceremonial site dating from AD 1100. There are also picnic areas and a nature trail. The park is open from 8 AM to dusk every day.

Apalachicola National Forest comes right up to the city's southwest limit, which makes Tallahassee a good base to explore the forest and enjoy its unparalleled fishing, hiking, canoeing, swimming and picnics facilities. Get more information from the Tallahassee Visitor's Bureau ☾ (850) 413-9200 TOLL-FREE (800) 628-2866.

10 miles (16 km) south of Tallahassee is **Wakulla Springs State Park** ☾ (850) 922-3633, at 1 Springs Drive, off Route 267, where you can swim in one of the world's deepest freshwater springs, take a riverboat tour, or walk the lovely grounds.

Sports

You can play a round of **golf** at the Seminole Golf Course ☾ (850) 644-2582, 2550 Pottsdamer Road. Or you can play a nine-hole course at the Jake Gaither Community Center and Golf Course ☾ (850) 891-3942, 801 Tanner Drive. The center also has **basketball** and **tennis courts**. Other tennis courts are available at Tom Brown Park ☾ (850) 891-3966, 501 Easterwood Drive and Forest Meadows Park ☾ (850) 891-3920, 4750 North Meridian Road.

Horseback Riding is offered at Trelawn Plantation Bed, Breakfast and Livery ☾ (850) 997-4786, in Monticello. Riding is also offered, together with **canoeing**, **fishing** and **boating**, at Steinhatchee Landing ☾ (352) 498-3513 TOLL-FREE (800) 584-1709, in Steinhatchee. **Boat charters** are also available from Captain Jerry Alexander Charters ☾ (850) 926-1768, and Laid Back Charters ☾ (850) 926-9531, both at Shell Point, and **cycling** and **in-line skating** equipment can be rented from About Bikes ☾ (350) 561-9090, 411 North Magnolia Street.

There is loads of family fun to be had at **Fun Station** ☾ (850) 383-0788, 2821 Sharer Road, including miniature golf, batting cages and bumper boats. **Q-Zar** ☾ (850) 383-2549, 2415 North Monroe, offers laser tag and has a large arcade.

Shopping

The place for gift shops and stalls selling local produce is **Market Square** ☾ (850) 893-9633, 415 Timberlane Road, while the **Tallahassee Mall** ☾ (850) 335-7145, 2415 North Monroe Street, has over 90 specialty shops plus 20 cinemas. The **Cannery** ☾ (850) 539-3800, 115 East Eighth Avenue, Havana, is a renovated historic canning plant which now houses 150 stalls selling antiques.

Nightlife

The Moon ☾ (850) 878-6900, at 1105 East Lafayette Street, is a multi-level nightclub that regularly presents with live music. There is country dancing on Fridays. **Dave's CC Club** ☾ (850) 894-0181, Sam's Lane, off Bradfordville Road, serves up legendary blues to go with their Cajun barbecue.

The **Buckhead Brewery & Grill** ☾ (850) 942-4947, 1900 Capital Circle, has a mountain lodge ambiance and home-brewed beers; while **Andrew's Capital Grill & Bar** ☾ (850) 222-3444, 228 South Adams Street offers live entertainment, dancing, and sports televisions.

WHERE TO STAY

Luxury

What sort of hotel serves complimentary breakfast, with the morning newspaper, in rooms with four-poster beds and antique furniture, has a free limousine service to any point within five miles (eight kilometers) of the hotel, allows free local calls, and serves complimentary cocktails in the evening? It's where the Governor of Florida stays when he's in town — the **Governor's Inn** ☎ (850) 681-6855 TOLL-FREE (800) 342-7717, next to the Old Capitol at 209 South Adams Street.

The **Radisson Hotel** ☎ (850) 224-6000 TOLL-FREE (800) 333-3333, is in a good downtown position at 415 North Monroe Street, and has very handsome rooms to go with its elegant lounge and restaurant. In nearby Monticello, **A Place in Time Lodge at Willow Pond** ☎ (850) 222-4440, West Lake Road, is set on 60 beautiful acres. Rooms have their own kitchen facilities.

Mid-range

In the downtown area, **Doubletree Tallahassee** ☎ (850) 224-5000, at 101 South Adams Street, has 246 attractive and spacious rooms, as well as 25 plush suites. **Quality Inn and Suites** ☎ (850) 877-4437 TOLL-FREE (800) 221-2222, at 2020 Apalachee Parkway, off Route 27, is a reasonably priced hotel with a tasteful sunken parlor where you can enjoy your complimentary continental breakfast.

Every room has a view over the city and surrounding countryside at the **Clarion Capital Hotel** ☎ (850) 222-9555, 316 West Tennessee Street. In Monticello, the **Palmer Place** Bed and Breakfast ☎ (850) 997-5519, 625 West Palmer Mill Road, is a 1830s home furnished with antiques.

Inexpensive

With free in-room movies and a children's playground among its amenities, the **Days Inn South** ☎ (850) 877-6121 TOLL-FREE (800) 325-2525, at 3100 Apalachee Parkway, off Route 27, is exceptional value.

There are also a good number of pleasant hotels on North Monroe Street, including No. 2726, the **Howard Johnson Express Inn** ☎ (850) 386-5000 TOLL-FREE (800) 356-7432, No. 2735, **Cabot Lodge North** ☎ (850) 386-8880 TOLL-FREE (800) 223-1964, and No. 2681, the **Econo Lodge North** ☎ (850) 385-6155 TOLL-FREE (800) 424-4777.

WHERE TO EAT

Expensive

At **Andrew's Second Act** ☎ (850) 222-3444, 2285 South Adams Street, do try the exceptional *tournedos St. Laurent* — lean tenderloin coated with garlic, scallion, and parsley butter, and served with asparagus.

The **Silver Slipper** ☎ (850) 386-9366, 531 Scotty' Lane, is a favorite in legislative circles and is especially popular for its steak, seafood and Greek specialties. The picturesque 1920s **Sweet Magnolia Inn** ☎ (850) 925-7670, 803 Port Leon Drive, St. Marks, offers delicious "fixed price" fusion cuisine, usually in seven courses.

At **Melhana Plantation** ☎ (912) 226-2290, 301 Showboat Lane, Thomasville, expect to find white linen, crystal, silver and all the trimmings. The Master chef's menu changes weekly and features refined Southern cuisine.

Moderate

Movers and Shakers ☎ (850) 222-9555, 316 West Tennessee Street in the Clarion Capital Hotel, is a Southern bistro with a variety of delicious and imaginative dishes on the menu. **Georgio's** ☎ (850) 893-4161, 3425 Thomasville Road, serves up mouth-watering seafood, and meat dishes in elegant surroundings. **The Melting Pot** ☎ (850) 386-7440, 2727 North Monroe Street, presents French-inspired meals in a romantic atmosphere, with good tableside cheeses and a fabulous chocolate fondue.

The Wharf ☎ (850) 894-4443, 1480 Timberlane Road, dishes up fresh seafood, pasta, and meat dishes in a relaxed, upscale environment. For lots of ambiance, visit **Nicholson**

Farmhouse Restaurant ☎ (850) 539-5931, State Route 12, with good home cooking. Bring your own bottle if you want to drink alcohol.

Inexpensive

Homemade dishes and hot sandwiches are offered with live entertainment at **Chef's Table** ☎ (850) 224-7441, R.A. Gray Building, 500 Bronough Street. Delicious grilled, blackened, and fried seafood is served at **Shell's** ☎ (850) 385-2774, 2136 North Monroe Street.

All your favorite Chinese dishes are served at great prices at **Golden Dragon** ☎ (850) 575-8868, 1964 West Tennessee Street, while the **Sparta Club & Grill** ☎ (850) 224-9711, 220 South Monroe Street, has classic Greek food at great prices.

The **Wakulla Springs Lodge** ☎ (850) 224-5950, in the state park with the same name, has quail, soft-shell crab, and fried shrimp among its menu items.

HOW TO GET THERE

The Tallahassee Regional Airport is served by a number of national airlines. Tallahassee Taxis and Yellow Cabs both operate from the airport, where you can also find the offices of the major car rental firms.

Approaching Tallahassee by car from the east or west, drivers should take Interstate 10. If coming from the north take Routes 27 and 319, and from the south take Route 319.

PANAMA CITY

The city lies on that stretch of coast often jokingly called the "Redneck Riviera" and is one of the Panhandle's most popular resorts, having a lively nightlife, an amusement park with arcades and rides overlooking one of the finest white-sand beaches anywhere, and good facilities for water sports. Quieter (even deserted) stretches of beach can be found to the east and west of Panama City, and two state parks — St. Andrews and Dead Lakes — are a short distance from the city. In short, there are attractions to suit all tastes and age groups, which is why Panama City is a particular favorite with tourists traveling *en famille*.

GENERAL INFORMATION

The **Panama City Beach Convention and Visitors Bureau** ☎ (850) 233-5070, 233-5070 TOLL-FREE (800) 722-3224 FAX (850) 233-5072 E-MAIL pcb@interoz.com, is at 12015 Front Beach Road, PO Box 9473, Panama City Beach, FL 32417-9473. It can provide you with all the information you may need about the area. Otherwise you can log onto their web site at www.panamacitybeachguide.com, for information about hotels, restaurants and shopping.

OPPOSITE: The Governor's Inn in downtown Tallahassee, next door to the Old Capitol, ABOVE, where visitors can take in the view from the dome.

Airline information is available from the Panama City-Bay County International Airport ☎ (850) 763-6751, or the Tallahassee Regional Airport ☎ (850) 891-7802. For a taxi try Executive Beach Taxis ☎ (850) 233-8299

In case of a medical emergency, call the Bay Medical Center ☎ (850) 769-1511.

WHAT TO SEE AND DO

Panama City's biggest attraction is the beach. But if sun and sand get boring, the waterfront offers several ticky-tacky fun parks, a couple of interesting museums and lots of water sport opportunities.

The **Miracle Strip Amusement Park** ☎ (850) 234-5810 TOLL-FREE (800) 538-7395, at 12000 West Highway 98-A, the biggest along the Gulf-front road, has arcades, roller-coasters, carousels, and dozens of other rides.

Great Adventures Amusements Co ☎ (850) 230-1223, 15236 Front Beach Road, counters with go-carts, bumper boats, and bungee jumping. **Coconut Creek Family Fun Park** ☎ (850) 234-2625, 9807 Front Beach Road, has two 18-hole mini golf courses, a grand maze and bumper boats.

Meanwhile, you can see performing porpoises and sea lions at **Gulf World** ☎ (850) 234-5271, 15421 West Highway 98-A, Panama City Beach, from 9 AM to 7 PM daily in the summer. **Zooworld** ☎ (850) 230-1243, 9008 Front Beach Road, has tropical animals, a petting zoo, and botanical gardens. **Shipwreck Island** ☎ (850) 234-0368 TOLL-FREE (800) 538-7395, 12000 Front Beach Road, is a typical waterpark.

Spring Break at Panama City.

Panama City tenders two interesting collections. The **Museum of Man and the Sea** ☎ (850) 235-4101, on 17314 Hutchinson Road, has exhibits of early diving equipment, treasures from Spanish shipwrecks, and great moments in our exploration of the ocean. The **Junior Museum of Bay County** ☎ (850) 769-6128, 1731 Jenks Avenue, offers exhibits on how local native Americans and early settlers worked and lived.

St. Andrews State Recreation Area ☎ (850) 233-5140, at 4607 State Park Lane, southwest of the city at the end of Route 392, includes marshes, pinewoods, dunes and beaches, as well as campsites. **Dead Lakes State Recreation Area** ☎ (850) 639-2702, about 30 miles (48 km) east of Panama City on Route 22, near the village of Wewahitchka, has some lovely nature trails and wonderful fishing.

Boat trips to the wonderfully scenic Shell Island off the coast of Panama City (part of St. Andrew State Recreation Area) are available at **Captain Anderson's Marina** ☎ (850) 234-3435, at 5550 North Lagoon Drive. Excursions depart at 9 AM and 1 PM daily. Dolphin encounters and glass-bottomed boat rides are also available.

For thrills and spills on the water, go for a ride with **Sea Screamer** ☎ (850) 233-9107, 3605 Thomas Drive, Treasure Island Marina, Slip 41, or a sightseeing tour with **Island Waverunner Tours** ☎ (850) 234-7245, 6400 West Highway 98. For a more sedate time, you can take a sightseeing trip on a glass-bottomed boat from **Treasure Island Marina** ☎ (850) 234-8944.

For more ideas on what to do during your visit to Panama City, call the Chamber of Commerce referral line ☎ (850) 234-3191.

Sports

Golf enthusiasts can take on the challenge of the par-71 Signal Hill Golf Course ☎ (850) 234-3218, at 9516 North Thomas Drive, Panama City Beach, or try the attractive course at the Hombre ☎ (850) 234-3673, 120 Coyote Pass. Another good course is the Holiday Golf and Tennis Club ☎ (850) 234-1800, 100 Fairway Boulevard, Panama City Beach. The Sports Park ☎ (850) 235-1081, 15238 Front Beach Road, offers activities like tennis, **racquetball**, **basketball** and **aerobics**.

Panama City Beach offers a variety of water sports: Bob Zales Charters ☎ (850) 763-7249 FAX (850) 763-3558, has **sports fishing** trips on yachts that can accommodate up to 25 people. Captain Choice Charters ☎ (850) 230-0004 or (850) 814-0805, at 3927 Vega Street, will take you **spear fishing** and **deep sea trawling**, and fishing trips can also be arranged through Nick Nack ☎ (850) 234-8246 or Treasure Island ☎ (850) 230-9222, both located on Thomas Drive behind the Treasure Ship. Captain Choice Charters also offers **diving trips** offshore in waters with a choice of 85 dive sites, or trained divers from the Panama City Dive Center ☎ (850) 235-3390, at 4823 Thomas Drive, can take you diving in some of the freshwater springs in the area.

Pontoons can be rented from J&B Marine and Sales ☎ (850) 235-2411, Lighthouse Marina. The Front Beach Resort TOLL-FREE (800) 874-7101 WEB SITE www.pcbeachmotel.com, offers **waverunners**, **aqua cycles**, **hobiecats**, **pontoon boats**, **parasailing** and even beach chairs and umbrellas to rent. On Thomas Drive, Panama City Water Sports ☎ (850) 235-3390 will take you day or night diving, on **snorkeling** trips, swimming with dolphins and **parasailing**. They also have **wave runners** for rent.

Shopping

For swimwear and everything else for the beach, try the variety of shops in **Field's Plaza** at 12700 West Highway 98-A, Panama City Beach, open from 9 AM to 9 PM. **On the Beach Supply Shop** ☎ (850) 960-0130, 17554 Front Beach Road, Panama City Beach, has beach-appropriate jewelry, gifts and supplies.

The **Galleria** at 2303 Winona Drive, Panama City, is the place for gift and specialty shops. For local crafts and souvenirs check out the **Olde Towne Mini Mall** at 441 Grace Avenue, Panama City.

Before taking to the water you should visit the **Panama City Dive Center** ☎ (850) 235-3390 FAX (850) 233-0624, 4823 Thomas Drive, Panama City Beach, for all your diving gear.

The small town of Seaside rests quietly on the shores of the Gulf of Mexico.

Nightlife

Reputed by locals, at least, to be the world's largest nightclub, **Club La Vela** ☎ (850) 234-3866, 8813 Thomas Drive WEB SITE www.clublavela.com, has eight different party areas including the huge Thunderdome, the techno-rave/alternative Adventures Club and the more sedate Pub and Cigar Bar.

Spinnaker ☎ (850) 234-7882, is set among the dunes at 8795 Thomas Drive, Panama City Beach; the music and dance continue until 4 AM, and it opens at 11 AM to give you plenty of time to get warmed up.

At 5550 North Lagoon Drive, Panama City Beach, you can board a boat and enjoy **Captain Anderson's Dinner Cruise** ☎ (850) 234-5940. Fine dining is followed by music and dancing.

For drama, dance and music performances, contact the **Kaleidoscope Theater** ☎ (850) 256-3226 or **Historic Martin Theatre** ☎ (850) 763-8080, 409 Harrison Avenue, Panama City.

The place for live country music is the **Ocean Opry** ☎ (850) 234-5464, 8400 Front Beach Road, a large venue with more than a whiff of Nashville about it.

WHERE TO STAY

Luxury

Edgewater Beach Resort ☎ (850) 235-4977 TOLL-FREE (800) 874-8686, at 11212 Front Beach Road, Panama City Beach, is one of the best hotels in the Panhandle. The self-contained apartments have everything from marble sinks to washing machines, and overlook either the ocean or the beautifully landscaped grounds, which includes a swimming lagoon with waterfalls and a bar, nine tennis courts, a beachside clubhouse, and a nine-hole golf course.

Matching the Edgewater for luxury is **Marriott's Bay Point Resort** ☎ (850) 234-3307 TOLL-FREE (800) 874-7105, at 4200 Marriott Drive, Panama City Beach, which has a 200-room hotel as well as self-contained villas in its 1,000-acre (400-hectare) grounds. There are also two golf courses, over 30 lakes and ponds, a forest, and numerous restaurants and shops. The resort's boat takes patrons across St. Andrews Bay to the beaches of Shell Island.

The **Miracle Touch Bed and Breakfast Retreat** ☎ (850) 236-9149 TOLL-FREE (877) 236-9150 E-MAIL miracleb@bellsouth.net, 7016 Beach Drive, Panama City Beach, offers a personal training program for mature women including stress management and rejuvenation, with more than a hint of fun.

If you're looking for a house or condo to rent, contact **St Andrew Bay** ☎ (850) 235-4075 TOLL-FREE (800) 621-2462 WEB SITE www.panamabeachrentals.com.

Mid-range

The **Sugar Sands Hotel** TOLL-FREE (800) 367-9221, at 20723 Front Beach Road, is right on the beach, and has comfortable rooms and suites with kitchenettes, and a cook-it-yourself barbecue next to the hotel's swimming pool.

The nearby **Dolphin Inn** ☎ (850) 234-1788 TOLL-FREE (800) 234-1788, 19935 Front Beach Road, also on the beach, targets the whole family and has kitchens and a pool.

TradeWinds Resort TOLL-FREE (800) 222-7108 WEB SITE www.tradewindsmotel.net, has a large pool, and there is a beautiful pier off its private beach. At Panama City Beach, every room at **The Reef** ☎ (850) 847-7286 TOLL-FREE (800) 847-7286, 12011 Front Beach Road, overlooks the gulf and its beaches and comes with fully equipped kitchens.

Inexpensive

There is a reasonable choice of cheaper places to stay in Panama City Beach, including the **Bikini Beach Motel** ☎ (850) 234-3392, at 11001 Front Beach Road; the **Bright Star Motel** TOLL-FREE (800) 421-1295 E-MAIL bright-star@travelbase.com, 14705 Front Beach Road; and the **Sugar Beach Motel** ☎ (850) 234-2142 TOLL-FREE (800) 528-1273 E-MAIL sugar-beach@travelbase.com, 16819 Front Beach Road.

WHERE TO EAT

Expensive

The beamed ceiling, stone walls, and fireplace make for a genuinely English ambiance at the **Boar's Head** ☎ (850) 234-6628, 17290 Front Beach Road, Panama City Beach, where beef prime rib with Yorkshire pudding adds an English accent to an excellent continental menu, which also has very tasty Greek dishes.

A classic menu, with a focus on fresh seafood and Angus beef, is presented by Chef Debra Warren at **Breakers** ((850) 234-6060, 12627 Front Beach Road, Panama City Beach. Each table offers a spectacular view of the Gulf and the stage, which showcases the music of Mike Van Elsen nightly.

Moderate

Harbour House ((850) 785-9053, 3001-A West 10th Street, Panama City, puts on a luncheon buffet of salads, cold cuts and vegetables which I highly reccommend, as I do the charcoal-broiled steak served in the evening.

Continental cuisine with a French bias is on the menu at the café-like **Greenhouse** ((850) 784-9880, 443 Grace Avenue, Panama City. **Sweet Basil's Bistro** ((850) 654-5124, 104 Highway 98 East, Destin, has delicious pasta and other Italian dishes in a casual setting, while if you are craving ribs, **Pineapple Willies** ((850) 235-0928 has the best barbecued ones in town at 9875 South Tomas Drive, Panama City Beach. While you are waiting for your food there are televisions to keep you entertained.

Panama City Beach Brewery ((850) 230-2739, 11040 Middle Beach Road, Panama City Beach, is a fun place to have a casual meal, check out the home-brewed beers, and listen to the dueling pianos perform.

Inexpensive

There is a distinct Louisiana flavor to the interior and the menu of the **Cajun Inn** ((850) 233-0403, at 617 Azalea Street, Panama City Beach. Don't miss the Bayou Teche jambalaya with a side order of Cajun-spiced potatoes.

Pickle Patch ((850) 235-2000, 5700 Thomas Drive, Panama City Beach, serves the freshest omelets, gyros, and kebabs. If you want a quick sandwich, try **Peddlers Alley** ((305) 769-6080, 4601 West Highway 98.

HOW TO GET THERE

Several national airlines serve the Panama City-Bay County Regional Airport, notably Northwest and USAir. Arriving by car, Route 98 enters the city from the east and west, and Route 231 from the north.

ABOVE LEFT: An ornate wrought-iron balcony in the Seville Quarter of Pensacola. RIGHT: Vintage wheels enter a vintage part of town. OVERLEAF: Fishermen enjoy a tranquil evening Bass fishing on the Suwannee River.

PENSACOLA

Florida's western-most city has a population of over a quarter of a million people, who live mainly on the hillsides. The downtown area contains the historic district, whose heart is the Seville Quarter, where most of the museums, restaurants, and pre-civil war houses can be found.

BACKGROUND

A Spanish explorer named Tristan de Luna established a colony at Pensacola in 1559. Two years later, however, ferocious tropical storms destroyed much of his fleet and the colonists were forced to abandon the settlement. The Spanish did not return to Pensacola until the 1690s, when they formed a military garrison at the bay. They co-existed peacefully with the French, who were their main rivals in the region. However in 1821 they were forced to abandon Pensacola again — due to American military strength this time, rather than weather conditions. There is still a military presence in the city today: the Pensacola Naval Air Station became the United States Navy's first flight training center in 1914.

GENERAL INFORMATION

The **Pensacola Area Chamber of Commerce Visitor Information Center** ☎ (850) 438-4081,

is at 117 West Garden Street, Pensacola, FL 32593-0550. The **Pensacola Convention and Visitor Center** ℂ (850) 434-1234 TOLL-FREE (800) 874-1234, is at 1401 East Gregory Street, Pensacola, Fl 32501. For flight information call the **Pensacola Regional Airport** ℂ (904) 435-1746, and for a taxi try **Blue and White Cabs** ℂ (904) 438-1497.

WHAT TO SEE AND DO

Learn all about the area's past — Native American, European, and more recent — at the **Pensacola Historical Museum** ℂ (850) 433-1559, in the Old Christ Church at 405 South Adams Street, and the **West Florida Museum of History** ℂ (850) 444-8905, 200 East Zaragoza Street. At the intersection of Zaragoza and Tarragona you'll find the **Historic Pensacola Village**, full of old restored houses and stores.

The **Civil War Soldiers Museum** ℂ (850) 469-1900 FAX (850) 469-9328, 108 South Palafox Place, provides an in-depth trip back to the Civil War through a diverse collection of artifacts, life-size camp scenes, music and art.

Wall South, the nation's first, full-scale replica of the Vietnam Veterans Memorial in Washington D.C., is located in Pensacola's Veteran's Memorial Park, Bayfront Parkway, near Ninth Avenue.

Pensacola Museum of Art ℂ (850) 432-6247 FAX (850) 469-1532, 407 South Jefferson Street, offers diverse exhibits and art classes for all ages. The European and American glass, and the African tribal art collections are particularly worth seeing.

The **Pensacola Zoo and Botanical Gardens** ℂ (850) 932-2229, off Route 98, 10 miles (16 km) east of Pensacola at 5701 Gulf Breeze Parkway, Gulf Breeze, is home to more than 700 animals, including Colossus, a lowland gorilla who, at 600 lb (1,320 kg), is believed to be the largest in captivity in the world. Open daily from 9 AM to 5 PM in summer and until 4 PM in the winter.

Children will also enjoy **Adventures Unlimited** ℂ (850) 623-6197 TOLL-FREE (800) 239-6864, at the end of Tomahawk Landing Road and **Fast Eddie's Fun Center** (850) 433-7735, 505 Michigan Avenue, at the corner of W Street.

Aviation enthusiasts won't want to miss the **National Museum of Naval Aviation** ℂ (850) 453-2389 TOLL-FREE (800) 327-5002, which has over 50 aircraft on display, including the historic NC-4 (the first aircraft to cross the Atlantic, in 1919), jet fighters, and the Skylab command module. Take Route 98 west out of town to Navy Boulevard and turn off to enter the Naval Air Station. The museum is within the air base at 1750 Radford Boulevard. The famed air-display team, the Blue Angels, frequently perform at the base.

Southwest of Pensacola is the **Big Lagoon State Recreation Area** ℂ (850) 492-1595, at

The Panhandle coastline at Destin shows off its many shades of blue.

12301 Gulf Beach Highway, where you can swim, boat, fish, camp, and hike. **Gulf Island National Seashore** ☎ (850) 934-2600 is over the water, along Route 98, just east of downtown Gulf Breeze. The old Spanish fort **San Carlos de Barrancas** ☎ (850) 934-2604 is located inside the seashore boundaries. To the northeast of Pensacola is **Blackwater River State Park** ☎ (850) 623-2363, Route 1 off Route 90 at Holt, which is an excellent park for canoeing enthusiasts.

The **Navel Live Oaks** area in Gulf Breeze has more than 1000 acres of woods and waterfront for you to walk and wade through.

Three-hour nature sailing trips are offered aboard the **Daedalus** ☎ (334) 987-1228, Robert's Bayou, 6816 South Bay Drive, Elberta. Nearby is the **Biophilia Nature Center** ☎ (334) 987-1228, 12695 Country Road, where you can learn a surprising amount from their staff biologists. Learn about butterfly life-cycles, meat-eating plants, and lots of wildflowers. Another attraction in the Elberta area is the **Baldwin Heritage Museum**, on Highway 98.

Sports

You can play **golf** at the club at Hidden Creek ☎ (850) 939-4604, at 3070 PGA Boulevard, Navarre; the Lost Key Golf Club ☎ (850) 492-1300, at 625 Lost Key Drive, Perdido Key; or the Stonebrook Golf Club ☎ (850) 994-7171, at 3200 Cobblestone Drive, Pace, and there are several free courts for **Tennis** players in Bayview Park, the sprawling recreation center in the city's tree-shaded East Hill area.

Scuba diving and **snorkeling** off the coast of Pensacola can be arranged through the Scuba Shack ☎ (850) 433-4319, 711 South Palafox Street and AquaVenture Charters ☎ (850) 934-8382, Perdido Key Oyster Bar and Marina.

Fishing trips can be booked through AAA Charter ☎ (850) 438-1925, 600 South Barracks Street, or Moorings Charter Boat Service ☎ (850) 932-0304 FAX (850) 429-9289, and **canoes** can be rented from Blackwater Canoe Rental ☎ (850) 623-0235, 6974 Deaton Bridge Road, Milton. The **Bob Sikes Fishing Bridge** between Gulf Breeze and Pensacola Beach gives anglers a free deck from which to fish in Santa Rosa Sound.

Shopping

Seville Square and the surrounding streets boast numerous shops selling craft items, artwork, antiques, jewelry and gifts.

For fine art, you should head straight for the **Quayside Art Gallery** ☎ (850) 438-2363, 15-17 East Zarragosa Street, a co-operative of more than 200 artists, dedicated to fostering and promoting original art and crafts in the region.

If you're looking for designer boutiques, try the **Harbourtown Shopping Village**, a modern mall at 913 Gulf Breeze Parkway, Gulf Breeze. Bargain hunters may want to check out the **Flea Market** ☎ (850) 934-1971, 5760 Gulf Breeze Parkway.

Nightlife

Live bands play every night at **Flounder's Ale House** ☎ (850) 932-2003, 800 Quietwater Beach Road.

Lively local bars include the **Seville Inn** ☎ (850) 433-8331, at 223 East Garden Street and **McGuire's Irish Pub** ☎ (850) 433-6789, at 600 East Gregory Street, which has live Irish music and good food to go with the beer.

Buccaneer ☎ (334) 981-4818, 25125 Perdido Beach Boulevard, is the largest dining and dancing venue between Pensacola and Mobile. **Kooter Brown's West** ☎ (850) 453-3100, 7601 West Highway 98, features karaoke on Tuesdays and Fridays and a kids' night on Wednesdays. Four big-screen televisions broadcast most major sporting events via satellite.

WHERE TO STAY

Luxury

Pensacola's old railway station concourse has been restored and converted into the lobby of the **Pensacola Grand Hotel** ☎ (850) 433-3336, at 200 East Gregory Street. The hotel has penthouse suites with Jacuzzis and bars, and rooms on the upper floors have terrific views over the city.

There is an international flavor to the **New World Inn** ☎ (850) 432-4111 TOLL-FREE (800) 258-1103, 600 South Palafox Street, where the 16 tasteful rooms have American, French, Spanish, or English furnishings and decor. The hotel's restaurant also has a splendid continental menu.

The best place to stay on Pensacola Beach is **The Dunes** ☎ (850) 932-3536, 333 Fort Pickens Road, where children stay free. Most of the rooms here overlook the Gulf, and there are indoor and outdoor swimming pools.

Mid-range

Rooms at the **Residence Inn By Marriott** ☎ (850) 479-1000 TOLL-FREE (800) 331-3131, 7230 Plantation Road, Pensacola, are positioned around a courtyard that has basketball and tennis courts, a Jacuzzi, and a large swimming pool. Kitchenettes are available and the hotel serves a complimentary continental breakfast.

If you book in advance, the **Days Inn** ☎ (850) 438-4922 TOLL-FREE (800) 874-0710, will send a car to pick you up at the airport. The hotel is near the historic district at 710 North Palafox Street. Well-priced cottages and rooms with kitchenettes are available at the **Sandpiper Inn** ☎ (850) 932-2516, on Pensacola Beach at 23 Via de Luna.

If you're looking for a little more character in your accommodation, then you might want to stay in one of Pensacola's many charming bed-and-breakfast establishments. The **Marsh House** ☎ (850) 433-4866 E-MAIL marsh@dotstar.net, 205 Cevallos, offers a real homey feeling. The **Pensacola Victorian** ☎ (850) 434-2818 TOLL-FREE (800) 370-8354 FAX (850) 429-0675 E-MAIL pcolabedbrk@pcola.gulf.net, 203 West Gregory Street, is a well restored

Whatever type of fishing you are into the Panhandle caters for it.

Queen Anne mansion on a shady lot: it once was the home of sea captain William Northup.

Inexpensive

There are 120 small but comfortable rooms at **Motel 6** ☎ (850) 477-7522 TOLL-FREE (800) 466-8356, 5829 Pensacola Boulevard, Pensacola, and you will receive a similar deal at the **Days Inn North** ☎ (850) 476-7051 TOLL-FREE (800) 325-2525, 6911 Pensacola Boulevard. The **Paradise Gulf Aire Motel** ☎ (850) 932-2319, at 21 Via de Luna, Pensacola Beach, has rooms with kitchens and is close to the beach.

WHERE TO EAT

Expensive

There is nowhere in town with better French food than **Jamie's** ☎ (850) 434-2911, 424 East Zaragosa Street, situated in a cozy Victorian-style cottage.

The elegant **Jubilee** ☎ (850) 934-3108, at 400 Quietwater Beach Road, has a large skylight to accentuate the décor, and a menu that includes the most delicious sweetbreads around and sautéed chicken breasts with crayfish.

Driftwood ☎ (850) 433-4559, at 27 West Garden Street, successfully mixes an American atmosphere with continental cuisine, and the Perdido Beach Resort's **Voyager** ☎ (334) 981-9811, 27200 Perdido Beach Boulevard, offers "light Gulf Coast Creole" cuisine and a great view of the Gulf of Mexico.

Moderate

There is much to recommend at the **Angus Steak Ranch** ☎ (850) 432-0539, 1101 Scenic Highway, Pensacola, where chef Spero Athanasios hasn't limited himself to steaks; try his snapper casserole with oysters, shrimps, and scallops, accompanied by a Greek salad.

Some people say that **Keenan's Bar-B-Q Kabin** ☎ (850) 492-6848, 13818 Perdido Key Drive, has the best barbecue south of Memphis. Ribs are their specialty. The **Original Point Restaurant** ☎ (850) 492-3577, 14340 Innerarity Point Road, may not be as fancy as some, but it does have good, fresh, local seafood.

Characters Cafe ☎ (850) 492-2936, 14110 Perdido Key Drive, is a relaxed restaurant which promises no fried food on its menu of burgers, steaks, seafood and chicken. House specialties include jerk chicken and black bean soup.

Inexpensive

In 1948, Arkie Ma Hopkins established **Hopkins' Boarding House** ☎ (850) 438-3979, and her son Ed continues to serve your basic fried chicken, beef stew, and black-eyed peas at 900 North Spring Street, Pensacola.

The freshest and, for the quality, the cheapest seafood in Pensacola is at **Captain Joe Patti's** ☎ (850) 432-3315, 524 South B Street, while filling and tasty breakfasts and lunches are the specialty at **Coffee Cup** ☎ (850) 432-7060, 520 East Cervantes Street.

Excellent Mexican food with a difference is served at the **Screaming Coyote** ☎ (850) 435-9002, 196 Palafox Street. For a light lunch, you might like to try **Deli on the Beach** ☎ (850) 492-0700, 16495 Perdido Key Drive, where you can eat in or take-away.

HOW TO GET THERE

The Pensacola Regional Airport is served by several national airlines. Taxis and car rental firms operate from the airport.

If you are traveling by car, the principal east-west route into and out of Pensacola is Interstate 10. From Panama City, take Route 98. From the north, take Route 29.

Sand traps and sea views on a Panhandle golf course.

The Gulf Coast

FLORIDA'S GULF COAST, WHICH EXTENDS almost 200 miles (320 km) from Cedar Key in the north down to Marco Island in the south, is punctuated by offshore sandbars and numerous inlets, islands, lagoons, bayous, and estuaries. Ideal conditions, in other words, for the coast's first commercial enterprise: piracy. Pirates such as Black Caesar, José Gaspar, and others operated along this coast during the eighteenth century, using their knowledge of the labyrinthine coastline to spring attacks and avoid capture. Their activities played a large part in discouraging European settlement on the Gulf Coast. In any case, the Spanish, French, and English were more concerned with consolidating themselves on Florida's east coast and protecting its important sea routes.

The pirates and the regions' indigenous Timucuan, Calusas, and Seminole tribes remained relatively undisturbed until 1824, when United States Army bases were established at Tampa and Fort Myers for the purpose of subduing the Seminoles. The bases attracted civilian settlers, two towns were born, and then more settlements began to appear all along the coast once the army had defeated the Seminoles and gained complete control of the region. Many fishing villages emerged, some of which are still there today, between Naples and Marco Island, where the inhabitants live much as their forebears did.

From the 1880s onward, the Gulf Coast's story is similar to that of the East Coast. Developers suddenly realized that what Flagler was doing from Jacksonville to Miami could certainly be done from Tampa down to Naples —they could entice rich Northerners with prospects of good transportation, luxury hotels, and year-round sunshine. The last condition being guaranteed, Henry Plant got to work on the first two, bringing a railway to Tampa by 1884 and completing the Tampa Bay Hotel by 1891, and the Bellview Hotel in Clearwater by the end of the century. In Sarasota, further south, John Ringling, founder of the Ringling Brothers, Barnum and Bailey Circus, built hotels and an art museum (sometimes using circus elephants on the job), as well as his own winter home, which was modeled after the Doges Palace in Venice.

The tourists took the bait and the Gulf Coast has flourished ever since, to the extent that between Venice and Tampa towns are now gradually merging as their suburbs sprawl and overlap. To the south, the beaches of the Charlotte Harbor area and the coastline and offshore islands below Naples are largely protected areas or wildlife reserves. In these areas the laws on development are very strict, but the rest of the Gulf Coast continues to be developed, with Fort Myers being one of the fastest growing cities in the country.

TAMPA

Tampa is Florida's third largest city, with a population of 300,000, including the Hispanics of Ybor City, a western district, and a large number of Greeks who first arrived at the turn of the century to dive for sponges off the coast at Tarpon City — which became the largest sponge center in the world during the 1930s. Tampa is also the seventh largest port in the United States, and the most important commercial and industrial city in western Florida. Unfortunately, because of the volume of traffic in and out of the port (ships carrying 51 million tons of cargo annually), and industrial waste, Tampa Bay is seriously polluted and unfit for swimming. On the coast to the north of the city and around St. Petersburg there are beaches washed by clear seas.

BACKGROUND

In its early days during the first half of the nineteenth century, Tampa (a Native American word meaning "sticks of fire") was a small community of fishermen and farmers clustered around Fort Brooke. The city's growth accelerated dramatically in 1885 when Vincente Martínez Ybor, due to labor problems in Key West and the prospect of lower taxes in Tampa, moved his cigar factory to the city. This brought with it a wave of immigrant workers who settled in the area now known as Ybor City— whose clubs, restaurants, shops, and culture remain overwhelmingly Cuban-Hispanic.

East meets West in downtown Tampa.

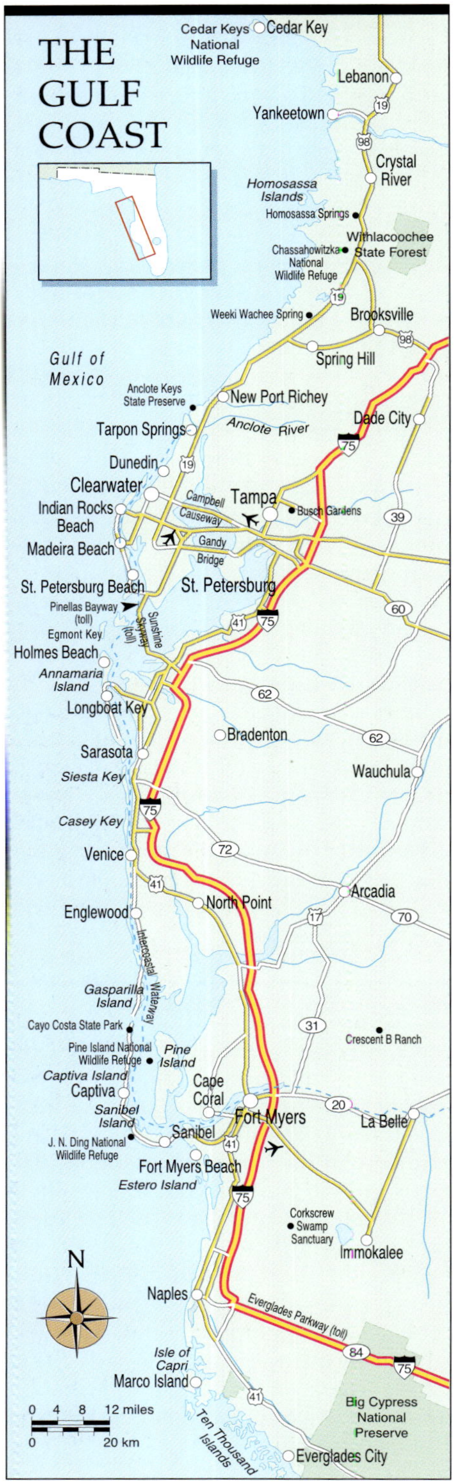

In 1898, the arrival of one man and his army of 30,000 gave Tampa its next big boost — both to the city's economy and to its status as one of Florida's most important cities. Theodore Roosevelt set up his headquarters in the Tampa Bay Hotel, and his force of "Rough Riders" trained in its grounds before going on to Cuba to fight in the Spanish-American War. The hotel now houses the University of Tampa administration offices and a museum.

GENERAL INFORMATION

The **Tampa/Hillsborough Convention and Visitors Association** ☎ (813) 223-1111 FAX (813) 229-6616 WEBSITE WWW.THCVA.COM, is at 400 North Tampa Street, Suite 1010, Tampa, FL 33602; and you can contact the **Greater Tampa Chamber of Commerce** ☎ (813) 228-7777, at PO Box 420, Tampa, FL 33601-0420.

Two newspapers, the *Tampa Tribune* and the *Tampa Times*, and a magazine, *Tampa Bay*, are full of information on local attractions and upcoming events.

Tampa International Airport ☎ (813) 870-8700 handles international and domestic flights, and **Yellow Cabs** can be contacted on ☎ (813) 253-0121.

In case of a medical emergency, call Tampa's**Physician Service Referral** ☎ (813) 253-4040

WHAT TO SEE AND DO

Busch Gardens ☎ (813) 987-5082 TOLL-FREE (800) 423-8368 WEB SITE www.buschgardens .com, at 3000 East Busch Boulevard, is an entertainment park with eight different theme areas. The newest is "Edge of Africa" which brings visitors face-to-face with lions, giraffes, hyenas and other animals from the Serengeti Plain. Also new is a dual wooden roller coaster, "Gwazi," which will take riders through almost 7000 ft (2000 m) of track at speeds exceeding 50 mph (85 kph). Another area, called "Egypt," has a huge inverted steel roller coaster and a replica of King Tut's Tomb. There are also stalls, shops and restaurants. The park is open from 9:30 AM to 6 PM daily.

Near the Busch Gardens, at 4500 Bougainvillea Avenue, is **Adventure Island** ☎ (813) 987-5000 TOLL-FREE (800) 423-8368 WEB SITE www.adventureisland.com — a water theme park for all the family. The fun includes wave-pools, beaches, water slides, inner-tube runs, swimming pools, stalls, and shops. In the peak vacation season between May 26 and August 19 the park is open from 9 AM to 8 PM daily.

The **Lowry Park Zoo** ☎ (813) 932-0245 WEB SITE www.lowryparkzoo.com, 7530 North Boulevard, is a 24 acre garden with over 1500 animals, including manatees, rare white tigers and a Tasmanian devil, in a tropical setting, and sunrise **hot air balloon rides** are offered by Big Red Balloon Sightseeing Adventures ☎ (813) 969-1518 WEB SITE www.bigredballoon.com, 16302 East Course Drive.

The city is home to a couple of interesting collections. The **Tampa Museum of Art** ☎ (813) 274-8130, 600 North Ashley Drive, houses contemporary American art as well as exhibits from ancient Rome, Greece, and Egypt. Free **walking tours** of Tampa's art and architecture are offered twice a month, starting at the museum ☎ (813) 274-8130. Exhibits that chart out the history of the city and portray its culture are on display at the **Henry Plant Museum** ☎ (813) 254-1891 WEB SITE www.plantmuseum.com, which is in the old Tampa Bay Hotel at 401 West Kennedy Boulevard. The site is now a national historical landmark. The **Tampa Bay History Center** ☎ (813) 228-0097, Tampa Bay Convention Center Annex, showcases the geographical, historical and multicultural influences that have shaped the Tampa Bay region. The **Museum of Science and Industry** ☎ (813) 987-6100 WEB SITE www.mosi.org, 4801 East Fowler Avenue, is the largest science center in the southeastern United States, and includes an IMAX theater. The excellent **Children's Museum of Tampa** ☎ (813) 935-8441, 7550 North Boulevard, offers hands-on, interactive fun for the kids to learn through. **The Florida Aquarium** ☎ (813) 273-4000 WEB SITE www.sptimes.com/aquarium, 701 Channelside Drive, features 600 species of plant and aquatic creatures in four galleries. There are behind-the-scenes and audio tours as well as dive shows and a touch tank.

For lots of fresh air and views of Davis Island in Tampa Bay, stroll along the longest continuous sidewalk in the world — six and a half miles (10.5 km) alongside Bayshore Boulevard.

Celebration Station ☎ (813) 661-4557, 10230 Palm River Road, is a popular family fun center, with go-karts, bumper boats, a video arcade, and a pizza restaurant.

The heart of the substantially restored Ybor City, Tampa's old Cuban and Hispanic quarter, is **Ybor Square** at Eighth Avenue and 13th Street, where there is a selection of arts and crafts shops, boutiques, very good restaurants and electric night clubs. At **Tampa Rico Cigars** ☎ (813) 248-0218 in the square at 1901 North 13th Street, you can watch Orlando Adad rolling cigars by hand from 10 AM to 4:30 PM and then you can try one. The **Ybor City State Museum** at 1818 East Ninth Avenue will show you how this district originated and how it has changed over the years. The museum also offers area walking tours ☎ (813) 247-6323. For a different perspective, **Ybor City Ghost Walk Inc** ☎ (813) 242-9255 FAX (813) 251-5475 offers a entertaining tour of this district and shares information about the colorful characters who gave it its colorful history.

Boats stacked in Dunedin.

For more information on this fascinating part of town, call the **Ybor City Visitors Center** (813) 248-3712.

The best beaches near Tampa are **Clearwater Beach**, on an island 15 miles (24 km) west of Clearwater across the Memorial Causeway; **Dunedin Beach**, north of Clearwater, near the charming neo-Scottish village of Dunedin (you can take ferries to the beautiful Caladesi or Honeymoon islands from the village); and **Sand Key Beaches**, just south of Clearwater off Gulf Boulevard.

Sports

Baseball fans will be interested to know that the New York Yankees hold their spring training at Legends Field (813) 879-2244, 1 Steinbrenner Drive.

You can see NFL **football** from August to January at Raymond James Stadium (813) 879-2827 WEB SITE www.nfl.

The Tampa Bay Lightning NHL team play their home games at the Ice Palace (813) 290-2658 WEB SITE www.tampabaylightning.com, during the October to April **ice hockey** season.

The two municipal **golf courses**, both of which offer lessons and have a lounge/snack bar among their facilities, are Rocky Point (813) 673-4316, at 4151 Dana Shores Road; and Rogers Park (813) 673-4396, at 7910 North 30th Street. There are also several private clubs around the city that welcome non-members. There are numerous **tennis courts** in Tampa, including eight courts at the Sandy Freeman Tennis Center (813) 259-1664, on Davis Island, south of downtown Tampa, and good facilities at the City of Tampa Courts (813) 870-2383, 15 Columbia Drive. For details on all golf courses and tennis courts, call the city's recreation department (813) 274-8615.

In-line skating and **ice skating** are both available at 12th Street Park (813) 301-0375, 209 12th Street.

For **water sports** check out Tidalwave Watersports (813) 223-2222, 200 North Ashley Drive at the Radisson Riverwalk Hotel.

Skydiving training and equipment is offered by Skydive City (813) 783-9399 WEB SITE www.skydivecity.com, 4241 Skydive Lane, Zephyrhills.

For recreation at a more leisurely pace, Canoe Escape (813) 986-2067, 9335 East Fowler Avenue, Thonotosassa, offers **canoes** for family fun through the 16,000 acre wilderness park on the Hillsborough River. Combination horseback/canoe tours are on offer by Horseback River Safaris (813) 659-0743.

Fishing expeditions can be arranged through Captain Dave Markett's Sports Fishing Guide Services (813) 962-1435, 14913 Warman Street.

Shopping

The city has several large shopping malls, but you can find the best range of shops — including four major department stores — at the **Citrus Park Town Center** (813) 926-4644 WEB SITE www.citrusparktowncenter.com, at GunnHighway and Veteran's Expressway. **Old Hyde Park Village** (813) 251-3500, features 65 shops, restaurants and outdoor cafes in a village atmosphere on West Swann and South Dakota Avenues.

The Big Top Flea Market (813) 986-4004, 9250 East Fowler Avenue, Thonotosassa has over 600 covered, bargained-filled booths with new and used merchandise. Open Saturdays and Sundays.

Book lovers should visit the **Old Tampa Book Company** (813) 209-2151, 507 North Tampa Street, for antiquarian, out-of-print and used treasures. You can rummage through antiques of all sorts at 4004 **South MacDill Antique Mall** on the corner of West Bayview Avenue or at **Village Antiques** (813) 839-1761, 4323 El Prado Boulevard and you are bound to find something authentically Cuban to take home with you in the gift shops of **Ybor Square** at Eighth Avenue and 13th Street.

Nightlife

Ybor really is the place to be at night in Tampa. On Fridays and Saturdays they close 7th street to through traffic so that the partying can spill out into the street from the myriad of restaurants and clubs in the area. The hot spots to head for in this area include the **Amphitheater** (813) 248-2331, 1609 East 7th Street, which has a revolving dance floor and a great laser light set-up and **Green Iguana** (813) 248-9555 WEB SITE www.greeniguana.net, 1708 East Seventh

Avenue, which features live entertainment served up with appetizers, burgers and sandwiches. Irish-themed entertainment is offered at **The Irish Pub** ☎ (813) 248-2099, 1721 East Seventh Street; while the **Atomic Age Cafe** ☎ (813) 247-6547, 1518 East Seventh Avenue, has hybridized foot plus experimental music and performances. **Fat Tuesday** ☎ (813) 248-9755, 1722 East Seventh Avenue, serves 17 kinds of daiquiris and live music on weekends. For a more sophisticated time, check out **Bernini** ☎ (813) 248-0099, 1702 East Seventh Avenue, which features a cigar and martini bar upstairs and for just plain people-watching, the tiny **Zion** ☎ (813) 248-3834, 1802 East Seventh Avenue, is a funky bar with an array of DJ characters.

The other main area of nightlife in Tampa is **Soho** — but here it stands for South Howard Avenue (and surrounding areas). Spots to visit include **Ceviche Tapas Bar and Restaurant** ☎ (813) 250-0203, 2109 Bayshore Boulevard, where the pitchers of sangria are particularly popular and for a completely different ambiance, there is the elegant lounge at **Le Bordeaux** ☎ (813) 254-4387, 1502 South Howard. There is also the night club **Hollywood Nites** ☎ (813) 254-7194, on 3001 North Howard Avenue, and the relaxed lounge of **Sideberns** ☎ (813) 258-2233, at 1002 South Howard.

Another popular venue which serves up live jazz, reggae, blues, and new wave music

A windsurfer's sail echoes the geometric shape of the Sunshine Skyway Bridge, over Tampa Bay.

is the **Skipper's Smokehouse** ☎ (813) 971-0666, at 910 Skipper Road.

For more cultural pursuits, call the **Tampa Bay Performing Arts Center** ☎ (813) 229-7827 TOLL-FREE (800) 955-1045 WEB SITE www.tampacenter.com, 1010 North Mac Innes Place, and choose between currently performing operas, drama, comedy, and dance.

WHERE TO STAY

Luxury

A first-class place to stay around Tampa Bay is the **Wyndham Harbour Island Hotel** ☎ (813) 229-5000 TOLL-FREE (800) 996-3426, at 725 South Harbour Island Boulevard, creatively designed and tastfully furnished, with attentive and friendly staff. Fifteen miles (24 km) north of Tampa, off Route 54 (exit 58) at 100 Saddlebrook Way, Wesley Chapel, is the award-winning **Saddlebrook Resort** ☎ (813) 973-1111 TOLL-FREE (800) 729-8383 WEB SITE www.saddlebrookresort.com, which is regularly ranked among the top 50 resorts in the world. The extensive sports facilities in the scenic wooded grounds include a golf course designed by Arnold Palmer, 17 tennis courts, an Olympic-size swimming pool and a large, soothing spa.

A sleek downtown hotel is the **Hyatt Regency** ☎ (813) 225-1234 TOLL-FREE (800) 233-1234 WEB SITE www/hyatt.com, at Two Tampa City Center, where there are suites with Jacuzzis and kitchenettes, and complimentary continental breakfasts are served in the stylish Regency Club.

The Radisson Hotel Tampa at Sabal Park ☎ (813) 623-6363 TOLL-FREE (800) 333-3333 WEB SITE www.radisson.com, 10221 Princess Palm Avenue offer oversized guest rooms with balconies and amenities including pool, tennis and fitness center.

By early 2000, the $105 million **Tampa Marriott Waterside** ☎ (813) 221-4900 FAX (813) 221-0923 WEB SITE www.marriott.com, is scheduled to open on the waterfront right next to the Tampa Convention Center, Tampa Street. The hotel will have huge conference facilities, and also offer 717 rooms, restaurant choices, pool, fitness center and spa.

Mid-range

Tampa' newest hotel at the time of writing is in the heart of Ybor City, The **Hilton Garden Inn Tampa** ☎ (813) 769-9267 WEB SITE www.tampayborcity.gardeninn.com, at 1700 East Ninth Avenue. This 95 room establishment has a pool, business center, exercise room and a mini marketplace. This hotel doesn't charge for children under 18 staying in the same room as their parents.

The **Holiday Inn Busch Gardens** ☎ (813) 971-4710 FAX (813) 977-0155, at 2701 East Fowler Avenue, has just undergone extensive renovation and it is especially welcoming to families with kids. There are suites with bunk beds, private television, and video games added to some guest rooms. It also has a swimming pool with a great kids waterplay area, sauna, health club, in-room movies, game arcade and a free shuttle service to Busch Gardens.

You can take a free shuttle to local shopping malls and golf courses from the **Days Inn** ☎ (813) 281-0000 TOLL-FREE (800) 237-2555, at 7627 Courtney Campbell Causeway, on Rocky Point Island, has tennis courts and a swimming pool, and a lounge featuring evening disco. In the heart of the downtown area, on the riverfront, is the **Holiday Inn Ashley Plaza Hotel** ☎ (813) 223-1351 TOLL-FREE (800) 513-8940, at 111 West Fortune Street, whose modern and attractive rooms are very reasonably priced, considering the enviable location of the hotel.

One of the few Tampa hotels with its own beach is the **Radisson Bay Harbor Inn** ☎ (813) 281-8900 TOLL-FREE (800) 333-3333, at 7700 Courtney Campbell Causeway, on the eastern shore of Tampa Bay, which most of the rooms' balconies overlook. Free sailing and windsurfing lessons are among the amenities.

Inexpensive

The **Budget Host Tampa Motel** ☎ (813) 876-8673 TOLL-FREE (800) 283-4678, 3110 West Hillsborough Avenue has simple, but well-furnished rooms and a swimming pool. The same facilities can be found at the **Tahitian Inn** ☎ (813) 877-6721, 601 South Dale Mabry Highway. Conveniently located near the airport is the **Home Gate Studios and Suites** ☎ (813) 637-8990 TOLL-FREE (888) 456-

4283, 1805 North Westshore Boulevard has a pool, fitness center, laundry facilities with kitchenettes available.

WHERE TO EAT

Expensive

At **Bern's Steak House** ✆ (813) 251-2421, 1208 South Howard Avenue, there are 38 different cuts of beef to choose from and nearly 700 different wines to compliment. **Donatello** ✆ (813) 875-6660 TOLL-FREE (888) 801-3463, at 232 North Dale Mabry Highway, is regarded as one of the best Italian restaurants in west Florida. Boca means mouth in Spanish, and the **Boca** restaurant ✆ (813) 241-2622, 1930 North Seventh Avenue, Ybor, claims that yours will smile when you sample their cuisine. Imaginative dishes include oak-grilled duck breast with a citrus glaze and tempura-fried snapper with spiced-soy butter. Just across from the University of Tampa at **Mise En Place** ✆ (813) 254-5373, 442 West Kennedy Boulevard, owners Marty and Marianne Blitz create New American Cuisine with fresh, local ingredients. The friendly staff really know their food and it is recommended that you take any menu suggestions that they are always more than happy to make.

Moderate

The pick of the Hispanic restaurants in Ybor City is the **Columbia** ✆ (813) 248-4961, at 2117 East Seventh Avenue, which features traditional Spanish dishes such as paella, pork salteado, and delicious bean soups all served in a romantic setting with tableside serenades by Spanish troubadours. You don't have to worry too much about getting a table, this restaurant seats 1,660 in 11 rooms, it extends over one city block. The popular **Cafe Pepe** ✆ (813) 253-6501, is a very lively Spanish-Cuban restaurant at 2006 West Kennedy Boulevard, which serves up spicy food in a cosmopolitan atmosphere. It is generally a good idea to reserve ahead.

For masterful and creative Thai cuisine, such as chicken, seafood, or vegetarian curry laksa soup, or curried crab meat in wonton pockets, go to the nearby **Jasmine Thai** ✆ (813) 968-1501, at 13248 North Dale Mabry Highway.

At the **Monte Carlo** ✆ (813) 879-6245, 3940 West Cypress Street, the chef specializes in seafood and, in particular, in new ways to serve lobster. The creamy lobster bisque is exquisite. **Ovo Café** ✆ (813) 248-6979, 1901 East Seventh Street, Ybor, is black,

ABOVE: Tall masts and skyscrapers jut into the evening sky at Tampa Bay.

white, and chic all over — but it's not just a place to be seen, the food is also very good here. The smoked gouda sandwich is a marvel, likewise their decadent deserts, and live acoustic music provides an entertaining background.

Nestled in a 35-acre nature reserve on the shores of Old Tampa Bay, behind the Hyatt Regency Westshore, is **Oystercatchers** ☎ (813) 281-9116, where you will get the freshest array of irresistible seafood available. The fabulous views serve as the perfect backdrop for the copious servings.

Inexpensive

If you want a jolly bohemian atmosphere in which to enjoy a masterpiece like *capelli di l'Angelo* — smoked salmon and caviar, tossed with spinach and pasta in a vodka and cream sauce — at unbelievable poor-student prices, go to **Bella's Italian Cafe** ☎ (813) 254-3355, at 1413 South Howard Avenue.

Also in the Soho area, you'll find **Le Bordeaux** ☎ (813) 254-4387, 1502 South Howard Avenue, which offers an intimate atmosphere and tableside cabaret singing. This bungalow turned bistro has a chalk board menu of imaginative French dishes that changes daily.

In Ybor City there are many cheap Cuban restaurants. I like **La Tropicana** ☎ (813) 247-4040 at 1822 East Seventh Avenue and Don Quijote Cafeteria ☎ (813) 248-3080 at 1901 13th Street.

After a visit to the Ice Palace stop by **Newk's Cafe** ☎ (813) 307-6395, 514 Channelside Drive, for seafood, salads, sandwiches and pasta in a casual, nautical setting inside or on the deck.

It may be a little out of town but **AJ Catfish** ☎ (813) 932-3474 at 8751 North Himes Avenue specializes (as you can guess) in catfish, but also serves other types of seafood, pasta, and chicken in a fun surrounding.

How to Get There

The modern Tampa International Airport is served by a large number of national and international airlines, and there are half a dozen car rental companies with offices at the airport.

Motorists approaching Tampa from the Panhandle should take Route 19. From the northeast or the south you want Interstate 75; from the east take either Interstate 4 (from Orlando) or Route 60 (from Lake Wales).

ST. PETERSBURG AND CLEARWATER

For many years, St. Petersburg had the image of a retirement town, because of the many elderly citezens who began to arrive in large numbers after the American Medical Association declared the area's environment and sea air to be good for the constitution. In recent years, however, St. Petersburg Beach and other beaches to the north have been developed, giving the area a younger, sprightlier image. Tourists — not just retirees — now come to the city in even greater numbers, lured by the wonderful beaches and beautiful waters of the "Suncoast" between St. Petersburg and Clearwater. The city itself has a developing downtown area and some delightful parks and gardens.

General Information

The **St. Petersburg Area Chamber of Commerce** ☎ (727) 821-4715, is at 100 Second Avenue North, Suite 150, and the **City of Gulport Chamber of Commerce** can be reached at ☎ (727) 327-2062. **The Pier Visitor Information Center** ☎ (727) 821-6164, is at 800 Second Avenue Northeast and the **Suncoast Welcome Center** ☎ (727) 573-1449 is at 2001 Ulmerton Road. For information about the resorts and beaches north of St. Petersburg, contact **Pinellas County Information** ☎ (727) 464-4861.

What to See and Do

The city's cultural renaissance is happening down on the cosmopolitan bayfront, where in the **Salvador Dali Museum** ☎ (727) 823-3767 TOLL-FREE (8000 422-3254 WEB SITE www.daliweb.com, at 1000 Third Street South, you can see the largest collection in the world of the Spanish surrealist's works, including oils, watercolors, drawings, and graphics. The museum is open from 10 AM

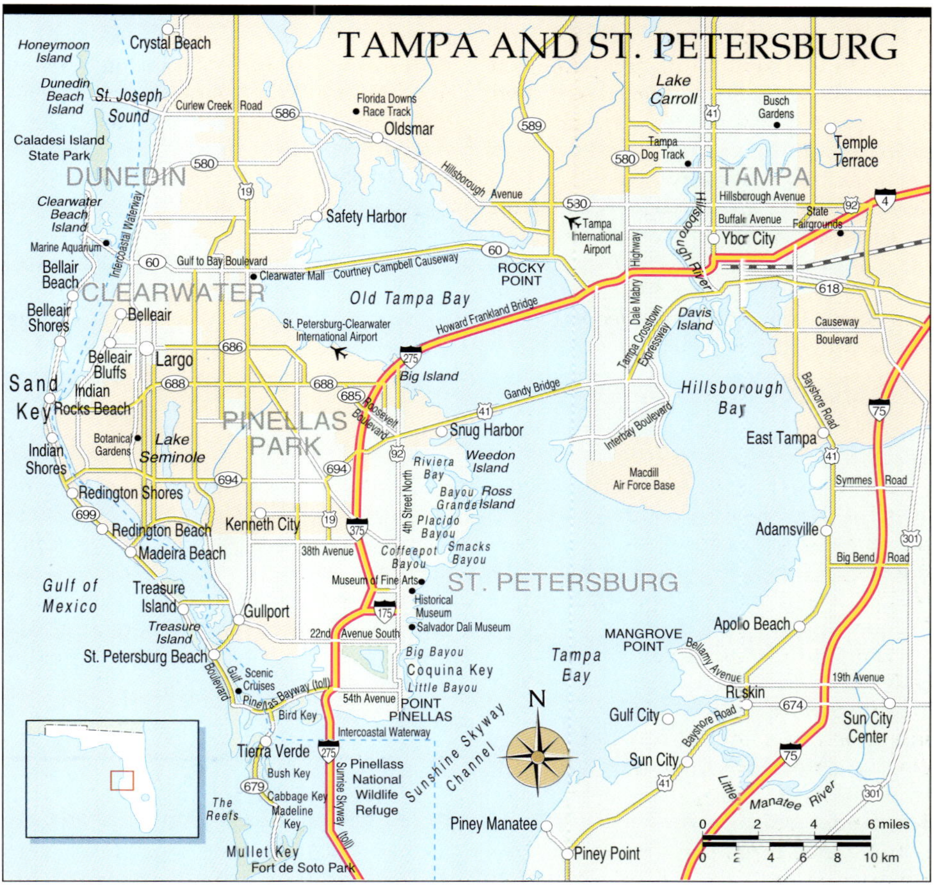

to 5 PM Tuesday to Saturday, from noon to 5 PM on Sunday. Many excellent paintings by the French Impressionists are on exhibit at the **Museum of Fine Arts** ✆ (727) 896-2667 WEB SITE www.fine-arts.org, at 225 Beach Drive North East, alongside oriental and American art, and photographic exhibits. The opening hours are the same as those at the Dali museum, and admission is free.

The renowned, and extensive, **Tampa Bay Holocaust Museum** ✆ (727) 820-0100 WEB SITE www.tampabayholocaust.org, at 55 Fifth Street South, is the fourth largest Holocaust museum in the country, and features Holocaust art and related special exhibitions. The **Florida International Museum** ✆ (727) 822-3693 TOLL-FREE (800) 777-9882, 100 Second Street North, houses the world's largest private collection of personal items of the late president John F. Kennedy. The **Florida World Museum of Natural History** is a 121,000 square-foot section of the Clearwater Mall. An affiliate of the Smithsonian Institution of Washington D.C., the museum features dinosaurs and other natural history exhibits. Also of interest to the kids is the **Great Explorations Museum** ✆ (727) 821-8885, 1120 Forth Street South, which is packed with interactive exhibits.

One of the strangest sights on the bayfront is **The Pier** ✆ (727) 821-6164 WEB SITE www.stpete-pier.com, which has a five-story inverted pyramid structure at the end of it, containing continental stores and restaurants; there is a viewing platform at the top affording great views over the bay, which The Pier juts into from 800 Second Avenue. The Juliett Class Russian guided-missile submarine U-484, the only submarine designed by a woman and the only Russian submarine available for public tours in the United States, is also based here.

Among the most beautiful on the Gulf Coast, the **Sunken Gardens** ☎ (727) 896-3187, is a well-ordered tropical jungle with over 50,000 varieties of plants, flowers, and trees, and an exotic bird aviary. The gardens are downtown at 1825 Fourth Street North, and are open from 9 AM to 5:30 PM daily. There are numerous cruises to choose from in the area, **Captain Memo's Pirate Cruise** ☎ (727) 446-2587 or (727) 446-2587 FAX (727) 447-3033 WEB SITE www.pirateflorida.com, leaves from the Clearwater Marina, 25 Causeway Boulevard, dock 3, Clearwater Beach on daytime and evening "swashbuckling" cruises aboard the *Pirate's Ransom* **Starlight Cruises** ☎ (727) 462-2628 leave from both St. Petersburg, 3400 Pasadena Avenue South and Clearwater at 25 Causeway Boulevard for sightseeing, Dixieland Jazz as well as dinner and dancing cruises. The two **Dolphin Encounter** cruises with guaranteed dolphin sightings leave from Clearwater Beach ☎ (727) 442-7433, at the West end of Clearwater Beach Marina and Caladesi Island ☎ (727) 734-5263, from the Honeymoon Island Recreation Area. **Hubbards Sea Adventures** ☎ (727) 398-6577 at Hubbards Marina, 150 128th John's Pass Village, Madeira Beach offers wildlife cruises, while **Merry Pier** ☎ (727) 360-1348, 801 Pass-A-Grille Way, St. Petersburg Beach, offers ecotours on unspoiled Shell Key. **Destiny Yacht Charters** ☎ (727) 319-2628, Tierra Verde Hi and Dry Marina, 100 Pinellas Bayway, has both sailing and motor boats for area cruises. **Sea Screamers** ☎ (727) 447-7200, Clearwater Municipal Marina, Slip 10, Clearwater Beach has a 73-foot speedboat which takes you on a scenic nature cruise and a thrillingly fast ride in the Gulf of Mexico.

There are over 20 parks in this area for the enjoyment of nature and the exploration of diverse ecosystems. Fort **DeSoto Park** at 34th Street on Mullet Key is in the mouth of the bay. You can explore the fort, which was built during the Spanish-American War, or simply relax on the island's beaches.

If you head north from Mullet Key on Route 679 and then join Gulf Boulevard you will reach St. Petersburg Beach. Gulf Boulevard continues north along an island chain which includes Madeira Beach, Indian Rocks Beach, Belleair Beach, and Clearwater Beach, which with St. Petersburg Beach comprise the "Suncoast".

Weedon Island Preserve ☎ (727) 579-8360, Weedon Island, is a 1500-acre nature preserve near St. Petersburg. The park has a 45-foot observation tower and a marked four-mile canoe trail and nine-mile hiking trail.

Philippe Park, in Old Tampa Bay near the Safety Harbor community, is of particular interest to history buffs, as it was the site of three distinct settlement periods: remains have been found of a large Native American Village, and the park includes evidence of Spanish exploration and of a European settlement.

Caladesi Island State Park is accessible only by boat, a factor which contributes to this park's pristine condition. Ferry service to the island is available from Honeymoon Island ☎ (727) 734-1501.

Honeymoon Island State Recreation Area Dunedin, is perfect for swimming, fishing, picnics and nature study. Like Caladesi Island State Park, this Island is one of the state's few undisturbed barrier islands.

The **Suncoast Seabird Sanctuary** ☎ (727) 391-6211, 18328 Gulf Boulevard, Indian Shores, is the busiest wild bird hospital in the county, caring for about 5000 sick or injured birds a year. Those with permanent injuries are housed at the sanctuary, giving guests the opportunity of seeing over 500 birds up close.

The **Clearwater Marine Aquarium** ☎ (727) 447-0980, 249 Windward Passage, Clearwater, is certainly not your average showcase for marine life. In addition to live and model displays of area marine life, they also offer three different adventures trips. Their Sea Life Safari Cruise ☎ (727) 462-2628 is a two-hour tour guided by a marine biologist where guests catch and touch sea-creatures and visit bird sanctuaries; their Kayak Adventure ☎ (727) 441-1970 is a three-hour trip, again led by a marine biologist, through Clearwater Harbor and St. Joseph's Sound — on which there is a good chance of seeing dolphins and Great Blue Herons — and their Marine Life Adventure ☎ (727) 441-1790, extension 31, is either a one- or a four-day trip where visitors team with marine biologists to study endangered animals and plants, and can even join in the rescue and rehabilitation of marine animals. Excursions include snorkeling and beachcombing.

The **Sunshine Skyway Bridge** south of St. Petersburg, connecting Pinellas and Manatee Counties, has to be seen to be believed. Modeled after the Brotonne Bridge over the Seine in France, it is 4.1 miles long and soars 183 feet above Tampa Bay. The bridges cables resemble an inverted fan and are painted yellow and illuminated at night.

The Don CeSar Beach Resort OPPOSITE in St. Petersburg and the Belleview Biltmore Hotel ABOVE in Clearwater are two shining examples of the luxurious accommodations found along the Gulf Coast.

For a quick side-trip to Greece without leaving Florida, you must make the journey to **Tarpon Springs** (((727) 937-6109 FAX (727) 937-6100 WEB SITE www.tarponsprings.com, north of Clearwater. Byzantine architecture and traditional blue and white buildings dot the landscape, Greek restaurants abound, the smell of freshly baked Greek pastries and festive Greek melodies fill the air, and sponge-diving is a major industry. The **St. Nicolas Boat Line** ((727) 942-6425, 693 Dodecanese Boulevard, provides a half-hour cruise with the opportunity to learn about the industry and to see how the hard-hat divers "fish" for sponges. **Spongeorama** ((727) 942-3771, 510 Dodecanese Boulevard, captures the history of the sponge industry, while the **Tarpon Springs Cultural Center** ((727) 942-5605, 101 South Pinellas Avenue, outlines the city's heritage.

Sports

Baseball fans can watch the Tampa Bay Devil Rays in training at Al Lang Stadium ((727) 825-3250, 180 Second Avenue; the Philadelphia Phillies at Jack Russell Stadium ((727) 442-8496, 800 Phillies Drive, Clearwater and the Toronto Blue Jays at Dunedin Stadium ((727) 733-0429, 373 Douglas Avenue at Beltrees, Dunedin.

Also for the spectators, is **greyhound racing** at Derby Lane ((727) 812-3339, 10490 Gandy Boulevard, St. Petersburg.

There are over 30 **golf courses** in the St. Petersburg area (Pinellas County), including Tides Golf Club ((727) 393-8483 or (727) 392-5345, 11832 66th Avenue North, overlooking beautiful Boca Ciega Bay in Seminole, this course has been a favorite with locals and visitors since 1973. Tarpon Springs Golf Club ((727) 934-5191, at 1310 Pinellas Avenue South; and Pasadena Golf Club ((727) 381-7922, at 6100 Gulfport Boulevard, St. Petersburg, are two of 15 public courses. Advanced Tee Time Reservations TOLL-FREE (800) 374-8633 can get you all set to play a round whenever, wherever you want.

Skydiving instruction is available at Skydive City ((813) 783-9399 TOLL-FREE (800) 783-9399, 4241 Skydive Lane, Zephyrhills. **Go-Kart Racing** competition, instruction and coaching is available for those over 12 years at MoKart Moretti Indoor Karting ((727) 866-3757 FAX (727) 865-9304 WEB SITE www.mokartusa.com, 4301 34thStreet South, St. Petersburg. **Bowling** is on offer at Sunrise Lanes ((727) 522-2174, 6393 Ninth Street North, St. Petersburg.

Sailboats, motorboats and **waverunners** are rented by the hour, half/full days for cruising, skiing or fishing at Tierra Verde Boat Rentals ((727) 867-0077, 100 Pinellas Bayway, Tierra Verde. **Parasailing** and equipment for other **water sports** are available at Captain Mike's (((727) 360-1998 TOLL-FREE (800) 330-1053, 4900 Gulf Boulevard, St. Petersburg Beach.

Flyfishing and **light tackle flats fishing** guided trips are offered by Fly the Flats Fishing Charts TOLL-FREE (800) 521-2872, 209 East Knights Griffin Road, Plant City; while **deep sea fishing** charters can be arranged with Far Horizons Sport ((727) 367-7252, 9610 Gulf Boulevard, Treasure Island. For fishing off terra firma, try North Pier ((727) 865-0668, St. Petersburg or South Pier ((941) 729-0117, Palmetto.

Shopping

The Pier (see WHAT TO SEE AND DO, above) at 800 Second Avenue contains exclusive boutiques and expensive gift shops. On Madeira Beach at 12,925 East Gulf Boulevard is the **Hubbard's Marina Boardwalk Shops** ((727) 398-6577, at Johns Pass Boardwalk is the home to gift shops and sportswear outlets. For outlet shops, head to the **Bay Area Outlet Mall** ((727) 535-2337, 15579 US Highway 19 North, Clearwater or **Prime Outlets at Ellenton** ((941) 723-1150, 5461 Factory Shops Boulevard, Ellenton. Further north you can find shops selling Greek products in the fishing village of Tarpon Springs, and Scottish tartan in Dunedin.

Nightlife

Downtown tends to be rather supine in the evenings, but sports fan will get a kick out of visiting Extra Inning ((727) 896-9872, 1850 Central Avenue, which is a sports bar with six levels of seating showing every sporting event available on satellite or television. As if this wasn't enough, they also have video games, pool tables, and pinball machines. At the Ringside Cafe ((727) 894-8465, 2742 Fourth Street North, you hear local and national rhythm and blues acts nightly in this funky old wooden house.

Most of the action is on the islands, especially at **The Beach Place** ☎ (727) 596-5633, 2405 Gulf Boulevard, Indian Rocks Beach, and **Cadillac Jack's** ☎ (727) 360-2099, at 145 107th Avenue, Treasure Island. Also recommended on Treasure Island is **Margo's** 11595 Gulf Boulevard, for live rock 'n' roll and **Gators on the Pass**, 12754 Kingfish Drive. A Bay Area mainstay for dancing and live classic rock bands is **Boomerz & Boulevard Grille & Sports Bar** ☎ (727) 391-7066, 6990 Seminole Boulevard, Seminole. For a good laugh, the **Coconuts Comedy Club** ☎ (727) 797-5653 or (727) 515-8059, at Cinema Café, 24095 US Highway 19 North, Clearwater. **Mahaffey Theater for the Arts** ☎ (727) 892-5767, 400 First Street South, St. Petersburg is host to quality, performing Arts in an intimate setting. For 24-hour information on what's happening at the Pier, the Times Bayfront Center and Mahaffey Theatre, the Coliseum and Tropicana Field ☎ (727) 825-3333.

WHERE TO STAY

Luxury

The **Renaissance Vinoy Resort** ☎ (727) 894-1000 FAX (727) 894-1970 WEB SITE www.renaissancehotels.com, 501 Fifth Avenue North East, St. Petersburg offers the style and glamour of another era combined with the opulence of a modern resort. The centerpiece of this waterfront hotel is the extensively renovated Vinoy Park Hotel, a building that is included on the National Register of Historic Places and is a member of the Historic Hotels of America. The resort has a private marina, 18-hole golf course, 14-court tennis complex and health spa. The pink, Mediterranean-style **Don CeSar Beach Resort and Spa** ☎ (727) 360-1881 TOLL-FREE (800) 282-1116 FAX (727) 367-6952 WEB SITE www.doncesar.com, 3400 Gulf Boulevard, is home of the celebrated Maritana Grille restaurant and a pampering spa. It's no wonder that this hotel has long been frequented by celebrities ranging from Scott Fitzgerald to Babe Ruth.

At the **Trade winds** ☎ (727) 562-1212 TOLL-FREE (888) 266-1233 FAX (727) 562-1222 WEB SITE www.tradewindsresort.com, at 5500 Gulf Boulevard, gondolas or paddleboats, operating on an internal canal system, deliver guests to their rooms. The recreational facilities feature a water sports center on the hotel's own beach, which has equipment for windsurfing, jet-skiing, water biking, and parasailing. Luxurious or tacky? It's a matter of personal opinion.

The **Belleview Biltmore Resort and Spa** ☎ (727) 442-6171 TOLL-FREE (727) 441-4173 WEB SITE www.belleviewbiltmore.com, 25 Belleview Boulevard, Clearwater, offers

guests Victorian accommodation with world-class amenities which include private docks, a golf course that opened in 1925, red-clay tennis courts, and a 14,000 sq ft (1,300 sq m) fitness center with spa.

Mid-range

In St. Petersburg, the **Orleans Bishop Bed and Breakfast** ☎ (727) 894-4312 TOLL-FREE (800) 676-4848 FAX 727) 822-1499 E-MAIL orleansbb@aol.com, is a quiet and comfortable hostelry at 256 First Avenue North. A long verandah with wicker chairs is provided for post-prandial relaxation, and all of the rooms are well maintained. At 105 Fifth

Sponges like these in Tarpon Springs can be bought for a fraction of the normal price.

Avenue North East, St. Petersburg, the **Mansion House** ☎ (727) 821-9391 TOLL-FREE (800) 274-7520 WEB SITE www.mansionbandb.com, offers bed and breakfast accommodation with the ambiance of the old North East. The **Bayboro House** ☎/FAX (727) 823-4955, is one of the city's oldest buildings, with conch shells lining the porch, and marble tables and grandfather clocks dotting the interior. The hotel is situated at 1719 Beach Drive Southeast.

There are 43 rooms and apartments overlooking the sea at the **Long Key Beach**

Resort ☎ (727) 360-1748 TOLL-FREE (888) 566-4539 FAX (727) 367-9026, 3828 Gulf Boulevard, and the **Dolphin Beach Resort** ☎ (727) 360-7011 TOLL-FREE (800) 237-8916 FAX (727) 367-5909 WEB SITE www.dolphinbeach.com, boasts 174 spacious rooms and its very own swath of white sandy beach at 4900 Gulf Boulevard. **Pasa Tiempo** ☎ (727) 367-9907 FAX (727) 367-9906 WEB SITE www.pasa-tiempo.com, 7141 Bay Street, St. Petersburg Beach, is a relaxed, Mediterranean style bed-and-breakfast with a deck over the bay and a private dock for fishing. For those who prefer a holiday without the kids, the **Shoreline Island Resort** ☎ (727) 397-6641 TOLL-FREE (800) 635-8373 FAX (727) 393-9157 WEB SITE www.shorelineislandresort.com, at 14200 Gulf Boulevard, Madeira Beach, is the perfect choice as no one under 21 is allowed. Tranquillity is the word at this beachfront hotel which has no restaurant, lounge or bar. The **Seabreeze Manor** ☎ (727) 343-4445 TOLL-FREE (888) 343-4445 FAX (727) 343-4447 WEB SITE www.seabreezemanor.com, 5701 Shore Boulevard, Gulport, was built in 1923 and is one of Florida's grand old homes, overlooking the park bordering Boca Ciega Bay. This bed-and-breakfast establishment offers private balconies, afternoon tea and an evening social hour with wine and cheese. Just minutes from Tarpon Springs, the Mediterranean style **Sheraton Four Points Hotel** ☎ (727) 942-0358 FAX(727) 938-9826, has comfortable, lakeside rooms at 37611 US Highway 19 North, Palm Harbor.

Inexpensive

For more economical rates in St. Petersburg you should check out **Grant Motel and Apartments** ☎ (727) 576-1369, at 9046 Fourth Street North; or the **Beach Park Motel** ☎ (727) 898-6325 TOLL-FREE (800) 657-7687, at 300 Northeast Beach Drive. Dormitory and semi-private accommodation is available at **St. Petersburg Hostel** ☎ (727) 822-4141 which is located at the McCarthy Hotel, 326 First Avenue North. In Clearwater Beach, try the white and yellow **Ivy League Motel** ☎ (727) 446-3477, at 600 Bayway Boulevard, directly on the bay, which stands out for its good value. Another good deal in this area can be found at **Sta 'N' Pla** ☎ (727) 442-4582 FAX (727) 442-6300 WEB SITE www.clearwaterbeach.com/STAPLA/stapla.html, 345 Hamden Drive. In Treasure Island, The **Molloy Gulf Motel and Cottages** ☎ (727) 367-1053 FAX (727) 367-6901, is on the Gulf of Mexico at 10164 Gulf Boulevard. Economical lodging can be found in Tarpon springs at **Scottish Inns** ☎ (727) 937-6121, 110 West Tarpon Avenue.

WHERE TO EAT

Expensive

The Keystone Club ☎ (727) 822-6600, 320 Fourth Street North, St. Petersburg, is a steak and chop house par excellence. Their prime rib is delicious, and so is their two pound pork chop. The Wine Cellar ☎ (727) 393-3491 WEB SITE www.thewinecellar.com,

17307 Gulf Boulevard, North Redington Beach, has been around for twenty years serving up outstanding Continental and American cuisine with attentive service in an old world setting. Another treasure is Domenicí Capri ☎ (727) 441-1111, at 411 Mandalay Avenue, Clearwater Bay, which has a delicious linguine with fresh clams, veal pizzaiola and seafood misto. If you are looking for fine dining in an intimate eatery, try Fetishes ☎ (727) 363-3700, 6690 Gulf Boulevard, St. Petersburg Beach, where you can dine on stuffed mussels, grilled shrimp on pesto and lobster-stuffed artichokes. The Grill at Feather Sound ☎ (727) 571-3400, 2325 Ulmerton Road, Clearwater, has a menu which includes fabulous steaks, succulent lumfin crab cakes and desserts that you just can't miss, including creme brulee and chocolate torte.

On the St. Petersburg side of the Gandy Bridge stands a run-down shack filled with the freshest crabs imaginable. Choose from blue, gold, soft-shell or stone crab at the **Crab Shack** ☎ (727) 576-7813, 11400 Gandy Boulevard. Those who prefer non-shellfish seafood should go to **Ted Peters** ☎ (727) 381-7931, at 1350 Pasadena Avenue South, St. Petersburg, where mullet and mackerel are smoked over red oak. Go past the Wagon Wheel Flea Market, you need to pull off onto the dirt road to 8285 Park Boulevard, Pinellas Park to find **Cajun Cafe** ☎ (727) 576-6732. Don't miss the crawfish cornbread, the po-boy sandwiches or the gator bites. And don't forget to wash it all down with ice-cold Dixie beer. **Seafood and Sunsets at Julies** ☎ (727) 441-2548, 351 South Gulfview Boulevard, Clearwater Beach offers Bahamian cracked crab, blackened gator and barbecue shrimp. Good chowder, hot wings and burgers can be had at Indian Rocks Beach at **Whitney's Beach Place** ☎ (727) 596-5633, 2405 Gulf Boulevard. Count yourself lucky if you are able to get a reservation at **Six Tables** ☎ (727) 786-8821, 1153 Main Street, Dunedin. Here there are only six tables with two sittings of a different six-course, fixed-price meal nightly. Authentic Greek cooking at its finest can be found at **Mykonos** ☎ (727) 934-4306 on the Sponge Docks at 628 Dodecanese Boulevard, Tarpon Springs.

Inexpensive

There are numerous inexpensive restaurants in St. Petersburg, among the best is **Sunset Grill** ☎ (727) 823-2382, 2996 Ninth Street North, which has hearty home-made burgers and thick milkshakes with live music on the weekends. You should also try Hilda La Tropicana ☎ (727) 898-9902, 320 First Avenue North, which serves up huge portions of Cuban sandwiches, yucca with mojo, fried plantain and black bean soup. The **Tamarind Tree Cafe** ☎ (727) 898-2115, 537 Central avenue, offers savory and satisfying vegetarian food, including chili, lasagna and macaroni and cheese. In North Redington Beach, The **Sweet Sage Cafe** ☎ (727) 391-0453, 16725 Gulf Beach Boulevard is an art gallery and bistro with gourmet coffees, soups, salads and decadent desserts. And in Clearwater Beach, **Shephard's Restaurant** ☎ (727) 441-6875, 601 South Gulfview Boulevard, has a huge seafood and prime rib buffets with a 31-item salad bar.

How to Get There

The St. Petersburg-Clearwater International Airport, 10 miles (16 km) southeast of Clearwater, is served by a reasonable number of national and international airlines. You will probably prefer to fly in to Tampa International Airport, on the eastern side of Old Tampa Bay.

Motorists should use the same roads for St. Petersburg as for Tampa. If you are coming from the south you can leave Interstate 75 north of Ellenton and take the Sunshine Skyway over the mouth of Tampa Bay to reach St. Petersburg.

SARASOTA

Known as the "Culture Capital" of Florida, Sarasota offers theater, classical music, opera, and a number of respected art galleries. Over the years, increasing numbers of artists, musicians, and writers have settled in Sarasota, attracted by the city's reputation for being hospitable to the arts. So if you are looking for culture to go with your sand, sea, and sun, this is the place for you.

Exterior view of John Ringling's winter residence, Ca'd'Zan in Sarasota.

BACKGROUND

Sarasota began to be noticed in 1927, when John Ringling, famous for the circus, established a winter residence for his family — and his circus — in the city. An avid art collector, with a special passion for Italian Renaissance and Baroque works, he built a museum to house his acquisitions. He also invested heavily in civic improvements for his adopted city, building hotels and island causeways and generally subsidizing the arts. The theaters and art galleries which proliferate in the city today testify to Ringling's enthusiastic patronage.

GENERAL INFORMATION

The Sarasota Convention and Visitors Center ☎ (941) 957-1877, is at 655 North Tamiami Trail, Sarasota, FL 34236, and the Sarasota Chamber of Commerce ☎ (941) 955-2508, is at 1551 Second Street, Sarasota, FL 33577.

For those of you flying into Sarasota, flight times are available from Sarasota-Bradenton Airport ☎ (941) 355-5200. For a taxi call Yellow Cabs ☎ (941) 955-3341, or to and from the airport try Airport Taxi ☎ (941) 365-1360.

For medical attention, call Jo Mills Reis Urgent Care Center ☎ (941) 917-7777

WHAT TO SEE AND DO

Sports

Baseball fans should know that the Cincinnati Reds hold their spring training and play their exhibition games here, at Ed Smith Stadium ☎ (941) 955-6501, 12th Street and Tuttle Avenue, Sarasota.

There is a good choice of **golf courses** in Sarasota, including the Sarasota Golf Club ☎ (941) 371-2431, at 7280 Leeswynn Drive, off Route 301, and the Bobby Jones Golf Club ☎ (941) 955-8097, at 1000 Circus Boulevard.

For **water sports** go to Don and Mike's Boat and Ski Rental ☎ (941) 966-4000, at Casey Key Marina on the waterfront downtown, where you can get surfboards, water skis, jet skis, wave jammers, miniboats, as well as windsurfing and water skiing instruction. Sailing enthusiasts should go to O'Leary's Sarasota Sailing School ☎ (941) 953-7505, 5 Bayfront Drive, Bayfront Park, near Marina Jack's restaurant, where you can rent sailboats and receive instruction on how to sail them. If you have the need for more power, C.B.'s Boat Rentals ☎ (941) 349-4400, 1249 Stickney Point Road at the Stickney Point Bridge rents out runabouts, deck and pontoons boats. **Fishing trips** can be arranged by Flying Fish Fleet ☎ (941) 366-3373, Marina Jacks, Sarasota Bayfront.

Biplane flights over Florida's Gulf Coast are available from GulfCoast Waco Bi-Planes ☎ (941) 359-2246, Sarasota/Bradenton Airport. Don't worry, the Waco planes are new, merely reproductions of the 1935 classic.

Sports equipment of many varieties, including rollarblades, bikes, kayaks and even beach chairs can be rented from Siesta Sports Rental ☎ (941) 346-1797, 6551 Midnight Pass Road, Southbridge Mall, Siesta Key.

Shopping

One of the best-known — and exclusive — shopping complexes on the Gulf Coast, **St. Armand's Circle** has over 100 specialty stores, including expensive gift shops and designer fashion outlets. Take Route 41 south to Route 789, turn right and cross Ringling Causeway to reach the circle of shops. For an equally wide choice at considerably lower prices head for the **Sarasota Square Mall** at 8201 South Tamiami Trail, or **Siesta Key** at 5000 Ocean Boulevard on Siesta Key. Or for real bargains, check out the Sarasota Outlet Center, just off exit 40 on University Parkway.

If you are looking for art, what better way to find it than by touring the **Towles Court Artist Colony** ☎ (941) 362-0960, 1945 Morrill Street, Sarasota and see the artists at work on your new piece.

Nightlife

The **Asolo Theatre Company** ☎ (941) 351-8000, at 5555 North Tamiami Trail, is a 40-year-old theater company that performs a well balanced repertoire during a season that runs from November through May at the Harold E. and Esther M. Mertz Theatre. A small professional company presents contemporary drama, comedies, and musicals at the **Florida Studio Theater** ☎ (941) 366-9796, 1241 North Palm Avenue; and the **Players of Sarasota** ☎ (941) 365-2494, enact comedies, thrillers, and musicals in a community theater at Route 41 and Ninth Street.

The **Florida West Coast Symphony** ✆ (941) 953-4252, Beatrice Friedman Symphony Center, 709 North Tamiami Trail, perform a variety of symphonic and chamber music from September through June, and you can hear internationally known artists, supported by young in-house apprentice singers, at the **Sarasota Opera House** ✆ (941) 953-7030 FAX (941) 954-1362, in a charming old theater at 61 North Pineapple Avenue.

For more information of the wealth of art available, contact the Sarasota County Arts Council ✆ (941) 365-5118, 1351 Fruitville Road, downtown.

For rawer entertainment, try **Geckos Grill and Pub** ✆ (941) 923-8896 at the Landings, home of the "famous bucket o' beer", which rocks until 2 AM nightly. **Captain Curt's Back Room** ✆ (941) 349-3885, Old Stickney Point and Midnight Pass Roads, is a sports bar and lounge with entertainment that includes live music, karaoke and sports events on television.

From September to April the **Sarasota Ballet of Florida** ✆ (941) 351-8000, 555 North Tamiami Trail, performs classical, modern and original ballets at the FSU Center, the Van Wezel, and the Sarasota Opera House.

Established in 1980, the **Jazz Club of Sarasota** ✆ (941) 366-1552 FAX (941) 366-1553, 290 Coconut Avenue, Building Three, is a non-profit organization hosting internationally known musicians in concerts and festivals.

The 50-plus professional members of the **Sarasota Concert Band** ✆ (941) 955-6660, 1345 Main Street, Suite E, perform from Broadway scores to Sousa marches in appearances at Van Wezel Hall from October through May.

At **Cafe Gardens & the Daiquiri Deck** ✆ (941) 349-8697, 5250 Ocean Boulevard, Siesta Key Village, you can enjoy 25 flavors of daiquiris while watching college and NFL football. For an evening on the water, arrange a cruise with **Fat Cat** ✆ (941) 362-7565 or **The Enterprise** ✆ (941) 951-1833, Marina Jack.

WHERE TO STAY

Luxury

The **Hyatt Sarasota** ✆ (941) 953-1234 TOLL-FREE (800) 228-9000 FAX (941) 952-1987 WEB SITE www.hyatt.com, is downtown next to a marina at 1000 Boulevard of the Arts. The hotel's fine restaurant, Scalini's, is much acclaimed,

The Ringling Museum of Art.

and its other amenities include a sauna, health club, and sailboats, as well as an excellent selection of water sports. There are 232 beach houses, villas, and apartments set in scenic grounds next to the ocean at the **Colony Beach and Tennis Resort** ☎ (941) 383-6464 TOLL-FREE (800) 282-1138 FAX (941) 383-7549 WEB SITE www.colonybeachresort.com, on Longboat Key north of Sarasota. All the accommodations are modern and self contained with full conveniences, and the resort's 21 tennis courts, fitness center, sporting and beach facilities are outstanding.

For more intimate surroundings, you might want to stay at **The Cypress** bed-and-breakfast ☎ (941) 955-4683 WEB SITE www.bbonline.com/fl/cypress, 621 Gulfstream Avenue, South Sarasota. All five guest rooms are tastefully decorated with American and European antiques, while the grounds overlook Sarasota Bay.

Mid-range

On South Tamiami Trail at No. 6660, is the modern and very comfortable **Days Inn Sarasota** ☎ (941) 993-4558, which is only a mile (1.6 km) from the beach. Facing the ocean at 459 Beach Road, on Siesta Key is a small, comfortable hotel with friendly service, the **Crescent House** ☎ (941) 346-0857 WEB SITE www.cresenthouse.com, which serves a complimentary continental breakfast each morning. The **Rolling Waves Cottages** ☎ (941) 383-1323 FAX (941) 383-7973 WEB SITE www.visitlongboatkey.com/rollingwaves, 6351 Gulf of Mexico Drive, Longboat Key, offers eight rustic cottages in an environment of simple beach pleasures. Cottages have full kitchen, cable television and air-conditioning. Also on Longboat Key is the **Sea Horse Beach Resort** ☎ (941) 383-2417 FAX (941) 387-8771 E-MAIL sresort@aol.com, 3453 Gulf of Mexico Drive, which has beachfront studio to two-bedroom apartments overlooking the gulf waters. On Anna Maria Island, **Palm Tree Villas** ☎ (941) 778-0910 FAX (941) 779-1066, 207 66th street, Holmes Beach, offers individually decorated apartments just 150 yards from the beach. Heated pool and private patios.

Inexpensive

With its own swimming pool and pleasant tropical gardens, the **Tides Inn** ☎ (941) 924-7541, is great value at 1800 Stickney Point Road. There are several inexpensive hotels on North Tamiami Trail, among them the Sarasota Motor Inn ☎ (941) 355-7747, at No. 7251; and the **Quayside Inn** ☎ (941) 366-0414 FAX (941) 954-3379, at No. 270.

Where to Eat

Expensive

Fresh seafood with crisp salads are served at **Marina Jack's** ☎ (941) 365-4232, 2 Marina Plaza, downtown, which affords a marvelous view over Sarasota Bay. The ***Marina Jack II*** is a paddle-wheel boat which leaves from Marina Plaza on lunch and dinner cruises. There is a northern Italian bias to the food at **Osteria** ☎ (941) 388-3671, 29 1/2 North Boulevard of Presidents, a charming restaurant bedecked with flowers, where the house specialty is their wonderful veal layered with prosciutto. One of the best continental restaurants in the area is the **Café L'Europe** ☎ (941) 388-4415 WEB SITE www.cafeleurope.net, at 431 Harding Circle on Lido Key, where I would urge you to try the wild mushroom strudel and the potato-crusted grouper. **Francoise et Henri** ☎ (941) 951-1510, 1359 Main Street, must be a contender for the most romantic restaurant in this area. Classic French cuisine, cooked perfectly, includes chateaubriand, crispy duck and Grand Marnier soufflé. For good solid American cuisine try **Michael's on East** ☎ (941) 366-0007 WEB SITE www.bestfood.com, at 1212 East Avenue South, Sarasota, where the desserts are sensational.

Moderate

The **Bistro at Island's End** ☎ (941) 779-2444, 204 Pine Avenue serves inspired dishes at a very low cost. The braised boneless short ribs with red wine sauce is delicious, so is the apple smoked salmon. For the kids, there is a "build your own pizza" offering. **Althea's** ☎ (941) 484-5187, 220 West Miami Avenue, Venice serves up an amazing breakfast of pancakes, steak and eggs or omelets. Lunch and dinner comprises salads, sandwiches and burgers, and also a good selection of vegetarian mains. **Fishnet Inc** ☎ (941) 795-5976, 4628 199th Street West, is a relaxing seafood restaurant that has a bar in the center which is an actual fishing boat. Here you'll get old favorites like conch chowder and crab cakes, but also more imaginative dishes like grapefruit grilled salmon. For seafood and Italian favorites, try **Poki Joe's Greatest Hits** ☎ (941) 922-5915, at 6614 Superior Avenue, which boasts Sarasota's most creative Sunday brunch.

Inexpensive

Everything on the menu is homemade, café-like at **Der Dutchman** ☎ (941) 955-8007 WEB SITE www.derdutchmanfl.com, 3713 Bahia Vista. **Johnny Leverock's Seafood** House ☎ (941) 794-8900, 12320 Manatee Avenue, serves up imaginative seafood dishes, like grilled mahi mahi primavera, at surprisingly reasonable prices. Another great place for seafood is **Walt's Fish and Chips Restaurant** ☎ (941) 921-4605,4144 South Tamiami Trail, where you should try the original combination platter or the steamed crabs. If you feel like some good old Amish home cooking, head to **Yoder's** ☎ (941) 955-7771, 3434 Bahia Vista Street, where you can find meatloaf, breaded veal, and liver and onions on the menu. For hot dogs and barbecued ribs and mountains of fries, head out to Siesta Key and the **Old Salty Dog Pub** ☎ (941) 349-0158, at 5023 Ocean Boulevard.

How to Get There

The Sarasota-Bradenton Airport is served by most of the major national airlines; in any case, the larger Tampa and St. Petersburg airports are also both convenient for Sarasota.

By car, Interstate 75 is the main route in from the north and south (the more picturesque Route 41 also comes in from the south). Routes 64 and 70 enter Sarasota from the east.

THE SHELL COAST

The Shell Coast runs from Captiva Island, near Fort Myers, to Ten Thousand Islands in the south, near Everglades City. Fort Myers is one of the fastest growing cities in the United States and an important center of commerce, while Fort Myers Beach is a resort community on the offshore island of Estero. There are also luxury resort facilities on the islands of Captiva and Sanibel.

Further south, the city of Naples has 41 miles (66 km) of beaches and some of the best shopping on the entire Gulf Coast. Continuing down the coast, you come to Marco Island, with its modern Gulf-front

Working boats temporarily lie at rest, moored at Tarpon Springs.

condominiums and its carefully preserved fishing villages such as Goodland. At the southern end of the Shell Coast are the "Ten Thousand Islands", which are still largely undeveloped and provide a home for a dazzling array of wildlife.

GENERAL INFORMATION

The Fort Myers Chamber of Commerce ☎ (941) 332-3624 WEB SITE www.fortmyers.org, is at 2310 Edwards Street, PO Box 9289, Fort Myers, FL 33902; and the Fort Myers Beach Chamber of Commerce ☎ (941) 454-7500 WEB SITE www.coconet.com/fmbeach, is at 17200 San Carlos Boulevard, Fort Myers Beach, FL 33931. The Visitors Welcome Center is at 6900 Daniels Parkway. The Sanibel-Captiva Chamber of Commerce ☎ (941) 472-1080 FAX (941) 472-1070, is at 1159 Causeway Road, Sanibel, FL 33957; and the Lee Island Coast Convention and Visitors Bureau (941) 338-3500 TOLL-FREE (800) 237-6444 FAX (941) 334-1106 WEB SITE www.LeeIslandCoast.com, is at 2180 West First Street, Suite 100, Fort Myers, FL33901. The Naples Chamber of Commerce ☎ (941) 262-6376 FAX (941) 262-8374, is at 3620 Tamiami Trail North, Naples, FL 33940. The Chamber Visitor Center ☎ (941) 262-6141 FAX (941) 435-9910 WEB SITE www.naples-on-line.com, 895 Fifth Avenue South, Naples and Visit Naples Inc ☎ (941) 403-0600 WEB SITE www.visitnaples.com, is located at 1400 Gulfshore Boulevard North, Suite 218, Naples, Fl 34102.

WHAT TO SEE AND DO

Sports

Baseball fans can see the Boston Red Sox in spring training at the City of Palms Park ☎ (941) 334-4700, 2201 Edion Avenue and the Minnesota Twins at the Six Mile Cypress Road, between Daniels Parkway and US Highway 41.

There is no shortage of **golf courses** along the Shell Coast, including the Bay Beach Golf Club ☎ (941) 463-2064, at 7401 Estero Boulevard in Fort Myers Beach; the Beachview Golf Club ☎ (941) 472-2626, at 1110 Parview Drive South on Sanibel Island, and Boyne South Golf Club ☎ (941) 732-0034, at 18100 Royal Tree Parkway, Naples.

There are literally hundreds of outfits in this area where you can rent a **canoe**, **kayak**, **sailboat**, **jetski**, or **power boat**, the ones listed here have the some of the greatest range of craft for rental. Adventures in Paradise ☎ (941) 472-8443 FAX (941) 472-3922 WEB SITE www.portsanibelmarina.com, 14341 Port Comfort Road, Fort Myers; Captiva Kayak & Wildlife Adventures ☎ (941) 395-2925 FAX (941) 472-5837, 15041 Captiva Drive, Captiva; Tarpon Bay Recreation Inc ☎ (941) 472-8900 FAX (941) 395-2772, 900 Tarpon Bay Road, Sanibel; Estero River Outfitters ☎ (941) 992-4050 FAX (941) 992-9023 WEB SITE www.all-florida.com/swestero.htm, 20991 South Tamiami Trail, Estero.

Fly fishing trips can be arranged through Back Bay Flats Fishing Charters ☎ (941) 458-0300, 15051 Punta Rassa Road, Fort Myers; West Coast Fishing Charters ☎ (941) 283-9340 WEB SITE www.cees.net/fishing, 1804 North West 26th Avenue, Cape Coral and Estero Bay Boat Tours ☎ (941) 992-2200 WEB SITE www.ecotours-esterobay.com, 5231 Mamie Street South West, Bonita Springs, who can also arrange **deep sea fishing** trips.

You can receive instruction and arrange **scuba diving** trips with Underseas Diving Academy ☎ (941) 262-0707, 998 Sixth Avenue South, Naples or with Scuba Adventures ☎ (941) 434-7477, 971 Creech Road, also in Naples.

M&H Stables ☎ (941) 455-8764 FAX (941) 352-1186 WEB SITE www.mhstables.com, 2750 Newman Drive, Naples, will take you on supervised trail rides on **horseback** and even give you cowboy style riding lessons.

Off-road bike and **swamp buggy tours** are available at Babcock Wilderness Adventures TOLL-FREE (800) 500-5583, 8000 State Road 31, North Fort Myers. Call for directions.

Shopping

For the best selection of shops in Fort Myers go to the **Royal Palm Square Shopping Center** located at 1400 Colonial Boulevard. In Estero, there is great shopping at Miromar Outlets ☎ (941) 948-3766, exit 19 off Interstate 75, Corkscrew Road.

On Sanibel Island, **Periwinkle Way** is lined with gift shops, shell shops, and a good selection of stores for sports and swimwear.

For upscale shopping in Bonita Bay, there is realy only one place to go, and that's the **Promenade** ☎ (941) 261-6100 on US Highway 41 in Bonita Springs.

The best-quality shops in Naples can be found at the **Old Marine Market Place**, 1200 Fifth Avenue South, while **Prime Outlets** TOLL-FREE (877) 466-8853, 10 minutes South of Exit 15 off Interstate 75 is good value.

Nightlife

In Fort Myers, the **Broadway Palm Dinner Theatre** ☎ (941) 278-4422 TOLL-FREE (800) 475-7256, 1380 Colonial Boulevard, puts on a good buffet followed by a high-quality Broadway-style performance. Call the **Alliance of the Arts** ☎ (941) 939-2787, to find out what is currently running at their 500-seat theater or outdoor amphitheater. They are situated at 10091 McGregor Boulevard in Fort Myers. Likewise, call the **Old Schoolhouse Theatre** ☎ (941) 472-6862 to find out what is on at this little schoolhouse, which has been recycled to a house community theater and has cabaret performances year-round. The theater is at 1905 Periwindle Way, Sanibel. Very close is the **Pirate Playhouse** ☎ (941) 472-0006, 2200 Periwinkle Way, which offers a variety of comedy, musical and dramatic performances.

In Naples call the **United Arts Council of Collier County** ☎ (941) 263-8242, 1051 Fifth Avenue South, to find out what is happening on the arts scene in this area. The **Philharmonic Center for the Arts** ☎ (941) 597-1111, 5833 Pelican Bay Boulevard, is home to the Naples Philharmonic symphony orchestra and chorale, the Philharmonic Galleries and the Miami City Ballet. Contact them to find out what's playing, from Broadway, ballet, Big Band Sound, chamber music and children's programs. The local theater group, **Sugden Community Theater** ☎ (941) 263-7990, 701 Fifth Avenue South, entertains year-round.

There is an array of dinner cruises to choose from. On Fort Myers Beach, there is **Europa SeaKruz** ☎ (941) 463-5000 FAX (941) 463-7111, 645 San Carlos Boulevard; in Sanibel, try **Captain Joe's Charters** ☎ (941) 472-8658 FAX (941) 472-8951, 6460 Sanibel-Captiva Road, and in Naples, try **Naples Princess** ☎ (941) 649-2275, 1001 Tenth Avenue South.

The Fort Myers area is the best place for living it up after dark on the Shell Coast. In Fort Myers itself there is **Crazy Bob's House of Sound** ☎ (941) 334-2229, 2240 McGregor Boulevard which has the feel of a concert

People and pelicans wind up a tranquil evening of fishing on a Sarasota pier.

hall where you can dance to live performances of well-known classic rock artists and bands. **Shooter Waterfront Cafe** ☾ (941) 334-2727 in the Holiday Inn SunSpree, 2220 West First Street, is one of the area's most popular nightspots, with a casual outdoor Tiki bar and regular live music on the Caloosahatchee River. In Fort Myers Beach, go along Estero Boulevard and sooner or later you will find what you're looking for.

WHERE TO STAY

Luxury

In Fort Myers the **Sanibel Harbor Resort and Spa** ☾ (941) 466-4000 TOLL-FREE (800) 767-7777 FAX (941) 466-6050 WEB SITE www sanibel-resort.com, 17260 Harbour Point Drive, offers luxurious hotel rooms and spacious condominiums amid 80 acres of unspoiled surroundings overlooking Sanibel and Captiva islands. **Collier Inn** ☾ (941) 283-4443, is an exclusive inn on Useppa Island in the former home of advertising magnet Barron Collier. The inn has three luxury suites and four deluxe rooms all furnished in the finest antiques with themes tied to the history of the island. Boats to the island are arranged through the reception center at ☾ (941) 283-1061. In Naples there is the deluxe **Ritz-Carlton** ☾ (941) 598-3300 FAX (941) 598-6691 WEB SITE www .ritzcarlton.com, at 280 Vanderbilt Beach Road, on a private peninsula overlooking Sanibel and Captive Islands. The **Registry Resort** ☾ (941) 597-3232 TOLL-FREE (800) 247-9810 FAX (941) 597-9151 WEB SITE www.registryhotels.com, at 475 Seagate Drive, Naples, is decorated with Italian marble and sparkling chandeliers in surprisingly unpretentious surroundings. This beachfront property has tennis courts, three pools and a fitness center.

Mid-range

The comfortable **Fountain Motel** ☾ (941) 481-0429, at 14621 McGregor Boulevard, Fort Myers, has both rooms and apartments. **Fairfiel Inn** ☾ (941) 437-5600 FAX (941) 437-5616, 7090 Cypress Terrace, Fort Myers, has comfortable, spacious rooms with a heated outdoor pool, exercise room and serves a hearty continental breakfast; and the **Outrigger Beach Resort** ☾ (941) 463-6577, at 6200 Estero Boulevard, is on the oceanfront in Fort Myers Beach. On Sanibel Island, Beachview Cottages ☾ (941) 472-1202 TOLL-FREE (800)860-0532 E-MAIL www.castaway@castawayssanibel.com, 3325 West Gulf Drive have simple but well-equipped apartments right on the beach. **La Playa Beach/Racquet Inn** ☾ (941) 597-3123 TOLL-FREE (800) 237-6883 FAX (941) 597-6278, near Vanderbilt Beach at 9891 Gulf Shore Drive, Naples, is particularly recommended for families. The **Lemon Tree Inn** ☾ (941) 262-1414 TOLL-FREE (888) 800-5366 FAX (941) 262-2638, 250 Ninth Street South Naples has a relaxed and secluded atmosphere in an Old Florida-style house. At the upper end of the moderate category is the comfortable **Trianon** ☾ (941) 435-9600 FAX (941)261-0025 WEB SITE www.trianon .com, on 955 Seventh Avenue South, which is located in the residential neighborhood of Old Naples.Also in Old Naples, **The Inn on Fifth** ☾ (941) 403-8777 FAX (941) 403-8778 WEB SITE www.naplesinn.com, 699 Fifth Avenue, is a boutique hotel with lots of old world Mediterranean charm.

Inexpensive

There are not too many budget deals on the Shell Coast, but three places that I know to be good value for the money are the **Ta Ki Ki Motel** ☾ (941) 334-2135, at 2631 First Street, Fort Myers; the Dolphin Inn ☾ (941) 463-6049 FAX (941) 463-2148 E-MAIL dolphin @olsusa.com, 6555 Estero Boulevard, Fort Myers Beach and the Flamingo Apartment Motel ☾ (941) 261-7017 FAX (941) 261-7769 383 Sixth Avenue South, Naples-on-the-Gulf.

WHERE TO EAT

Expensive

In Fort Myers Beach, the **Snug Harbor Restaurant and Lounge** ☾ (941) 463-8077, at 645 San Carlos Boulevard, features wonderful seafood from local waters. **Morgan's Forest** ☾ (941) 472-4100, 1231 Middle Gulf Drive, Sanibel Island, is an "authentic reproduction" of a South American Rainforest on Sanibel Island, and a multiple area award winner. Their Pescado Yucateco — snapper and crab meat in garlic butter, rolled in romaine lettuce leaves and topped with mushrooms and bernaise sauce, is delicious. The **Grill Room** ☎ (941) 598-3300 at the Ritz-Carlton Hotel, 280 Vanderbilt Beach Road, serves wonderful traditional continental cuisine.

Moderate

The seafood is impeccably prepared and presented at **The Prawnbroker** ☎ (941) 489-2226, 13451-16 McGregor Boulevard, in Fort Myers. For good, honest just-about-everything in Fort Myers you should head for the **Riverwalk Fish and Ale House** ☎ (941) 263-2734, at 1200 Fifth Avenue South. On Fort Myers Beach **Pappa Mondo** ☎ (941) 765-9660, serves up fresh homemade pasta and other Italian delights at 1821 Estero Boulevard. In Naples, The **Swan River** ☎ (941) 403-7002, 3741 Tamiami Trail North, has the freshest seafood, bought directly from local boats, and the **Silver Spoon** ☎ (941) 591-2123 FAX (941) 591-3231, 5375 Tamiami Trail North #210, is an American café with good burgers, pizza, and pasta.

Inexpensive

In Fort Myers, **Woody's Bar-B-Q** ☎ (941) 997-1424, at 6701 North Tamiami Trail, is exactly what you might expect, and it is excellent. In Fort Myers Beach, **Pete's Time Out Café** ☎ (941) 463-5900, 1005 Estero Boulevard, has good homemade soup, salads and sandwiches, while **Dusseldorf's on the Beach** ☎ (941) 463-5251, Seafarers Village Mall, 1113 Estero Boulevard, has a menu "that has been tested by thousands of beer drinkers around the world".

HOW TO GET THERE

The Southwest Florida Regional Airport is 10 miles (16 km) southeast of Fort Myers and is served by many national airlines.

The principal north-south roads through the region are Interstate 75 and Route 41. Route 17 approaches the Shell Coast from the northeast, and Everglades Parkway ("Alligator Alley") is the main road from the east into Naples. Route 80 enters Fort Myers from the east.

A picket-fenced walkway leads down to a pristine beach for an early morning dip.

The Everglades

EVERGLADES NATIONAL PARK

Many, if not most, people imagine a swamp filled with alligators when they think of the Everglades. But the reality is something that more closely resembles a vast mid-western wheat field: an expanse of sawgrass, interrupted by copses of hardwood and cypress trees, which, at the end of winter before the spring rains, appears totally dry. When the rains do come, and the water levels rise, this grassy plain is transformed into a unique river — over 60 miles (100 km) wide and six inches (15 cm) deep — which flows slowly southward to the Gulf Coast and Florida Bay. The river drops only 13 ft (four meters) over its 100-mile (160-km) length, which gives you some idea of the flatness of the Everglades.

The Indian name for the region is *Pa-hay-okee*, meaning the "grassy waters". An early white surveyor came up with the name River Glades, but later maps changed River to Ever, and the new name stuck. The water sources of the Everglades start with the rivers of central Florida's Kissimmee Valley, which runs into the huge Lake Okeechobee, which in turn feeds the grassy waters. On its course southwards, the river passes through a zone where temperate and subtropical climates blend: this is one of the reasons for the great diversity of animal and plant life in the region, which includes such rarities as the manatee and the Florida panther, not to mention half of the 650 species of birds found in North America, as well as 45 kinds of flora that cannot be found anywhere else in the world.

ABOVE: In the Everglades, a pelican thinks things over. OPPOSITE: Alligators flourish in the Florida swamplands.

The Everglades are also a source of water for farmlands to the east around the city of Homestead and Florida City, and for the homes of millions of people who live along Florida's southeast coast. The drainage involved has had its effect on the ecological balance of the Everglades, with water levels dropping in recent years as demands increase from the thirsty and booming city populations on both coasts.

Everglades National Park consists of approximately 1.5 million acres (500,000 hectares) of protected land and coastline stretching from Everglades City in the northwest down to the coast near Key Largo in the southeast, all policed by park rangers and carefully tended by conservationists.

BACKGROUND

Calusas, Tequestas, and Mayaimis lived in Pa-hay-okee for two thousand years before white settlers arrived in the latter half of the nineteenth century and set about requisitioning the marshland for agricultural purposes. By 1909, a canal running from Lake Okeechobee to Miami was completed, and numerous dikes and irrigation canals had been installed across the plains, impeding the natural rise and fall of water levels. In the 1920s a series of hurricanes whipped up the waters of Lake Okeechobee, causing floods in the surrounding area, killing 2,000 people. In response, the United States Army Corps of Engineers ringed the lake with the Hoover Dike and constructed a further 1,400 miles (2,254 km) of canals and levees to control and channel the waters of the lake and the Everglades.

All of this drastically upset the eco-sys-

tem, which demands that the marshes are "dry" in winter and crossed by the river in the summer. Sometimes, due to water mismanagement, the cycle was reversed, with devastating results for flora and fauna alike. Since 1930 the Everglades have lost about 90 percent of their marsh and wading birds, and without great conservation efforts even the alligator would have disappeared.

A conservationist named Marjorie Stoneman Douglas published a book in 1947 entitled: *The Everglades: River of Grass*, which began: "There are no other Everglades in the world." She went on to warn that the region was in danger of being destroyed if action wasn't taken urgently. The book had an unforeseen effect. That same year President Truman created the Everglades National Park, to the north, and then in 1989, a further 107,000 acres (42,800 hectares) of the ecologically crucial Shark River Slough in the northeast was added to the park.

Meanwhile, and perhaps more importantly, politicians have realized that the protection of the Everglades is a popular voting issue. The "grassy waters" may survive after all.

GENERAL INFORMATION

In case of an **emergency** while in the park call ☎ (305) 242-7272. Outside of the park and in nearby Florida City, you can call the **Physicians Office of Florida City** ☎ (305) 245-0110, 646 W. Palm Drive, Florida City.

The best time of year to visit the Everglades is winter — the "dry" season — when you will see the greatest concentration of bird life and far fewer mosquitoes and other biting insects, which can be a real problem at other times of the year. (If you do visit in summer, be sure to take plenty of insect repellent, because there are plenty of repellent insects.) At any time of the year you should be aware of the presence of poisonous plants and snakes (particularly coral snakes, water moccasins, diamondback and pigmy rattlesnakes), guide booklets to the park will clearly identify them for you. If you keep to the official trails and follow all written and oral instructions, you should have no problems.

If you do decide to head out on your own, be sure to file your planned walking or boating route at the nearest ranger station. The park is vast and there are very few navigational points of reference; reckless amateur explorers have been known to disappear without a trace in the Everglades. What you have to remember is that this is not a theme park or a zoo; this is the real thing: one of the great wild areas in the world.

Most importantly, *don't* (yes, it has been known to happen) go near or try to touch the alligators, however somnolent they may appear. They have an incredible turn of speed and leaping ability, which could well be your last great surprise if you get too close to one.

The federal custodian of the Everglades is the **National Park Service** ☎ (305) 242-7700 WEB SITE www.nps.gov/ever, whose headquarters are located at 40001 State Road 9336, in Homestead. Another useful source of information to help plan a trip to the Everglades is the **Tropical Everglades Visitor Association** ☎ (305) 245-9180 FAX (305) 247-4335 TOLL-FREE (800) 388-9669 WEB SITE www.tropicalevergaldes.com, 160 US Highway 1, Florida City.

For lodging information in neighboring cities outside the park, try calling the **Homestead and Florida City Chamber of Commerce** ☎ (305) 247-2332, 540 North Homestead Boulevard, Homestead, FL 33030. The **Everglades Area Chamber of Commerce** ☎ (941) 695-3941, is at 32016 East Tamiami Trail, Everglades City, and the **Marco Island and the Everglades Convention and Visitors Bureau** ☎ (800) 788-MARCO, is at 1102 North Collier Boulevard, Marco Island.

WHAT TO SEE AND DO

More than one million people visit the Everglades annually. There are three main entrances to the park — at Shark Valley in the northeast, off Route 41; at Everglades City in the northwest on Route 29, off Route 41; and the entrance southwest of Homestead on Route 9336, where the **Ernest F. Coe Visitor Center** is located. I would recommend the latter entrance if you can spend only one day in the park. The visitor center offers exhibits on the wildlife and ecology of the Everglades, and there are free brochures and maps explaining the attractions and trails you can find in the park. Naturalists lead numerous hikes or canoe trips throughout the park, and these are highly recommended for those interested in this unique and fragile eco-system, but you are free to make your own way from the visitor center along a 38-mile (61 km) park road called the Ingraham Highway. You pass through sawgrass plains, hardwood and cypress copses, and mangrove swamps on the way to the fishing village of Flamingo, 35 miles (56 km) to the southwest.

Branching off from the road are trails and boardwalks, some of which lead to "hammocks" — raised, tree-clad mounds in the swamps. The first turning on the left takes you to the **Royal Palm Visitor Center**, which has slide shows with recorded commentaries and rangers who will direct you along the various nature trails that branch out from the center. The Anhinga and Gumbo Limbo trails are particularly popular boardwalks, from which you can see alligators, egrets, herons, raccoons, opossums, and lizards, among other wildlife. There are several more twists and turns along Ingraham Highway before you reach Flamingo; the maps and official guides will tell you where they are and what you can expect to see.

OPPOSITE: An osprey keeps a lookout from its lofty vantage point. ABOVE: A boat operator in Everglades National Park.

When you arrive in Flamingo, at the park's southern end, go to the visitor center for information about trails, boat routes, picnic areas, campsites, and special attractions in the area. There is a restaurant, shop, motel, and marina in the village, plus a bayfront observation deck with telescopes to view the islands and wildlife offshore. At the Gulf Coast Visitor Center at Everglades City you can board a narrated boat tour and explore the coastal mangroves, as well as Ten Thousand Islands, since this is the park's western entrance to the ocean.

Located at the northern end of the park is the **Shark Valley Information Center,** where you can board tram tours, rent bicycles or visit the book shop.

The Tamiami Trail (Route 41) runs from Miami to Everglades City on the Gulf Coast, and is a good way to view the park's northern attractions. Twenty-five miles (40 km) west of Miami you will find the **Miccosukee Indian Village** ((305) 223-8380 or 223-8388 FAX (305) 223-1011, where 500 contemporary Miccosukees live and work. You can watch native Miccosukee women at work and buy their handmade ornaments and crafts. Or you can watch a trainer "wrestle" an alligator using the same techniques that the Miccosukee used for decades to tie up the gators. You can take a stroll on the boardwalks or an airboat ride into the surrounding wilderness. The village is open daily from 9 AM to 5 PM. A mile (1.6 km) down the road from the village is **Shark Valley** ((305) 221-8455 from where you can take a tram ride around a 15-mile (24-km) loop road. The tram stops at an observation tower, which allows panoramic views of the surrounding countryside and such local denizens as alligators, otters, wood storks, and kites. Reservations are advisable for the December–March period.

In Everglades City you can take a 12-mile (19-km) boat tour through the offshore Ten Thousand Islands region. The **Everglades National Park Boat Tours** ((941) 695-2591 TOLL-FREE (800) 445-7724, leave from Parks Docks on Chokoloskee Causeway, half a mile south (1.6 km) of the Gulf Coast Ranger Station on Route 29, off Route 41. If you are in Chokoloskee Bay at sunset, you will be treated to the sight of as many as 20,000 birds returning to the mainland to roost.

Farther south down the coast, **boat trips** aboard the *Bald Eagle* leave from Flamingo Marina ((941) 695-3101 TOLL-FREE (800) 600-3813 FAX (813) 695-3921, on a 90-minute tour of the islands in Florida Bay, providing close-up views of the fascinating birdlife.

A two-hour cruise aboard the *Pelican* (at the same phone numbers) out of Flamingo Marina explores the tropical estuaries and mangrove swamps of the coast, giving you a chance to see manatees, dolphins, sharks, and a variety of birds, among them the bald eagle. There is also a three-hour ride onboard the *Everglades Queen;* a replica of an old steam launch from the turn of the century. Reservations can be made — and are strongly recommended — in the winter season for all the boat tours.

There is also an inland water route, called the Wilderness Waterway, from Flamingo to Everglades City. The route's course is marked with posts along its 99-mile (159-km) length. You can receive more information about it from the visitor center in the village. Outboard motorboats take about six hours to make the trip, and can be rented from Flamingo Marina.

Coopertown Airboat Rides ☎ (305) 226-6048, 22700 Southwest Eighth Street, off Krome Avenue, west of Miami, offers 30-minute excursions that take in hardwood hammocks and alligator holes.

For a comprehensive guided tour of the park, including an airboat ride, the Indian Village, Shark Valley, nature trails, and lunch, contact **Everglades Excursions** ☎ (941) 262-1914 TOLL-FREE (800) 592-0848, 1100 Sixth Avenue South, Suite 227A, Naples. This all-day tour takes you on a jungle cruise through the park, to historic Everglades City and a gator exhibit.

Everglades Alligator Farm ☎ (305) 247-2628 FAX (305) 248-9711 E-MAIL gatorfarmr@aol.com WEB SITE www.everglades.com, 40351 Southwest 192 Avenue, Homestead, is located on the edge of the Everglades National Park and is a great place to learn about the life cycle of the alligator, of which you'll see thousands in breeding ponds. The farm rehabilitates animals that cannot be released back into the wild, and you can also take in an alligator show. The airboat ride is one of Florida's fastest, and drivers give you a thrill by doing 360-degree turns in the swampy waters.

If visiting the Everglades park does not fulfill your wildlife experience, then drive north on Interstate 75 from either Miami or Fort Lauderdale and visit the **Big Cypress National Preserve**: 2,400 square miles of huge cypress trees with a similar eco-system as the Everglades. U.S. Highway 41 (Tamiami Trail) and I-75 both cross the preserve, but the Tamiami Trail provides better access to the **Oasis Visitor Center** ☎ (941) 695-4111 WEB SITE

OPPOSITE: Roadside veetable stand.
ABOVE: A squadron of black skimmers.

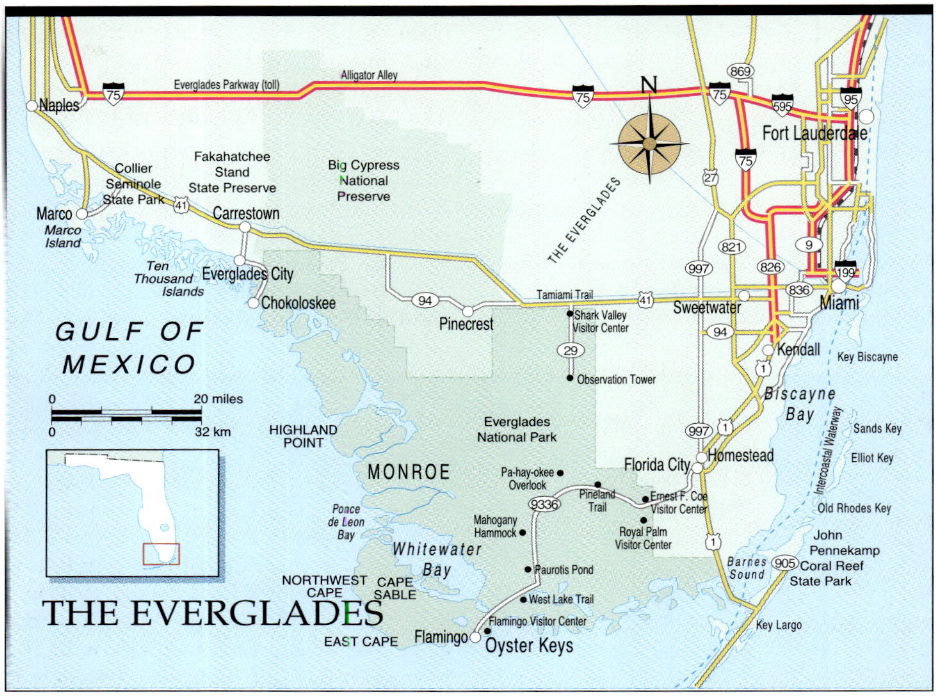

www.nps.gov/bicy, in Ochopee.

You can immerse yourself in the native culture of Florida's Seminole tribe at the **Billie Swamp Safari** TOLL-FREE (800) 949-6101 WEB SITE www.seminoletribe.com/safari. Turn off I-75 exit 14, then drive north 19 miles to the park entrance on the Big Cypress Reservation. You can enjoy airboat rides with close-up views of water buffalo and alligators. The facility also has a rustic camping village where visitors can stay in native-style *chickees* overnight.

The **Ah-Tah-Thi-Ki Museum** ☎ (941) 902-1113, E-MAIL museum@semtribe.com WEB SITE www.seminoletribe.com/museum, on Country Road 833 to West Boundary Road, Clewiston, provides an introduction to the culture of the Seminoles. Take Interstate 75 from Naples or Fort Lauderdale to exit 14, then continue north 17 miles.

Sports

If you want to take a **guided tour of the park by canoe, kayak, or motorboat** contact the NACT. Everglades Canoe/Kayak Outpost ☎ (941) 695-4666 FAX (941) 695-4155, 107 Camellia Street, Everglades City. There are six canoe trails in the Flamingo area, including the southern end of the Wilderness Waterway. Canoes can be rented at the Flamingo Marina, along with skiffs and houseboats. For **fishing**, contact the Back Country Sports Fishing ☎ (305) 248-9470, 28230 Southwest 136th Place, Homestead. For fishing charters, try the Captain Adam Redford Inc. ☎ (305) 255-7618 FAX (305) 254-3012, 8701 Southwest 148th Street, Flamingo, within the Everglades National Park.

Golfers have a choice of two courses that are open to the public: Redland Golf and Country Club ☎ (305) 247-8503, 24451 S.W. 177 Avenue, Homestead and Keys Gate Golf & Tennis Club ☎ (800) KEYS-GATE, 888 Kingman Rd., Homestead, an 18-hole championship, par 71 course.

Shopping

The shop at Flamingo Marina sells the usual gifts and souvenirs, guides to the Everglades, local crafts, film, sun lotion, and insect repellent. Homestead is the only place in the vicinity of the Everglades with any significant selection of shops.

One of the places you must stop at is the **Robert Is Here Fruit Stand** ☎ (305) 246-1592 FAX (305) 246-6273 E-MAIL fresh@robertishere

.com WEB SITE www.robertishere.com, 19900 Southwest 144th Street, Homestead, which is famous for key lime milkshakes and key lime pies. You are encouraged to pick your own fresh tropical fruit and you can purchase rare produce from this family-owned stand that has been at this junction for more than 25 years.

Homestead is becoming known as an antique shopping district. One of the places to check out is the **Homestead Antique Federation** ((305) 247-1771, 41 North Krome Avenue.

For some of Florida's best bargains on designer labels and other fashion, pop into **Prime Outlets** ((305) 248-4727, 250 East Palm Drive, Florida City.

Where to Stay

Many Everglades visitors choose to stay at hotels in the Greater Miami area, but struggling through heavy traffic to reach one of the park's entrances seriously reduces one's "quality time" in the park. The town of Homestead offers several comfortable and moderately-priced hotels, including the **Budget Express Inn** ((305) 245-4330 FAX (305) 248-0470 E-MAIL budget@ambertides.com WEB SITE www.ambertides.com, 27707 South Dixie Highway (US Highway 1), Homestead, located 20 minutes from both the Everglades park and the Homestead Motorsport Race Track. The **Holiday Inn Express** ((305) 247-7020 FAX (305) 247-7020, 990 North Homestead Boulevard, Homestead, also near the Motorsport complex and convenient to the park, is more on the upscale end and has a relaxing poolside bar. The **Green Stone Motel** ((305) 247-8334 TOLL-FREE (888) 223-3460, 304 North Krome Avenue, is a historic motel in downtown Hoemestead with 24 spacious smoking and non-smoking rooms.

Katy's Place B&B ((305) 247-0201 FAX (305) 247-4588 E-MAIL Info@Katysplace.com WEB SITE www.katysplace.com, 31850 Southwest 195 Avenue, Homestead, offers three bed-and-breakfast rooms, with a full kitchen and an exercise facility. Right next door you will find the **Ten Oaks Bed & Breakfast** ((305) 247-7035 FAX (305) 247-7433 E-MAIL Nancy@ten_oaks.com WEB SITE www.tenoaks.com, 31800 Southwest 195th Avenue, Homestead, a private home with three bed-and-breakfast rooms.

Another suitable bed-and-breakfast is the **Country Grove Guesthouse** ((305) 247-6572 E-MAIL info@groveinn.com WEB SITE www.groveinn.com, 22540 Southwest Krome Avenue, Redlands. The 14-room inn has private baths, and live music during a Friday Happy Hour from 7pm.

In Everglades City, there are tasteful rooms and self-catering villas at the **Captain's Table Lodge and Villas** ((941) 695-4211 TOLL-FREE (800) 741-6430, FAX (941) 695-2633, 102 Broadway Street. Probably the best-known hotel, and the only one actually inside Everglades National Park, is the **Flamingo Lodge, Marina, and Outpost Resort** ((941) 695-3101 TOLL-FREE (800) 600-3813 FAX (941) 695-3921 WEB SITE www.amfac.com, 38 miles southwest of park headquarters in Flamingo. It offers 103 rooms and 24 cottages with kitchenettes, a very friendly staff, rooms overlooking Florida Bay, and a marina. Reservations are strongly advised for the winter season. Like the Captain's Table, the Flamingo Lodge is moderately priced.

On the Banks of the Everglades... A B&B Inn ((941) 695-3151 TOLL-FREE (888) 431-1977 FAX (941) 695-3335, 201 West Broadway, Everglades City, features eight moderate apartments with full kitchens, and not too far away from Everglades City is the **Port of the Islands Resort and Marina** ((941) 394-3101 TOLL-FREE (800) 237-4173, 25000 Tamiami Trail East, with two pools and suites available.

A low-cost alternative is the **Everglades International Hostel** ((305) 248-1122 TOLL-FREE (800) 372-3874 FAX (305) 245-7622 E-MAIL gladeshostel@hotmail.com WEB SITE www.members.xoom.com/gladeshostel, 20 Southwest Second Avenue, Florida City. Housed in a 1930's boarding house, the dorm beds and family rooms are very affordable, and the hostel is convenient to the Everglades and the Florida Keys. Canoe rentals are also available.

All three **Campgrounds** in the Everglades are basic (no electricity). You must provide your own food and water (and insect repellent). Note: the park rangers come down justifiably hard on litterbugs. Anything you bring in you must take back out with you. Information on the campsites, and permits to stay in them, are available from the ranger stations in Flamingo and Everglades City, or at any of the visitor centers at the entrances to the park and inside the park grounds.

Three campsites are accessible by foot, and almost 43 additional sites are accessible only by canoe or boat, along Florida Bay, the Gulf Coast, and on inland rivers and waterways Reservations can be made in person up to 24 hours before entry. Fees

are $10 for 1-6 people, $20 for 7-12 people, $30 for a group of 13 or more. An official camping permit is required for registration purposes and to control the number of campers. Call the **National Park Service** at TOLL-FREE (800) 365-2267, or ☎ (888) 530-9796 for the hearing impaired.

WHERE TO EAT

The Tamiami Trail (Route 41) between Miami and Shark Valley and the area from Homestead to Florida City offer the best dining possibilities in or near the Everglades.

The **Miccosukee Restaurant** ☎ (305) 223-8388, Tamiami Trail, has such native American specialties as pumpkin bread, tacos, breaded catfish, and frogs' legs. The restaurant is by the Shark Valley entrance on Route 41, and it is very reasonably priced. By contrast, the expensive **Oyster House Restaurant** ☎ (941) 695-2073 or (941) 695-3423, Highway 29, across the street from the entrance station in Everglades City serves alligator and prime rib and other local delicacies. **El Toro Taco** ☎ (305) 245-8182, 1 South Krome Avenue, Homestead, has superb Mexican food at superbly low prices.

In Florida City, you have three choices: **Angie's Café** ☎ (305) 245-8939, 404 Southeast First Avenue, **Beethoven Restaurant** ☎ (305) 247-6655, 321 West Palm Drive, and the nearby **Mutineer Restaurant**.

In Everglades City you must try the **Rod and Gun Club** ☎ (941) 695-2101, at 200 Riverside Drive, which serves delicious steaks, poultry, and seafood on a porch where you can watch boats drift by as you eat. On the second floor of the visitor center in Flamingo, the **Flamingo Restaurant** ☎ (941) 695-3101, has wonderful views over Florida Bay, and an eclectic menu featuring Cuban pork loin roasted with garlic and lime, and delicious pan fried marlin.

HOW TO GET THERE

Most visitors to the Everglades fly into Miami International Airport. Greyhound offers bus service from the airport to Homestead, but from there you will have to find your own way into the park. You can rent a car at the airport. An alternative is to fly into Fort Myers International Airport north of Everglades City.

The easiest way to reach the park from Miami by car is to drive from the Florida Turnpike to the Homestead-Florida City area, where it merges with US Highway 1. Turn right at the first traffic light onto Palm Drive. Continue to Route 9336 and turn right: this will take you to the main visitor center and Flamingo. Route 41 — also known as the Tamiami Trail — runs from Miami to the Shark Valley entrance, and then on to Everglades City. Route 41 is also the principal highway down the Gulf Coast to the Everglades.

ABOVE: Visitors focus on the local fauna.
RIGHT: Anhinga nest in the Everglades.

JOE'S
JOE'S
SLOP
Hemingway's
FAVORITE
Bar
MUST HAVE DRIVERS LICENSE OR STATE I.D.
SHOES
AND
SHIRT
REQUIRED
2.00
COVER
COCKTAILS

Florida Keys

THE SEQUENCE OF CORAL AND LIMESTONE ISLANDS known as the Florida Keys runs in a southwesterly curve from Biscayne Bay almost 124 miles (200 km) down to Key West. The Keys appears on a map like a long sea wall, battered and breached, but still preventing the waters of the Atlantic from washing over southern Florida's marshlands.

In fact, the Keys have their own sunken defensive wall, in the form of a live coral reef (the only one in the United States) that lies off their eastern coasts. This protective reef means that there is little surf and surprisingly few beaches on the eastern shores.

The name "Key" is derived from the Spanish word *cayo*, meaning "little island." The islands have been known as the Keys since the early nineteenth century. The name first given to them, by the sixteenth-century explorer Ponce de León, was *Los Martires*, and throughout the seventeenth and eighteenth centuries the coves and inlets of Los Martires were ideal bases for infamous pirates such as Blackbeard and Lafitte, who regularly attacked treasure-laden Spanish ships traveling from South America.

By the early nineteenth century, piracy had died out and the islands were renamed the Florida Keys. The first community of European settlers on the islands was at Key West which, with its deep-water port, soon became a major salvaging town. The town continued to boom throughout the nineteenth century, while the rest of the Keys remained virtually undeveloped and largely uninhabited — except for a few very small groups of native Americans and a handful of tiny salvaging villages in the Middle and Upper Keys.

It was in 1905 that the Keys attracted the attention of Henry Flagler, who decided to extend his Florida East Coast Railroad to Key West. He envisioned the railway would carry wealthy sportsmen to lavish resorts, as well as export cargo to Key West. The railroad was completed in 1916, and it included one bridge that was over seven miles (11 km) long.

In 1935, much of the railroad was destroyed by a terrible hurricane, but within a few years a road developed following literally in the tracks of the railroad. The Ocean Highway — Route 1 — remains to this day the world's longest entirely coastal road. The Ocean Highway is lined with green mile-markers (MMs), and as it is the only major road through the Keys, most hotels, restaurants, and shops have the number of the nearest mile-marker as their address (e.g., The Caribbean Club, Route 1, MM 104). The MMs start on Route 1 a mile (1.6 km) south of Florida City, with MM 126, and end with MM 0 in Key West. If an address falls between two mile-markers, the designation 5 is used.

Nowadays, the Keys are extremely popular vacation destinations, offering all kinds of fishing, diving, and water sports facilities. You can also enjoy the uniquely romantic experience of watching the sun rise over the Atlantic. Later in the day, after you have wandered over to the other side of the Key, you can watch the sun set into the Gulf of Mexico. At the tip of the Ocean Highway, is America's southernmost city, with one of the most evocative names on the entire continent: Key West, once the home of Ernest Hemingway, Tennessee Williams, Wallace Stevens, and a host of other great American writers.

KEY LARGO TO LONG KEY

The string of islands from Key Largo to Long Key are known as the Upper Keys. These are the islands that attract the most tourists, as they are within a few hours' drive of Miami and Palm Beach. Key Largo is the starting point of the 113 mile (182 km) journey along the Ocean Highway to Key West. It is best known as the setting for the Bogart-Bacall film. Key Largo is also the nearest island to the John Pennekamp Coral Reef State Park — the world's first underwater park — and is the main diving site in the Keys.

Further south are the Upper and Lower Matecumbe Keys, the name derives from the Spanish *matar* ("to kill") and *hombre* ("man"), which is a self-explanatory reference to the welcome originally given to shipwrecked sailors by the islands' original native inhabitants. These Keys are particularly renowned for their first class fishing. Islamorada is known as the "purple

A favorite local pastime; cruising the Keys.

island" because of the color of the snails that once thrived on its shores; Indian Key is an island of particularly lush tropical growth; Long Key is noted for the quality of its beaches and camping facilities.

GENERAL INFORMATION

The Key **Largo Chamber of Commerce** ((305) 451-1414 TOLL-FREE (800) 822-1088, is at MM 106 bayside, Key Largo. The **Islamorada Chamber of Commerce** ((305) 664-4503 TOLL-FREE (800) 322-5397, can be found at MM 82.5 bayside, Islamorada. The **Florida Keys and Key West Visitors Bureau** ((305) 296-1552 TOLL-FREE (800) 352-5397 WEB SITE www.fla-keys.com, can be contacted by writing to PO Box 1147, Key West, FL 33041.

WHAT TO SEE AND DO

The **Key Largo Undersea Park** ((305) 451-2353, Route 1, MM 103.2, 51 Shoreland Drive, is an acre-wide enclosed lagoon, designed to emulate the ocean's natural ecology and environment while providing easy access to divers and snorkellers of all skill levels. There is a working subaquatic marine research center, an underwater art studio, even an underwater hotel (see WHERE TO STAY, below).

The main attraction in the Key Largo area, however, is the **John Pennekamp Coral Reef State Park** ((305) 451-1202 or (305) 451-1621, Route 1, MM 102.5. It is 21 miles (34 km) long and eight miles (13 km) wide, covering over 2,000 acres (800 hectares) of land and 178 sq miles (287 sq km) of water, and containing 40 types of coral and 650 species of fish. Scuba and snorkeling tours, as well as glass-bottom boat tours, are available for you to view the coral, fish, and shipwrecks in the park's waters. There are also beaches and nature trails on the park's coast. An aquarium, gift shop, and Visitor Center can be found in the park, which is open from 8 AM to 5 PM every day. There is a small charge for admission and prices vary greatly for the diving and boat tours, for which you are urged to make reservations. You can also arrange a glass-bottom boat ride to the John Pennekamp Coral Reef State Park with Key Largo Glass Bottom Boat ((305) 451-4655.

Off this park and the adjacent Key Largo National Marine Sanctuary is the 4,000-pound (1,800-kg) bronze statue "**Christ is Deep**", standing on a 20-ton concrete base in 25 feet (7.5 meters) of water. A gift from industrialist and undersea sportsman Egidi

Cressi, it has become one of the most photographed underwater sites in the world.

Fans of Humphrey Bogart will be interested to know that the original boat used in the film, ***African Queen***, is on display outside the Holiday Inn Dock, Route 1, MM 100. Visitors can set up an appointment with the boat's owner, James Hendricks ☎ (305) 451-2121, to go aboard for a ride.

At Dolphins Plus ☎ (305) 451-1993, Route 1, MM 99.5, visitors enjoy **swimming with dolphins** plus a special marine orientation program which is designed to make people more aware of the plight of endangered marine species. Extended group programs up to six days long are offered.

Florida Keys Wild Bird Rehabilitation Center ☎ (305) 852-4486, Route 1, MM 93.6, rescues and rehabilitates injured birds and releases them to the wild. Recovering birds can be seen at the center.

In Islamorada you can visit the **Theater of the Sea** ☎ (305) 664-2431, Route 1, MM 84.5, which is one of the nation's top marine parks; here you will find dolphin and sea lion shows, as well as collections of sharks and stingrays. Reservations are required to swim with the dolphins or stingrays. The park is open from 9:30 AM to 4 PM daily.

The **Indian Key State Historic Site** ☎ (305) 664-9814 WEB SITE www.dep.state.fl.us/parks, can be reached by taking a boat from MM 77.5, Indian Key Fill, between Upper and Lower Matecumbe Keys, to the 10-acre (four-hectare) **Indian Key** ☎ (305) 664-9814 from where tour boats leave. Guides lead you on a tour of a reconstructed salvaging village and of the surrounding tropical vegetation. Boats also leave MM 77.5 for **Lignumvitae Key** ☎ (305) 664-4815, an uninhabited virgin hammock with tropical growth of the kind that once covered most of the Keys. A maximum of 50 people can visit the island between 10:00 AM AND 2:00 PM, ALTHOUGH IT IS closed Tuesdays and Wednesdays. On Long Key, the **Long Key State Park** ☎ (305) 664-4815, Route 1, MM 67.5, is popular for its beaches and its canoe and camping facilities.

Sports

Water sports, not surprisingly, are *the* sports on the Keys. **Fishing trips** are arranged in Key Largo at Sailors Choice ☎ (305) 451-1802 or (305) 451-0041, Route 1, MM 100, and in Islamorada at the Holiday Isle Resort Marina ☎ (305) 664-2321 TOLL-FREE (800) 327-7070

OPPOSITE: Crab floats. ABOVE: Sportfishing boats at Key West.

WEB SITE www.theisle.com, Route 1, MM 84.5. The marina also offers **diving courses** and **wreck trips**, and has diving and snorkelling equipment for rent, as well as boats and yachts. The John Pennekamp Coral Reef State Park ☎ (305) 451-1621, Route 1, MM 102.5, has a water sports center, which has **snorkeling tours** three times a day, **scuba diving** trips twice a day and a **combined sailing and snorkeling** trip daily. The center's dive shop also rents all sorts of equipment, including sailboats, canoes, and windsurfing boards.

Caribbean Water Sports ☎ (305) 852-4707, at the Westin Resort, Route 1, MM 97, offers **waverunners**, **windsurfers**, **sailing lessons**, **parasailing**, **diving**, **snorkeling**, **Jamaican bobsled** and more. Papa Joe's Maria ☎ (305) 664-5505, Route 1, MM 79.7, has single and double **kayaks** for rent, and all along Route 1 in the Key Largo area you will find shops catering to anglers and those interested in water sports.

Florida Bay Outfitters ☎ (305) 451-3018, 104050 Overseas Highway, Key Largo, also offers a variety of **backcountry adventures** into the Everglades National Park, Florida State parks on Lignumvitae Key and the Indian Key historic site.

Shopping

Key Largo's streets are lined with department and grocery stores, hardware stores, gift shops, fishing shops, and shops selling everything you might need for the beach — in other words, here you will find the best selection of shops in the Upper Keys. Diving enthusiasts may want to visit **Divers Outlet** ☎ (305) 451-0815 WEB SITE www.diversoutlet.com, 105410 Overseas Highway, which offers discount dive and snorkel gear. In Islamorada, **H.T. Chittum** ☎ (305) 664-4421, 82748 Overseas Highway offers casual, sophisticated clothing along with gifts and even fishing equipment. The **Bimini Town Shops** alongside the Holiday Isle Resort, Route 1, MM 84, have an excellent range of beach and swimwear.

Nightlife

At the **Caribbean Club** ☎ (305) 451-9970, Route 1, MM 104, you can sit on the verandah with a drink and watch the sun fall into the Gulf of Mexico. This, by the way, is the club where part of the film *Key Largo* was shot. Bogart would have liked the place now, as it is open 24 hours a day. The liveliest night spot in Key Largo, though, is **Coconuts** ☎ (305) 451-4107, MM 100 next to Marina del Mar, which features disco music and live reggae bands. In Islamorada, the nightlife centers around the **Holiday Isle Resort** ☎ (305) 664-2321, Route 1, MM 84, where you can find the **Tiki Bar**, the **Bilge Bar**, the **Kokomo Beach Bar**, and the **Horizon Restaurant** at the top of the hotel, which has mellow, but nonetheless live, music for dancing.

WHERE TO STAY

Luxury

Marriott Key Largo Bay Beach ☎ (305) 453-0000 TOLL-FREE (800) 932-9332, Route I, MM 103.8, 103800 Overseas Highway, offers 153 rooms and suites on the beach with kitchen facilities, and a pool, fitness center, dockage, game room, and *tiki* bar.

For an experience you'll never forget, **Jules Undersea Lodge** ☎ (305) 451-2352 FAX (315) 451-4789 WEB SITE www.jul.com, Key Largo Undersea Park, 51 Shoreland Drive, is the world's first and only underwater hotel. Guests have to actually scuba dive to enter the lodge. For guests who are not certified, there is a three-hour course available. The lodge is the size of a cottage with two bedrooms, and can accommodate up to six people. Belongings are transferred to the lodge in a waterproof suitcase.

Offering some of the best facilities in Key Largo, the **Marina del Mar** ☎ (305) 451-4107 TOLL-FREE (800) 451-3483 FAX (305) 451-1891 WEB SITE www.marinadelmar.com, Route 1, MM 100, 527 Caribbean Drive, has a marina with water sports equipment, several tennis courts, a fitness center, a swimming pool, a night club, and spacious, well-equipped rooms. The hotel is also in an excellent position near the offshore diving areas. Another top hotel in Key Largo is the **Westin Key Largo** ☎ (305) 852-5553 TOLL-FREE (800) 539-5274 WEB SITE www.1800keylargo.com, Route 1, MM 97, 97000 South Overseas Highway, which faces the Gulf.

In Islamorada, an alternative to regular hotel rooms is offered in the form of luxury houseboats. **Luxurious Houseboat-Villas**, TOLL-FREE (800) 749-2911 E-MAIL fun@pyh.com, Plantation Yacht Harbor Resort and Marina, 87000 Overseas Highway, have houseboats that sleep up to eight people, with full-sized kitchens, cable television, and full resort facilities just steps away.

The **Holiday Isle Resort** ☎ (305) 664-2321 TOLL-FREE (800) 327-7070, off of Route 1 at MM 84, has just about everything: seven lounge bars, five different restaurants, beachside shops, two swimming pools, a famous marine park next door, and accommodation ranging from luxurious rooms to fully-equipped suites and apartments. The **Chesapeake Resort** ☎ (305) 664-4662 TOLL-FREE (800) 338-3395 FAX (305) 664-8595 E-MAIL Chesapea@aol.com, Route 1, MM 83.5, is an oceanfront resort with two pools, tennis, playground, deepwater lagoon, dock, watersports, and gardens. A little further down Route 1, at MM 82 in Islamorada, is the **Cheeca Lodge** ☎ (305) 664-4651 TOLL-FREE (800) 327-2888 FAX (305) 664-2893, an old fishing lodge that has recently been renovated. It has a health spa, tennis courts, and a nine-hole golf course in its 25 acre (10 hectare) grounds. A pier poking out into the Atlantic affords fishing, diving, and snorkeling facilities.

Mid-range

There are seven very pretty two- and three-bedroom cottages set in tropical gardens at **Largo Lodge** ☎ (305) 451-0424 TOLL-FREE (800) 468-4378, Route 1, MM 101.7, next to the beach. The nearby **Kona Kai Bayfront Resort** ☎ (305) 852-7200 TOLL-FREE (800) 365-7829 FAX (305) 852-4629 E-MAIL Konakai@aol.com, a restored 1940s bayfront resort, has a lush tropical landscaping, hammocks, and an attractive swimming pool. The stucco-style **Stone Ledge Lodge** ☎ (305) 852-8114, Route 1, MM 95 3, 95320 Overseas Highway, offers

simple rooms or studios overlooking a small beach, while the **Coconut Bay Resort** ☎ (305) 852-1625 TOLL-FREE (800) 385-0986, Route 1, MM 97.7 bayside, 97770 Overseas Highway, has six units on a sandy beach with pool, tiki hut, dock and boat ramp. **Lookout Lodge** ☎ (305) 852-9915 TOLL-FREE (800) 870-1772 FAX (303) 852-3035. Route 1, MM 87.7, 87770 Overseas Highway, is a charming and intimate waterfront resort with nine rooms.

Inexpensive

There are not many cheap hotels in the Keys, especially the nearer one gets to Key

OPPOSITE: The southernmost house in the United States. ABOVE: A typical old Key West residence stands proud amid the semi-tropical vegetation.

West, but in Key Largo there is **the comfortable Ed & Ellen's** ☎ (305) 451-4712 TOLL-FREE (800) 889-5905, ROUTE 1, MM 103.4, which has six units; the **Sea Trail Motel** ☎ (305) 852-8001, Route 1, MM 98.5 with eight units, and the **Tropic Vista Motel** ☎ (305) 852-8799 TOLL-FREE (800) 537-3253, Route 1, MM 90.5, which has 24 units. All three are well-kept and spacious.

Camping is another inexpensive alternative and there are many well-kept sites to choose from in this area. The **Key Largo Campground** ☎ (305) 451-1431 TOLL-FREE (800) 526-7688, Route 1, MM 101.5 is 10 minutes from the ocean, while **America Outdoors** ☎ (305) 852-8054, also on Route 1, at MM 97.5, has 154 camping spaces and a sandy beach.

Such is the reputation of **Marker 88** ☎ (305) 852-9315, that you should book well in advance if you are to have any hope of getting a table. The reputation is well-deserved, and the address is predictable: MM 88, Route 1, Plantation Key. Atop the Holiday Isle Resort in Islamorada at MM 84 is the **Horizon Restaurant** ☎ (305) 664-2321, with wonderful views over the ocean; and the very popular **Atlantic Edge** ☎ (305) 664-4651 is within the Cheeca Lodge Hotel at MM 82. George Bush once had a meal here, descibing it as "real swell".

WHERE TO EAT

Expensive

The Quay ☎ (305) 451-0943 TOLL-FREE (800) 927-7126 WEB SITE www.quayrest.com, Route 1, MM 102.5 bayside, Key Largo, is in a particularly special location, overlooking the gulf. The menu features numerous French-inspired seafood dishes, along with alligator meat sautéed in garlic and lemon butter.

Moderate

The very popular **Ziggy's Conch Restaurant** ☎ (305) 664-3391, Route 1, MM 83.5, Islamorada, offers some of the best seafood in the Keys. Some of the rest of the best is available at the **Italian Fisherman** ☎ (305) 451-4471, Route 1, MM 104 bayside, Key Largo, where you should definitely try the *linguini marechiaro:* clams, scallops, and shrimps in a garlic butter sauce and served with linguini. Steaks and excellent prime rib are offered along with the seafood at the **Green Turtle Inn Restaurant** ☎ (305) 664-9031, Route 1, MM 81.5, Islamorada, and the two-level **Coral Grill** ☎ (305) 664-4803, Route 1, MM 83.5, Islamorada, has a gourmet buffet on Sundays (it's wise to book ahead).

Inexpensive

In Key Largo, **Ganim's Kountry Kitchen** has two popular locations that both serve hearty country-style breakfasts, lunches and dinners at affordable prices. Both are on Route 1, the first at MM 102 ☎ (305) 451-3337, and the second a little further down, at MM 99.6 ☎ (305) 451-2895. In Islamorada there are two places I'm particularly fond of: **Lor-e-lei on the Gulf** ☎ (305) 664-4656, at MM 82, which overlooks a small harbor and specializes in lamb and ribs; and **Papa Joe's** ☎ (305) 664-8109, at MM 79.7, where the seafood is Italianate.

HOW TO GET THERE

A number of national airlines, including Delta, have regular flights out of Miami International Airport into Marathon Regional Airport, which is about 20 miles (32 km) southwest of Long Key. Most people, however, drive from Miami down Route 1.

GRASSY KEY TO STOCK ISLAND

The islands between Grassy Key and Stock Island constitute the chain known as the Middle and Lower Keys. The population centers here are **Marathon** in the Middle Keys and **Big Pine** in the Lower Keys. Marathon, on Vaca Key, is a resort and fishing center, and the start of the Seven mile Bridge — the country's longest, it reaches all the way to Sunshine Key, next to Bahia Honda Key. Bahia Honda has some of the best beaches you'll find between Key Largo and Key West.

The vegetation is more lush in the Lower Keys, due to the slightly warmer and more tropical climate, but the activities are the same as anywhere else in the Keys: water sports, fishing, beachcombing, swimming. On Big Pine Key and the surrounding islands you can see a unique and wonderful sight: the tiny, endangered Key Deer which, as you are frequently reminded by road signs, you should watch out for when driving, particularly at night. From Big Pine Key the highway passes over various wild-looking Keys with wide expanses of beach. Roadside motels, resorts, and restaurants begin to increase in number as you approach Key West.

GENERAL INFORMATION

The **Greater Marathon Chamber of Commerce** ☎ (305) 743-5417 TOLL-FREE (800) 842-9580, is at Route 1, MM 53.5 bayside, Marathon, FL 33043, and the **Lower Keys Chamber of Commerce** ☎ (305) 872-2411 TOLL-FREE (800) 872-3722, is in Big Pine at MM 31, on the ocean side.

WHAT TO SEE AND DO

Grassy Key is the home of the **Dolphin Research Center** ☎ (305) 289-1121, Route 1, MM 59, which — I am not joking — rehabilitates show dolphins suffering from stress-related conditions brought on by overwork, pressure to perform, and cramped pools. You can swim with one of these sweet, long-suffering creatures if you like. The Center is closed on Mondays and Tuesdays. In the town of Marathon is the 63-acre (25.2-hectare) **Tropical Crane Point Hammock** ☎ (305) 743-9100, on Route 1, MM 50, which has the largest native Florida thatch palm hammock. Visit too the historic Adderley House at MM 51, which houses a **Natural History Museum** and the **Children's Museum of the Florida Keys**.

OPPOSITE: One form of transport in Key West.
ABOVE: Another form — the Conch Tour Train.

There are also archaeological sites and renovated conch-style houses in its grounds.

The **Seven Mile Bridge** between Vaca Key and Sunshine Key is a wonder to behold, as indeed is the vastness of the seas to either side of it.

On Bahia Honda Key at the **Bahia Honda State Park** ((305) 872-3210, MM 37, you can find white sand beaches, tropical plants and birds, a nature trail, picnic areas, and a very picturesque marina. Big Pine Key — which is covered in pines and cacti — contains the **National Key Deer Refuge**. In 1954 there were only 50 deer left in the park, but protection and careful management have enabled their numbers to reach something approaching 300, despite well-meaning tourists feeding them often-lethal snacks. (If you see a deer, please don't feed it anything: deers have a fragile metabolism, and the fines for feeding them are heavy.)

Guided tours of the out-islands, as well as a variety of **wildlife** and **snorkeling tours** are offered by Island Excursions ((305) 872-9863, at MM 29.5 and by Strike Zoen Charters ((305) 872-9863 also at MM 29.5, bayside.

Just a few miles offshore from Route 1 MM 30, the **Looe Key National Marine Sanctuary** is a protected reef area. The water is reasonably shallow, and there is a brilliant array of underwater landscapes, making for a perfect place for either snorkelling or scuba-diving.

Sports

You can go on **fishing trips** out of Marathon with Marathon Lady ((305) 743-5580, Route 1 MM 53, at Vaca Cut Bridge, or Starlight ((305) 743-8436, also on Route 1, MM 53. For offshore trips, instruction, and rental of **diving** equipment, try Paradise Diver ((305) 872-1114 TOLL-FREE (800) 852-0348 WEB SITE www.diveguideint.com/P0865.htm at MM 39, Sunshine Key Resort; or Innerspace ((305) 872-2319 TOLL-FREE (800) 538-2896 E-MAIL swansea@aol.com, Route 1, MM 29.5 Big Pine Key. You can rent **boats** in Marathon at Rick's Watercraft Rental ((305) 743-2450, Banana Bay Resort, Route 1, MM 49.5

Wet Willy's Watersports ((305) 743-9822, has a large selection of **boats**, **waverunners**, **hydro bikes**, **hobiecats** and **windsurfers** for rent on the beach of the Buccaneer Resort, Route 1, MM 48.5. Sombrero Reef Explorers ((305) 743-0536, 19 Sombrero Boulevard at the Sombrero Resort and Lighthouse Marina offers two **snorkel** trips daily, and Spirit Snorkeling ((305) 289-0614, at MM 47.5 next to Porky's Bayside Restaurant, Marathon, specializes in family snorkeling trips.

Reflections Kayak Nature Tours ☎ (305) 872-2896, PO Box 430861, Big Pine Key arranges **kayak** excursions into the Great White Heron National Wildlife Refuge and the Everglades National Park. Lost World Adventures ☎ (305) 872-1040 provides **guided tours** into the islands of the Great White Heron Refuge, Key Deer Refuge and the Coupon Bight Aquatic Preserve.

Harley Davidson **motorcycles** are for rent at Island Cycle Motor Company ☎ (305) 289-3012, Route 1, MM 50.5, and Key Colony Beach ☎ (305) 289-1533, in Marathon, has a **golf course** and **tennis courts** open to the public.

Shopping

The only real shopping center in the Middle and Lower Keys is in Marathon, which has several shopping malls and a selection of shops selling gifts, souvenirs, sportswear, and swimwear.

Nightlife

At the Faro Blanco Resort, 1966 Overseas Highway, MM 48.5, you'll find **Angler's Lounge** ☎ (305) 743-9018, which features live entertainment by local performers. For exceptional sushi with live music to go with it try **Shuckers Raw Bar** ☎ (305) 743-8686 at MM 46 oceanside. **Gary's Pub & Billiards** ☎ (305) 743-0622, is located at 5271 Overseas Highway, oceanside, and is known locally as the "adult day-care center of the Keys" — with pool tables, video games, pinball machines and television for watching sports. At the popular **No Name Pub** ☎ (305) 872-9115, on Big Pine Key at the north end of Watson Boulevard, you can play darts and pool, hear live bands, eat hearty pub grub and choose from over 70 beers. Rock bands also perform regularly at the **Looe Key Reef Resort** ☎ (305) 872-2215 at MM 27.5, on Ramrod Key.

Further south, **Mangrove Mama's** ☎ (305) 745-3030, Route 1, MM 20, has live entertainment on Friday, Saturday and Sunday evenings.

Many of the watersports companies offer **sunset cruises**. Try All Aqua Adventures ☎ (305) 743-6628, located bayside at Faro Blanco Marine Resort, 1966 Overseas Highway, MM 48.5.

OPPOSITE: Diners enjoy a Key West sunset.
ABOVE: A Key West memorial to Cubans who fled the 1959 revolution.

WHERE TO STAY

Luxury

Occupying its own 60 acre (24 hectare) island, the **Hawk's Cay Resort** ✆ (305) 743-7000 TOLL-FREE (800) 432-2242, at MM 61 in Marathon, is in a tropical setting — which is cleverly echoed in the decor and furnishings of the rooms and suites. The resort has its own Atlantic lagoon, with a pretty beach, where you can swim or windsurf or take your boat out to sea. There are also tennis courts and a golf course in the grounds.

The **Faro Blanco Marine Resort** ✆ (305) 743-9018 TOLL-FREE (800) 759-3276, 1966 Overseas Highway, MM 48.5, offers lodgings for every taste and budget, from 2000-sq-foot (180-sq-meter) luxury condos to floating houseboat staterooms to two lighthouse apartments.

On Key Colony Beach at 351 Ocean Drive East, is the **Ocean Beach Club** ✆ (305) 289-0525, with its own beach, a swimming pool, and apartments. One of the most pleasant residences in the Lower Keys is the **Little Palm Island** ✆ (305) 872-2524, FAX (305) 872-4843 WEB SITE www.noblehousehotel.com, at MM 28.5 on Little Torch Key, which has 28 oceanfront, one-bedroom, thatched-roof bungalow suites in beautiful grounds, designed for absolute privacy and seclusion. Children under 16 are not allowed, and the resort has a full range of water sports facilities.

Mid-range

At **The Buccaneer Hotel** ☎ (305) 743-9071 TOLL-FREE (800) 237-3329 FAX (305) 743-5470 WEB SITE www.floridakey.com, MM 48.5, Marathon, you have the choice of renting a room, a cottage, or a villa. You can rent windsurfer boards, powerboats, yachts, and other boats, including bareboat charters, at the nearby marina.

On Little Torch Key there is the moderately-priced **Palmer's Resort** ☎ (305) 872-2157 FAX (305) 872-2014 WEB SITE www.parmersplace .com, 565 Barry Avenue, which offers cottages and motel rooms in lush seclusion. On Sugarloaf Key, the **Sugar Loaf Lodge** ☎ (305) 745-3211 FAX (305) 745-3389 has pretty hotel rooms that all face the water, offering relaxation in wonderful tropical surroundings. Diving enthusiasts, however, might prefer to stay at **Looe Key Resort and Dive Center** ☎ (305) 872-3786 TOLL-FREE (800) 942-5397 FAX (305) 872-3736 WEB SITE www .diveflakeys.com, on Ramrod Key MM 27.5, where you can board the dive boat just outside the back door of your room. The resort has a large swimming pool, a good seafood restaurant, and a Tiki bar. The **Conch Key Cottages** ☎ (305) 289-1377, just off Route 1 at MM 62.5, occupy their own lovely island, reached by a causeway. The delightful wooden cottages are fully-fitted and are near a small private beach.

Inexpensive

The **Valhalla Beach Motel** ☎ (305) 289-0616, which is by the ocean in Marathon at MM 57, 56243 Ocean Drive, has 12 fairly basic but clean rooms. Somewhat more expensive, but still in the inexpensive category, **Tropical Cottages** ☎ (305) 743-6048 MM50, 243 61st Street gulfside, offers ten cozy cottages with kitchenettes.

WHERE TO EAT

Expensive

The **Hideaway Café** ☎ (305) 289-1554, at the Rainbow Bend Resort, 57784 Overseas Highway, MM 58, has been a local treasure for close to ten years. The gnocchi with lobster, the roasted whole duck and the veal marsala are all truly amazing.

Overlooking the marina, **Kelsey's** ☎ (305) 743-9018 is the restaurant of the Faro Blanco Resort at Overseas Highway, MM 48.5, and offers some wonderful seafood dishes, along with an excellent chateaubriand and rack of lamb. **Crocodiles on the Water** ☎ (305) 743-9018, Route 1, MM 47.5, at the end of 15th street, has fresh seafood, juicy steaks and highly recommended daily specials. A boat will take you from MM 28.5 on Little Torch Key to the restaurant of **Little Palm Island** ☎ (305) 872-2524, where the gourmet French cuisine with a Caribbean flair is essentially only an accompaniment to the deliciously exotic before- and after-dinner cocktails on the beach.

A seaside bar at Key West provides plenty of maritime atmosphere.

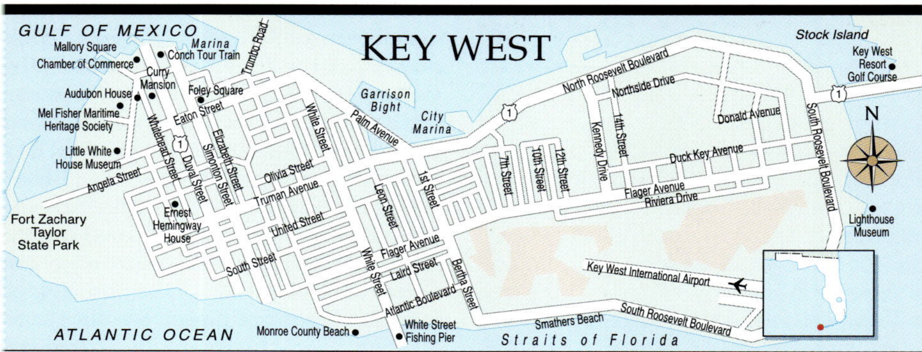

Moderate

Chef's ✆ (305) 743-2250, at the Sombrero Resort, 19 Sombrero Boulevard, Marathon, is as unpretentious as its name, and very good.

Sunset Café ✆ (305) 743-9071, at the Buccaneer Resort, MM 48.5, has a great bay view from a wrap-around deck and serves chicken, seafood, and sandwiches. **Monteís Restaurant and Fish Market** ✆ (305) 745-3731, at MM 25 on Summerland Key, has lovely conch chowders and fritters. **Sandbar** ✆ (305) 872-9989, MM 28.5, Barry Avenue, Little Torch Key, has waterfront dining, with dishes that include seafood, steak, burgers and sandwiches.

Inexpensive

Marathon Pizza and Pasta ✆ (305) 743-9338, in the Publix Shopping Center, MM 50, Marathon, has excellent New York-style pizza and authentic Italian food at budget prices, while the intimate **Grassy Key Dairy Bar** ✆ (305) 743-3816, at MM 58.5, is unusual in that it puts on a different menu — Italian, Mexican, etc. — every night.

A broad range of fresh seafood and copious salads are justifiably popular at **Shockers Raw Bar & Grill** ✆ (305) 743-8686, 1415 15th Street, Marathon. **Cocoa's Cantina** ✆ (305) 745-1564, MM 21.5, serves up some of the finest down-home Spanish-American food in the Florida Keys.

KEY WEST

Key West, the southernmost city in the United States, has a permanent population of 24,000 on a sub-tropical island four miles (six and a half kilometers) long and two miles (three kilometers) wide. The inhabitants are a mixed bunch: retired military personnel and their families, a long-established West Indian community, a large number of writers and artists, Cuban exiles — and the Conchs (pronounced "conks") who are the descendants of the island's original settlers. Only genuine Conchs are permitted to call themselves Conchs, although if you live there for seven years you can become an honorary "freshwater Conch".

The original Conchs came to the island from the Bahamas late in the eighteenth century. It became a part of the future state of Florida in 1822 when one of the settlers, John Simonton, bought it in a Cuban bar for $2,000. Also around this time a United States Navy commodore named David Porter finally managed to clear the Keys of its pirates, enabling the settlers to establish their own form of *ex post facto* piracy: shipwreck-plundering, or "wrecking". So profitable was wrecking that by 1830, the Conchs of Key West could claim the highest per-capita income in the country. By 1850, the Conch community (pop. 600) was earning a million dollars a year from wrecking. Then came a cigar-making factory set up by Cuban immigrants, and then a United States naval station. By 1880 Key West had a population of 10,000 and was the biggest city in the state.

But the cigar business packed up and moved to Tampa, which together with the Depression meant that by 1934, 80 percent of Key West's inhabitants were on welfare. Economic aid from the state eventually bailed the city out and enabled it to survive even the hurricane that destroyed Flagler's railway. And when the Ocean Highway reached the Keys, so did the tourists.

GENERAL INFORMATION

The **Greater Key West Chamber of Commerce** ☎ (305) 294-2587 TOLL-FREE (800) 527-8539, is at 402 Wall Street, Key West, FL 33040. The **Florida Keys Visitors Bureau**, TOLL-FREE (800) FLA-KEYS, which covers all the Keys, is at 416 Fleming Street, Key West, FL 33040. Visitor information can be found on-line at their comprehensive WEB SITE: www.fla-keys.com.

WHAT TO SEE AND DO

A good way to see Key West and many of its sights is to take a ride on the **Conch Tour Train** ☎ (305) 294-5161, which has boarding points at Mallory Square, Roosevelt Avenue, and Duval and Angela Streets. It runs at regular intervals from 9 AM to 4 PM daily. On the tour you will pass through the restored **Old Town** centered around Duval Street, which is lined with Spanish, Southern, and old Conch buildings (including the city's oldest house), and several old bars, among them **Sloppy Joe's** ☎ (305) 294-5717, 201 Duval Street, where Hemingway used to drink and, occasionally, write.

Earnest Hemingway's House ☎ (305) 294-1135, at 907 Whitehead Street, is where the great man lived and worked during the 1930s. Here he wrote, among other works, *The Green Hills of Africa* and *To Have and Have Not*. You can see some of Hemingway's possessions in the study where he wrote, which is open from 9 AM to 5 PM daily. Tennessee Williams' House is not open to the public, but you can see it from the outside at least, at 1431 Duncan Street. Another of Key West's famous citizens was the painter and naturalist John James Audubon, who painted the local bird life and also made engravings and prints; many of his works are on display in **Audubon House** ☎ (305) 294-2116, at 205 Whitehead Street. The house is open from 9:30 AM to 5 PM daily.

A number of operators offer **tours** of Key West. Old Town Trolley Tours ☎ (305) 296-6688, 1910 North Roosevelt Boulevard, offers a 90 minute tour with 14 stops which gives a good introduction to the city's shopping, dining, and attractions. Perfect Pedicabs ☎ (305) 292-0077, offers unique local tours without contributing to air pollution, while Island City Strolls ☎ (305) 294-8380, offers walking or bike tours as well as personalized group tours that cater to special interests.

For a truly unique tour, contact the **Historic Florida Keys Preservation Board** ☎ (305) 292-6829, to arrange for a guide to meet you at Margaret Street for a tour of the Key West Cemetery. It's picturesque and historic and not at all morbid, as the headstones are full of humor.

You can visit 22 rooms, porches and verandahs , all packed with antiques and Tiffany glass, at **Curry Mansion** ☎ (305) 294-4349, 511 Caroline Street, Key West's architectural landmark.

Harry S. Truman's Little White House Museum ☎ (305) 294-9911, 111 Front Street, is at the historic Winter White House used by Presidents Truman, Eisenhower and Kennedy. The museum is open daily from 9 AM to 5 PM.

The world's largest display of treasure taken from shipwrecks is at the **Mel Fisher Museum** ☎ (305) 294-2633, at 200 Greene Street. The museum was named after the man who found the wreck of the *Atocha*, a seventeenth-century Spanish ship, which carried treasure with a modern value of $400 million. The *Atocha*'s gold and silver bullion, coins, diamonds, and precious stones are on display in the museum, which is open from 9:30 AM to 5 PM.

At **The Wrecker's Museum/The Oldest House** ☎ (305) 294-9502, 322 Duval Street, you can tour the oldest house in southern Florida, and learn about nineteenth century shipwrecks, as well as see detailed model ships and historic documents.

Model ships are also on display, along with sundry maritime artifacts, at the Key West **Lighthouse Museum** ☎ (305) 294-0012, 938 Whitehead Street. The museum also houses such military peculiarities as a two-man Japanese submarine captured at Pearl Harbor. The view from the top of the lighthouse alone is worth the entrance charge. It is open from 9:30 AM to 5 PM.

For more military history, go to the **Fort Zachary Taylor State Historic Site** ☎ (305) 292-6713, at the western end of Southard Street. This museum has a lot of historic weaponry, including the nation's largest collection of Civil War cannons. Here you can also learn the story of the fort, which was occupied by Union troops during the Civil War and re-armed in 1898 for the Spanish-American War. The park around the fort has picnic sites and one of the finest beaches on the island.

After a day visiting the museums, the kids may be ready to let off a little steam. Try **Laser Tag and Arcade** ✆ (305) 292-2330, 416 Eaton Street, for a big adrenaline rush.

West. Contact Seaplanes of Key West ✆ (305) 294-0709 TOLL-FREE (800) 950-2359 WEB SITE www.conch.net/-seaplane, Key West Airport, and arrange to fly the 68 miles (109 km) west to the **Fort Jefferson National Monument** in the Dry Tortugas, a group of small coral islands. The plane passes over the Marquesas Keys atoll and a number of coral reefs, and shipwrecks before landing at the Dry Tortugas, where you can explore both the fort and the island. A boat to the Dry Tortugas also leaves Key West, from Lands End Marina, at 8 AM daily ✆ (305) 294-7009 TOLL-FREE (800) 634-0939.

Glass-bottom boat tours of the sensational reefs off Key West are offered by The Pride of Key West ✆ (305) 296-6293, 2 Duval Street, and Discovery Glass Bottom Boat ✆ (305) 293-0099, 251 Margaret Street, Lands End Marina. **Cruises** are offered throughout the day by Fury Catamarans ✆ (305) 294-8899, and on the Liberty Schooner ✆ (305) 292-0332, both at the Key West Hilton Resort and Marina. These two outfits also offer **snorkeling** trips. Or you can purchase an all day pass on the Curry Princess ✆ (305) 293-1999 which allows you unlimited boarding and re-boarding while it circumnavigates Key West.

If you are feeling adventurous, a **seaplane** flight will give you a novel perspective of Key

Sports

For **fishing trips** out of Key West to both Gulf and Atlantic waters, or to the Dry Tortugas, try Linda D ✆ (305) 296-9798 TOLL-FREE (800) 299-9798, Dock 19 & 20, Amberjack Pier, City Marina; or Yankee Cruise and Fishing, TOLL-FREE (800) 634-0939, Lands End Marina at the foot of Margaret Street. **Scuba diving** and **snorkeling** trips and lessons can be arranged, and equipment rented, at the Captain's Corner Diver Center ✆ (305) 296-7701, Zero Duval Street at Ocean Key House Suite Resort and Marina; or at Subtropic Dive Center ✆ (305) 296-9914 TOLL-FREE (888) 471-3483 WEB SITE www.subtropic.com, 1605 North Roosevelt Boulevard. Mosquito

Coast Island Outfitters and Kayak Guides ☎ (305) 294-7178, 1107 Duval Street take **kayakers** to Geiger Key or Sugarloaf key for near-shore natural history tours. **Parasailing** is available through Sebago Watersports ☎ (305) 294-5687, Key West Bight Marina, 200 William Street, and **Jet skis** can be rented through Island Watersports ☎ (305) 296-1754 WEB SITE www.keywest.com/islandws.html, 245 Front Street, Hilton Resort and Marina.

There is a **golf course** on Stock Island at the Key West Resort ☎ (305) 294-5232, and public **tennis courts** at Island City Tennis ☎ (305) 294-1346, on Truman Avenue.

Shopping

Most of the shopping in Key West is done in the Old Town area around Duval Street, where you will find numerous souvenir and gift shops, boutiques, designer outlets, and arts-and-craft shops. For all sort of curios, visit Mac's Sea Garden ☎ (305) 293-7240, 280 Margaret Street. There are several **galleries** in the Old Town with quite decent works by resident and visiting artists. The Guild Hall Gallery ☎ (305) 296-6076, 614 Duval Street, showcases the very best of local artists and is Key's West's original artists' co-op. Key West Aloe ☎ (305) 294-5592, 40 Greene Street, is a skincare and cosmetics company that has the most wonderful natural products made right in this factory outlet.

Nightlife

Key West offers the most colorful and varied nightlife in the Keys. You mustn't miss, for example, **Sloppy Joe's** ☎ (305) 294-5717, at 201 Duval Street, Hemingway's favorite watering hole. On the wall is a sailfish that Hemingway is reputed to have caught. Short drinks and tall stories still abound here, as well as live rhythm-and-blues bands. The **Hogs Breath Saloon** ☎ (305) 296-4222 WEB SITE www.hogsbreath.com, corner of Duval and Front streets has live entertainment from 1 PM to 2 AM DAILY. Another Key West landmark is **Captain Tony's Saloon** ☎ (305) 294-1838, at 428 Greene Street, where many of the town's bohemian characters hang out. There is a lively happy hour at the **Half Shell Raw Bar** ☎ (305) 294-7496, 231 Margaret Street, and **Jimmy Buffett's Margaritaville** ☎ (305) 292-1435, 500 Duvall Street, offers, what else but, great margaritas and live music from 10 30 PM. This place really gets wild whenever Buffet is in town (usually in February) and all the Parrot heads come out to play. **Club International** ☎ (305) 296-9230, 900 Simonton Street, is a locally owned gay and lesbian bar. For dancing, visit **Channel Zero** ☎ (305) 294-4060, 218 Duval Street, where 70s, 80s and 90s music is spun nightly by DJs. **Rumrunner Key** ☎ (305) 293-1999, 210 William Street, is a 171-passenger party boat which offers a tiki bar, Jacuzzi, and live reggae at sunset.

For a much more laid-back evening, stop by the **Sunset Pier Bar and Raw Bar**, zero Duvall Street (really), for live local entertainment and great sunset views.

Dance and musical performances are presented Wednesdays through Saturdays at **Eight O One Cabaret** ☎ (305) 294-4737, 801 Duval.

But a Key West sunset would not be complete without a visit to **Mallory Square** pier, which turns into a celebration each evening, where buskers abound, showing off all sorts of talent, from the traditional to one regular who balances a stove on his chin.

WHERE TO STAY

Luxury

Among the destinations for travelers on Flagler's railway was the **Wyndham Casa Marina Resort** ☎ (305) 296-3535 TOLL-FREE (800) 626-0777, at 1500 Reynolds Street, which is still one of the city's most elegant hotels. It has its own beach with extensive water-sports facilities, lighted tennis courts, a swimming pool, and a private fishing pier.

There are some exceptional old Victorian guesthouses in Key West, including **Eaton Lodge** ☎ (305) 294-3800 FAX (305) 294-4018 WEB SITE www.eatonlodge.com, at 511 Eaton Street, where every room has a large balcony overlooking a central tropical garden. Another very fine guest house, with rooms facing the ocean, is **La Mer Hotel** ☎ (305) 296-6577 TOLL-FREE (800) 354-4455 WEB SITE www.oldtownresorts.com, at 506 South Street. At the edge of the Old Town at 601 Front Street, you can find the **Hyatt Key**

A watering hole near the water.

West ✆ (305) 296-9900 TOLL-FREE (800) 554-9288 FAX (305) 292-1038 WEB SITE www.hyatt.com, which has a beach, a marina, a swimming pool, Jacuzzis, and an exercise room among its amenities, as well as rooms offering magnificent views of Key West's famous sunsets.

Mid-range

The charming **Nassau House** ✆ (305) 296-8513 TOLL-FREE (800) 296-8513 FAX (305) 293-8423 WEB SITE www.keywestinns.com/nassau.html, is in the heart of the old town

at 1016 Fleming Street. This 100 year old house was remodeled in 1995 and now offers comfortable rooms, some with full kitchens. There is a lagoon pool incorporating a spa, bicycle rentals are available, and the continental breakfast is delicious.

The **South Beach Motel** ✆ (305) 296-5611 TOLL-FREE (800) 354-4455 FAX (305) 294-8272 WEB SITE www.oldtownresorts.com, with a small pier for swimming and fishing, and bright and neatly furnished rooms, is at 508 South Street. At the 130-year-old **Duval House Historic Inn** ✆ (305) 294-1666 FAX (305) 292-1701 WEB SITE www.kwflorida.com/duvalhse.html, the 22 antique-furnished rooms surround a garden and swimming pool in the heart of the Old Town at 815 Duval Street. Another small and friendly guest house, **Eden House** ✆ (305) 296-6868 TOLL-FREE (800) 533-5397 FAX (305) 294-1221 WEB SITE www.edenhouse.com, at 1015 Fleming Street, has Roaring 'Twenties decor, and a lovely swimming pool. **Deja Vu** ✆ (305) 292-9339 TOLL-FREE (800) 724-5351 FAX (305) 292-2258 WEB SITE www.dejavukeys.com, is a clothing optional resort, at 611 Truman Avenue, with 27 rooms, a large swimming pool, and a 14 person hot tub.

Inexpensive

Inexpensive accommodation can be very difficult to find in Key West, but there are a few possibilities.

On Simonton Street there is the **Santa Maria** ✆ (305) 296-5678 TOLL-FREE (800) 821-5397 FAX (305) 294-0010, at No. 1401, which is simple but clean. Also good value is the friendly **Atlantic Shores**, TOLL-FREE (800) 778-7711 WEB SITE www.atlanticshoresresort.com, at 510 South Street, which has its own pier and swimming pool.

Hostelling International Key West ✆ (305) 296-5719 TOLL-FREE (800) 514-6783 FAX (305) 296-0672, offers clean, comfortable single-sex and co-ed dormitories, as well as private rooms, near the beach at 718 South Street. As an alternative, you may want to pitch a tent at either **Boyd's Key West Campground** ✆ (305) 294-1465 FAX (305) 293-9301 WEB SITE www.gocampingamerica.com/boydskeywest, 6401 Maloney Avenue, which has a heated pool and a good camp store, or **Jabour's Campground** ✆ (305) 294-5723 FAX (305) 296-7965, in the Old Town seaport district.

For complete information on lodging in Key West, get in touch with the Key West Chamber of Commerce (see GENERAL INFORMATION, above), which will be happy to supply you with a guide to hotels and guest houses, or **AA Accommodations Center** TOLL-FREE (800) 732-2006, at 628 Fleming Street, Key West, FL 33040.

WHERE TO EAT

Expensive

Louie's Backyard ✆ (305) 294-1061, at 700 Wadell Street, is a Revival Conch House listed in the National Register of Historic

Places. The fascinating menu features local seafood with a Caribbean flair and includes such delights as grilled sour orange-rubbed *garoupa* with black bean pancakes. **The Rooftop Café** ☎ (305) 294-2042, 310 Front Street, is nestled in the treetops, overlooking historic buildings and with wonderful sunset views. Its imaginative American menu features such dishes as shrimp and crab cake accented with citrus *beurre blanc* and roast duck with jalapeno plum sauce. The **Café des Artistes** ☎ (305) 294-7100, at 1007 Simonton Street, specializes in Provençal cooking, with dishes including pan-roasted veal rib served in wild mushroom sauce with seasonal wild mushrooms, and lobster *flambéed* in cognac and saffron butter with mango and basil.

Moderate

Lovers of sushi, sashimi, teriyaki, sukiyaki, and other Japanese delights should try **Kyu Shu** ☎ (305) 294-2995, at 921 Truman Street. You can eat outside under a straw roof or in a traditional tatami dining room. **La-Te-Da** ☎ (305) 296-6706, is the restaurant in the hotel with the same name at 1125 Duval Street, and offers mostly continental cuisine. **Antonia's** ☎ (305) 294-6565, at 615 Duval Street, has masterfully prepared northern Italian food, and cleverly offers half-servings of various pasta dishes. **The Bagatelle** ☎ (305) 296-6609, is in a restored Conch house at 115 Duval Street, and serves a mixture of local seafood and more exotic Bahamian cooking. For good old southern-fried cooking go to **Pepe's Café** ☎ (305) 294-7192, down near the old waterfront at 806 Caroline Street. Lovers of good Italian food should try **La Trattoria** ☎ (305) 296-1075, 524 Duval Street, which has a Northern Italian menu featuring such dishes as pasta sautéed with mushrooms, sundried tomatoes and crabmeat in cream sauce. Another excellent Italian restaurant is **Mangia Mangia** ☎ (305) 294-2469, 900 Southard Street, which has house specialties including *pollo con funchi e piselli* and *bollito misto di mare*. **Kelly's Caribbean Bar and Grill** ☎ (305) 293-8484 301 Whitehead is owned by movie star Kelly McGillis of *Top Gun* fame, and is situated in the building where Pan Am Airlines was started.

Inexpensive

Camille's, 703 Duval street, serves up delicious breakfasts and lunches as well as Sunday brunch.

Duds n' Suds ☎ (305) 292-1959, 829 Fleming Street, is not the most obvious place to eat, situated as it is adjoining a Laundromat, but if you like spinach, you've got to grab a meal here, as Ellen makes the best spinach salad ever. Another takeout with good food is **Lobo Mixed Grill** ☎ (305) 294-3294, Five Key Lime Square, which offers roll-up sandwiches and a variety of quesadillas.

For Tex-Mex dishes, visit **Gato Gordo** Cafe ☎ (305) 294-0888, 404 Southard Street, where you have an overwhelming choice of 86 brands of tequila.

For the ultimate in Key lime pie, stop by the **Key West Lime Shoppe** ☎ (305) 296-0806 WEB SITE www.keylimeshop.com, 200 A Elizabeth Street, and try a slice that has been dipped in chocolate and then frozen on a stick.

How to Get There

Delta Airlines has regular flights to Key West. Motorists simply follow Route 1 to the end, at the Key West Lighthouse. If you get this far, you have gone as far south as it is possible to go in the continental United States.

Self-captioning landmark in Key West.

Travelers' Tips

THE BEST TIP OF ALL: FIND A GOOD TRAVEL AGENT. How? Ask the same questions of several different agents — questions that can't be answered out of a brochure. You can answer those questions yourself. The point of the exercise is not to find a travel agent who has all the answers — nobody does — but to find one who is willing to take the time and trouble to get the answers for you.

GETTING THERE

BY AIR

All major cities in Florida are served daily (often many times daily) by airlines from all corners of the United States Likewise, many international airlines have regularly-scheduled flights to Florida. These include: **British Airways** TOLL-FREE (800) 247-9297 WEB SITE www.british-airways.com; **Continental** TOLL-FREE (800) 523-3273 WEB SITE www.flycontinental.com; **Virgin Atlantic** TOLL-FREE (800) 862-8621 WEB SITE www.flyvirgin.com; **Lufthansa** TOLL-FREE (800) 645-3880 WEB SITE www.lufthansa.com; **Delta** TOLL-FREE (800) 221-1212 WEB SITE www.delta-air.com; **American Airlines** TOLL-FREE (800) 433-7300 WEB SITE www.americanair.com; **KLM** ((800) 374-7747 WEB SITE www.klm.nl; **Air France** TOLL-FREE (800) 237-2747 WEB SITE www.airfrance.com.

There are an infinite variety of special discount fares and package deals. Every airline has at least one, as does American Express and other travel companies. In addition, charter flights are available.

BY RAIL

Not to be outdone by the airlines, Amtrak now offers a variety of special fares (and much improved food and service) in an effort to bring Florida-bound travelers back to earth. In particular, ask your travel agent about the USA Rail Pass, which is offered to international visitors only and offers six different passes that range between 15 and 30 days validity. The North America Rail Pass offers unlimited stops over 30 consecutive days in the US to and Canada to Americans

and visitors alike. Amtrack also offers promotions with United Airlines and Carnival Cruise Lines. Information about timetables and special fares, including tour packages, is available directly from **Amtrak** TOLL-FREE (800) USA-RAIL WEB SITE www.amtrack.com, P.O. Box 311, Addison, Illinois 60101. On the web site, consult "Rail Sale" for the latest discounts on selected Amtrack routes.

BY BUS

Greyhound offers discounts on 21, 14 and seven-day advance bookings plus a free companion ticket for three-day advance purchases. Ameripass is Greyhound's one-price unlimited travel ticket, valid for 60 consecutive days. The **Greyhound Inter-**

national Office ((212) 971-0492 TOLL-FREE (800) 231-2222 WEB SITE www.greyhound.com, is at Port Authority Bus Terminal, 625 Eighth Avenue, New York, NY 10018.

BY CAR

By far the most popular way to reach Florida from other states is driving. Interstate highways make the cross-country journey a breeze, although it still takes two days to drive all the way from New York or Chicago and at least three days to drive from the West Coast. Major interstate routes:

Interstate 95: Boston, New York, Philadelphia, Baltimore, Washington DC, Virginia, North Carolina, Savannah, Jacksonville, Space Coast, Miami.

Interstate 75: Detroit, Cincinnati, Kentucky, Tennessee, Atlanta, Tampa, Sarasota, Fort Myers, Miami.

Interstate 10: Los Angeles, Phoenix, San Antonio, Houston, New Orleans, Mobile, Pensacola, Tallahassee, Jacksonville.

ARRIVING

VISA AND TRAVEL DOCUMENTS

When arriving in the United States, Canadian citizens who plan to stay less than 90 days need only show proof of identity and residence (a driver's license will do); a passport isn't necessary, but it might be useful as identification for financial transactions.

The seaside at Seaside, Florida.

A number of countries are participating in the visa waiver pilot program whereby citizens of participating countries can travel to the United States for 90 days or less without obtaining a visa. A valid passport and return ticket are required. Check with your travel agent for the current rules and participating countries. (At the time of writing there were 26 participating countries including: Australia, France, Germany, Italy, the Netherlands, New Zealand, Spain, and the United Kingdom.)

Visitors from other countries should contact the United States embassy or consulate in their country for the exact details for obtaining a visa.

CUSTOMS

United States customs allows you to bring in, duty-free, 200 cigarettes or 50 cigars or three pounds (1.4 kg) of tobacco. I should add, however, that you would be stark raving mad to bring tobacco (especially cigars) into a state where you can buy all kinds of excellent tobacco products for a fraction of their price in the duty-free shops of the world's airports. The same goes for alcohol: you can bring in one United States quart (a liter), but it would be wiser and more economical to buy it when you get there. You may also bring in duty-free gifts up to $100 in value.

Carrying non-prescription narcotic drugs into the country may well result in a long prison sentence.

EMBASSIES AND CONSULATES

Foreign embassies are located in Washington, DC. To obtain the phone number of an embassy not mentioned below, call directory assistance ((202) 555-1212.

Embassy of France ((202) 944-6000, 4101 Reservoir Road, Washington D.C., NW 200007.

Embassy of Italy ((202) 328-5500 FAX (202) 328-5593, 1601 Fuller Street, Washington D.C., NW 20009.

Royal Netherlands Embassy ((202) 244-5300 FAX (202) 362-3430, 4200 Linnean Avenue, Washington D.C., NW 20008.

British Consulate ((407) 426-7855, 200 South Orange Avenue Orlando, FL 32801

Consulado General De Espana ((305) 446-5511, 151 Sevilla Avenue, Coral Gables, FL 33134.

TOURIST INFORMATION

There are more than 200 Chambers of Commerce and Convention and Visitor Bureaus scattered around the state. In the GENERAL INFORMATION sections of the preceding chapters I have listed the local agencies; each will be more than happy to answer any queries or supply any information about their area.

All you need do to find yourself caught in a blizzard of facts and figures, maps and pictures, brochures and pamphlets, is to contact one of the following:

The Florida **Association of Convention and Visitors Bureaux** WEB SITE www.facvb.org, provides links to regional CVBs.

Florida **Chamber of Commerce** ((850) 425-1200 FAX (850) 425-1260, WEB SITE www.flchamb.com, 136 South Bronough Street, P.O. Box 11309, Tallahassee, FL 32302-3309.

Florida Department of Environmental Protection **Division of Recreation and Parks** ((850) 488-9872 WEB SITE www.dep.state.fl.us/parks, 3900 Commonwealth Boulevard, Tallahassee, FL 32399.

Southeast Region **National Park Service** ☎ (404) 562-3100, 100 Alabama Street SW, 1924 Building, Atlanta, GA 30303.

Florida **Fish and Wildlife Conservation Commission** WEB SITE www.state.fl.us/gfc, 620 South meridian Street, Tallahassee, FL 32399-1600.

Florida **Association of Recreational Vehicle Parks and Campgrounds** ☎ (850) 562-7151 FAX (850) 562-7179 E-MAIL FlaARVC @aol.com. 1340 Vicker Drive, Tallahassee, FL 32303.

GETTING AROUND

The best way to get around Florida is by automobile. For one thing, Florida is the cheapest place in the world to rent a car. All the major car rental firms (Hertz, Avis, Budget) offer special deals, and the others don't need to. For another thing, fuel is astonishingly cheap by European standards. And lastly, of course, American roads and highways are a motorist's dream.

If you prefer to travel by train, Amtrak serves 22 cities in the state. Your travel agent will have timetables and pricing details, or you can phone Amtrak General Information and Reservations TOLL-FREE (800) 872-7245 WEB SITE www.greyhound.com. Greyhound has buses going to every nook and cranny of the state, with several package tours. Write to their International Office at Port Authority Bus Terminal, 625 Eighth Avenue, New York, NY 10018.

For air travel within Florida, ask your travel agent about the availability of specially-priced Visit USA tickets and the many domestic shuttle flights between cities.

Car rental offices are located convenient to the baggage check out or customs offices in all major airports in the state. However, most travelers will want to make reservations for a car rental at the same time reservations are made for air travel; this is the only way to insure that the particular car you want to rent will be ready and waiting when you arrive. Travelers to the Sunshine State may want to take advantage of the convertible cars that can be rented from some agencies.The services offered by rental car agencies throughout Florida vary from place to place, even within the same agency.

The following is a list of the toll-free numbers of the major agencies found in every part of the state. If you're looking for budget prices, the best deals can usually be made through the small local agencies. For long-term leases, the best bets are the major auto dealers such as Ford or Chevrolet.
Alamo: TOLL-FREE ☎ (800) 327-9633
Avis: TOLL-FREE ☎ (800) 331-1212
Budget: TOLL-FREE ☎ (800) 527-0700
Dollar: TOLL-FREE ☎ (800) 421-6878
Hertz: TOLL-FREE ☎ (800) 654-3131
National: TOLL-FREE ☎ (800) 328-4567.

The most frustrating thing about driving in Florida, or in the United States generally, is that the nation with the best roads in the world has the lowest speed limits in the world: 65 mph (95 kph) on many highways and 20 to 40 mph (32 to 64 kph) in cities and residential areas. Speed limits, which are clearly marked, do go up to 70 mph (113 kph) on some main roads in some rural areas only. Obey the signs, for the speed limits are strictly enforced.

It is legal to turn right at red rights in Florida, provided that you come to a full stop first and there is no sign prohibiting a

OPPOSITE: Taking to the water is one of the best ways to explore Sanibel Island. ABOVE: Interior view of John Ringling's winter residence.

right turn. Two other laws with which visitors may not be familiar require all drivers to carry proof of personal injury insurance coverage; and secure children five years old and younger or any child under 40 lbs (regardless of age) in child restraint seats. All persons driving in a car should wear seat belts. For more detailed information contact the **Florida Highway Safety and Motor Vehicles Department** ☎ (850) 488-2276, 2900 Apalachee Parkway, B441, WEB SITE www.state.fl.us/hsmv. For help or travel information while on the road, call the **American Automobile Association** ☎ (407) 444-7000, 1000 AAA Drive, Lake Mary, FL 32746.

ACCOMMODATION

A full range of accommodation is available in Florida, from major luxury resorts and quaint bed & breakfast inns to national park campgrounds and the ubiquitous motels that border many highways. Major international chains like Hilton, Sheraton and Hyatt are well represented, as are America's top budget motel chains like Days Inn, Travelodge and Motel 6. The choice is almost endless, especially in major tourist destinations like Miami and Orlando.

Advance reservations are absolutely necessary during the summer months (June, July, August) and peak holiday periods during the remainder of the year (Christmas, Thanksgiving, Easter, Memorial Day, Labor Day). The best way to make reservations is calling the toll-free (800) number of the hotel/motel chain or individual property where you want to stay. Ask plenty of questions before confirming your room: Find out the exact location of the hotel or motel, its distance from the places you want to see, and the facilities it has to offer.

Florida hotel and restaurant prices can fluctuate enormously depending on a number of factors (see WELCOME TO FLORIDA on page 69 for additional commentary). For the purposes of this guide, I have therefore divided hotels into three categories according to the range of prices you can expect.

Luxury: over (sometimes way over) $120 for a double room;

Mid-range: between $60 and $120;

Inexpensive: under (sometimes way under) $60 for a double room.

LUXURY AND UPMARKET HOTEL CHAINS:

Hilton: ☎ (800) 445-8667
Holiday Inn: ☎ (800) 465-4329
Howard Johnson: ☎ (800) 654-2000
Hyatt: ☎ (800) 233-1234
Marriott: ☎ (800) 228-9290
Ramada: ☎ (800) 228-2828
Sheraton: ☎ (800) 325-3535

Inexpensive hotels and motels:
Comfort Inn: ☎ (800) 228-5150
Days Inn: ☎ (800) DAYS INN
Motel 6: ☎ (800) 4-MOTEL-6
Quality Inn: ☎ (800) 228-5151
Super 8: ☎ (800) 843-1991
Travelodge: ☎ (800) 255-3050

Camping

There are more than 100 state parks in Florida, as well as campsites for recreational vehicles and wilderness areas, all of which provide camping facilities. For further information, contact the **National Park Service**, Southeast Region ☎ (404) 562-3100, 100 Alabama Street, Southwest, 1924 Building, Atlanta, GA 30303. There is also the valuable *Florida Camping Directory* published by the Florida Association of RV Parks and Campgrounds ☎ (850) 562-7151, 1340 Vickers Drive, Tallahassee FL 32303.

EATING OUT

There are many fine restaurants in Florida featuring continental cuisine, and indeed I have already recommended quite a few of them, but as a general rule, to enjoy the best meals in Florida you should stick to what is uniquely — or at least distinctively — Floridian. (See GALLOPING GOURMETS, page 60, in YOUR CHOICE,).

Price categories used in this book for restaurants are:

Expensive: over $50 per person, excluding wine;

Moderate: between $20 and $50;

Inexpensive: below $20, and often well below.

TIPPING

Because a tip is an acknowledgment of a service rendered, the size of the tip depends ultimately on your opinion of the quality of the service. However, assuming that the service performed was at least adequate, and that no service charge has already been included in your bill (which it only rarely is in Florida), you should tip about 15 percent in restaurants and for room service. Porters and doormen who help with your bags should get 50 cents to a dollar per bag, depending on the size and weight; taxi drivers will expect a tip of 10 to 15 percent. Most hotel rooms in Florida now come with an envelope with advice on how much to tip the chambermaids. Remember that almost everyone employed in a service industry in Florida is on the minimum wage and so they rely heavily on, and work hard at earning their tips.

BASICS

The language spoken in Florida is English, right? Wrong, if you're in those parts of south Florida where Spanish (or, occasionally, Yiddish) is the *lingua franca*. And even the English that is spoken is very different from the British version; however, the differences are either so well-known or so easily decipherable ("elevator" for "lift") that it would be a waste of time to catalogue them.

The electric current is 110–115 volts AC. Unless you buy your electrical appliances in the Unitd States you will need an adapter.

Except for the extreme western part of the Panhandle, Florida is on Eastern Standard Time, which is five hours behind Greenwich Mean Time (i.e., when it is noon in London it is 7 am in Miami). If for some reason you feel the need to know the precise time (and also the temperature), you can call (305) 324-8811.

MONEY

The old joke about the American tourist who asks, "How much is that in real money" is not so funny when a bank teller in America looks at your foreign currency as if it were a bank robber's note demanding cash. The dollar may have fallen on relatively hard times in recent years, but it is still the only currency that Americans understand and trust. Therefore you should really only travel with dollars or travelers'

The boardwalk at Madeira Beach.

checks in dollars. Also, in the land that invented plastic money, it's a very good idea to have a Visa Card or MasterCard or some other internationally recognized card with you. A *very* good idea, in fact, because many American firms prefer cards to cash — and some even insist on cards rather than cash.

MAIL

United States post offices are generally open 8:30 AM to 5 PM Monday to Friday, but hours can vary greatly from one branch to another. Some are open 9:30 AM to noon on Saturday. A growing number of commercial communications centers provide similar services (stamps, registered mail, air courier, PO boxes and packaging, plus notary services, photocopies and stationery supplies) including the Mailbox USA and Postal Annex chains. For the location and opening hours of United States Post Offices, as well as ZIP code information, call ✆ (800) 275-8777.

TELEPHONES

Florida has one of the most modern telephone systems in the world, although the choice of different phone companies and services can sometimes seem overwhelming for foreign visitors. Most pay phone accept coins or calling card numbers and there is an increased number that accept credit cards. The flat fee for most local calls is 35 cents.

For local calls in your same area code, dial the phone number without any prefix. For direct dial calls outside of your area code, dial one (1) plus the area code and local phone number. For direct dial international calls, dial the United States overseas access number (011) plus the country code, city code and local number of the place you are trying to ring. To make an operator assisted call (collect, person-to-person, third party, etc.) dial zero (0) followed by the area code and phone number, and then follow the recorded instructions. If you don't know the area code, country code or city code of the place you're trying to call, dial double zero (00).

Phone Service Numbers:
Directory assistance (information): 411; different area code dial 1 + area code + 555-1212; toll-free numbers dial (800) 555-1212.

Emergency Phone Numbers:
Police, Fire, Paramedic: 911
Poison Control Center: (800) 876-4766
Crisis Team Hotline (suicide counseling): (800) 479-3339.

HEALTH AND SAFETY

Health care in Florida is excellent, as you would expect, but unbelievably expensive, so don't even *think* about going to Florida without some kind of short-term medical insurance. Your travel agent or private health insurance company will be able to advise you on the insurance you will need while visiting the state.

The only other general advice I can offer is: don't underestimate the capacity of the local insects to ruin your vacation. Mosquitoes, ants (especially fire ants), flies (especially sand flies), and other tiny pests are abundant and obnoxiously happy to welcome you unless you have some kind of insect repellent with you.

A bad sunburn could also very easily ruin your vacation, so treat the Florida sun with respect. It is very strong. Additionally, always remember Noel Coward's memorable phrase, only mad dogs and Englishmen go out in the midday sun: from 11 AM to 2 PM you are well advised to stay inside. As we all now know that a suntan is just as bad for you as a sunburn, my advice is simple: wear sunscreen at all times, even if the weather is overcast.

Another point to bear in mind is that some parts of the body are more sensitive to the sun's rays than others. Your nose, knees, and the tops of your feet should be particularly well protected by sun lotion, and your eyes should be protected by "proper" sunglasses. By proper sunglasses I mean ones that are UV-coated to keep out the harmful ultraviolet rays, and preferably with Polarized filters if you are planning to spend much time on the water, where your eyes are vulnerable to reflected light.

SECURITY

A string of notorious incidents in the late 1980s and early 1990s — including the murder of half a dozen foreign visitors and several violent carjackings — earned Florida a world-wide reputation for tourist-related crime. Since then state and local law enforcement authorities have gone out of their way to make Florida just as safe as other major United States tourist destinations.

The good news is that crime dropped dramatically in Florida over the latter half of the 90s, reflecting both this increased vigilance and the booming economy. According to the Florida Department of Law Enforcement, overall crime dropped for six consecutive years leading up to 1999 (the last year for which full figures are available) including the state's lowest murder rate since 1933. Even Miami — one of the most crime plagued cities in America, is undergoing a rapid decline in villainy (with a 23% drop in major crime between 1996 and '99 according to the mayor's office).

The bad news is that crime hasn't vanished completely. In recent years there has been an explosion of new criminals who use highly sophisticated, computerized fraud schemes to victimize residents and visitors alike. If your credit cards, check books, passports or other ID are lost or stolen, report the loss immediately to the appropriate authorities.

Although Florida's tourist areas are generally safe (especially the high-security Disney World area) visitors should still take precautions in order to avoid becoming a victim. Avoid high-crime areas like Miami's Liberty City neighborhood. If you don't know the location of these areas, ask the locals — hotel personnel, rental car employees or tourist office clerks. Avoid deserted, poorly-lit and marginal areas at night, especially in big cities. Avoid parks and beaches at night, unless there is a large crowd of people or an event in progress. But be aware that crowds attract pickpockets and bag-snatchers.

Needless to say, you should never carry valuables in public, especially expensive jewelry. Leave the baubles behind in your hotel safe deposit box or room safe. Don't flash large amounts of money when paying bills. Beware of strangers who approach you on the street, especially anyone who offers to be your guide. Keep your hotel room and car doors locked at all times.

When traveling between destinations, keep your valuables locked in the vehicle trunk — not on a seat where they are easy prey to criminals. Only take taxis clearly identified with official company logos and emblems. Never pickup hitchhikers and never hitchhike yourself. If your car breaks down, beware of people stopping to offer assistance; use emergency telephones to summon either a tow truck or law enforcement and wait for them to arrive.

Women travelers are no more vulnerable to crime or harassment in Florida than anywhere else in the United States The best advice is never travel alone. If that's not possible, then following the steps listed above should keep you secure in most areas and most situations. Solo women travelers should generally avoid cruising bars or beaches at night, even in popular tourist areas. They should also stay at hotels with valet or on-site parking.

Florida's police officers are well trained to assist the state's 47 million annual visitors.

If you are confronted by criminals, the rule of thumb is give them what they want — your passport, wallet, camera, etc. Usually they will take the item and leave without harming you. Only if physical harm is imminent should you take evasive action.

THE INTERNET

Just about everywhere you go in Florida, you will find a bookstore, café, or public library offering access to the Internet for a nominal fee (and sometimes for free). If

you've signed up for one of the global **e-mail** accounts before leaving home (e.g., HotMail or Yahoo!, for example) then you are wired, too.

While some public libraries offer access, the actual availability varies greatly because of lack of equipment and high demand. If the library lets you down, ask around for an Internet café where you can settle down with a coffee and get some warming news from home.

The Internet is also becoming a powerful tool for researching and planning trips. Many, if not most, organizations, hotels, and tour operators listed in this book have home pages on the **World Wide Web**. Finding one of these home pages is usually a simple matter of logging on to your web browser (e.g., Netscape Navigator™ or Microsoft Internet Explorer™), locating the search function and typing in the name of the organization you are looking for. You can also do keyword searches if you don't have a specific organization name in mind. Essentially, once on the web, your access to information is limited only by your ability to ask the right question.

Web sites are of varying quality. Some are quite useful, allowing you to retrieve information quickly, make contact via e-mail direct from the site, or even make a reservation at the touch of a button. Others will have you pulling out your cyber hair.

The following sites are ones that I found useful in my research on this book. They offer pertinent information and essential services, as well as links to other home pages that will set you on your way into cyberspace.

WEB SITES

The official web site of the **State of Florida** is www.state.fl.us. Here you'll find state government-related information as well as a link to the web site of **Visit Florida** — the state's official tourism promotion agency (a private/public partnership between the Florida Commission of Tourism and the state government) at www.flausa.com. The Visit Florida site includes virtual tours, radar and satellite weather images, maps and even the opportunity of buying souvenirs before you go on your vacation.

Billing itself as the (almost) **Official City Site,** www.209.41.76.173/florida.html offers links to discounted airfare, hotel reservations, car rentals as well as city newspapers and information about various cities within Florida.

For more general information, www.mapsonus.switchboard.com has maps, routes and yellow pages listings for all areas in America, including Florida.

RADIO AND TELEVISION

Media is not hard to come by in Florida. Every major city has its own television stations, most of them affiliated with the nationwide networks (ABC, CBS, NBC, Fox, UPN and WB). Cable and satellite provides another 60 or so channels including all-news (CNN, MSNBC), all-sports (ESPN) and children's (Disney, Cartoon, Fox Family, Nickelodeon) formats. Programs are listed in daily newspapers and the weekly magazine *TV Guide* available at newsstands and supermarkets.

Radio stations are also abundant, with formats that range from rock and jazz to country and western and talk. FM tends to be more music oriented, whereas AM leans toward all-news and talk show formats. All-news radio is your best bet for traffic reports like WINZ 940 and WIOD 610 in Miami.

Major newspapers in Florida include the *Miami Herald, St. Petersburg Times, Orlando Sentinel, Fort Lauderdale Sun-Sentinel,* Jacksonville Times-Union and the *Palm Beach Post*. National papers like the ultra-conservative *Wall Street Journal* and colorful *USA Today* are available on most newsstands, as is the highly respected *New York Times*. Overseas papers can be found at larger newsstands and book stores in Greater Miami.

WHEN TO GO

Most people, like most birds, tend to flock to Florida in the winter. In the coldest month, January, the average daytime temperatures in the southern part of the state are 74°F (23°C) on land and 72°F (22°C) in the water. It is cooler, of course, in the evenings, but pleasantly so.

The summers are hot — but not that hot; it seldom gets over 90°F (32°C). It's the humidity that's bothersome, although the late afternoon showers tend to wring the moisture out of the air. And the ubiquitous air conditioning blow-dries as it cools the air indoors.

As with most places in these latitudes, spring and autumn are the most agreeable times to visit.

PUBLIC HOLIDAYS & FESTIVALS

New Year's Day	January 1
Martin Luther King, Jr. Day	January 15
President's Day	February 20
Memorial Day	Last Monday in May
Independence Day	July 4
Labor Day	1st Monday in September
Columbus Day	2nd Monday in October
Veterans' Day	November 11
Thanksgiving	4th Thursday in November
Christmas Day	December 25

During these holidays, federal, state and city offices close, as more importantly, do the banks. Whether shops and restaurants are open during public holidays depends on the region, but anywhere you go, shopping malls are likely to be open seven days a week, including holidays.

Other holidays, such as St. Patrick's Day (March 17), Easter Sunday (late March or early April), Mother's Day (May), Father's Day (June), and Halloween (October 31) may be celebrated in various ways by different communities. (See FESTIVE FLINGS in YOUR CHOICE, page 55 for statewide and regional celebrations.)

WHAT TO TAKE

As always, the oldest advice is the best: take half the clothes and twice the money you think you will need. This applies especially in Florida's case, because everything you could possibly need or want is available, at prices — here's the good news — that are much cheaper than you might expect.

Having said that, let me list a few of the things I personally would never travel in Florida without: number one is a good, high-factor, sunscreen and a wide-brimmed hat, which are especially important if you are traveling with children (Florida is a good place to buy that perfect summer hat); insect repellent; eyedrops; aspirin; antiseptic ointment; a Swiss Army knife; tissues; a sewing kit; and a good, comfortable, pair of walking shoes.

OPPOSITE: Fishing boats at Tarpon Springs.
ABOVE: This South Walton course is just one of the reasons Florida is the golfing capital of the world.

Recommended Reading

BARTRAM, WILLIAM. *Travels*. Penguin Books, New York 1988.

BENNETT, CHARLES E. *Settlement of Florida*. University of Florida Press, Gainesville 1968.

BIRNBAUM, STEVE. *Walt Disney World: The Official Guide*. Houghton Mifflin, Boston 1999.

BURNETT, GENE M. *Florida's Past*. Pineapple Press, Sarasota 1986.

DASMAN, RAYMOND F. *No Further Retreat: The Fight to Save Florida*. Macmillan, New York 1971.

DIDION, JOAN. *Miami*. Pocket Books, New York 1993.

DOUGLAS, MARJORY STONEMAN. *Florida: The Long Frontier*. Harper and Row, New York 1967.

FICHTER, GEORGE S. *Birds of Florida*. E.A. Seamann, Miami 1971.

Florida Outdoor Guide. The Miami Herald, Miami 1989.

HALL, JAMES. *Mean High Tide*. Mandarin, London 1994.

HATTON, HAP. *Tropical Splendor: An Architectural History of Florida*. Alfred A. Knopf, New York 1987.

HEMINGWAY, ERNEST. *Islands in the Stream*. Scribner's, New York 1970. *To Have and Have Not*. Scribner's, New York 1937.

HIAASEN, CARL. *Native Tongue*. Fawcett Crest, New York 1991. *Skintight*. Pan Books, London 1991

JAHODA, GLORIA. *Florida: A bicentennial History*. W.W. Norton, New York 1976.

Kennedy Space Center Story. NASA, Cape Canaveral 1986.

LUMMUS, JOHN N. *The Miracle of Miami Beach*. Teacher Publishing, Miami 1940.

MACDONALD, JOHN D. *Condominium*. Lippincott, New York 1977. *The Deep Blue Good-by*. Fawcett, New York 1964

MCGUANE, THOMAS. *Ninety-two in the Shade*. Farrar, Straus, New York 1973.

MCLENDON, JAMES. *Papa Hemingway in Key West*. E. A. Seamann, Miami 1972.

MARTH, DEL and MARTHA. *Florida Almanac*. A.S. Barnes, St. Petersburg 1988.

MORRIS, ALLEN. *The Florida Handbook*. Peninsula Publishing, Tallahassee 1992.

NEY, JOHN. *Palm Beach*. Little, Brown, Boston 1966.

RABKIN, RICHARD and JACOB. *Nature Guide to Florida*. Banyan Books, Miami 1978.

SMILEY, NIXON. *Florida: Land of Images*. E.A. Seamann, Miami 1977. *Yesterday's Florida*. E.A. Seamann, Miami 1974.

STACHOWITZ, JIM. *Diver's Guide to Florida and the Florida Keys*. Windward Publishing, Miami 1976.

WILLIAMS, TENNESSEE. *Memoirs*. Doubleday, New York 1975.

Quick Reference A–Z Guide to Places and Topics of Interest with Listed Accommodation, Restaurants and Useful Telephone Numbers

The symbols Ⓕ FAX, Ⓣ TOLL-FREE, Ⓔ E-MAIL, Ⓦ WEB-SITE refer to additional contact information found in the chapter listings.

The symbols Ⓕ FAX, Ⓣ TOLL-FREE, Ⓔ E-MAIL, Ⓦ WEB-SITE refer to additional contact information found in the chapter listings.

The symbols Ⓕ FAX, Ⓣ TOLL-FREE, Ⓔ E-MAIL, Ⓦ WEB-SITE refer to additional contact information found in the chapter listings.

The symbols Ⓕ FAX, Ⓣ TOLL-FREE, Ⓔ E-MAIL, Ⓦ WEB-SITE *refer to additional contact information found in the chapter listings.*

The symbols Ⓕ FAX, Ⓣ TOLL-FREE, Ⓔ E-MAIL, Ⓦ WEB-SITE *refer to additional contact information found in the chapter listings.*

The symbols Ⓕ FAX, Ⓣ TOLL-FREE, Ⓔ E-MAIL, Ⓦ WEB-SITE refer to additional contact information found in the chapter listings.

The symbols Ⓕ FAX, Ⓣ TOLL-FREE, Ⓔ E-MAIL, Ⓦ WEB-SITE *refer to additional contact information found in the chapter listings.*

The symbols Ⓕ FAX, Ⓣ TOLL-FREE, Ⓔ E-MAIL, Ⓦ WEB-SITE *refer to additional contact information found in the chapter listings.*

The symbols Ⓕ FAX, Ⓣ TOLL-FREE, Ⓔ E-MAIL, Ⓦ WEB-SITE refer to additional contact information found in the chapter listings.

The symbols Ⓕ FAX, Ⓣ TOLL-FREE, Ⓔ E-MAIL, Ⓦ WEB-SITE refer to additional contact information found in the chapter listings.

The symbols Ⓕ FAX, Ⓣ TOLL-FREE, Ⓔ E-MAIL, Ⓦ WEB-SITE refer to additional contact information found in the chapter listings.

The symbols Ⓕ FAX, Ⓣ TOLL-FREE, Ⓔ E-MAIL, Ⓦ WEB-SITE *refer to additional contact information found in the chapter listings.*

The symbols (F) FAX, (T) TOLL-FREE, (E) E-MAIL, (W) WEB-SITE refer to additional contact information found in the chapter listings.

The symbols Ⓕ FAX, Ⓣ TOLL-FREE, Ⓔ E-MAIL, Ⓦ WEB-SITE refer to additional contact information found in the chapter listings.

The symbols Ⓕ FAX, Ⓣ TOLL-FREE, Ⓔ E-MAIL, Ⓦ WEB-SITE *refer to additional contact information found in the chapter listings.*

The symbols Ⓕ FAX, Ⓣ TOLL-FREE, Ⓔ E-MAIL, Ⓦ WEB-SITE refer to additional contact information found in the chapter listings.

The symbols Ⓕ FAX, Ⓣ TOLL-FREE, Ⓔ E-MAIL, Ⓦ WEB-SITE refer to additional contact information found in the chapter listings.

The symbols Ⓕ FAX, Ⓣ TOLL-FREE, Ⓔ E-MAIL, Ⓦ WEB-SITE *refer to additional contact information found in the chapter listings.*